THE ATLANTIC SYSTEM

THE
ATLANTIC SYSTEM

The Story of Anglo-American
Control of the Seas

BY FORREST DAVIS

REYNAL & HITCHCOCK · NEW YORK

To the Memory of

DWIGHT W. MORROW

A GOOD NEIGHBOR WHO UNDERSTOOD
THE ATLANTIC SYSTEM

ACKNOWLEDGMENTS

THE AUTHOR wishes to acknowledge with thanks the kind permission of the Houghton Mifflin Company for the use of numerous quotations from three copyrighted books published by them: *The Education of Henry Adams, The Letters of Henry Adams (1858-1918)*, and *The Intimate Papers of Colonel House*.

He also wishes similarly to thank Little, Brown & Company for permission to quote freely from the works of Admiral Mahan, notably: *The Interest of America in International Conditions, The Influence of Sea Power upon History, 1660-1783, The Influence of Sea Power upon the French Revolution and Empire, 1793-1812, Lessons of the War with Spain,* and *The Problem of Asia and its Effect on International Policies*.

"We have got to fortify the Atlantic System . . . for if Germany breaks down England . . . she becomes the center of a military world, and we are lost. The course of concentration must be decided by force—whether military or industrial matters not much to the end."

—From a letter written by Henry Adams to a friend in 1906.

Contents

Foreword

UNLIKE THE AXIS blueprints for a New World Order, a sterile prisonhouse inhabited by robotlike heroes and faceless subject races, the Atlantic System is old, rational, and pragmatic. Growing organically out of strategic and political realities in a congenially free climate, its roots run deep and strong into the American tradition. It was Henry Adams, endlessly seeking form and design in history, who first gave a name to the community of interest binding the self-governing peoples around the Atlantic basin. That was as recently as 1906. But back of Adams stood the great nineteenth-century forefathers of the Atlantic System. In the Americas they were Thomas Jefferson, James Madison, and James Monroe as well as that reluctant progenitor, John Quincy Adams, and the Venezuelan liberator Simon Bolivar, who brought independence to one-quarter of South America. George Canning, the English Foreign Secretary who professed himself alternately fascinated and repelled by the "hard features of trans-Atlantic democracy," was likewise a forefather, although his parenthood had a cynical cast.

Jefferson, terming it the "American system," was foremost in accepting England's adherence. To all these wise gentlemen it was apparent—as it is again today—that the Atlantic world, pre-eminently the legatee of the liberal revolutions of the eighteenth and early nineteenth centuries, had a set of political institutions and interests essentially in conflict with those of Central and Eastern Europe. It was not lost on the Presidents of the Virginia succession, and on Adams, Bolivar, and Canning, that modern democracy was flourishing best in the states of the Atlantic seaboard—in both

xi

Europe and America. The forefathers likewise were aware, as we are today, that the peaceful development of the Atlantic world depended upon sea power. Then the shield of the Americas was British sea power. Today it is the concert of Anglo-American power, an English-speaking entente that has grown to maturity within the last half-century.

It was in 1823 that Jefferson, Madison, and President Monroe defined the Atlantic System in a memorable exchange of letters dealing with Canning's proposal of an Anglo-American alliance to safeguard the independence of the New World against the Quadruple Alliance, secular arm of the Holy Alliance. Canning wished, on behalf of the English merchants, to forestall revival of Spanish trade monopolies in Latin America. The Americans had a wider interest. Agreeing that the incipient Monroe Doctrine was more than a double-edged policy forbidding the Americas to European conquest and forswearing our interference in purely Old World Affairs, the three Founding Fathers had no doubt that it was also a lever prying England away from the autocratic Continental System, and a clamp attaching her to the Atlantic world. To these democratic Virginia gentlemen, liberty and tyranny still had the ring and the sharp contours of freshly minted coins, and the authoritarian league of sovereigns under Alexander I and Metternich was morally repugnant as well as a threat to the peace of this hemisphere. Seeking counsel of his predecessors, Monroe wrote: "Has not the epoch arrived when Great Britain must take her stand, either on the side of the monarchs of Europe or on the side of the United States, and, in consequence, either in favor of despotism or of liberty?"

Both former Presidents advised acceptance of Canning's tender, for as Madison (who had fought England in 1812) pointed out, "with the British power and navy combined with our own, we have nothing to fear from the rest of the world; and in the great struggle of the epoch between liberty and despotism we owe it to ourselves to maintain the former, in this hemisphere *at least*." The Sage of Monticello, a land-hungry, democratic imperialist who bought the Louisiana

Territory, coveted Cuba and Florida, and anticipated a transisthmian canal, was at once more definitive and more militant. Europe, as Jefferson saw it, was "laboring to become the domicil[e] of despotism," and America should therefore surely be making "our hemisphere that of freedom," arguing further: "One nation, most of all, could disturb us in this pursuit. She now offers to lead, aid, and accompany us in it. By acceding to her proposition, we detach her from the band, bring her mighty weight into the scale of free government, and emancipate a continent at one stroke, which might otherwise linger long in doubt and difficulty."

Twice Jefferson had witnessed war between the Americans and the British. Yet now, impelled by recognition of a common enemy and therefore common English-speaking interests, he advocated that with Britain "we should the most sedulously nourish a cordial friendship, and nothing would tend more to knit our affections than to be fighting once more, side by side, in the same cause." Moreover, a war in defense of the "American system" would not be alone "her [England's] war, but ours" as well.

Three years after this correspondence Bolivar held the first inter-American conference at Panama. There he sought unsuccessfully to bring Great Britain and the United States into a political structure spanning the Atlantic, one based on Bolivar's belief in the political solidarity of the American republics with the British Empire.

Monroe and his Secretary of State, the knotty John Quincy Adams, elected to make the Monroe Doctrine unilateral. Canning's bitter strictures against the United States and his aggressive part in the recent war made him unwelcome to Adams as a collaborator. Yet the fact that England and America were partners in erecting this barrier to Continental reaction was implicitly recognized by the authors and the sponsors of the Monroe Doctrine. While the admonishing declaration came from Washington, the power of enforcement lay with the British fleet. Not for two generations would we begin to accumulate sufficient sea power to defend the dictum. Meanwhile Canning, with truthful arrogance, could boast in Parliament that he had "called the New World into being to redress the balance of the Old"; the Latin republics were able to consummate their independence in the lee of British sea power and American assertion; and this country rounded out its self-allotted portion of North America undisturbed.

History, as everyone knows, simulates itself. Substitute Hitler for Czar Alexander, the Nazi New Order for the Holy Alliance, and you have a continental Europe again "laboring to become the domicil[e] of despotism." The parallel cannot, however, be pushed too far, the earlier league of kings having lacked the demonic, concentrated will of the contemporary tyranny. Yet a significant point of similarity does exist in England's case. As in Napoleon's time, as in 1823, and also as in 1898, when she balked attempts to revive the Holy Alliance—this time against the United States—England again has placed herself outside a despotic Continental System.

From the 1820's to 1890, in which year the United States began to put forth strength beyond its own borders, Anglo-American collaboration on even terms in Atlantic affairs remained in the germinal stage. The Atlantic was prevailingly an English sea, as it had been except for brief interruptions since Elizabeth's freebooters and the elements scattered Philip II's "invincible" Armada in 1558; and England, having the power, was not disposed to share the authority. During the American Civil War, it is true, the North developed enough naval strength to blockade the Confederacy effectually and to command the American seas, but that was only an episode of a period in which, to the outside world, whatever Atlantic System existed was preponderantly British. Only when the United States undertook a part in the world commensurate with its internal strength did there push above the ground the shoots of the Atlantic System as a genuine partnership of the English-speaking Powers committed to guardianship of a common ocean and a common, humane civilization.

As it thrived—in 1896, during the Spanish War of 1898, in 1903, at Algeciras in 1906, and of course in 1917—the Atlantic System increasingly gained the approval of instructed Americans as a beneficent, sheltering growth. Not until 1939, however, with the Americas again threatened by a despotism far grimmer, far more brutal and reactionary, than the Continental System that sent the Virginia Presidents hurriedly to the side of the recent enemy, would it become widely apparent that defense of the Atlantic world inextricably involved defense of the English-speaking world. Again Great Britain was the eastern outpost of the Atlantic System. This time the peril was more urgent. In partial realization of that strategic fact, the United States Government undertook to wage a quasi-war; a "white war," half in, half out. The reason for that tentative behavior on the part of an Administration believing this to be also our war is that many citizens, as usual, were unprepared psychologically for the defense of their vital interests by force—unless and until the enemy, bearing convincing credentials, appeared on our doorstep. For so many years we have lived with a lie that it too has entered into our tradition.

The lie is that the United States has led an isolated existence. Each generation sees its revival to comfort the fainthearted, fortify the pacifist and the fifth-columnist, confuse the thoughtless, and supply ammunition to partisans, in spite of the demonstrable facts that (1) we have intervened morally, politically, and economically in Europe and Asia whenever it suited our purposes; and (2) we have not remained apart, either as colonies or as republic, from any general European war since 1689. They are all in the school histories: King William's, Queen Anne's, King George's, the French and Indian, the Napoleonic Wars, and the First World War.[1] The first five being American segments of the intermittent struggle between England and France from Louis XIV to Napoleon.

We have, moreover, maintained two provocative international policies. The Monroe Doctrine, underwriting the territorial integrity of a fabulously rich, underpopulated,

---

[1] The First World War was really, of course, only the first phase of a world war of which we are now seeing the second phase.

inadequately defended continent extending for many thousand miles, is by no means self-enforcing. For four decades the Open Door policy has been a forcible assertion in the relations of China with other Powers. It was bearing us toward war in 1921. Had England joined hands with us, we might easily have become embroiled with Japan ten years later. Under isolationist impulses we compelled abrogation of the Anglo-Japanese Alliance in 1921, dictated terms of sea power around the globe, and interfered with power relationships in Europe as well as Asia. A great Sea Power, we have shouldered defense commitments sweeping from Iceland to Cape Horn and westward across the Pacific to Asia and for two decades we have shared command of the seas with Britain.

The result of this contradiction between profession and deed is an often unrealistic and usually infirm foreign policy. It explains why in both phases of world war we have seemed to "drift" toward war. Twice within this generation, after vowing neutrality we have gravitated into the support of a beleaguered Britain from motives strictly American and in defense of the Atlantic System. In neither case did our Government have any option if it wished to preserve the true security afforded by our oceans. The wonder, given the history of the Atlantic System, is not that we went to the side of Britain; it is that we did not go earlier.

The history of the Atlantic System is the story of Anglo-American relations during the last half-century: the quarrels and misunderstandings; the forces operating both to attract and to repel; the "broad entente" (as André Siegfried describes the bond) existing between these strongheaded, individualized peoples. A secondary theme is the rise of the United States from an inferior place in the council of nations into a junior partnership, then a full partnership, with England in the Atlantic System, with intimations of larger leadership to come.

FORREST DAVIS

Cornwall, New York,
September, 1941.

I. America Returns to the Sea:
The Prophet Mahan

THE WORLD OF 1890 sunned itself in the Indian summer of the Pax Britannica, that great, liberal century stretching from Waterloo to Sarajevo. A year notable for peace, 1890 was also remarkable for portents, events half-hidden or only dimly apprehended which nevertheless foreshadowed, among other things, the world-wide convulsions of 1914 and 1939, with America's relationship to them. William II, only thirty-one and barely seated on the German throne, wrote his grandmother at Windsor that Europe was at its "most peaceful for a long time." More prudently, the Marquis of Salisbury, the Tory squire who governed Victoria's realm four times with shrewd negligence, observed "several clouds" ominously on the horizon, seeing fit to caution the Queen that "any day one of them may rise."

It was, however, the Kaiser who first identified one of the omens of that year. This cloud was arising over the United States, which in 1890 signified a return to the sea in force after an absence dating, roughly, from Appomattox. Noting from afar a controversy in Washington over a battleship program, with the Secretary of the Navy proposing the building of twenty and his Policy Board recommending thirty-eight for a navy that had at the moment precisely no battleships, the Emperor scratched out an urgent note to his grandmother. What, he asked, were the Americans up to? Did they intend to become a first-rate Sea Power overnight? Victoria, immersed in dynastic routine, episcopal politics, and her Albertine memories, knew an omen when it was called to her attention, particularly if it related to sea power. Anxiously she passed William's note on to Salisbury. In his

1

desire to soothe his sovereign's alarm the Prime Minister minimized the portent, replying that it would take many years to build so many capital ships, that "many changes of administration" would intervene, and that on the whole the Americans themselves, suspicious of large armaments, could be trusted to veto the ambitions of their navy. Complacently he added that in any case the British "could always catch them up."

When Congress, after a searching debate, rejected both Navy Department recommendations, authorizing only three "sea going, coast line" battleships (the terminology being a sop to the isolationists of 1890, who believed the country could best be defended at the three-mile limit), the Queen was further comforted. Those three ships of the line, the *Oregon,* the *Indiana* and the *Massachusetts,* formed nevertheless the nucleus of the "fighting fleet" which, as much as any factor, projected this country first into the thick of Atlantic affairs, and then into the stormy waters of power politics on a world scale. The United States was not to become a major Sea Power for sixteen years, but in far less time than that it would enter the Anglo-American concert underlying the Atlantic System, establishing a power partnership on the seas that has become one of the most impressive facts of modern times. In that light, the Naval Act of 1890 must be taken as the point of departure for English-speaking collaboration, and it may be doubted if any other happening of that precursory year exerted an equal influence on American life and destiny in the next half-century.

The return of the Americans to blue water had larger significance abroad than at home. Captain Alfred Thayer Mahan, U.S.N. (by a pertinent coincidence, Mahan gained world-wide authority in 1890 as a military historian and power theorist), might infer that the United States, having subdued the continent and recuperated from the Civil War, was again "looking outward." His was a lone if prophetic voice. Soon a New York newspaper, the *Commercial Advertiser,* would discover the country standing "on the thresh-

old of new policies as surely as it did in 1803, when
Jefferson annexed Louisiana and the United States realized
that it must govern it." But at the moment even the big-
navy men in Congress shrank from reading expansionist
meanings into their desire for an offensive fleet. There was,
as Mahan perceived, "no aggression in our pious souls."

Outside America, the Naval Act was generally taken as
evidence of an intention to become a great Sea Power.
Robert Louis Stevenson thought the "modern navy of the
States" opened a "new epoch in world history." A witness
to American colonial disinterestedness in Samoa, where he
was waging his losing battle for life, the Scottish author
expected America's new power to be exercised benevolently.

Another British poet and novelist, Rudyard Kipling, who
saw all power matters in terms of the British Empire, supposed that with a fleet an American "alliance will be worth
having—if the alliance of any republic can be relied upon."
The poet, fresh from India, was twenty-five. In his *American Notes,* which were singularly bereft of sympathy, Kipling poured contempt on the state of our defenses. The
"big, fat Republic," he wrote, is "as unprotected as a jelly
fish. . . . From five miles out at sea . . . a ship of the power
of *H.M.S. Collingwood* would wipe out any or every town
from San Francisco to Long Branch; and three first-class
ironclads would account for New York, Bartholdi's statue
and all." Mindful of India's treasure, Kipling gloatingly
described the "ransom and loot past the counting of man
on [the] seaboard alone," with "neither a navy, nor half a
dozen first-class forts to guard the whole." His pitiless ex-
posure of our military weakness, published in 1891, flayed
America's self-esteem, but it sank home. The facts were
with Kipling. We had no ship that could match a *Collingwood.*

Afloat, the nation of John Paul Jones, of the Tripoli
campaign, of Isaac Hull and the *Constitution,* of the
brothers Perry—Oliver Hazard, who met the British on Lake
Erie, and Matthew, opening Japan to the world—of the

clippers and of Farragut—that nation had fallen on evil days. A revival of naval interest in the 1880's had provided a small fleet, but it was built around monitors, unwieldy floating forts whose conception dated from Jefferson's day, and fast cruisers, "cavalry of the sea," unprotected and designed only to raid enemy commerce. Strategically we still dwelt in the era of the War of 1812. At the close of the Civil War we had, briefly, the most effective striking force on the seas; in 1890 our navy was at best third-rate.

So also with the merchant marine. In 1861 it included nearly 2,500,000 tons, a fleet second only to Britain's in size and excelling Britain's in speed and efficiency. Of all our ocean-borne commerce, more than three-quarters traveled in American bottoms. But steam and steel had passed us by while the sections fought and the best energies of the country forged westward, and by 1890 we had only a fraction of the prewar registry.

The full story could not be told, however, in merchant tonnages and naval statistics. They were merely the premise; the conclusion was even more disquieting. Although the world marveled at and envied our mushroomlike growth in population, wealth, and industrial capacity, outside the three-mile limit it accorded us little weight as a nation. The taunt of a British military journal that the "scream of the eagle had become no more alarming than that of a parrot" expressed a common European viewpoint.

Even in the hemisphere we had sworn to protect our word went for naught. In the early 1880's Chile, possessing armor-clads and rifled cannon against our unprotected hulks armed with smoothbores, thumbed her nose at our attempted intervention in the war that cost Bolivia her seacoast and her nitrate beds. In 1880 President Hayes designated the Panama Isthmus a "part of the coast line of the United States"; in his inaugural in 1881 Garfield declared it our "right and duty" to build a transisthmian ship channel; the House Foreign Affairs Committee that same year termed a foreign-built canal a "violation of the spirit and letter of the Monroe Doctrine," yet we were compelled to sit by in glum impotence as De Lesseps and his Frenchmen undertook the task. It was during this time that Prince Bismarck began referring to the Monroe Doctrine as a piece of "international impudence." In 1890, for a quarter-century we had lacked the means of defending it.

Everywhere we turned, moreover, we encountered British sea power, sometimes constraining, sometimes helpful. However we regarded Great Britain, the United States depended upon the British. The Monroe Doctrine itself was shadowy without the substance of the English fleet, and in the outer world the United States, because it lacked the strength to enforce its will, passed for a ward of Great Britain. When the President of France, Jules Grévy, proposed intervention in the Chile-Bolivia War by his country, England, and the United States, our pride was pricked. Coldly we replied that inasmuch as our "commercial and political interests . . . on this Continent transcend in extent and importance those of any other power," we "must preserve" an independent "position." But official Washington knew in its heart that England's veto rather than ours restrained the French.

2

A consciousness of weakness in relation to Great Britain and other Powers, including Chile, helped launch the battleship program. Since the Chilean War, the West coast had shivered periodically in fear of raids by the superior Chilean warcraft. "I confess with a sense of shame," . . . said Senator Eugene Hale, chairman of the Naval Committee, ". . . [that] there is nothing whatever to prevent Chile . . . from steaming along the Pacific coast and laying our towns under contribution . . . burning and destroying the metropolis of the Pacific coast." In 1891 a clash with Chile over an attack on American sailors in Valparaiso revived trepidation in Washington and on the West coast, and prompted Theodore Roosevelt to consider organizing a cavalry troop. The South American republic had one cruiser under construction in Toulon that could sink any ship in our navy; the 1890-class

American battleships were barely laid down. A genuine war scare was only ended with Chile's apology.

There were, naturally, other factors represented in our return to the sea. We could well afford it. The country waxed richer year by year and the Government had a Treasury surplus, although currency trouble lay just ahead. Also we had begun the march across the Pacific that within a decade would place us on the China Sea. Since 1778 we had maintained a naval station at Pago Pago in the Samoa Islands, sharing the oversight of that archipelago with the Germans and the British. In 1887 Grover Cleveland had acquired exclusive rights to Pearl Harbor in Hawaii as a naval base, staking a claim to American ascendancy in those islands. The Samoan venture brought us grief in 1889 when a hurricane wrecked in the harbor of Apia, Samoa, most of our Pacific naval force, a cruiser and two smaller men-of-war, with the loss of nearly half a hundred lives. Robert Louis Stevenson, historian of the storm and the civil war preceding it, maintained that the shock of that loss brought about the naval awakening of 1890. In this view he was by no means alone.

As an incident to the hurricane there occurred one of those events attesting what the London *Times* described—in another connection—as the "native affinity between the American and British fleets." In March, 1889, seven warships rode at anchor in the tiny, unprotected harbor at Apia—a show of strength reflecting the fact that three great countries were grimly interfering in the native affairs of the islands, a set of dots in the South Pacific nearly 5,000 miles from San Francisco. Three ships were German, three American—the *Trenton,* flagship of Admiral Kimberly, the *Vandalia,* and the *Nipsic*—and one British, the *Calliope.* They had been assembled there because the Germans, whose commercial interests exceeded those of both other Powers, had provoked native strife by deposing King Laupepa Malietoa and enthroning his rival Tamamese. Whereupon a strong outlying chief, Mataafa, challenged the German choice. Finally, with Mataafa victorious everywhere, the German consul, in violation of treaty, proclaimed martial law and landed Marines. In a night sortie the Germans were repulsed and lost 20 killed, 30 wounded to the Samoans.

The United States bore a special relationship to Samoa. Our treaty, antedating those of the other Powers, created a vague protectorate, which we were loath to acknowledge but which lay nevertheless on our conscience. In exchange for Pago Pago we had agreed to use our good offices on behalf of the Samoans with any third party. The civil war, reported by American correspondents, had aroused American sympathy. There was a report that the flag had been fired on by the Germans. Congress, aroused, had voted $500,000, and President Harrison had ordered Kimberly to Apia.

The hostilities had ceased and Bismarck (who had been under sharp attack in the American press) was in course of recalling his consul, but international tension stood high in the harbor as the hurricane arrived. For forty-eight hours it swept the islands, driving all the German and American ships on reef or beach. The German loss of life was greater than the American. The British escaped unscathed because as the other vessels slowly were being driven ashore the *Calliope,* Captain Kane, made a run for the sea to escape being fouled by the *Nipsic*—made a crawl, rather, the ship being unable to advance as much as a mile an hour. Riding at the harbor's mouth was the *Trenton,* with 450 men aboard, half-flooded and with her wheel and rudder carried away. As the *Calliope* inched alongside the *Trenton* the Americans gathered at the rails. In *A Footnote to History* Stevenson thus recorded the scene: "From the doomed flagship, the Americans hailed the success of the English with a cheer. It was led by the old Admiral in person, rang out over the storm with holiday vigor and was answered by the *Calliope's* men with an emotion easily conceived. This ship of their kinsfolk was almost the last external object seen from the *Calliope.*"

Gradually the *Trenton* was borne toward shore, coming to rest alongside the beached *Vandalia.* One man only was lost from the flagship. When the rescued crew had been lined up ashore, Kimberly paraded the ship's band. Into the teeth of the storm they hurled "Hail Columbia." Kane wrote the

Admiralty that he and his men had been "much affected."
The story ran round the globe, inspiring many editorialists
and versifiers, including Charles Roberts, a Canadian poet,
who predicted that

> The memory of those cheers
> Shall ring in English ears
> Where'er this English blood and speech extend.

In reply to a letter from Kane, Admiral Kimberly wrote:
"We could not have been gladder if it was one of our own
ships, for in a time like this, I can say truly with old Admiral
Josiah Tattnall that 'blood is thicker than water.' " [1]

A man of resolution as well as sentiment, Kimberly established a camp on the beach, disposed of his dead, restored
peace, and issued a proclamation calling upon the Samoans
to "bury war in so deep a grave that it will sleep forever,
unseen and forgot." Later that year England, Germany, and
the United States negotiated the Act of Berlin, re-enforcing
the condominium and exiling Mataafa.

Whatever effect the Samoa shipwreck, with its collateral
gallantry, had in preparing the American mind for a modern
navy, there can be little doubt where the credit for reaching
Congress rested. The man uniquely behind the battleship
program was Captain Mahan. As professor of history, strategy,
and tactics at the Naval War College since its foundation in
1884, Mahan had formulated for the navy the thesis of the
"fighting fleet," putting into systematic form for the officers
of the Naval Policy Board the arguments used in their report.
Benjamin F. Tracy, the Secretary of the Navy, who leaned
on Mahan's dialectical skill, paraphrased him in his request
for battleships. Mahan wrote that war, "however defensive
in character, must be waged aggressively if it is to hope for
success," and again that "no purely defensive attitude can be
successfully maintained." In Tracy's report he asserted that
"a war, although defensive in principle, may be conducted

---

[1] Tattnall, flag officer of the Asiatic station, violated neutrality in 1857
by fighting his ships with the British in a difficult assault on the forts at
Taku, below Tientsin. The phrase was his excuse before a General Board,
which exoneratetd him.

most effectively by being offensive in its operations." Truisms now, those utterances were widely challenged in 1890, not only by an uninformed public, but in the United States Navy itself.

In asking for a force capable not only of beating off an enemy but of also threatening his shores, Tracy shivered the timbers of conservatism. The Naval Policy Board's recommendation of battleships able "to attack points on the other side of the Atlantic" drove retired admirals and fresh-water Senators into indignant tremors. Versed only in commerce-raiding and blockade tactics, they saw naval warfare still in terms of hit-and-run engagements between single antagonists. As for defending the coast, they relied on shooting it out at the mouth of the harbor. It was Mahan who taught (a lesson not yet comprehended by large sections of the public) that war should be fought in the enemy's waters and ports—not in one's own. Mahan and like-minded officers, such as Rear Admiral Stephen B. Luce, a great sea power theorist who founded the Naval War College and discovered Mahan, permeated the navy with the "heretical" doctrine that the best defense (navally) is offense. It remained for Mahan to reduce technical jargon to crackling phrases that penetrated lay indifference, in Congress and out. "There must be," he reiterated at Newport and in his writings, "the power to strike, as well as to shield." Never since Andrew Jackson in his 1837 inaugural demanded a fleet that could "reach and annoy the enemy" had the matter been put more trenchantly.

3

The rise of Mahan into international influence was without doubt one of the major happenings of 1890. Its import was far-reaching in time and space. Accepted at once as a prophet, Mahan undertook without delay to propagate his doctrines. These included American strategical expansion and Anglo-American solidarity at sea. To Mahan command of the seas was a prerequisite of world power, and his gospel therefore had its fullest sway in England and in the three

countries which in 1890 put forth signs of future greatness on
the sea—Germany, Japan, and the United States. None was a
Naval Power in that year.

Mahan came of a background both bookish and military.
His father Dennis, the son of Irish immigrants, taught at
West Point for a generation. A scholar and a mathematician,
not a soldier, he instructed Grant, Lee, and most of the other
Civil War generals in tactics.

In 1884 Mahan, then forty-four, was idling up the west
coast of South America in command of the *U.S.S. Wachusett,*
a wooden man-of-war forced by the decrepitude of its engine,
to rely on sail power—one of the units in what the *Army
and Navy Journal* had called a "heterogeneous collection of
naval trash." He had written a thorough but uninspired
account of his service in the Gulf of Mexico during the Civil
War. Sufficient it was, however, to recommend his scholar-
ship and grasp to Admiral Luce, just now organizing the
Naval War College, who telegraphed the offer of the first
professorship. Accepting, Mahan found the study more to his
liking than the quarterdeck. Six years later publication of
his first great work, *The Influence of Sea Power upon History, 1660-1783,* brought him into world-wide notice. He was
a thoughtful, rather somber officer, Spartan as to duty, pious,
with a formidable literary equipment consisting of a capacity
for sweeping historical synthesis and convincing exposition.
His words were respected in imperial courts, chancelleries
both royal and republican, the universities, and wherever
men handled and thought about fighting ships.

The British Prime Minister however, may be forgiven if he
overlooked the dynamic import of Mahan. There were more
obvious omens in 1890, nearer at hand. Prince Bismarck (the
New York Herald's "grim demigod of Europe") fell in March,
an event of evil significance to the British Empire, and sec-
ondarily to the United States. The Iron Chancellor stamped
out of the Schloss in Berlin muttering about the "psychiatric
questions" that rose to mind whenever he saw the young
Emperor, leaving the Empire's tiller to yaw with every
Hohenzollern gust. Within a few years the Kaiser would

prophesy fatefully to a German audience that "Germany's future lies on the water."

Halfway around the world at Yokohama impressed diplomats for the first time saw the fleet which in 1894 would destroy the Chinese at Yalu, bringing into being a new Naval Power. At Washington, by passing the stiffly protectionist McKinley tariff act, Congress soured the ascending industrial class in Germany, and inspired a campaign of contempt in the German press against all things American. The act distorted German understanding of this country and prompted the Kaiser in 1897 to solicit the Czar's help in forming a Continental league aimed at the "yellow races" and America because, on our part, we had "declared hostilities against Europe" by our tariff policies.

Of more remote consequence, a band of minor intellectuals (to the mystic number of seven) organized at Frankfort-on-the-Main a racial cult to be known as the Pan-German League, the teachings of which partially prefigured the Gothic broodings of Berchtesgaden. In refreshing contrast the year likewise witnessed the foundation of the Pan-American Union, an inclusive association, hemisphere-wide, linking Latin and Anglo-Saxon civilizations in the New World. A Pan-American Congress, through which James G. Blaine, as Secretary of State, helped to effectuate the vision of Bolivar, established in Washington a permanent secretariat for the American republics. A half-century later these antipodal abstractions, clothed in power, would confront each other across the Atlantic.

4

A further circumstance of 1890 casting its shadow before was the extreme preoccupation manifested in America with England and in England with America. Each country was engaged, not always happily, in discovering the other. The *North American Review,* for example, with a shrewd sense of the topical, published a symposium under the title "Do Americans Hate England?" The answers were equivocal.

Colonel Thomas Wentworth Higginson wrote that while
"common motherhood was too strong a tie to permit of anything like hatred . . . Americans of the purest English descent
must admit that the mother country has been a . . . stern
parent." A general worked off a string of epithets against
the "insulting, domineering, aggressive policies of the British
Government and the supercilious and patronizing airs" of
the upper classes. General Horace Porter, who had been
Grant's aide and secretary, put a better face on the matter,
referring to England's literature and gallant deeds, "in which
Americans justly feel they have a common heritage, for it is
only bastards who manifest no regard for their parents."

Andrew Carnegie, the "Star-Spangled Scot," conceded a
general ill will in America toward the British, laying it to
ultrapatriotic schoolbooks. "The masses of the English people," on the contrary, "cordially loved and admired
America." Carnegie ended with a warning which would not
prove too wide of the mark a generation hence: "woe betide
the race that attempts to go too far against one branch of the
English race or the other."

The truth was that England stood low in American esteem
as we entered the last decade of the nineteenth century.
James Bryce, writing his monumental *The American Commonwealth* in 1888, thought American animosity considerably diminished from the "venomous hatred" against
Britannia discovered by De Tocqueville in the 1830's. But
Kipling, reminiscencing in *Something of Myself,* published
in 1937, recalled that England in those years was "still the
dark and fearful enemy, to be feared and guarded against."
Nor were Americans, including those who would bear a part
in the coming rapprochement, backward about speaking their
pieces. Theodore Roosevelt, who as President played power
politics hand in hand with Downing Street to a degree un-
surpassed by any President before or after, was then railing
at "feeble folk" who betrayed "Anglo-maniac tendencies."

New and revived grievances fanned the ancient grudge.
Canadian seal fishermen encroached on the American monopoly in the Bering Sea, losing their ships in a Sitka prize

court for their temerity. On the East coast the Canadians
were again hampering New Englanders fishing the Grand
Banks, in retaliation against discriminatory tariffs, with
Maine and New Brunswick squabbling lengthily over Passa-
maquoddy Bay. Under all Anglo-American relations, of
course, ran a fierce drumfire of antagonism from the transplanted Irish Nationalists, who followed the fortunes of
Parnell far more avidly than the major politics of their
adopted land. Moreover, literate folk with tender memories
were finding in Kipling's caricatures of American life unpleasant reminders of Charles Dickens and Mrs. Trollope.

These, however, were pinpricks. The underlying motives
were fear and a sense of frustration. Since 1783 the United
States had obtained title to a considerable wedge of this
continent; yet as long as Great Britain encircled us with
military and naval power we could not feel wholly at ease.
Canada stretched to the north, a potential base of operations,
however lightly we might try to dismiss its menace, while in
the seas around us the British maintained eleven naval bases
and thirty-three coaling stations. Always the Admiralty had
greater strength in American waters than we could muster.
At Halifax and Bermuda, it was suspected, were guns and
stores with which to arm transatlantic liners speedily for
blockade and raiding duty. Against whom were these bases
to be used? There was only one answer, an answer readily
given in the battleship debate of 1890. Senators, such as
M. C. Butler, and Representatives, typified by Henry Cabot
Lodge, the young Massachusetts scholar, politician, and disciple of Mahan, repeatedly called the country's attention to
Britain's overweening naval strength off our shores. Secretary
Tracy in his 1891 report likewise gave that fact its due.

A group of alarmed Senators proposed to Chairman Hale
that a deal be attempted: England to dismantle the great
bases at Halifax, Bermuda, Jamaica, and Esquimault on the
British Columbia coast in exchange for abandonment of our
battleship projects. Hale dismissed the suggestion as worth-
less, being confident that England would not trade.

Nor was that all. The Esquimault base had been recently

equipped with twenty eighty-ton Armstrong guns. This base
threatened our route to the Orient. Why, asked a despairing
Congressman, had we gone to the expense of building trans-
continental railways if our Pacific trade lanes were to lie in
the shadow of another Power? The rapid completion of the
Canadian Pacific and the enlargement of the Welland Canal
were viewed by big-navy members of Congress with suspicion, the *Army and Navy Journal* regarding that railway as
"only a military creation."

Small-navy men might decry such alarms, cheerfully maintaining that Britain's investments in this country, the difficulty of defending Canada, and fear of Russia in her rear
protected us from British aggressiveness. But prestige as well
as security was at issue. With Britain present in superior
force, the United States, for all its size and riches, was not
master on this continent. Moreover, with England regnant
on both shores her command of the Atlantic was indisputable.

In 1890 President Benjamin Harrison made a fresh at-
tempt to mediate a long-standing boundary dispute between
British Guiana and Venezuela. Robert Todd Lincoln, United
States Minister in London, approached Lord Salisbury as to
a triangular conference of England, Venezuela, and the
United States with a view to agreeing on a formula. The
Prime Minister, chronically dilatory, wore out Lincoln.
Blaine threatened direct intervention. Harrison expressed
anxiety over the "appearance of encroachment" on an Ameri-
can republic and sent the North Atlantic squadron into
Venezuelan waters on receipt of erroneous word that the
British meditated forcible persuasion at Caracas. Yet in the
end Harrison fell back before Salisbury's passive resistance.

The quarrel, vexing Anglo-American relations for well
over a decade, turned on yellowed Dutch and Spanish maps
and Britain's steadfast refusal to submit their definition to
any but her own judgment. Venezuela had sought a settlement early in the 1880's. Failing in London, she appealed to
Washington. Lord Granville, Gladstone's Foreign Secretary,
accepted President Grover Cleveland's good offices in 1885,
but Gladstone fell before a preliminary convention could be

drafted. On returning to power, Salisbury repudiated the accord. Thereafter in Cleveland's first term the Foreign Office, abetted by Edward J. Phelps, the American Minister and previously a Yale law professor, successfully skirted the question. Phelps, doubting that we had a legitimate interest in a piece of "jungle, bush and water" near the equator, took the liberty of pocketing one of the President's notes. He would not be the last legal scholar to misunderstand this country's preoccupation with the Venezuelan border.

Still another problem troubled Anglo-American relations. In general this referred to this country's long-time desire for a transisthmian canal, specifically to the Clayton-Bulwer Treaty. That treaty, negotiated in 1850, neutralized Central America, binding the United States and Great Britain not to acquire territory there and not to dig a canal separately. In effect, the treaty inhibited both countries from undertaking the canal. This was especially irksome to the United States, which had contemplated the project since the 1820's. The treaty grew out of a state of tension that followed the discovery of gold in California and the Mexican War. The gold rush had again focused attention on the isthmian passage (we obtained from Nicaragua in 1849 a treaty ceding canal rights) and the war, setting its sanction on the acquisition of Texas, California, and the Southwest, alarmed Britain as to our further intentions toward the south. For our part, we were fearful of British encroachments on Nicaragua and Honduras. British power was paramount in the Carribbean, incidents affecting American trade and shipping multiplied, and John M. Clayton, Secretary of State, negotiated the convention with Sir Henry Bulwer, the British Minister, in momentary dread of a "collision."

Although the treaty met a need of the weaker Sea Power, it had never been popular in this country. James Buchanan, Clayton's predecessor and soon to be President, thought Bulwer "deserved a peerage" for what he had obtained, while Stephen A. Douglas charged the Secretary of State with "truckling to the British." Repeated attempts, the most recent by James G. Blaine as Secretary of State, had failed to lift the yoke. The Frenchmen came and went from Panama, and by 1890 the question of an all-American canal was by no means academic. With a show of bravado, Congress actually chartered a company to build a canal across Nicaragua, but that act did not abrogate the treaty. In January, 1891, the Senate Foreign Relations Committee resolved that the United States was no longer bound in law and morality to uphold the treaty, which should now be declared null and void. Although only a committee pronouncement, this reflected a widespread exasperation, as did Senator John Sherman's protest against the possibility of an English canal. Such a development, said Sherman, would create a zone "more formidable than Gibraltar and more troublesome than Canada." England had made no move in that direction; the Senator merely included that among the evils capable of flowing from the treaty.

Out of mingled wrath, pride, and impotence there swelled a boldly recurrent demand for the expulsion of Great Britain from this continent. The annexation of Canada was perennially mooted in the press. Lodge, coming from Boston, a focus of Anglophobia, epitomized the "on to Canada" mood by urging the United States to be "as insolent and overbearing and ready to show fight as the others" (meaning England), to the end that "from the Rio Grande to the Arctic Ocean there shall be but one flag, and one country." To the *New York Sun* it seemed there could be "no middle place for Canada. For us, she must be either incorporated with our own union or be deemed a foreign country. It is for the Canadians to say whether they choose to be treated as brothers or strangers."

The agitation gave the British some concern, as it provoked a steady controversy in Canada itself. A writer in the London *Fortnightly Review* took note of a widespread belief in England that the Bering Sea disputes were but "precursors of the annexation of Canada to the United States." Sir Charles Dilke's challenging book, *The Problem of Greater Britain*, which recommended imperial federation, came out in 1890. Reviewing it in the *North American Re-*

view, the Marquis of Lorne remarked on the "prevailing belief in the States . . . [that] ultimately all the Anglo-Saxons in North America will range themselves under the banner of one huge republic."

5

On both sides of the Atlantic the unhealthy state of Anglo-American relations caused alarm, strong voices being raised in behalf of closer ties. There was even ill-timed talk of alliance or federation, Carnegie and Cecil Rhodes advocating English-speaking union. The steelmaster, however, rubbed salt into whatever wounds existed on that side, advising the English to ship the royal family "back to Germany" and apply for entrance into the American republic as a regional subdivision of eight states, the capital to remain at Washington. Said Carnegie: "The only course for Britain seems to be reunion with her giant child, or sure decline to a secondary place, and then to comparative insignificance in the English-speaking race." Carnegie saw power in terms of industrial productivity, not in naval tonnage and bases. His reflections appeared in a book, *A Look Ahead,* which gave rise to protracted discussion in the press of both countries. Rhodes took a more moderate line, the other eminent precursor of Union Now suggesting that the capital alternate between London and Washington. Where Carnegie appealed to "race patriotism," Rhodes preferred "imperial patriotism," the American seeing the future in republican terms, the South African builder envisaging, as did Dilke, a magnified empire.

The prevailing note of English comment on America was one of pained surprise, in the vein of the London *Telegraph's* reproach that "American diplomacy still seems to be affected with a curious dislike of England, while every Englishman now feels a kind of family pride in the strength of America." A writer in the *Fortnightly Review* might call it a "pity that . . . inflation and boastfulness, arising partly . . .

from a sense of their own deficiency, should be so rife amongst Americans, for it is unnecessary"; but Lord Lorne, in the review before mentioned, saluted the "noble American nation, of whom it is our proudest boast that they have sprung from the same ancestry and are working out a kindred future of good to all mankind." And Viscount Wolseley, in a letter to a Baltimore friend published in the American press, fervently declared that "the closer the bonds uniting England to the United States, the better for both countries and for the whole civilized world. A war between the two countries . . . [would] afford a triumph to the foes of the Anglo-Saxon race."

These were not utterances to be dismissed lightly, coming as they did from the topmost drawer of the aristocracy and the army. Lord Lorne (later the Duke of Argyll), who had been Governor-General of Canada from 1878 to 1883, was a son-in-law of Victoria's, having married her fourth daughter, Princess Louise. Wolseley, Dublin-born, likewise knew this continent, having served as an observer with the Confederate armies in 1862 and commanded the Red River expedition that suppressed the Riel Rebellion in 1870. A great soldier and military commentator, Lord Wolseley was commander in chief in Ireland in 1890.

It was in such powerful circles that Mahan appeared as the most realistic, authoritative, and congenial American protagonist of collaboration. The naval officer's first book had struck the British—in the words of the *New York Post*—with the "force of revelation." Impressively, Mahan confirmed Sir Walter Raleigh's syllogism that world power rested on sea power and commerce. He rationalized every Englishman's instinctive certainty that England's might lay on the sea, and elaborated brilliantly John Adams's terse generalization of 1802 that "the trident of Neptune is the sceptre of the world." Tracing that course of empire during which the British swept Holland and France from the seas, acquiring India and Canada by the way, Mahan protested (as the *Literary Digest* reviewer pointed out) the "tendency of the closet historians to deal almost entirely with the phenomena of land movements . . . and of armies."

The British felt that much could be forgiven a man who reasoned thus cogently, even his declarations that America must prevail in her own part of the world. On any subject Mahan was heard with respect. When in his first published counsel in 1890 he avowed a "cordial understanding with Britain" to be "one of the first of our external interests," the British ruling class reacted approvingly. He penetrated their indifference by describing the British Empire baldly as "our greatest potential enemy." That circumstance, based upon encirclement, need not, however, stand against a "cordial recognition of the similarity of character and ideas" existing between the two countries.

Unemotional as a gun turret, Mahan assumed that "both nations . . . properly seek their own interest." It was "as true now as when Washington penned the words, and will always be true, that it is vain to expect nations to act . . . from any motive other than that of interest." Furthermore, false expectations should not be aroused, for "sentiment, although powerful in nations, is excessively undependable." Others might drape Anglo-American comity with garlands. Mahan, his name, his character, and his reasoning as rugged as the silhouette of a battle wagon, placed it on practical grounds.

He proposed a partnership, but one with limited liability. He wished no federation, dreading the irksome "bondage of the letter." Countries, he held, should not bind their action permanently because they had been drawn together in a specific crisis; mutual undertakings should be confined to matters of mutual interest. At other times each country should "stand clear of the other," realizing that "misplaced meddling separates the closest friends." His rationalism did not altogether exclude "sentimental" reasons for Anglo-American cohesion. Mahan's paternal grandparents came from the south of Ireland, his maternal grandparents being of Huguenot and English stock. Himself, he was uncompromisingly American. The intangible case for Anglo-American

affinity he placed less on grounds of race than on those of a
shared civilization, saying that

play with words and facts as we may, assert the composite character of the population of the United States, which none will
deny, the truth remains that the strength of our people, as of
Great Britain—herself a congeries of races—rests in a common
political and legal tradition, preserved and intensified under
conditions of separation nothing less than insular, which both
have inherited from the old home, where the forefathers of the
one race dwelt when history first knew them.

A publicist as well as a historian, writing often for the
periodical press here and in England, Mahan saw that our
expansion in the Caribbean would have to be primarily at
the expense of the British. As much as any American he
brought the British to agree that such a sacrifice might well
be compensated by the existence of a strong, satisfied, and
friendly Power at their rear and on Canada's flank. More
than any other single emollient, it may be supposed, Mahan's
cool arguments soothed the pain of Britain's Tories and sea
dogs over the successive amputations through which they
were to retire peaceably from the Caribbean and from their
prospective partnership in an isthmian canal, at length sharing their treasured sovereignty of the seas.

On this side of the Atlantic also Mahan, certainly as influ-
entially as any American, helped shape the new orientation.
Many of the Americans and the Britons who were to form
their country's external policies in the crucial years figura-
tively went to school to the shy, spare, silent naval officer.
His counsel, moreover, would extend into the great wars
of the twentieth century. His text in the matter of Anglo-
American relations never varied. Neither country, he held,
need fear the other, once the points of friction in this
continent had been removed; once England recognized our
command of our hemispheric waters. We would build the
canal, and automatically the Caribbean must become our
sphere. Elsewhere our strategic requirements were com-
plementary.

In his measured prose, beating with the cadence of his lifetime love, Mahan disclosed the unifying factor, the common denominator, that bound Anglo-American interests—Anglo-Saxon supremacy on the seas. For him the sea was the "nursing mother" of America as well as of England—our shield of security, our means of hemispheric prestige, and our road to destiny. In his first work he welcomed the "not far distant day when the people of the United States must again betake themselves to the sea and to external action, as did their forefathers, alike in their old home and in the new." Upon that theme he played many variations. The Anglo-Saxon Powers, confronting each other across the Atlantic, must keep that ocean under their command at all costs. That was the core of Mahan's reasoning, as it became the basis for the collaboration he so devoutly preached.

In 1886 Mahan asked Theodore Roosevelt to lecture at Newport. Out of that occasion grew a firm friendship. Upon reading the first sea-power book Roosevelt hailed it as a "naval classic" and vowed that he had passed the better part of two days absorbing it. He reviewed the book for the *Atlantic,* Lodge for the *North American Review.* In the 1890's Mahan served also as "philosophical mentor" to John Hay, the gifted journalist, author, and statesman who had been Lincoln's secretary; to Henry White, the diplomatist; to successive Secretaries of the Navy and members of Congress.

Walter Hines Page, one of the first magazine editors to solicit contributions from Mahan, as Ambassador to England in the First World War, foresaw the necessity of American participation if command of the Atlantic were not to pass. A naval enthusiast, steeped in Mahan's history, biography, and commentary, Franklin D. Roosevelt, was Assistant Secretary of the Navy during the Admiral's last few months in Washington. There were many other followers. No naval debates for many years but rang with Mahan's precepts.

On Mahan's first visit to England in 1894 he found himself regarded not only as a man of letters, a historian, and the world's leading authority on sea power—a field wherein

the British acknowledged some proficiency—but also as a
personal pledge of Anglo-American amity. No other American ever won so swiftly the respect of another nation; no
other American intellectual, unless it was Emerson, obtained so firm a hold on British thought. The prime reason,
naturally, was that Mahan wrote expertly on Britain's vital
interest, seagoing. His findings both explained and justified
the method by which England had gained imperial domination. As Mahan was a politico-military historian, moreover,
and not a social critic, he dealt only with the techniques by
which power was acquired and maintained, ignoring considerations of the wisdom of its use.

He was overwhelmed by Britons who wished, in addition
to honoring him, to obtain further enlightenment on England's chief preoccupation. The demands for his time exceeded the supply. As his stay neared its end Lord Rosebery, the Liberal Prime Minister, sent word: "I write in the
forlorn hope of being able to persuade you to dine with me
quietly . . . when we might have a conversation less inter-
rupted than was possible the other night; but I know it is
a forlorn hope." Lord Salisbury, who was out of power, had
better luck, carrying Mahan off to Hatfield, the famous
country seat of the Cecils, for a long week end.

The Prince of Wales, having dined him on the royal
yacht at Cowes, commanded Mahan's presence at a levee at
St. James's Palace so that they might protract their discus-
sion of sea power. Another of Victoria's sons, the Duke of
Connaught, a serious military theorist, dropped in on
Mahan unannounced aboard the cruiser *Chicago,* which
Mahan was commanding on the European station, and
thereafter sought other opportunities for informal talk. His
interviewers included Lord Roberts, the hero of Kandahar,
Lord Spencer, First Lord of the Admiralty, and Admiral
Lord Charles Beresford, who declared roundly that the
American had turned "sea power" into a household word.

In accepting degrees from Oxford and Cambridge within
one week Mahan was, Rosebery wrote him, "setting a
record." At Cambridge the public orator, welcoming him in

the ritualistic Latin, "thoroughly appreciated that we are of
the same blood, the same language, and the same glorious history," stretching "forth across the sea, which happily separates us no longer, our right hand in a bond of friendship
which we hope is destined to be for all time." The implication, of course, was that Mahan had bridged the Atlantic
for the Anglo-Saxons. He was seriously sounded on a project
to provide him with a chair of history at Oxford. In the
London press, daily and periodical, which had hailed his
first two books (the *Edinburgh Review* used thirty-two pages
to describe the first), the visit called for superlatives. None
excelled the *Times,* to which Mahan was another Coperni-
cus, his new, if mundane, system being based on sea power.

The climax of Mahan's pragmatic apostolate came on the
Queen's birthday, May 24, 1894, when princes of the blood
and Cabinet Ministers honored him at a banquet. A large
banner proclaiming "Blood Is Thicker than Water" draped
one end of the hall. Lord George Hamilton, the chairman,
who had been and again would be First Lord of the Admiralty, feelingly toasted Anglo-American reunion: "England and the United States are not two nations, but one;
for they are bound together by Heaven's act of Parliament
and the everlasting law of nature and fact."

Mahan, his power doctrines and his visit, inspired a brief
and unrealistic movement toward an alliance of the English-
speaking Powers based on sea power. The premature movement, important because it was the first sprouting of a concept that would show a sturdy growth a generation later,
was unrealistic because an important issue of ascendancy in
the New World still had to be settled between the two
Powers; it was brief because that issue would soon obtrude
itself on their relations.

Carnegie's inflated proposal had stimulated dinner talk,
but few Britons were as yet ready to take a back seat to the
Americans, especially if that meant exiling the Widow of
Windsor. Sir George Clarke (later Lord Sydenham), finding
Carnegie's projected federation "too remote to appeal to the
practical mind of either nation," suggested a substitute

based on common sense. Since the Americans intended becoming a Sea Power, why not, asked Sir George, form an English-speaking "naval league" for defense and peace? Sir George was an English Mahanite, a friend with whom the American naval officer carried on correspondence.

The Clarke formula gained its greatest triumphs in the service journals. A flight into prophecy by the *Army and Navy Gazette* foretold a day when the allied navies would "give peace to the world through that predominance of race, which is as strong in action as it is close-knitted in kinship." And the *Admiralty and Horse Guards Gazette*, preferring a "practical" and limited seagoing alliance, felt sure that the United States would "take up arms in our defense" were the "continental powers to attack the British empire." A wide hearing was given the idea in the periodicals, and a novel—*Blood Is Thicker than Water* by Geoffrey Danvers—forecast a "naval union," placing its consummation at the beginning of this century. By coincidence a British squadron visited Boston late in May, and its commander, Admiral Sir John Hopkins, predicted for the press a coming "federation" of British and American sea power.

Mahan joined the public discussion that fall, taking part with Lord Charles Beresford in a friendly debate—"Possible Anglo-American Reunion"—in the *North American Review*. Both seafaring men favored an informal naval accord; neither thought the time ripe for an alliance—if, in truth, the time ever would be ripe for hard-and-fast political unity. Mahan opposed a forced growth, wishing to await the processes of democracy in any case, saying: "When, if ever, an Anglo-American alliance, naval or otherwise, does come, may it be rather as a yielding to an irresistible popular impulse than as a scheme, however ingeniously wrought, imposed by the adroitness of statesmen." In conclusion, he urged that the "two nations should act together cordially on the seas."

6

Unfortunately for the British and, as it transpired, for the Americans also, the great sea tracts of Mahan were conned elsewhere than in the English-speaking countries. Translated into other tongues, they became standard fare for all the Naval Powers, including Japan and Russia. The French, observing that Mahan respected their major authorities, paid him intellectual compliments. The Kaiser paid him the deference of pupil to master. In Germany Mahan became required reading for statesmen and bureaucrats as well as navy men.

In the Kaiser's study at the New Palace in Potsdam, copies of Mahan in English could be seen, their margins annotated. After the second work, *The Influence of Sea Power on the French Revolution and the French Empire,* came from the presses, William telegraphed his American friend Poultney Bigelow that he was "just now not reading, but devouring, Captain Mahan's book and am trying to learn it by heart. It is a first-class work and classical in all parts . . . constantly quoted by my captains and officers." The major lessons of the first two books for an ambitious ruler lay in Mahan's explanation of the loss of Louis XIV's empire to the British, and of the eventual defeat of Napoleon. That these lessons struck home at Potsdam may be deduced from the Kaiser's subsequent naval policy. Rejecting the advice of his great Minister Colbert, Louis XIV fatefully turned his back on the sea, as Mahan pointed out. As for Napoleon:

On the land, State after State went down before the great soldier who wielded the armies of France. . . . Victory after victory graced his eagles, city after city and province after province were embodied in his empire, peace after peace was wrested from the conquered; but one enemy remained ever erect, unsubdued, defiant; and on the ocean there was neither peace nor truce, until the day when he himself fell under a host of foes, aroused by his vain attempt to overthrow . . . the power that rested upon the sea.

And again, a bit of prose that has become famous: "Those far-distant, storm-beaten ships, upon which the Grand Army never looked, stood between it and domination of the world."

It may be assumed that the vivid, egocentric William II wished to avoid the common fate of the Sun King and the Corsican—defeat at the water's edge. His desire for a challenging navy, a desire that came to consume him, had however to be deferred. His almost landlocked people could not be brought at once to the sea. His Ministers lagged also. Count von Caprivi, Bismarck's successor, and still under his spell, opposed naval expansion until he too fell in 1894. With Caprivi "the only naval question was how small our fleet can be, not how big." Prince von Hohenlohe, Caprivi's successor, a kinsman of Victoria's and a cynic with his major estates in Russia, understood that the Germans had a besetting fault, as Tacitus had divined—envy; but he did not understand sea power. It was only when in 1898 the Kaiser got as Chancellor the supple-minded Count (later Prince) von Bülow—"*my* Bismarck"—that the naval race with Britain would begin.

The next year, 1899, when William by doubling his naval estimates contributed to the inevitability of 1914, Mahan attended the First Hague Conference as a delegate from America. Alongside Mahan's name on the cabled list the Kaiser penciled, in what must have been a flash of clairvoyance: "Our greatest and most dangerous foe." A corresponding footnote from Salisbury would have its own historical interest.

A measured judgment on Mahan cannot be passed with too much confidence. His sea-power dogmas, confirmed as they have been in every trial, are again being tested in the most decisive of ordeals. Mahan was much more than a naval expert, however, or than a protagonist of expansion, a prose Whitman calling for "passage to more than India," bidding Americans "Sail forth, steer for the deep water only!" Theodore Roosevelt, who at various times hailed him "mas-

ter" and "genius," in a more definitive moment ascribed to
him the "mind of a first-class statesman."

A statesman Mahan undoubtedly was. He defined for the
United States a foreign policy consisting of four principles
of action: (1) supremacy in the Caribbean; (2) co-operation
in the Orient; (3) abstention from European affairs; and
(4) collaboration with Great Britain. As this narrative pro-
gresses it will be seen how closely we have hewed to the
Mahan line. It was in realms of high strategy, the disposition of the power of the state, that Mahan most influenced
events. He understood not only the external relations, but
the internal structure of the state, being always aware that
in a "nation of more complex organization . . . the wills
of the citizens have to be brought not to submission merely,
but to accord."

Like Clausewitz, Mahan regarded force as an attribute of
statecraft to be employed on all appropriate occasions and
not reserved for crises. War to him also was a continuation
of policy "by other means." "The surest way to maintain
peace," he held, "is to occupy a position of menace." He
regarded war as an evil too vast to be trifled with, the
preservation of peace as a task requiring all the experience,
skill, and hard sense available. A clear understanding of the
country's strategic position; the full utilization of offensive
and defensive association with countries whose interests
tallied with ours; just and honorable dealings with the weak
as well as the strong outside our borders; the will to resist
aggression wherever offered, and the arms suitable for that
task—that might be submitted as Mahan's prescription for
peace.

Mahan foresaw in the 1890's, before the dreadnought, the
submarine, air power, and even the wireless, the larger magnitudes into which war was evolving. The United States, between its two oceans and the two "old worlds," was "to all
intents an insular power like Great Britain." (Japan had not
then risen to a position of potential enmity.) Since America
was insular, Mahan taught, "every danger . . . to which
the United States may be exposed can be met best outside

her own territories." To Mahan the ocean was not a barrier but a highway, not a huge, inert bastion, but a broad, smooth plain over which an enemy, unless hindered, might move more swiftly than over broken ground.

With the piercing of the isthmus, a "historical imperative," we would become committed to the protection of a great sea gate. From being an abstraction that we had felt ourselves powerless to defend, the Monroe Doctrine would become a genuine necessity for our own continental security. Woven through his thought was the implicit belief that prudence dictated sharing our enlarging defense burdens with our neighbor and kinsman, the mightiest Sea Power.

The shadow cast by Mahan over the twentieth century was to exceed that of any other military or naval man of the nineteenth—surpassing also, perhaps, that of any political thinker, with the possible exception of Karl Marx. Certainly no one can assess with exactitude how much his teachings prompted the Kaiser to challenge British sea power in the years before 1914, or to what degree his precepts influenced the Anglo-American sea-power coalition of 1917 and 1941. Upon his death in 1914 the Paris *Figaro* said of Mahan that he had "called a new age into being" and that "as the supreme philosopher of history . . . he profoundly modified the history of the age in which he lived." The appraisal may be suspect as rhetoric, yet there can be no doubt that Mahan, both as exponent of sea power and as prophet of Anglo-American collaboration, greatly modified the power equations of the last half-century.

7

Our first Ambassador to England,[1] Thomas F. Bayard, wrote the State Department in 1894: "The United States is the last nation on earth with whom the British people or

---

[1] In 1893 the Administration "smuggled" through an isolationist Congress an act raising the rank of our envoys to the principal Powers to that of Ambassador.

rulers desire to quarrel; and of this I have new proofs every day in my intercourse with them." Bayard's note, no doubt wholly truthful, came nevertheless in the midst of a fresh Caribbean incident, a British intervention in Nicaragua that paraded again before American eyes the bogey of encirclement.

For more than a century Great Britain had maintained a protectorate, sometimes legal, sometimes implied, over the Mosquito Indians of Nicaragua's Mosquito coast. In 1860, responding to representations from Washington, the British surrendered suzerainty by the Treaty of Managua. Friction persisted, however, and in 1881 the Emperor Francis Joseph, called in as arbitrator under the terms of the treaty, deprived the Nicaraguans of most of their sovereignty over the Mosquito coast. Thereafter the British, with the moral support of the Americans on that coast, virtually governed the Reservation in the name of the Indian King of the Mosquitos. The British consular officers presumed to act on behalf of the King because his $5,000 annuity from Nicaragua was in arrears although American banana interests predominated in the Reservation and in the city of Bluefields.

In 1893, a new Nicaraguan dictator, José Santos Zelaya, arose. He was soon at war with Honduras and, proclaiming it a war measure, he sent troops into the Reservation. The troops took over, and when the British consuls protested they locked up a vice-consul. Americans and British alike welcomed the British man-of-war *Cleopatra* when she arrived in March, landing marines and Gatling guns, driving out the Nicaraguan troops, restoring order—and the consular regime. A minor colonial brush to the Foreign Office, which levied a demand for $75,000 in damages from Zelaya, the incident annoyed the United States Government, especially as the British were now stipulating with Zelaya that no representative of another American state could sit in on the adjudication.

Furthermore, the Mosquito coast contained the eastern terminus of any Nicaraguan canal, and the Bluefields inci-

dent re-enforced American feeling that the British were
poaching in the neighborhood of the prospective canal.
Therefore Cleveland instituted diplomatic inquiries through
Ambassador Bayard. The President considered that somehow we were being trampled upon.

II. The Last Quarrel

At Christmas time in 1895 the English-speaking Powers stood for three days poised on the ragged edge of hostilities, nearer to war than at any moment since Andrew Jackson had saved New Orleans from Sir Edward Pakenham and his red-coats. Cleveland, aiming over Venezuela's shoulder, had dealt a stout blow at British encirclement, and in all the eighty years since New Orleans no international issue had so aroused the truculence of Washington—and the country. Defiantly unanimous, Congress promptly authorized the President to run his own Venezuela-British Guiana boundary without regard to the English, voting $100,000 to speed the job. Not in the memory of the oldest Senator, reported the London *Times* with moderation, had there been such "spontaneous demonstrations." At the Navy Department lights burned late as the North Atlantic squadron, under orders for the West Indies, was detained in Hampton Roads. Two days after the presidential message of December 17 the *Washington Post,* reflecting the capital's overwrought condition, promised the British: "Let but a drum tap be heard from the White House grounds and in every city of the land a host will rise, and in every rural neighborhood and countryside battalions will start up."

In London also the Government bristled over what the *Times* termed a "monstrous and insulting" procedure. A flying squadron of twelve vessels was ordered by the Admiralty to stand by for possible duty in the Caribbean, the press calling it a "naval mobilization." The War Office inquired about Sikhs and Ghurkas for the South American jungles. Soon, however, pacific voices rose above the incip-

ient clash of arms. "Only common sense is needed," rumbled
Gladstone from his retirement, calling the thought of war
"astounding folly." Lord Rosebery stigmatized an Anglo-
American war as the "greatest crime on record," and the
Prince of Wales and the Duke of York bespoke in a message
to the *New York World* a return to the "same warm friendship" that had existed.

Although Lord Salisbury predicted on December 19 that
the war spirit would soon "fizzle away," American blood
was up. A Wall Street panic on "Dismal Friday," December
20, 1895, dropped $350,000,000 out of security values, ruined
eight firms, moved the London *Times* to a not ungratified
comment on the "commercial and financial disaster" wrought
by the President, and helped to sober the country. But
jingoes were yet to mob a peace meeting addressed by Henry
George and Dr. Lyman Abbott in New York, and an Irish-
American group, assuming the cloak of extraterritoriality,
offered Cleveland 100,000 volunteers. Sir Julian Pauncefote,
the British Ambassador in Washington, truthfully reported,
however, a week after the message that a "strong undercur-
rent" had begun to flow "in opposition to the warlike attitude of the President."

The fever ran its course in about two weeks—a counter-
irritant unwittingly applied by the Kaiser helped to abate
it in England—whereupon responsible Britons and Americans alike gave thanks. "A family quarrel," in the words of
one of the principals, it lacked none of the virulence of domestic strife. Fortunately its termination was more har-
monious and lasting than that of many such quarrels. Arising nominally over the boundary question, the difference
went, of course, far deeper. The dispute stood squarely in
the path to that accord on which alone an Atlantic concert
might be based. In effect, Cleveland was asking the British,
none too politely, to call off their sea-power cordon, leaving
to us these shores of the Atlantic. This the British were to do,
and in view of the result the diplomatic passage at arms over
Venezuela may have been the most fruitful in the whole history of Anglo-American relations.

Being ahead of the story, we must now retrace our steps to see how the long-standing dispute reached crisis proportions. Upon recrossing the White House threshold in 1893, Cleveland found the Venezuela matter no nearer solution than in 1889. Gladstone, soon to retire after more than sixty years in the House of Commons, was briefly in power, a circumstance heartening to the President, that "four-square, firm, solid, magnificent Titan" (as Gamaliel Bradford saw him), when he patiently resumed diplomatic entreaty. But this was not the Gladstone of the 1880's, and his Foreign Secretary, Rosebery, who, Ambassador Bayard was convinced, "would rather win the Derby than carry through an important public matter," proved less amenable than Lord Granville had in 1885.

The President now determined to haul the issue out of the diplomatic pouches and into the light. In his annual message of December 3, 1894, Cleveland accordingly begged the British to arbitrate, a "resort," he threw in placatingly, "which Great Britain so conspicuously favors in principle and respects in practice." Although his patience scraped bottom, the President, thoroughly aware of our naval ineffectiveness, also sang low. (He had once warned the country that "inability to resist aggression" enfeebled a foreign policy.) An arbitration proposal introduced by a member struck fire in Congress, which on Washington's Birthday, 1895, passed a joint resolution calling on England and Venezuela to compose their long-standing differences.

Whereupon the glorified "line fence quarrel," as Cleveland would describe it in a memoir published eight years later, entered a new magnitude. The United States had officially declared itself in, it had become (again quoting the President's memoir) this Government's plain "duty and obligation to protect our own national rights." Taken in conjunction with the state of anti-English feeling, the congressional action was an unmistakable warning—a signal which Rosebery, who had meantime succeeded Gladstone, and Lord Kimberley, his Foreign Secretary, ignored. Worse than that, Kimberley, progressing from polite evasiveness to firm assertion, responded by initiating a strong policy in the Caribbean.

In April, 1895, Cleveland had before him a blunt refusal by Kimberley to heed the request of the United States Government. With his refusal was a note from Bayard, describing a "pink line" the Foreign Secretary had traced on a map, a line extending British Guiana's claims to a mouth of the Orinoco River. The President, seeing in the "pink line" a new encroachment, was not soothed when Bayard, often more British than the Queen, advised him in the face of Kimberley's obduracy to call it a day.

At this juncture Kimberly's policy produced a sequel to the Nicaraguan incident of 1894. On April 22 three British warships entered the Nicaraguan west-coast port of Corinto, demanding immediate payment of the $75,000 reparations assessed by London over the Bluefields trouble. All other conditions, including a salute to the flag, had been met. When the improvident Nicaraguan Government confessed itself unable to raise the money, the naval commander declared a blockade, and five days later—after the Nicaraguan authorities refused him access to their cable—he landed Marines, seized the customhouse, occupied the town, quelled rioting by force, and remained in occupation until the money was on the barrel head.

As if by reflex action, a wave of antagonism swept America. The Senate rang with charges of British aggressiveness at Corinto. In Albany the Assembly of Cleveland's own state adopted a resolution decrying the lack of patriotic spirit "which has characterized the Administration at Washington in its dealing with the complications at Corinto." The Connecticut Senate engrossed similar reflections. Theodore Roosevelt informed the Washington correspondent of the London *Times* as "plainly as a mortal can, that the general sentiment of this country is . . . hostile to England and . . . very strong in support of the Monroe Doctrine."

Up and down the Atlantic seaboard the press bayed England with one voice. The *Baltimore American* called Britain's conduct "brutal," her "claim unjustified." In Philadelphia the *Press* inquired, in comment on our weakness at sea: "If England chooses to hold on, how is she to be dispossessed?" The *New York Tribune* termed the "bullying" of Nicaragua one of the "wanton crimes against civilization," and called for a new "marginal reading of the Monroe Doctrine." But it was the *New York World* that exposed the gravamen of the American objections to Corinto: "England cannot have another rood of ground on the American hemisphere, and in the neighborhood of the trans-Isthmian routes, she cannot have an inch."

John B. McMaster, the historian, attempted to explain in the *New York Herald* that the Monroe Doctrine did not apply at Corinto. Few informed Americans believed that it did. Most of them, including the State Department experts, knew that it did not. The Monroe Doctrine, however, could be and was loosely referred to as a means of covering American chagrin.

In England the Corinto incident was mildly deplored as an excessive demonstration of force. Sir William Harcourt, Chancellor of the Exchequer, government leader in the House of Commons and a notable Liberal, raged privately at the Prime Minister and Kimberley for their ineptitude in "using . . . arms to settle a paltry amount" at the risk of incurring ill will in America. Carnegie cautioned his friend John Morley (the biographer of Burke, Voltaire, Rousseau, and Emerson), then Chief Secretary for Ireland, that the Ministry was "playing with fire" in the Caribbean. It is almost certain, however, that if the Ministry thought of the explosive opposition here, it minimized it. Even Harcourt was unprepared for the storm when it burst.

Cleveland could not, if he would, ignore the public temper. In the spring of 1895 a considerable part of his nation was marching as to war. The jingoes, reproducing the hasty conduct of Henry Clay's "war hawks" in 1812, were nudging the President to action. "Inflammable materials," as Henry White would describe them to Salisbury and others in London, lay about everywhere. Cleveland himself supplied a spark by unburdening his perplexities to Don M. Dickinson, who had been Postmaster General in the first Cleveland Cabinet. On May 10 Dickinson, in a speech at Detroit, after hinting that Britain was strengthening her West Indies strongholds, gave utterance to a circumlocutory warning to England against further interference in this hemisphere.

In London, Bayard disparaged Dickinson's speech as a "flow of contentious bosh," but the "war hawks" approved. Senator John T. Morgan, the expansionist from Alabama, led the attack on the "British occupation of Nicaragua," and when the fight petered out upon British withdrawal, Bayard rejoiced that "Morgan's swords of lath and shields of pasteboard" had been made "ridiculous." Bayard was not alone in reprehending the jingoes. John Bassett Moore, who was to become the foremost American authority on international law and was then teaching at Columbia University, applauded Bayard's course, writing him to London that the war party that had "grown up since the panic of two years ago" seemed determined to bring on a war "to crown their wicked insanity"—some because they thought it a "good thing for the country," others in the hope of speculative profits.

Deprived of Nicaragua as an issue, the warmongers recurred to Venezuela, beating the drums for the Monroe Doctrine. Senator Lodge, warning the country that if Britain succeeded in crowding Venezuela, there would be no barrier to European colonization to the south of us, cried: "South America must not become a second Africa!" The Monroe Doctrine, he declared, must be upheld, "peaceably" if possible, "forcibly" if need be. The war party was, in truth, bipartisan. Theodore Roosevelt might wring cheers from the National Republican Club in New York by emphatic appeals to the Monroe Doctrine; downtown, a former Governor of Ohio, Campbell, aroused Tammany to a like enthusiasm by demanding that the Government invoke the "spirit of 1866" —when Napoleon III was required to withdraw his support from Maximilian in Mexico. And Joseph B. Foraker, a former Republican Governor of Ohio soon to go to the Senate, called for application of the Monroe Doctrine "boldly" throughout the Western Hemisphere.

The old demands that Britain strike her flag on this continent ran through the press that spring. The *Army and Navy Journal* remarked meaningfully that England may one day stand in need of friends, and she may as well know now that the "appearance of any European flag on this Continent is a constant offense to American sentiment." Senator William E. Chandler spoke the authentic accents of the war party when in a signed editorial in his *Concord* (New Hampshire) *Monitor* he called war with England "inevitable"; encirclement had created an irrepressible issue, hostilities would develop over the mouth of the Orinoco.

The President, hands to ears, groaned that it was "very provoking to have such matters . . . prematurely and blunderingly discussed in the newspapers," but by now his own mood was not meek, and Dickinson's speech presumably had mirrored his state of mind with accuracy. The uproar disturbed Lawrence Godkin, who deplored in the *New York Post* the "number of men and officials in this country who are now mad to fight . . . navy officers dream of war and talk and lecture about it . . . Senate debates are filled with predictions of the impending war and with talk of preparing for it at once." His father, the Irish-born, irascible E. L. Godkin, writing in the *Nation*, characterized the warlike American democracy as "mostly ignorant and completely secluded from foreign influence." In such a martial atmosphere did Cleveland prepare his next sortie on behalf of the Monroe Doctrine.

Rosebery's Ministry fell in June (not, however, on account of its American policy), and the Olympian Salisbury returned to power in time to sustain the brunt of Cleveland's gathering wrath. In that month the President gained an ally when upon the death of Secretary Walter Q. Gresham he promoted Richard Olney, Attorney General, to the State Department. A Massachusetts lawyer with a marching mind, piercing black eyes, and a gift for the forcible phrase, Olney it was who by suggesting the injunction in the Chicago

railroad strike had assisted Eugene V. Debs on his self-sought
road of martyrdom. Bold to the point of rashness, Olney
could put a point to the President's sprawling determination.

The President in all but this crisis was a "Little American," unsympathetic with the expansionists, averse to jingoism. Olney, on the contrary, favored expansionism, was a bit
of a jingo himself, and likewise a friend of England. Believing with all the influential men who were to shape the
coming pro-English orientation in the encirclement thesis,
Olney held, however, that this quarrel had to be resolved first.

Escaping the heat of the capital, the President and the
Secretary of State fled to the Massachusetts coast, Cleveland
to Buzzards Bay, Olney to near-by Falmouth, where he prepared a note and delivered the draft by his own hand to
Buzzards Bay. Cleveland approved, calling the note the "best
thing of its kind I ever read." Olney, he thought, had put
the case for our right to intervene under the Monroe Doctrine "on better and more defensible grounds than any of
your predecessors—or mine." After minor revisions the note,
withheld for the present from publication, went into a
pouch for Bayard. As the pouch closed Olney realized that
it would be "difficult to retrace" that step.

2

The note was a bugle call set to legal terms. Few diplomatic communications passing from one friendly Power to
another have ever had its ringing quality. Since Olney was
not a trained diplomat but a lawyer, the note read like a
brief, the argument being marshaled in two parts. First the
Secretary urged England to have done with this border dispute that did her no credit. He stressed Venezuela's weakness, her inability to match force with the British Empire,
and then appealed to the "love of justice and fair play so
eminently characteristic of the English race." That was familiar ground. Then, dismissing Venezuela, he came to the
heart of the matter—the stake of his own country. The
United States was pledged not to permit a European coun-

try to enlarge its territories in this hemisphere by no matter what means. Encroachment on a self-governing Latin American neighbor stood in our view precisely on the same footing as conquest or pre-emption of empty land by colonization. By what warrant did we interpose? By virtue of the Monroe Doctrine, a part of our "public law."

The United States, Olney next generalized, was "practically sovereign on this Continent . . . its fiat law upon subjects to which it confines its interposition." Three thousand miles of ocean "make any permanent political union between a European and an American State unnatural and inexpedient." That, of course, meant Canada. Then came a threat. With the "powers of Europe permanently encamped on American soil," we would have to alter our military policies.

Olney's vehemence violated the diplomatic canon. He asked for a reply within a specific time (so that the President might comment in his December message), and that made the note ultimative in character. It was "shirt-sleeve" diplomacy at its most spirited. Years later Olney acknowledged the "bumptiousness" of the note, explaining that he had chosen words "the equivalent of blows" as the only means of penetrating Foreign Office opacity. The British, Olney felt, reflecting a widespread American opinion, held us much too negligibly.

The President called the note "Olney's 20-inch gun," and critics of the Venezuelan policy have maintained that the caliber was excessive. As a rule, Americans who felt moved to apologize for the Secretary's rugged boastfulness were those who restricted the issue to the boundary question, ignoring, or perhaps minimizing, the incendiary background out of which it came. In estimating the collateral circumstances, it should not be overlooked that in 1895 the Monroe Doctrine enjoyed little prestige abroad. At best, Europe tolerated without acknowledging it, largely because of a tradition that Britain, mistress of all the sea lanes leading to the Americas, wished it upheld. As his ambitions waxed the Kaiser was to find it more and more irksome. Soon a generation of German militarists, nourished on Pan-German assertiveness, would agree with Dr. W. Wintzer, a colonial authority, that Germany "cannot allow herself to be simply dispossessed of her inheritance in one of the most thinly peopled and richest quarters of the globe, South America."

In 1895 a great many Americans believed, rightly or wrongly, that England was undermining the Monroe Doctrine and that prompt and strong action was needed to shore it up. Nor was it difficult to arouse public anxiety over the Monroe Doctrine. A symbol of national prestige, its name was a rallying cry. Mahan doubted that its "precise value" was understood by most Americans, but "the effect of the familiar phrase has been to develop a national sensitiveness which is a more frequent cause of war than material interests."

Since the Monroe Doctrine was the broadest of generalizations, covering this country's relations to Europe and the republics to the south like an umbrella, few Americans could hope to understand its "precise value." It had, moreover, an organic nature, having been enlarged, interpreted, and invoked several times. Reinterpreted by Cleveland and Olney, it was now being invoked in reality to enlarge the gains of the American Revolution. In 1783 the colonists had won sovereignty over the thirteen colonies. Their descendants were now seeking acknowledged hegemony over a continent and the continental waters.

Olney's note went forward on July 20. In London Bayard read it to Salisbury, preserving the amenities by suggesting to the Prime Minister the "importance of keeping such questions in an atmosphere of serene and elevated effort." In reply, Salisbury expressed "surprise and regret" that it covered so much ground. A member of a distinguished Delaware family, Bayard had served his party as Senate leader during part of Reconstruction and as Secretary of State in Cleveland's first Administration. He believed his forte to be conciliation. In May, when the Venezuelan crisis was gathering day by day, he had written from London that "no questions now open between the United States and Great Britain . . .

need any but frank, amicable and just treatment." The former Secretary of State deprecated Olney's statesmanship; Olney, in turn, held Bayard in scorn. "The constant stream of taffy played by Mr. Bayard on the English people tickled them," Olney put in a letter, "where it did not sicken them."

Cleveland and Salisbury, both large, reserved, slow-speaking, stubborn men careless of their appearance, now confronted each other. The Prime Minister also had gained a coadjutor in June, Joseph Chamberlain, a match for Olney in audacity, the "republican ex-mayor of Birmingham," a Radical Home-Ruler who had turned Liberal Unionist. As Colonial Secretary, a hitherto second-grade rank in the Ministry that he had chosen, Chamberlain would virtually share the Premiership with Salisbury for seven years, contribute more than his part toward letting England in for the Boer War, muddy England's relations with Germany, and create as glittering a dash in his way as the Kaiser and Theodore Roosevelt did in theirs.

A middle-class ironmaster from Birmingham, Chamberlain entered Parliament as a vociferating reformer, hell-bent against the Established Church and the House of Lords, agitating for an income tax and "three acres and a cow" for the agricultural laborers. By 1895 he had been transformed into the leader of British imperialism. He was the greatest toff in the West End, identifiable anywhere by his silver-rimmed eyeglasses and the orchid in his buttonhole. He had married (the second time) an Endicott from Massachusetts and hence qualified for what Harcourt, who had married a daughter of John Lothrop Motley, called the company of "semi-Americans." The first businessman to rise into the top flight of British power circles, Chamberlain would be the most puzzling and uncertain figure in the Venezuelan crisis. Effusively pro-American in public, behind the scenes he would be threatening, dilatory, and obstructive. Salisbury, "that old bulldog," as Olney dubbed him, although a master of the arts of procrastination was a miracle of translucence beside the Colonial Secretary.

The Prime Minister received the note on August 7, then

went to the Continent for a holiday. Olney, returning to Washington in September, grew impatient when by mid-October he had received no acknowledgment. He cabled Bayard without result. In that month divergent expressions in the two countries illustrated the difference in their attitudes toward the chasm widening between them. The British press, still under the moderating influence of Mahan's visit, revived talk of Anglo-American collaboration. Mindful of the profound changes in the Far East flowing out of the Sino-Japanese War of 1894-95, the *Westminster Gazette* suggested that the English-speaking peoples had better stop wasting their energies "squabbling over such petty matters as the boundaries of Venezuela and Nicaragua." The *Spectator* urged an Anglo-American treaty recognizing the Monroe Doctrine, and the London *Morning Post,* organ of the squirarchy, conceded that the United States would regard an enlargement of Britain's territories at the expense of Venezuela as "an infringement of the Monroe Doctrine."

In the United States a report that Olney had sent Britain a stiff note leaked out and produced a fresh anti-English barrage in the press. The *New York Times* saw Britain robbing Venezuela of a sixth of her lands "on no better title than the highwayman establishes to the traveler's purse." Anticipating the President, the *Washington Post* would have the United States draw a boundary and then "plant ourselves upon that line sword in hand." The *Chicago Tribune* foresaw a defense of the Monroe Doctrine "not only with rifles, but with cannon." But it was the *Atlanta Constitution* that went to the essence of the quarrel, predicting that "if we do not wake up very soon, England will have all of Central and South America under her control, and the United States will be forced back into the ranks of the third and fourth class commercial powers."

At this point Britain served Venezuela with an ultimatum based on a border attack on Guiana police. A spatter of reproof in the London press and new attacks here caused the Foreign Office to notify Bayard promptly that the incident in no way affected the boundary. Nerves on both sides of the Atlantic were drawing tight. When the *New York World* published a report that Salisbury had received Olney's note "curtly," advising the American Ambassador that he rejected the Monroe Doctrine as a basis for our intervention, Bayard rushed into print with a circumstantial denial. An article by Roosevelt, now a New York City police commissioner, in the *Century Magazine* prompted Moorfield Storey, the Boston Liberal, to exchange letters with Carl Schurz, the German who became an American statesman. Storey thought it "hardly safe to let the demagogues go too far in arousing the jingo feeling," and Schurz complained that Roosevelt "gives too much rein to his restless and combative temperament."

On November 20 Olney again cabled Bayard, saying that it would not be regarded as "courteous if the British Government did not answer [soon] or give any reason" for the delay, but Bayard was unable to mail Salisbury's reply until November 27, too late for the annual message. Cleveland, deeply irritated, wrote his message, making only passing reference to the Venezuela matter, and went to North Carolina duck-shooting. He instructed Olney to receive the note from Sir Julian Pauncefote in his absence and draft a reply against his return.

In time Olney would learn that Salisbury's slight was in part intentional. Relying on representations from high American quarters in London, official and unofficial, Salisbury believed that he could ignore the President's time limit with impunity. He had been told that Olney was a clever lawyer who with a presidential campaign in the offing wished merely to "twist the lion's tail" for political purposes. The hope that a change in administration would weaken the American position was to linger in the Ministry. In addition to all this Salisbury resented in Olney's note the suggestion of an ultimatum. Later it would be explained that the Prime Minister had delayed because the Turkish persecution of Armenians, then in full stride under Abdul Hamid (Gladstone's "Great Assassin"), engrossed his attention. Likewise, that subordinates had misled him about the date for the opening of Congress. Neither explanation soothed American asperities.

3

Salisbury's reply, in two separate notes, reached Washington on December 6. If the Olney note had the force of a blow, Salisbury's rejoinder was no less crushing. In prose sterner than Olney's the Prime Minister rejected each argument in detail. Great Britain would not arbitrate with Venezuela; Salisbury regarded the American assumption of a voice in a border dispute between a European Power and an American republic as the assertion of a "novel prerogative"; he coldly rebuked Olney's annoyance at the presence in the Western Hemisphere of the British flag; he declared the Monroe Doctrine unknown to international law, and in any case inapplicable here. The Prime Minister "offered no solution and invited no further discussion."

After five months Lord Salisbury had replied in kind, in what Andrew D. White, the president of Cornell University and a former Minister and future Ambassador to Germany, described as Salisbury's "cynical, 'Saturday Review,' high Tory way." The President, returning on Sunday the fifteenth, read the note and announced that he would have a special message for Congress on Tuesday. Olney's proposed reply was ready and Cleveland's dander was up. After conferring with Olney and Secretary Lamont, Cleveland sat up all night, alone in the White House, redrafting his message, following substantially Olney's line. On Monday he read it to the Cabinet. The Cabinet, although realizing the gravity of the message, gave their unreserved approval.

On Tuesday a Congress at first startled, then swept by warlike enthusiasm, heard the President's blunt declaration that he proposed taking the Anglo-Venezuelan quarrel into his own hands. Come what may, "fully alive to the responsibility incurred," Cleveland, that "staunch old boy" (as his successor, McKinley, called him) was going to run the boundary—and stand behind it when run! He declared it the duty of the Government to "resist by every means in its power, as a wilful aggression upon its rights and interests, the appropriation by Great Britain of any lands, or the exercise of any governmental jurisdiction over any territory which, after investigation, we have determined of right belongs to Venezuela." And in justification of his course he stated that "there is no calamity which a great nation can invite which equals that which follows supine submission to wrong and injustice."

This was war talk, so interpreted at once and in both countries. The cheers of Congress found a loud echo in the press. A sort of hysteria swept the people, the jingoes denouncing England extravagantly, the Anglophiles of the exclusive city clubs going to equal lengths in condemnation of the "war spirit." Thus Theodore Roosevelt, polishing his sword in the *New York Evening Sun,* prophesied the early seizure of Canada, and declared it "infinitely better" that American cities should be "laid level" than that tribute be paid for the sake of safety. He put the affair on lofty grounds by charging the British with never permitting "considerations of abstract right or morality to interfere with the chance for national aggrandizement or mercenary gain." In a letter to Lodge, Roosevelt hoped the "fight will come soon."

Lodge charged that eminent friends of England, "ordinarily sane," had cabled London that the Senate was controlled by "a jingo mob in the galleries; 'gentlemen of the pavement' reminiscent of the French Revolution." Cleveland thanked Commissioner Roosevelt for his support. Among the host of obscure Americans writing their approval to the White House were Woodrow Wilson, a Princeton professor, and William McKinley, Governor of Ohio, who vouchsafed the "approval of the people of Ohio" for the "President's firm and dignified stand."

Carnegie, yielding to a surge of hostility, wrote the Duke of Devonshire, now Lord President of the Council, that English recalcitrance would force the United States to build a great navy and to take Canada. "The giant son," he crowed, "is his mother's child, down to the roots, and like her will boss things within what he feels to be his sphere of operations . . . which is rapidly expanding." Dining with a "lot of financiers, including Morgan," the night of the message, Chauncey Depew found them terrified, predicting that Europe would rush to sell the next morning and create a "financial cataclysm, the like of which had never before been witnessed."

The stock-market reaction was deferred three days. In the Senate, Lodge attributed the panic to an attempt by London to "frighten Congress." Writing to Henry White in Europe, he reported that "outside the moneyed interests . . . the American people, like Congress and the press, are solidly behind the President in defense of the Monroe Doctrine. We shall carry our point, and there will be no war."

In other quarters there was no such firm assurance that we would not be called on to fight. Sober men were shocked at evidence that so large and vocal a proportion of the people seemed to welcome another go at the British. In the Midwest and farther toward the Pacific the press confidently held that Britain would have to back down; she needed our foodstuffs, she had heavy investments in this country, she would not wish to lose Canada, and—the most clinching argument—she "couldn't get to us." But Americans such as Mahan, who understood our strategic problem in terms of sea power, reckoned the respective naval strength of the two countries in ships and available bases and prayed for deliverance.

The British, ringing us with bases, had forty-four battleships to our four, with other types in even greater disparity, and an overwhelming capacity to build ships. We were potentially the great Land Power of the West, but our armies could only reach Canada. With Britain in command of the seas, responsible military experts foresaw that if the British chose to fight, they might punish the coastal cities thoroughly and subject the country to a long and vitiating blockade. If war came, these men feared that it might be protracted, costly, and likely to end in a stalemate, with Canada back in the empire and British sea power aggrandized. The experts comforted themselves with reports that Europe's power relationships were highly unstable and the British might very well fear that an American war could grow into a general war, with Russia and even Germany taking a hand at her rear. As we shall see, Britain was pretty well isolated by the Continental Powers.

On the third day, as Congress authorized the President to run the border, the Senate heard a word of caution from the chaplain, who asked God to "forbid that the two foremost nations . . . which bear the name of Christ . . . should be embroiled in war with all its horror and barbarities." Thereafter, although talk of war would not stop entirely for some days, other voices echoing the chaplain's pious hopes would be heard increasingly. Dr. Lyman Abbott mounted an anti-war demonstration at Plymouth Church; Dr. Charles H. Parkhurst thundered against the war party; and a Newark, New Jersey, clergyman ringingly doubted that "all of South America" was "worth a drop of American blood."

Carl Schurz deprecated Cleveland's rigor, holding that it "grievously broke [with] his otherwise dignified and statesmanlike foreign policy." Joseph Pulitzer, who soon would be blowing the bellows for another war, this time exercised his journalistic ingenuity for peace. His *New York World,* branding the President's policy a "terrible blunder," cabled dozens of English leaders for peace messages in harmony with the season. The cables were burdened with their replies, which forthwith appeared on the first page of the *World.* Also beating against the current, the *Springfield Republican* condemned quarreling over a "beggarly plot of land."

The plain-spoken Charles W. Eliot poured a withering fire on Roosevelt and Lodge as "degenerated sons of Harvard" for exploiting "this jingoism, this chip-on-the-shoulder attitude of a ruffian and a bully." Roosevelt retorted by categorizing Eliot and Schurz as "futile sentimentalists" whose endeavors would contribute toward a "flabby, timid type of character, which eats away the great fighting qualities of the race."

In London the expatriate novelist Henry James struck a

note of dark dismay. The "American outbreak, the explosion of jingoism," he misread, ascribing warlike fervor exclusively to the rawboned West, discovering a "vast new cleavage . . . split almost, roughtly speaking, between the West and the East . . . really two civilizations side by side in one yoke; one civilization and a barbarism." He was correct to the extent that Eastern financial and business interests threw their weight overwhelmingly into the scale of appeasement. (Eight years later Cleveland was to level his contempt at the commercial classes that in the winter of 1895-96 preferred profits to the country's "honor.") The *Journal of Commerce* spoke for Wall Street when it charged that "Mr. Cleveland has outjingoed the jingoes."

Into the heat of the controversy the venerable Chamber of Commerce of the State of New York threw a resolution urging the President to conciliate Britain. A group of Boston financiers telegraphed asking Cleveland to put no Americans on his border commission. From many quarters came petitions that Gladstone be asked to preside over that body, but Cleveland's commission, headed by a Supreme Court Justice, was all-American. The deportment of entrenched capitalism disposed fairly well of John Bassett Moore's analysis of the economic basis of the war party, as well as of the Marxist explanation that in the Venezuelan crisis the American capitalists were seeking to divert public attention from hard times, the outcries of the bimetallists (among the most warlike of Anglophobes), and the Populist uprising in the Midwest.

A good many American intellectuals narrowed the issues to the single matter of Venezuela's boundary. Among those who ignored the provocative question of encirclement was John Bassett Moore, who doubted that the claims of the Latin American republic were "scrupulous," and feared that Cleveland had launched us on "numberless quarrels." (The United States Government, of course, had not prejudged the virtue of either side's claims, only requesting that they be adjudicated by an impartial body.) The historian James Ford Rhodes opposed application of the Monroe Doctrine to a "mere boundary dispute." Andrew White here and Bayard from London reproached the Venezuelans for their incapacity to govern themselves with Anglo-Saxon wisdom and orderliness. Robert Todd Lincoln also sought to calm the waters by a reflection on the Venezuelans. He asserted in a newspaper interview that once they had declined arbitration. This was denied by Lodge.

As the convulsive year neared its end these narrow constructionists were answered exhaustively. On December 30 Lodge, in the Senate only two years, summoned his historical and literary talents for a major effort, a full-dress arraignment of Great Britain's intransigeance. The preceding summer Lodge had passed in England, where under Henry White's chaperonage he had seen Chamberlain, Balfour, and others. First reviewing the boundary dispute from its earliest times, the Massachusetts Senator proceeded to America's case for ascendancy in the Western Hemisphere. Should Europe break the force of the Monroe Doctrine, "we shall have formidable rivals all about us; we shall be in constant danger of war. . . . The Monroe Doctrine rests primarily on the great law of self-preservation." At the last session he had called the Senate's attention to England's absorption of islands in the Pacific and stressed the necessity of annexing Hawaii before that archipelago fell to the great Sea Power. Said Lodge now:

I ask you . . . to look at the Caribbean sea . . . look at the strong naval station . . . at St. Lucia . . . thence . . . westward . . . you find Trinidad . . . then Jamaica, then British Honduras. . . . That line faces the South American coast. This territory claimed from Venezuela is being pushed steadily to the westward along that coast, and the point at which it aims is the control of the mouths of the Orinoco. . . . The purpose of all these moves is written plainly on the map. If successful, they will give Great Britain control of the Orinoco and the Spanish Main and make the Caribbean Sea little better than a British lake.

The United States, Lodge continued, had become a great nation. "We must be leaders in the Western Hemisphere." For thirty years we had been absorbed in "healing the rav-

ages of the Civil War and in completing the conquest of the
great continent which was our inheritance. That work is
done." Now Americans were turning their eyes outward,
"toward interests that lie beyond our borders and yet so near
our doors." What do they see?

They see those interests have been neglected. They see another
nation hemming them in with fortifications and encroaching
upon regions which must remain what they have always been—
American. They are resolved that there shall be an end to those
encroachments . . . that the United States shall not sink in the
scale of nations, that it shall not be menaced even by that nation
to which we are united by bonds of blood and speech.

Lodge could not believe that "any English ministry seriously intends" hostilities, and yet

their recent policy is . . . unfortunate. We have seen British
forces at Corinto. We know the attitude the British Government
assumes in Venezuela. They are attempting to take land on the
Alaskan boundary. They have just denounced the *modus vivendi,*
and reopened in that way, the perilous dispute of the north-
eastern fisheries.

The Senator ended on an ominous note: "It is not by acci-
dent that these events have all occurred, or all come to an
acute stage, within the last year." (In testimony to man's
chronic inability to penetrate the future, all the grievances
enumerated by Lodge were to be satisfied, peaceably, within
six years.) His speech, widely published in the press, hardened American determination to see the Venezuelan crisis
through.

4

The impact of Cleveland's message fell more heavily on
the British. They were unprepared either for trouble over
a distant and unconsidered South American republic or for
the American President's severity. James Bryce, indignantly
protesting Cleveland's shotgun language, reported to Henry
Villard, the American journalist and railway magnate, that
"not one man in ten . . . in the House of Commons" had

any idea that the boundary dispute was in crisis stage. The British public, even less aware of the long, tedious diplomatic prologue to the message, was undoubtedly taken by surprise.

All England, therefore, bristled as the Government prepared for hostile eventualities in the Caribbean. Chamberlain sprang to action in an interview in the London *Times,* saying: "Americans are not people to run away from; in fact, I do not know any people from whom we can afford to accept a kicking." The *Times* itself set a belligerent key: "When kinsmen fall out, they can quarrel very bitterly. As we cannot yield to the demands . . . without surrendering title to almost the whole of our empire, we must hold ourselves prepared to defend our rights in any quarter where they may be threatened." London music-hall crowds booed "Yankee Doodle."

Generally the British press took a lordly rather than a martial tone. The service journals, which after Mahan's visit had been advocating a naval alliance, now lectured their transatlantic cousins. American "brag," the *Army and Navy Gazette* admonished, might arouse the British lion. In like strain the *Admiralty and Horse Guards Gazette* counseled the United States to climb down ere the British lion gets "his back up at this recurring tail-twisting . . . and determines to lay about him with his paws." A London daily, the *Graphic,* asked if Cleveland seriously believed that the "frontiers of the European colonies in America are to be held at the good pleasure of a committee of Washington gentlemen." Exceptions were the *Times* and the *Telegraph,* which carefully considered dispatches from the United States such as those of George W. Smalley, who cabled the *Times* from Washington after Cleveland's message: "Senator Lodge bubbling over with delight . . . there could not be a more sinister indication of the sense in which this message is understood." In the political weeklies a less exigent note quickly appeared; the Tory *Saturday Review,* for example, on January 4, 1896, granting that the Ministry could "sub-

mit the dispute in Venezuela to arbitration, and American
arbitration at that, without loss of self-respect."

On the whole British bellicosity failed to reach the height
or the duration of its American counterpart. After all, it
was the Americans who considered themselves the aggrieved
(and encircled) party. Abram S. Hewitt, a former Mayor of
New York, might seek to cheer Salisbury by suggesting that
"Cleveland must have been drunk"; Bayard might wring
his hands publicly over the inelegance of "that MAN" Olney;
but as for the British themselves, Henry White observed that
they looked with "profound horror on the thought of war
with America."

White, a skilled diplomatist who had been legation secretary at London under Harrison and would return under
McKinley, disapproved of Cleveland's bluster, but strongly
upheld his objectives. It was, White wrote home at this time,
"to the interest of both branches of the Anglo-Saxon race
that we shall be supreme in both American continents; otherwise, there will always be questions between the two countries." John Hay, also in London during part of the crisis,
held the same views. Thus it was that the "scholars and
gentlemen" who would have much to do with orienting
American policy toward association with England in the
next few years—Hay, Roosevelt, Lodge, and White—were
united in confronting England in 1895-96, and for the same
reason. All wished the British to give over in the Caribbean,
believing the removal of friction in that area a prerequisite
to genuine friendship.

Salisbury and Chamberlain at first resisted appeasement.
The Colonial Office was inundated with messages from Canada and other British outposts in North America and the
West Indies angrily denouncing Cleveland and demanding
a strong policy against American "insolence." But the friends
of America, numerous in the City as well as in political quarters, rallied for peace as quickly as their opposite numbers
on this side. Bryce, although annoyed over the outburst of
Anglophobia in a country where he felt at home and had
been honored, Harcourt, Balfour, and others sought to mol-

lify the Prime Minister. There were some curious omissions. John Morley, regarded as a friend of the United States, repeated a story current in London that an American gold-mining syndicate, having obtained concessions from Venezuela in the disputed region, was "bullying the United States Government." (J. L. Garvin resurrected this story in his life of Chamberlain.) The theory was founded on an inadequate knowledge of Cleveland's character.[1]

In letters to Roosevelt and Villard, Bryce betrayed a lack of comprehension of public feeling in America. "What in the world is the reason" for the ill will? he inquired. "There is nothing but friendliness on this side. . . . The idea of making the Caribbean Sea an English lake [according to Lodge] is quite a novelty to us. Why should we be hated in the United States . . . we don't come into hostile contact . . . we are not rivals anywhere . . . we have the warmest feeling toward the people of the United States." At about this time Roosevelt wrote White of their mutual friend Lodge: "The Anglomaniac press and, of course, Smalley have utterly misrepresented him . . . it is to the interest of civilization that the United States . . . the greatest branch of the English-speaking race should be dominant in the Western Hemisphere."

Meanwhile the London Stock Exchange, which had been caught in the reflex of the New York panic as had those of Paris and Berlin, applied the balm of humor, cabling solicitously to the New York Stock Exchange: "When our warships enter New York Harbor, we hope your excursion boats will not interfere with them." The New York brokers replied: "For your sakes, it is to be hoped that your warships are better than your yachts." The reference was to an America Cup race sailed the preceding summer in New York Harbor, in which the challenger, Lord Dunraven, protested the crowding of the course by spectators' boats, claimed a foul,

[1] All through the controversy rumors cropped up of the activities of American and English gold syndicates. None disclosed any real relationship between gold and the actions of either Government. Bayard was a prolific source of these reports.

and then defaulted, giving rise to derogations in each country
on the sportsmanship of the other's yachtsmen.

On Christmas Eve Chamberlain's roving imagination
conceived a diversion in the spirit of the season. He wrote
Salisbury to suggest that both Americans and Britons might
find an outlet for their martial desires in a joint naval demonstration against the Sultan of Turkey. He reminded the
Prime Minister that after all "blood is thicker than water,"
but Salisbury doubted that the time was propitious for
sounding the American cousins on the subject.

The next day diversion appeared from another quarter.
Dr. Leander Starr Jameson, a hotheaded administrator for
Cecil Rhodes's South Africa Company, appeared on the
border of the Transvaal at the head of from 400 to 500
armed members of the company's constabulary and militia-
men. In the Boer South African Republic a revolt had been
timed for the end of the year, a rising by Uitlanders, predominantly British, against the rule of President Paul
Kruger. When the trouble began at Johannesburg, Jameson
was to march in. Rhodes and Chamberlain were thoroughly
familiar with the project. The Johannesburgers, however,
did not rise. Jameson was ordered not to advance across the
border, but on December 29 he disobeyed, and on New
Year's Day was surrounded by Kruger's bearded farmers and
taken prisoner at Krugersdorp. Jameson's headlong conduct
embarrassed Chamberlain, and he at once repudiated Jameson and set about extricating him and his men, several of
them officers in the British forces, from Kruger's positive
clutch. This took place on January 2, 1896.

The philosopher William James chose this moment to
excoriate Cleveland for arousing the "old fighting instincts
that lie so near the surface." Governments, he wrote, should
avoid "direct appeals" to man's pugnacity. "This your European governments know; but we, in our bottomless inno-
cence and ignorance . . . know nothing, and Cleveland, in my
opinion . . . has committed the biggest political crime I have
ever seen."

5

On January 3, 1896, British sensibilities were stirred to their deeps by the Kaiser's historic telegram to Kruger:

I express to you my sincere congratulations that without appealing to the help of friendly powers, you and your people have succeeded in repelling with your forces armed bands which had broken into your country and in maintaining the independence of your country against aggression.

Since 1881, the South African Republic had been under Great Britain's tutelage and hence the Transvaal had no foreign relations except as they passed through London. The telegram, therefore, was a flagrant intrusion between a European Power and its ward. A self-righteous document, it likewise passed judgment on an event concerning which the British were touchy, being uncertain over their moral ground. Further and more personally, the message was taken as an insult by a supposedly friendly monarch to his grandmother, the Queen.

The effect was felt instantly. From Queen to coster, England profoundly resented William's interference. Noting in her journal the German Emperor's "most unwarranted . . . outrageous and very unfriendly" act, Victoria penned him a grandmotherly note, suggesting that his agents had been misbehaving in South Africa and that his telegram had "made a very painful impression." The Prince of Wales, who had been busy stroking the American eagle, complained spiritedly of his nephew's "most gratuitous act."

The London populace, forgetting Cleveland's brusque war cry (although the Ministry did not), gave a physical point to its disapproval of the Kaiser. German sailors and dock workers were beaten. In shops, offices, hotels, and restaurants German workers suffered insults and sometimes dismissal. German clubs put up shutters and German residents kept to their homes. In some alarm, the Queen besought the Prime Minister to "hint to our respectable papers not to write violent articles," as "these newspaper wars often tend to provoke war—which would be too awful." She also "entreated" Salisbury to "prevent ill-usage of the innocent and good German residents." Led by the *Morning Post* calling for a fleet demonstration in the North Sea, the press indeed waged war on William II. "England," stormed the *Post,* "will not forget it, and her foreign policy will in the future be strongly influenced by the remembrance."

Lord Salisbury piecing the evidence together, concluded that the telegram really represented the climax of a six months' attempt by the Kaiser to "frighten England into joining the Triple Alliance." Placing this suspicion before the Queen, the Prime Minister added that such a pact would of course be "impossible . . . because the English people would never consent to go to war for a cause in which England was not manifestly interested." Her Majesty was not wholly convinced. She shared a view being widely advanced that "our isolation is dangerous."

6

The external pressures on the British Empire were concentrated at Number 10 Downing Street on January 11, 1896. Count von Hatzfeldt, the German Ambassador to the Court of St. James, called on the Prime Minister, as he had done before, to urge adherence to the Triple Alliance. He rather "forced" the matter, uttering "many warnings of the dangers of isolation," but leaving Salisbury unshaken, as he reported to the Queen. That day also Salisbury held a full Cabinet meeting, a device of government to which he resorted so seldom that two of his Ministers were certain the Prime Minister did not know them by sight. The Cabinet, summoned to discuss the American crisis, almost reached a crisis itself when Salisbury found a substantial majority so eager for accommodation with the Americans that they cared little or nothing about the terms.

Neither Salisbury nor Chamberlain had come prepared for so precipitate a backdown. Indeed, at eleven o'clock the night before, when Sir William Harcourt called on the Colonial Secretary at his house in Prince's Gardens, he had encountered resistance. Chamberlain was anything but "friendly" to arbitration. To that stanch friend of America, Sir William, Chamberlain would remain the "Spanish fly in the pot of ointment."

In the Cabinet meeting Salisbury, compelled to give some ground, held out for a negotiated peace, so to speak; and when the majority pressed him too closely, he won his point and time to work out a settlement on his own lines only by threatening to resign. He would not, he declared, tender Cleveland and Olney an "unconditional surrender." It was apparent, however, to both the strong men of the Ministry that surrender of some sort was inevitable.

In the Cabinet and outside, sentiment by now overwhelmingly supported a speedy composition of the differences. Two days before the Cabinet meeting, in fact, Bayard had heard from a Foreign Office source that Salisbury was preparing to "trim his views." With the public, William's telegram had eclipsed Cleveland's challenge to the British Empire. By a transposition perhaps unparalleled in the affairs of nations, overnight Germany had replaced the United States as the enemy, and as a sequel this country suddenly became popular with the English people. In the "halls" there were now cheers for "Yankee Doodle," jeers for "Die Wacht am Rhein." Press and pulpit alike confessed themselves revolted at the thought of war with the English-speaking republic.

Four days after the Cabinet meeting Balfour, then the First Treasury Lord, sounded the call to retreat. At Manchester, voicing his abhorrence of an Anglo-American war as suggestive of the "unnatural horror of civil strife," Balfour looked forward to that happy time "when some one, some statesman of authority more fortunate even than President Monroe, will lay down the doctrine that, between the English-speaking peoples, war is impossible." On that day Bayard cabled Olney about the "welcome and unmistakable difference" in English reactions toward a possible "conflict with the United States—and with Germany." The Ambassador had a letter from an English friend describing the contrast:

"In the first [contingency], incredulity, doubt, horror that England and America should go to war; in the second, the whole nation to a man . . . aroused at once to fever heat and ready for anything."

Forthwith Chamberlain also quieted public apprehensions in a speech at Birmingham:

We do not covet one single inch of American territory and war between the two nations would be an absurdity as well as a crime. . . . The two nations are allied, and more closely allied, in sentiment and in interest, than any other nations on the face of the earth. While I should look with horror on anything in the nature of fratricidal strife, I should look with pleasure to the possibility of the Stars and Stripes and the Union Jack floating together in the defense of a common cause, sanctioned by humanity and justice.

Salisbury made his "surrender" public in February. The speech from the throne at the opening of Parliament noted, with approval and a degree of understatement nothing short of remarkable, that the United States had "expressed a wish to co-operate in terminating the differences" over Venezuela's borders. In reply Lord Rosebery, Opposition leader in the Lords, declared it everyone's duty to help the chiefs of the two governments out of their "impasse." Sir William offered Liberal support in the Commons. Balfour, the tall, remote skeptic and amateur of spiritualism whose lot it would be to ruffle Anglo-American feelings more than any other British statesman of his generation, denied in the House any slightest intention on the part of the Ministry to violate the "substance, or the essence" of the Monroe Doctrine. But it fell to Salisbury to make the amende magnificent:

From some points of view, the mixture of the United States in this matter may conduce to results satisfactory to us more rapidly than if the United States had not interfered. I do think the bringing in of the Monroe Doctrine was, controversially, quite unnecessary. . . . Considering the position of Venezuela in the Caribbean Sea, it was no more unnatural that the United

States should take an interest in it, than that we should take an interest in Holland or Belgium.

Thus Salisbury conceded to the United States a primary position in the Caribbean. Carefully separating the American objective (recognition of the Caribbean as our sphere) from the instrument we had chosen to obtain it (the Monroe Doctrine), in his faintly querulous utterance, the disillusioned Prime Minister signified Britain's retirement from that sea.

In an exploratory conference with Henry White a few weeks later Salisbury gave evidence that the concession in his Venezuelan "surrender" speech represented a permanent policy. Asked by White for an indication of Britain's attitude in case we felt called upon to annex Cuba, Lord Salisbury replied that American relations with Cuba—then deep in the insurrection that led within two years to American intervention—were "no affair of ours." Friendly to Spain and reluctant to see her "humiliated," said Salisbury, the British Government did not "consider that we have anything to say in the matter, whatever . . . course the United States may decide to pursue."

In November (after the American election) Olney and Pauncefote signed the heads of a treaty between Great Britain and Venezuela. Cleveland observed that as the United States was not a party, the treaty would be saved the "customary disfigurement at the hands of the Senate." The American boundary commission stopped work at that time. Its fourteen volumes of maps and other documents went to the arbitration commission, and it was a source of satisfaction to Andrew White, a member of the American body, that the final disposition closely followed the findings of that commission. Venezuela and Britain each gained and lost lands they had claimed, the British being restrained back of the Orinoco delta.

The real gainers, of course, were the United States and Great Britain. The British began their retreat from the Caribbean and American waters, a retirement that would not halt until the naval bases encircling the United States of the 1890's were turned over to America in 1940. The Monroe Doctrine was acknowledged by the British Government, and the British Foreign Office initiated a policy, ascribed to an edict of Salisbury's, of never allowing any dispute with the United States to come to a head. Soon German diplomatists, as will be seen later, were to complain of an Anglo-American tie and to seek, under the Kaiser's definitive instructions, to break it.

Growing out of the last quarrel between the Anglo-Saxon Powers, a reliable friendship was obtained by the British, one standing them in good stead in their next three wars, one with the Boers, two against the Germans. Henceforward, as Olney was to assert in a speech at Harvard on March 1, 1898, the two countries in general would make common cause against any third party. At Harvard the stout protagonist of aggressive American action in 1895 said:

There is a patriotism of race as well as of country—and the Anglo-American is as little likely to be indifferent to one as to the other. Family quarrels there have been . . . and doubtless will be again, and the two peoples, at the safe distance which the broad Atlantic interposes, take with each other that liberty of speech which only the fondest and dearest relatives indulge in. Nevertheless, that they would be found standing together against any alien foe by whom either was menaced . . . it is not permissible to doubt.

The ancient animosities with Canada would slowly subside. The recurrent threats against the Dominion's British attachment would give way to a fixed acceptance of that status on this side of the border; and United States-Canadian relations would grow in warmth until in 1938 an American President underwriting Canada's defense against any hostile power aroused general approval in his country. By 1940 only Americans infected with Nazi megalomania would assert a claim to the great Dominion.

No other Power, Mahan suspected in 1896, would stand aside for American ambitions. The strategic and sentimental factors were not likely to be so conjoined again. The first hindrance to Anglo-American association in an axis extending across their common ocean had been removed. Others would fall soon. Balfour's "more fortunate Monroe" had not arisen, but a common consent, more potent than a written formula, would outlaw war between the greatest Atlantic Powers.

The rapprochement of 1896 was studied closely on the European continent. A conviction spread in German and French diplomatic circles that the two countries were bound by a secret understanding. Again and again until 1914 that suspicion was to cross the minds of European diplomatists. Prophetically, the *Cologne Gazette*, typifying Continental comment, supposed that the effects of the new accord would be "felt long after the British Guiana boundary question has been forgotten." All movements toward Anglo-American fellowship, here and in England, gained impetus. A characteristic utterance was the proposal by Professor George Burton Adams in the *North American Review* for a new "empire of the race." The unrealistic and somewhat lyrical emphasis on race, mildly reflecting the hysterics of the Pan-Germans and the Pan-Slavic *mystique* of Moscow, was a froth on the surface that would be skimmed off in the clearer light of the twentieth century. Underneath were unifying elements appealing to the hard, pragmatic sense of both peoples.

7

While Anglo-American relations pursued an ascending curve until 1914—and thereafter—Anglo-German relations were generally to trend downward, following a course marked by frequent jolts, and by occasional periods of concord, but moving steadily toward mortal conflict. German-American relations also were to deteriorate.

The rancors produced in England by the Kaiser's telegram to Kruger were prolonged and aggravated by economic stresses. In late January, 1896, the newly founded *Daily Mail* branded Germany a "semi-civilized nation" like Turkey—the

ultimate in epithet at the period of the Armenian mas-
sacres. By late spring German goods were boycotted in the
Midlands. Not only was the Kaiser thought inimical, but
Germany stood disclosed as the commercial enemy. A book
brought about that realization, a journalistic tract, *Made-
in-Germany,* written by a Socialistic thinker named Ernest
Williams, who hoped to prod England into adopting the
state-subsidized neomercantilism of Germany.

"A gigantic commercial state," said Williams, "is arising
to menace our prosperity and contend with us for the trade
of the world," by freight rebates given by German shipping
lines and the state railways, together with government encouragement of cartels, and consular help in the field. The
British, suffering from the practices, called them question-
able, if not actually "unsportsmanlike." The report also disclosed lower wage scales and better technical training across
the North Sea.

British pre-World War resentment of Germany's commercial strides reached its peak in midsummer, 1896. By August
a Board of Trade Blue Book soothed sensibilities. Pointing
out that the Germans had only made gains here and there,
the Blue Book attempted to prove that British world-wide
trade had not only held its own but was steadily gaining.
"The German trade bogey disappeared with the light," remarked the *Daily News,* chief free-trade organ. A year later
the *Contemporary Review* was pleased to report that British
trade had reached a new high-water mark in the fiscal year
1896-97, and that empire trade had increased faster during
the last twenty years than that of the rest of the world. This
made gratifying news for the Diamond Jubilee visitors.

Victoria had reigned sixty years in 1897. The "Captains
and the Kings" reviewed with her the home fleet of one hundred and sixty-five vessels stretching beyond the horizon at
Spithead. William II, believing against the evidence of his
eyes that British might had seen its best days, would soon
be penciling on the margin of Hatzfeldt's reports: "The
Jubilee swindle is . . . over," and "the dead ride fast."

Germany, like the United States, was on the march. In

1894 Erich von Tirpitz, then attached to the Oberkommando of the navy in Berlin, had furnished William with his first high-seas naval policy. Based on Mahan, it called for an aggressive battle fleet embodying "national power on the seas." Tirpitz argued that a "state which has . . . world interests must be able to uphold them and make its power felt beyond its own territorial waters. . . . World commerce . . . world industry . . . world intercourse and colonies are impossible without a fleet capable of taking the offensive."

Until then Germany had never acknowledged naval interests wider than the North and Baltic seas. In 1895 the Kiel Canal was opened. By 1897 Tirpitz, after a tour of duty in the Far East, had a seat of power in the Reichsmarineamt, and his presence there was accepted as evidence that the German Empire was embarked on an aggressive naval policy. In that year Great Britain first took alarm at German naval ambitions.

In 1897 the Kaiser seized a naval base in the Pacific from the Chinese and attempted to obtain another from the United States. In November the Germans descended on Kiaochow, on the Shantung Peninsula, using as excuse the death at the hands of Chinese bandits of two Roman Catholic missionaries attached to a German mission. While in Asiatic waters Tirpitz had recommended Kiaochow as the best Chinese port available and even drawn terms for a lease. "I am thoroughly resolved, with full severity and at need with the most brutal regardlessness," William instructed his naval commander, Rear Admiral von Diederichs, "to show the Chinese at last that the German Emperor does not allow himself to be played with; and that it is bad to have him for an enemy." The Chinese needed no "severity." (It was during a Reichstag debate on Kiaochow that Bülow first demanded for Germany a "place in the sun.") The Russians, who had a secret fifteen-year lease on the port, gave way, and Germany had a foothold across the Yellow Sea from Japan and around the corner from the Russians at Port Arthur.

Also arousing the Kaiser's—and Tirpitz's—desires was Pago

Pago, one of the choicest harbors in the Pacific. German cupidity, it turned out, was stimulated by a new American move to annex Hawaii, a collection of islands that had been attached to the United States sentimentally since 1820, economically since 1875, and as a naval outpost since 1887.

In the closing weeks of his Administration Harrison had sought to incorporate the islands in the American political system, but Cleveland set the effort aside. Negotiated with King Kalakaua, but in the interest of the American sugar planters, a reciprocal trade treaty of 1875 brought Hawaii within what James G. Blaine called the "American Zollverein (customs union)" and made them "an outlying district of the State of California." Then in 1887 Cleveland obtained from the King exclusive rights to Pearl Harbor as a naval base. At the same time he vetoed a British proposal to lend the Hawaiian Government $2,000,000 on the pledge of certain revenues.

No serious challenge to American ascendancy had ever arisen, although British Ministers in Honolulu and Washington had from time to time sought various leverages. There can be no doubt that Hawaii, a great sea bastion lying athwart an imperial life line from Canada to the antipodes and commanding the approach from the Orient to both North America and the Isthmus of Panama, represented a temptation to British naval strategists. It may even be doubted that Great Britain would have allowed any nation other than the United States to hold Hawaii without a struggle. The fact that the British offered so little obstruction (and that largely in the way of diplomatic intrigue on the spot) may be taken as an indication that the encirclement so disturbing to Americans in the early 1890's was less a matter of conscious, resolute policy in London than of habit and drift.

King Kalakaua died in 1891 while on a visit to the mainland. A close collaborator of the New England Congregational missionaries and their offspring, the sugar planters who dominated the islands economically, the King had sought the protection of the American flag. He wished to be annexed. His sister and successor, Queen Liliuokalani, attempted to break the grip of the Americans on the realm. Fearing the submergence of her people under the weight of American economic control and Asiatic immigration, she re-established native customs and announced a policy of "Hawaii for the Hawaiians." Her hostility to the Americans coincided with legislation on the mainland discriminating against Hawaiian sugar. Under the McKinley tariff all offshore sugar was admitted free; a bounty was established on the domestic crop. Heretofore Hawaiian sugar had been duty-free, West Indies and other sugar had paid a duty. The Hawaiian planters, facing heavy loss, saw their only hope for survival in annexation, which would include them in the domestic bounty.

The upshot was a coup promoted by the planters, assisted by the American Minister, John L. Stevens, and supported by United States Marines. Stevens at once recognized the provisional government, the American flag was raised over Government House, and a delegation departed for Washington to offer Hawaii to the Union. Within eleven days a treaty was drafted, and Harrison sent it to the Senate only a little more than two weeks before he left office on March 4, 1893.

Cleveland withdrew the treaty, sent an antiexpansionist former Congressman from Georgia, James H. Blount, to investigate the "revolution," and upon hearing the facts—that the natives had no voice and the Queen's government had been overawed by the Marines—he decided to undo the uprising and turn the islands back to the Queen. His envoy, however, encountered an obstacle in the Queen, who gravely informed him that if returned to power she would be obliged to behead the American conspirators and seize their property.

Cleveland was confronted, as Mahan saw it, with a "choice no less momentous than that of the Roman Senate when the Mamertines invited the Romans to occupy part of Sicily and thus abandon the policy of isolation that had confined them to the Peninsula." He elected the isolationist alternative, declining, as he told Congress in his annual message of December 3, 1893, to depart from the "unbroken American tradition" in order to "provide for the addition to our territories of islands of the sea more than two thousand miles removed from our nearest coast." The means by which the "sugar barons" had obtained power he characterized with a "familiar and unpleasant name when found in private transactions."

His repudiation of Manifest Destiny brought condemnation from the jingoes, the expansionists, and large numbers of plain Americans who objected to hauling down the flag in the Pacific. The press, notably that of his own party, dealt mercilessly with the abandonment of Hawaii. Pulitzer's *New York World* thought Cleveland "under no obligation to replace a highly aggressive throne." The *Atlanta Constitution* sniffed that the "Democratic party has not been in the habit of restoring monarchies anywhere." "In ordering Old Glory pulled down at Honolulu," the *New York Commercial Advertiser* averred, Cleveland had "turned back the hands on the dials of civilization" and "shattered" the "dream of an American Republic at the crossroads of the Pacific—a dream which Seward and Marcy and Blaine indulged." To this editor, Cleveland "was the Buffalo Lilliputian." There seems little doubt that the public favored annexation in the light-hearted mood of a current jingle:

> . . . Liliuokalani
> Give us your little brown hannie!

The big-navy party, led by Mahan, strongly opposed the President's "policy of scuttle." To Mahan, Hawaii was the "Gibraltar of America." In a letter to the *New York Times* on January 31, 1893, he called the islands a vitally strategic "outpost" that must be held for Western civilization against a "wave of barbaric invasion" that might some day be forthcoming out of the Far East. Holding Hawaii would, of course, call for enlargement of our naval power, he added. Japan made no objection in 1893, but in 1897, when McKinley introduced a new Hawaiian treaty, the Tokyo Government filed a pro forma protest. All sections of British sentiment in 1893 seemed favorable to American annexation, the *London Times,* the *Spectator,* and the *Saturday Review* bestowing their blessings.

Meanwhile, wheels had been whirring at the Foreign Office in the Wilhelmstrasse. Tirpitz and the Kaiser viewed the disposition of the Hawaiian stronghold disapprovingly, but doubted their ability to alter it. Pago Pago was next best. Friedrich von Holstein of the Foreign Office provided a modus vivendi, and Hatzfeldt called on Salisbury with a devious proposal. Germany and Great Britain, the Ambassador suggested, should declare a joint interest in the fate of Hawaii, making inquiries in Washington. Then, having aroused American apprehensions, they should offer to withdraw their scruples over annexation if the United States would surrender Pago Pago. "You ask me to put my hand into a wasps' nest," Salisbury grumbled, declining the proposal.

III. Atlantic Concert: "Our Natural Ally"

"ON THE 1ST of May, 1898, a gun was fired in the bay of Manila and, in response, the skirmish line crossed the Pacific, still pushing the frontier before it." A usually grim novelist, Frank Norris in untypical star-spangled prose, celebrating Dewey's victory, typified the mood of 1898—Mahan's "great year." A great year it was, both for a spread-eagled pride in "imperialism" and for the Atlantic System. While the United States Navy swept Spain from the East and West Indies, gaining strategic footholds in both Indies for America, England moved to the side of this country, joining diplomatic forces against the pro-Spanish Powers of the European continent.

The Atlantic concert thus formed, fulfilling the dream of Jefferson, his Virginia successors, and Bolivar, gratified the expansionist party in the United States. Captain Mahan, hailing the British Empire as "our natural, though not our formal ally," rejoiced in a letter to Admiral Sir Bouverie Clark that the English-speaking Powers were following "Dizzy's [Disraeli's] road to imperial democracy." Henry Adams, harking back to Jefferson, supposed that England was at last entering the "American system," and Albert Jeremiah Beveridge, the Indiana laureate of empire, saluted "this conquering race . . . the Anglo-Saxon peoples' league of God," which, as he saw it, stood ready to divide the backward regions of the earth in the name of progress and universal peace.

To Mr. Dooley it seemed that "ye could waltz to" Beveridge's rhapsody, but America was marching, not waltzing, to such music. The end of the century was at hand, men's thoughts quickened into epochal idioms, and the Americans,

as Adams noted, were not content to wait for the fin de
siècle: "whether consciously or not, the new American had
turned his back on the nineteenth century before he was
done with it." Bismarck, born three months before Waterloo,
Gladstone, and Bayard likewise failed to wait out the century, dying in 1898; the German Chancellor taking occasion
before his end to stigmatize as "disgraceful" America's war
on Spain.

In that war destiny outran expectations. Who had suspected that the remnants of empire imposed on the Americas
by Columbus and Ferdinand and Isabella, by Cortez and
Pizarro, would be so poorly, if gallantly, defended? Certainly
not the Kaiser, who gaily prophesied that the pure-blooded
"hidalgo [would] cut Brother Jonathan to pieces," nor Tirpitz, predicting that the Yankee fleet, if it did not run, would
be sunk by the Spaniards. The Germans were, as usual and
characteristically, underrating the prowess of the English-
speaking Powers. Even the friendly English thought the
Spaniards would put up a better fight. In the Hong Kong
club, before that May morning at Manila English officers
offered Dewey's men good odds that they wouldn't survive
the Spanish mines, the new Krupp guns at Corregidor in the
mouth of the harbor, and the shore batteries in sufficient
force to get at Montojo's squadron.

The "comic-opera war" did not appear so in advance. Yet
it lasted barely three months. The embattled Americans, inflamed by the sinking of the *Maine* and the cries of the
Cuban insurrectos (under arms since 1895), declared war
on April 25, 1898. Within a week Dewey had taken Manila.
The destruction of Admiral Cervera's fleet off Santiago de
Cuba in the first week of July removed the Spanish threat
from the Atlantic. With the fall of Santiago on July 17 the
war virtually came to an end, although a truce would not be
signed until August 12. Manila was occupied August 13,
and on the same day the American flag flew over Cuba (to
be a protectorate, then a republic), Puerto Rico, and the
Philippines—all taken from Spain. Meanwhile Hawaii had
been independently annexed.

There was ground for boastful rhetoric. But to the soldiers home from Cuba, marching to the quick beat of "There'll Be a Hot Time in the Old Town Tonight," to the press, talking of America's humanitarian role and of imperial destiny, the motives and implications of 1898 were not crystal-clear. The expansionists of the Mahan school understood, however, that the United States had not merely been flexing its muscles, succoring the Cubans, or driving circuitously for markets. They saw in the war a move for the enlargement of our strategical resources. Theodore Roosevelt rejoiced that another step had been taken "toward completely freeing America from European domination." The "expulsion of Spain from this continent" gratified Cabot Lodge, justifying and extending the evacuation order to British sea power served by Olney in 1895 and obligingly acknowledged by Lord Salisbury in 1896. Lodge pointed out that Cuba lay athwart the "line to the Isthmus." Mahan saw the reduction of Spain in Cuba as a momentous advance toward making the Caribbean unmistakably "mare nostrum."

To Mahan, Hawaii was a needful outpost, and although the Philippines made him catch his breath (he called their occupation "history in embryo"), on second thought he was willing for the United States to "share the tutelage of Asia" from its own advanced post. For the Philippines were more than a distant archipelago containing 7,000,000 of William Howard Taft's "little brown brothers," Christianized Malaysians, Mohammedan Sulus, and savage mountain tribes. The chain of islands flanked the South China Sea. At Manila the United States now had a potential stronghold commanding the sea route from Japan, Siberia, Manchuria, North China, and Central China to the Straits, the East Indies, and Europe by way of Suez. With the steppingstones of Hawaii, Guam, Midway, and Wake (intermediate bases that seemed adequate before air power and the submarine), and the overreaching Aleutians, this country, naval experts were not slow to observe, might restrain Japan to the seaward. Nor were the Japanese remiss in their own observations on that point.

Nearer home, Cuba, geographically a stopper in the bottle

of the Gulf of Mexico, had been the object of American desire since 1809, when the acquisition of that island became "Mr. Jefferson's hobby" just as he was leaving the White House. In the long view, the United States acted not precipitately but belatedly in striking the Spanish chains from Cuba. Although Madison renounced "Mr. Jefferson's new idea," sending word to that effect through Albert Gallatin to Napoleon's Minister Turreau, who was interested in the Spanish West Indies, American statesmen in each generation thereafter followed Jefferson rather than Madison.

Cuba alone of the important Spanish holdings in this hemisphere had remained loyal to Spain during the revolutionary cycle of the early nineteenth century. Beginning in 1868, however, the islanders had fought a ten-year war for independence. From this struggle the United States, spent by the Civil War and lacking the naval power to contest with Spain, remained aloof, disappointing liberal, antimonarchical elements in this country and abroad. The great Italian republican Mazzini represented this sentiment when he confessed himself "profoundly saddened" that the United States, "this child that has become a veritable giant amongst the nations," declined its "providential mission" of freeing the Cubans from their European yoke. It was not until 1898, when the battleship fleet inaugurated in 1890 had become more than a match for Spain, that the "great republic of the West" could fulfill Mazzini's hopes.

The principal value of Cuba to the United States, as of Hawaii also, was strategic. Both Cuba and Hawaii already lay within the American economic system. Economically, closer ties with the mainland were more advantageous to the islands than to this country. But Guantánamo in Cuba and Hawaii's various bases immeasurably strengthened the American system of defense.

Those who account for the 1898 excursion into "imperialism" by reference only to economics and psychology, ignoring the factor of sea power and strategy, find themselves at a loss to explain its brevity. The sudden burst of expansionist force subsided almost as rapidly as it had flared. Once this country had a Canal Zone and had made an unsuccessful bid for the Danish West Indies, the military "imperialism" of 1898 was at an end. The reason, no doubt, was that we had no further need for strategical expansion and no national policy urged us toward a colonial empire on the pattern of the British or the French. Great Britain gradually retired in force from our waters. The only other Power having possessions in the Caribbean was France, and these became neutralized, as far as we were concerned, early in the twentieth century when the Anglo-French Entente attached that country to the Atlantic System. Only Germany remained, as we shall discover, in a position of threat toward our security to the south. Until the First World War the United States was to watch Germany's moves in the Caribbean with hawklike vigilance, notifying Berlin from time to time with some asperity that we would fight any encroachments on this side of the Atlantic.

In the light of Mahan's sea-power interpretations, the "imperialism" of the period was strictly strategic. The events of 1898, equally with those of 1895-96, seem at bottom to have been motivated chiefly by a desire to supplement the Monroe Doctrine with a policy of hegemony in the Caribbean, a policy calculated to promote national security by ridding the American seas of possible military rivals and establishing there our own strongholds. In this expansion the Republican party took leadership.

The most active and intelligent fabricators of Republican policy in those years may be called in evidence on this point along with the Republican platform of 1896, which demanded the "eventual withdrawal of the European powers from this hemisphere and the ultimate union of all English-speaking parts of the Continent," the emancipation of Cuba, and the annexation of Hawaii. In Europe the Republican plank was taken at face value as a forecast of national policy. The strategical interpretation also explains the insistence on military intervention in Cuba. It was not enough, from our point of view, to have Cuba freed by Spain. American power requirements dictated that this country take a direct hand in order to obtain a naval foothold and acquire influence sufficient to check the penetration of any other Power.

Infused through the military happenings of 1898 were diplomatic strands that formed a pattern testifying unmistakably to English-speaking solidarity. The United States, fighting its first war for overseas objectives, found itself friendless on the Continent. An indefatigable Spanish Foreign Secretary, Carlos O'Donnell y Abreu, Duke of Tetuan, activated, as he said, by the threatening Republican platform, undertook to revive the Holy Alliance with the support of Francis Joseph, the French Government, and the Kaiser. The Duke of Tetuan predicated his league on what he supposed to be a fraternal desire by the European monarchs to bolster the Spanish throne and check the indicated drive of the United States on colonies in America. It will be noted that the aims of Tetuan approximated those of Prince Metternich after Waterloo.

The British, in opposition to the unconcealed pro-Spanish sympathies of Victoria, stanchly upheld the United States. A benevolent neutral, Britain by her course aided American interests at Madrid and Port Said, at London and Suez, at Washington, Ottawa, Hong Kong, and Manila, earning the reproaches of Maria Christina, the Spanish Queen Regent (Victoria's "poor thing") and convincing European chancelleries that the English-speaking Powers were bound in formal alliance.

The first fruits of an Atlantic System, outlined only two years earlier, brought to the United States the comforting protection of its rear, foreshadowing the like comfort the British would derive from the same unwritten understanding in 1914 and 1939. Great Britain therewith established a precedent of Anglo-Saxon solidarity in the presence of a third party that has not since been violated. Four years before Manila and Santiago, Mahan uttered this prophecy:
"Let each nation [England and America] be educated to realize the length and breadth of its own interest in the sea; when that is done the identity of these interests will become apparent."

Once America had returned to the sea, said Mahan, this Anglo-Saxon identity of interest would be "firmly" established in "men's minds." Thereupon, he added, the United States would "cast aside the . . . isolation which befitted its infancy." We shall see how truly the prophet spoke.

2

McKinley, who seemed to most Americans a simple little Ohioan kind to his wife and fond of flowers, but whose countenance reminded Hay of a "genuine Italian ecclesiastical face of the fifteenth century," had become President on March 4, 1897. With some misgivings, he had appointed Theodore Roosevelt Assistant Secretary of the Navy. Hay, the "Republican laureate," went to England, and Henry White, offered the post of Minister to Spain, chose to return to the secretaryship of legation in London.

Already, Hay was given to understand upon reaching London, Lord Salisbury had intervened diplomatically on behalf of the United States and against the Duke of Tetuan's project. In August, 1896, the Spanish Foreign Minister had drawn up a memorandum of Spain's position vis-à-vis America. A stinging indictment of the behavior of the North American republic in harboring Cuban filibusters, the memorandum suggested a set of demands to be levied on Washington by the Concert of Europe. Included were ingenious arguments why the Powers should join in maintaining the status quo of "political and commercial interests . . . about the Gulf of Mexico," especially with an isthmian canal in prospect. The paper had the approval of the Queen Regent, mother of Alphonso XIII, and of Canovas, the Prime Minister. The envoys of France, Austria, Germany, Italy, Russia, and England had been consulted. Sir Henry Drummond-Wolff, the English Ambassador, had been noncommittal, but the others gave Tetuan their cordial assent. In London Salisbury had discouraged the enterprise to the Spanish, Austrian, and French envoys, according to word reaching Tetuan.

Hannis Taylor, the American Minister, was in ignorance of the Duke's plans until a few hours before the memorandum was to have been submitted to the Powers by Spain's missions at their capitals. It being August, the Spanish court was at San Sebastian. That afternoon Taylor unsuspectingly paid his respects to the Duke in his box at the bullfight. At 10:30 that night the British Ambassador called at the Foreign Minister's house in a state of excitement to report that the American Minister had discovered the existence of the memorandum, had been to see him and the French Ambassador, and now threatened to expose the intrigue to the world. Tetuan arranged to see Taylor the next day and meanwhile instituted an inquiry into the source of the leak. The mechanics of disclosure had been simple. An English journalist in Sir Henry's confidence had informed Taylor, advising him to seek confirmation at the British Legation. The Briton had verified the report and sent Taylor on to the French Embassy. Thereafter during his stay in Madrid, as Sir Henry ironically noted in his memoirs, he observed a "tone of coldness" in official circles.

As the text of the memorandum was actually in the hands of the Spanish envoys, awaiting release, the Duke of Tetuan was required to telegraph new instructions after his interview with Taylor. Taylor, simulating diplomatic anger (as he informed the State Department), had warned the Duke that the United States would "take offense at any action of the Great Powers, whatever it might be; and nothing could inspire greater hostility toward Spain" than the circulation of the memorandum.

This "inopportune phase," as Tetuan termed it, ended for a year the formal effort to organize the Powers, but as Hispano-American stresses were intensified through 1897 the Spanish Foreign Secretary renewed, more subtly, his efforts to enlist the Concert of Europe. The Queen Regent being an Austrian Archduchess, Francis Joseph genuinely favored the cause. Gabriel Hanotaux, the brilliant historian and Minister for Foreign Affairs at Paris, acknowledged a pull in Spain's direction for two causes peculiar to France. One was

Hanotaux's fear that the American assertion of supremacy in the Caribbean placed Martinique, Guadaloupe, and French Guiana in jeopardy, and the other that the Paris Stock Exchange was sensitive to Spain's internal conditions, since the French had the largest foreign investments in the railroads, mines, and industries of the peninsula. Russia, interested only to the vague extent that Nicholas wished to assist another monarch, preferred to curry favor with a friendly United States, especially if strengthening of the traditionally friendly Russo-American ties might in any way serve to disquiet the British. Italy, although her statesmen blew hot and cold, was taken to be, in the final analysis, in Great Britain's orbit.

The line-up of the six Powers, then, during the last half of 1897 and the prewar weeks of 1898, consisted of Austria and France, pro-Spanish; England and Russia (by no means concertedly) pro-American; and Germany and Italy uncertain. Francis Joseph, with a tinge of bitterness, lamented to the Count Goluchowski, his Foreign Minister, at the outbreak of the war that only Austria and France had shown stanch sympathy with Spain. Even Goluchowski, as the Emperor suspected, had not entered with enthusiasm into the Spanish designs.

The Wilhelmstrasse was a house divided. The Kaiser, backed by the Junkers, the industrialists, and the press of the right and the center, might rant at America as a "covetous" upstart. He might brand America a mongrel and pusillanimous but at the same time a bold and dangerous nation, might confidently predict to the royalty and nobility at Francis Joseph's fall maneuvers in 1897 that Spain would swiftly humble "Brother Jonathan," openly snubbing the inoffensive American military attachés. But Count von Bülow, deft, realistic, and personable, appraised American strength more accurately, and though sharing the Kaiser's derogatory views of the United States, was not disposed to risk the enmity of that country on behalf of feeble Spain.

On September 28, 1897, the Kaiser directed Bülow by telegraph to prepare for intervention on Spain's side in concert with a European league. Both men were absent from Berlin and the Kaiser's message passed through the Foreign Office. Upon its receipt Bülow at once instructed the Foreign Office secretariat to dissuade the Kaiser from committing himself until at least Germany knew where France and Russia stood, suggesting that they impress upon him the danger Germany ran of incurring trade and tariff reprisals from the United States. Under the new Dingley tariff the Government at Washington had authority to discriminate between friend and foe. Neither the Kaiser nor Bülow referred to the possibility of England's joining the league; and Count Botho von und zu Eulenberg, Ambassador to Vienna, when enlisted by the Kaiser for the purpose of persuading the Foreign Secretary, expressly ruled England out.

So Bülow, hedging in his correspondence with Eulenberg, made Germany's entrance into the league conditional on that of both France and England, being adamant against any expression from the Foreign Office unless the "British and French naval forces" were willing "to take up an unambiguous position in favor of intervention." Meanwhile the Kaiser, failing to move his own Foreign Secretary, kept up a running flow of letters to Francis Joseph suggesting ways and means of enlisting France and Russia, and encouraging his fellow Kaiser. William's messages also heartened Tetuan and his Liberal successor, Moret—the Liberals succeeded the Conservatives after Canovas's assassination in August, 1897, by an Italian anarchist avenging the suppression of the Cuban rebels—as they crisscrossed Europe with appeals for a "cooperation which should be neither platonic nor fantastic, but strong, positive, and effective" in defense of "Spain's rights and her sovereignty over Cuba" against American "aggressions."

In Paris, Vienna, and Berlin a chill descended on American diplomatists, but at St. Petersburg the American Minister, Clifton R. Breckinridge, found himself singled out for attention at the same time that Count Muraviev, the Foreign Minister, informed the Spanish Ambassador that Russia must remain neutral in case of a Spanish-American war. Czar

Nicholas conversed meaningfully with Breckinridge on court
occasions, lingering over the handshake. Speaking of Cuba,
he assured the Minister of his loyalty come what may, saying
that "we are always in agreement with the United States and
I hope we shall always remain so." Breckinridge's dispatches
suspected that the Czar did "not object to his step causing
some anxiety to England."

The American diplomats, enlightened by friendly colleagues, were not in ignorance of the general course of events.
General Horace Porter reported from Paris to the State
Department the pro-Spanish bias of the Government; yet
he believed that France would balk at actual intervention
unless England could be brought in. From Berlin Dr. Andrew D. White, who was, as he confessed, unaware of the
Kaiser's animus, yet knew vaguely of the anti-American
machinations around him, wrote Washington at the beginning of 1898 that "ill will towards the United States had
never been so strong," but he doubted that a "coalition will
be formed against us."

Soon Ambassador White would be protesting to the Foreign Office the flagrantly abusive tone of the German press,
a part of which Bülow privately acknowledged his ability
to "inoculate" and all of which the Foreign Secretary believed had become "coarser than in any other country."
Advancing beyond the normal disparagement of American
morals, political, commercial, and private, and the slurs at
American manners and racial integrity current throughout
the 1890's, the important journals of the German Empire,
with only two exceptions, had descended into even lower
depths of defamation.

The mildest epithet applied to the United States Government was "bully." Spain was held up as the exemplar of
a superior civilization, in Cuba and at home. Spanish women,
it was gravely asserted, were not only more virtuous but more
beautiful than American women, and American life generally was a compound of "corrupt lawlessness and barbarism."
White found, he records in his memoirs, that as war drew
near the campaign of hatred was intensified, the editorialists

addressing themselves to the "cowardice of our [American] army and navy." American ships, it was said, would sink before meeting the enemy because corrupt builders had given them "sham plating"; American "sham guns" would explode in the faces of the American sailors, who "belonged to a deteriorated race of mongrels and could never stand against the pure-blooded Spanish sailors."

A scanning of the German and American press of the period confirms the Ambassador's recollections. Veering wide of the merits of the Spanish-American controversy over Cuba, the *Tägliche Rundschau* addressed itself to the character of the "American politicians," who it asserted were mere "pocketbook patriots, who allow themselves to be bought and sold by the industrial millionaires . . . their God is mammon and they betray their country." The *Vossische Zeitung*, with ties to the Foreign Office, was certain that the "whole American republic was founded upon the violation of the rights of other people," and the *Kreuzzeitung*, a Junker organ, announced that "the lowest motives brought on this war." Daily the passionately anti-American utterances of the German press were cabled to this country for publication, inspiring frequent comment here. Typically, the *Providence Journal* believed that the "contemptuous sneers at the 'Yankees' . . . represent the . . . real feeling of the German people. They try to despise us as seamen and say that we could not meet in naval battle an equal foe. Much of this is ignorance; but much of it is also envy and malice and all uncharitableness."

The German press was no more anti-American, no less indifferent to the cause of the Cuban insurrectos, than that of Vienna and Paris—or, indeed, all of the Continent. As the Vienna *Deutsche Zeitung*, in a moment of dissent, was to point out on April 24, the day Spain declared war, virtually all European newspapers had "given themselves over to hounding in a most shameful manner the North American republic. Liberal, conservative, and clerical organs, pro- and anti-Semitic, as well as nationalist organs, have joined to fly at poor Uncle Sam, whose policies are branded as a 'naked, brutal program of conquest,' the meanest lawlessness, and the most open greed for plunder."

It was perhaps because of the German gifts for heavy-handed thoroughness and dogmatic judgments that the Americans resented German press attacks more than those of the French. There was, however, another difference. The Germans, unwilling to confine their reactions to the political issue of the moment, vilified the personal courage, the honor, the decency, and the virtue of all Americans. The American press characteristically raked the Kaiser over the coals for what it considered his "saber-rattling," for his excessive vanity, truculence, and arrogance; it condemned evidences of a militaristic spirit in the German system, but demeaned neither itself nor the German people by reflecting on the character of the Germans as individuals or as a human society. Persons shocked by the irresponsible mendacity of the Nazi press may reflect that that quality, like almost everything in the Nazi regime, has its roots in German tradition.

In the early years of the new century, when the German Government sought methodically to drive a wedge between the English-speaking Powers, diplomatists and intellectuals regretted the excesses of 1898 as inexpedient. "The unfriendliness of German public opinion about Cuba was an undoubted political blunder," Dr. Ernst von Halle of the University of Berlin, propaganda chief of the Reichsmarineamt, wrote in 1902. It was then, however, late in the day.

Running counter to national sentiment, Bülow attempted to sidetrack the European league by proposing papal mediation and coldly advising the Spanish Ambassador in Berlin, Mendez Vigo, to back down. "I should," he said, "be acting disloyally if I should allow Your Excellency to believe there was any real prospect of active intervention by the Powers in Spain's favor." Bülow added with rigorous cynicism: "You are isolated because everybody wants to be pleasant to the United States or, at any rate, no one wants to arouse America's anger; the United States is a rich country, against which you simply cannot sustain a war; I admire the courage

Spain has shown, but I would admire more a display of practical common sense."

The deflated Spanish Ambassador replied that Spain would fight "for her honor" as she had done, successfully, many times in the past. Little remained for diplomacy as 1898 opened. Leo XIII and his Secretary of State, Cardinal Rampolla, explored the situation on Spain's request, after notifying the American Minister in Rome that the Vatican would do nothing prejudicial to American interests. Archbishop Ireland, a friend of President McKinley's was sent from St. Paul to Washington on a peace errand. He found his friend in the White House still hopeful that hostilities might be averted. Papal mediation, however, was not even attempted, as Rampolla encountered obstacles in Madrid.

3

In February the tempo of America's trend toward war was accelerated. The American people had been overwhelmingly convinced that Spain's conduct in Cuba was not, in McKinley's words, "civilized warfare," that it was in reality "extermination," and that the "only peace it can beget is a wilderness." They had adopted the Cuban cause as their own, especially after publication of a stolen letter in which the Spanish Minister, Dupuy de Lôme, characterized McKinley as a low politician.

Henry White, calling on Lord Salisbury, was sardonically informed by the Prime Minister that the preceding visitor, the Count de Rascon, the Spanish Ambassador, had "savagely attacked" the United States for its effrontery in stationing a battleship (the *Maine*) at Havana. The *Maine* was sunk on February 15, 1898. In the United States Theodore Roosevelt, having consulted throughout the winter with Mahan, busied himself with projects for taking Hawaii and defeating the Spanish at Manila. On February 25, with Secretary Long absent for the afternoon, he sent his famous order to Dewey at Hong Kong: "In event of declaration of war with Spain your duty will be to see that the Spanish squadron does not leave the Asiatic coast, and then offensive operations in the Philippine Islands." The purview of Roosevelt extended beyond the Caribbean. He had designs on the Pacific as well. To Mahan he wrote repeatedly of battle plans and the Pacific problems, which engrossed them both.

"If I had my way," wrote the Assistant Secretary, "I would annex those [the Hawaiian] islands tomorrow." He was "fully alive to the danger from Japan," a possibility against which Mahan, bearing in mind the Japanese protest of 1897, had warned him. Roosevelt wished to dig the Nicaraguan Canal at once and build a dozen new battleships, half on the Pacific coast. Mahan advised him concerning Hawaii: "Do nothing unrighteous but . . . take the islands first and solve the problem afterwards."

"I suppose I need not tell you," Roosevelt replied, "that as regards Hawaii, I take your view absolutely, as indeed I do on foreign policy generally." A motive for their urgency was the fact that Japan had building in Europe two new ships more powerful than any in the American battle line. At another time, asking for advice, Roosevelt wrote the naval officer: "All I can do toward pressing your ideas into effect will be done . . . there are many, many points you will see that I should miss." Acknowledging his indebtedness to Mahan, Roosevelt wrote in another letter: "There is no question that you stand head and shoulders above the rest of us!" The way to the China Sea was thus prepared in advance.

In London Hay and White observed a growing geniality on the part of public and press as well as the Government. The Ministry, especially Balfour and Chamberlain, openly avowed their sympathy with the American cause. In Salisbury's absence in the south of France Balfour acted as Prime Minister and Foreign Secretary. White was breakfasting with him one day when Sir Thomas Sanderson, the Permanent Under-Secretary for Foreign Affairs, arriving with dispatches, hesitated on the threshold. "Come in, Sanderson," said Balfour, "we have no secrets from Harry White."

Not only were the American diplomatists kept informed

on the progress of the Continental coalition but also Hay, calling on Balfour over a routine matter, was told that the Foreign Office had "formally instructed Sir Julian Paunce-fote to be guided by the wishes of the President in any action he may or may not take in the direction of collective repre-sentations by the diplomatic body in Washington." As Hay departed Balfour reassured him that "neither here nor in Washington did the British Government propose to take any steps which would not be acceptable to the Government of the United States." At this time Goluchowski in Vienna informed Hoyos, the Spanish Ambassador, that Great Britain had consented to a joint European offer of good offices "on condition that her Ambassador in Washington shall first discuss the matter of a friendly mediation by the Powers with the American State Department."

So delighted was Ambassador Hay by the evidences of a new cordiality in London that he bombarded Washington with reports. The British, he cabled, were standing solidly behind the United States. "Official opinion" advised that we "take Cuba at once; we [the British] wouldn't have stood it this long." Chamberlain was "extremely desirous of a close alliance with us, or, if that is prevented by our traditions, of an assurance of common action on important questions. 'Shoulder to shoulder,' he said, 'we would command peace the world over' and 'I should rejoice in an occasion in which we could fight side by side.'" Chamberlain was, he men-tioned, all for selling the United States such men-of-war as were needed, but others in the Cabinet doubted the legality of such an act. Sir Edward Grey, the Liberal M.P. who was to be the First World War Foreign Secretary, was suggesting that we "borrow the British fleet and do in Spain in a hurry, returning the favor some other time." Comprehensive among Hay's messages to America during the prewar period was this letter to Senator Lodge: "This is the only European country whose sympathy is not openly against us. . . . For the first time . . . I find the 'drawing room' sentiment altogether with us. If we wanted it—which, of course, we do not—we could have the practical assistance of the British navy—on the *do ut des* principle, naturally."

On his yearly leave White discovered that Americans were responding to such reports of British friendliness. In the Senate, Lodge, Morgan, Cushman K. Davis, and William B. Frye of Maine, the last three die-hards of Anglophobia, had softened to a point where Morgan described them as "pro-English." Lodge wanted to be known as the "promoter of a good understanding" between the countries, and Senator Foraker of Ohio regretted that the United States had not "joined England in stopping Russia in China." He referred to Russia's occupation of Manchuria beginning in March, 1898.

Coupling White's wartime visit home with persistent reports of an Anglo-American alliance, the *New York Herald* reported that he had brought with him the text of the treaty. The story ran through the American press. White denied it in an interview at his home in Baltimore, calling an alliance "undesirable" and expressing preference for a "thorough understanding," which would grow out of the belief in both countries that each had the other's sympathy and would have "at least its moral support in certain contingencies."

4

In March Spain, Austria, and the Kaiser renewed the protracted diplomatic struggle for a European league. The Kaiser, disregarding Bülow, communicated directly with his envoys at London, Paris, and Washington, urging collective action. Spain concentrated on England, Rascon being instructed to learn definitely "if Great Britain has really made a commitment with the United States with respect to the future, or if her attitude of reserve and silence is due merely to a wish to retain independence."

A moving appeal went from the Queen Regent to Victoria: "Now, when the insurrection is nearly over, America intends to provoke us and bring about war and this I would avoid at all cost," the Spanish Queen wrote. "But there are limits to everything and I cannot let my country be humbled by America." Maria Christina recalled how Victoria, "with greatest kindness," had always "interested yourself in my poor, fatherless son—for his sake, I beg you to help me." She besought the English Queen to join the European coalition under Francis Joseph. Victoria was in the south of France, at Cimiez with the Prime Minister at near-by Beaulieu when the Spanish Queen's letter reached her on March 17. She addressed the Prime Minister at once, strongly suggesting that Britain enter the league.

Lord Salisbury's reply, under date of April 1, conceded that the Queen Regent's plight was "most lamentable and grievous"; he agreed that his sovereign "would not refuse to join in any course taken by all the other Great Powers," and yet he doubted the expediency of such a move, saying that "the Spanish question is very grave. . . . Any communication from this country to the United States, in the way of remonstrances, might arouse their susceptible feelings and produce a condition of some danger without any corresponding advantage." A protest by the Powers, he added, would be "more likely to help the war party in the United States."

Underneath the elaborate formalities prescribed for the address of a Minister to his sovereign, that meant no. Victoria answered the Queen Regent on April 4, conveying Salisbury's dark view of the projected Holy Alliance. The delay from March 17 to the first week in April, together with Rascon's unsatisfactory reports from London and the puzzling, certainly unfriendly, absence of Sir Henry Drummond-Wolff from his post during the entire first quarter of 1898, finally convinced the Spanish Government that they could look for little help from that quarter. The British Foreign Office, the Spanish Ambassador wrote home, maintained a "correct" attitude toward Spain, yet never by word or intimation expressed censure of the United States. In retaliation the Madrid Ministry on March 24-25 omitted inviting the British chargé d'affaires and the Italian Ambassador (supposed to be taking London's initiative) to a conference of Ambassadors with the Queen Regent at which final emergency steps were considered.

Out of this meeting grew joint diplomatic action in Washington, in which Britain concurred with reservations; and there seems little doubt that the Queen Regent's appeal to Victoria helped bring about that limited participation. On April 6 the six Ambassadors and Ministers of the Powers submitted a note to McKinley at the White House, a perfunctory paper hoping that a way might be found to avert war. A stronger representation had been drawn by Pauncefote but, obeying instructions, he submitted it to the State Department for revision. McKinley thanked the envoys for their "good will" and in an informal chat assured them that no one had done more for peace than himself.

When next the six envoys met—only a week before the scales were irrevocably tipped toward war—it seemed, briefly, that the Holy Alliance stratagem had succeeded, that Europe was finally ranged against the United States as Ferdinand VII had sought in 1823 to organize Europe against the revolted Spanish possessions in America.

This time the British Ambassador, presumably without consulting the Foreign Office, certainly without seeing McKinley or the State Department, assumed leadership of the diplomatic concert. Pauncefote's change of face between April 6 and April 14, when the envoys met to reprobate the United States, may never be understood clearly. Questions in the House of Commons four years later, after the Kaiser had attempted to make capital in America of Pauncefote's leading part in the conference of April 14, failed to reveal whether the Ambassador acted on his own responsibility, on a request from the Queen (as was suggested at the time), on instructions from persons subordinate to Balfour and Salisbury, or on those of Balfour or Salisbury themselves. William II, seeking to convict the British Ministry of double-dealing, charged that Salisbury had promoted the diplomatic action. It was, however, Balfour who handled the matter in London.

Between the two meetings the House of Representatives had adopted a resolution calling for armed intervention in Cuba. The Senate, impeded by an isolationist bloc that insisted on a self-denying ordinance respecting the absorption of Cuba, had not yet acted. Observing what seemed to be divided counsels, the managers of the coalition in Europe cabled their envoys to reassemble. Goluchowski directed the Austrian Ambassador von Hengelmüller, to "proceed with vigor." Apologists for Pauncefote relate that the five other diplomats met first at the Austrian Embassy and then proceeded, at Pauncefote's invitation, in a body across Connecticut Avenue to the British Embassy. A note satisfactory to the United States was then drawn in English, these accounts continue, but when Jules Cambon, the French Ambassador, put it into French, its character changed so that it became offensive to the United States, and Pauncefote subscribed to it without studying the draft in French.

The drawback to that version lies in the circumstance that the note was made uniform and Sir Julian cabled the English text to the Foreign Office, urging its acceptance on a somewhat bewildered Balfour. This text contained the vital clause warning the United States that the Powers, wishing to disabuse this Government of the belief that the civilized world favored its course, "cannot give their approval to armed intervention, which seems to be entirely unjustified." Such sharp representations might have averted war, although in the light of the American temper at the time it is more likely that they would merely have broadened American antagonism into rancor against all Europe without relieving the plight of the decrepit Spanish monarchy. The Concert of Europe, unable to resolve the Greco-Turkish turmoil over Crete at that time, would not, in any human likelihood, have gone to war in the Caribbean or the China Sea, American isolationism would have gained wide new sanctions, and Anglo-American accord would have been set back immeasurably.

As it happened, no Power except Austria supported the note of the diplomatic bloc. In England Pauncefote's cable reached Balfour in the country. The acting Prime Minister, a man of tentative resolution, confessed himself in "great perplexity" in forwarding a copy of the message to Chamberlain. Salisbury's absence was unfortunate. Instead of grasping the magnitude of the mistake (from the point of view of Anglo-American amity) Balfour recoiled from a decision. "At once spinsterish and architectural," Harold Begbie described Balfour in the mordant *Mirrors of Downing Street,* with "slackness in his blood and no vital enthusiasm in his heart." At that moment in Berlin the Kaiser, as unfavorable to America as Balfour professed himself favorable, was penciling on the margin of his Ambassador's telegram: "I regard it as completely futile and purposeless and therefore prejudicial. I am against this step."

Balfour, calling it a "strong order" to reject Pauncefote's advice, directed Sir Thomas Sanderson at London to cable Pauncefote that while Great Britain favored peace and had not formed a "judgment adverse to Spain as is assumed apparently by Congress," it seemed doubtful "whether we ought to commit ourselves to a judgment adverse to the United States, and whether, in the interest of peace, anything will be gained by doing so." The acting Prime Minister's confusion was disclosed equally in his note to Chamberlain: "The whole thing had to be done in a quarter hour and it was just possible that I ought to have been more peremptory . . . but when your own Ambassador on the spot and all the Great Powers are in agreement, one does not feel disposed to be too rough in one's antagonism." The Powers, of course, were not in agreement—only their representatives at Washington, under the presidency of the British Ambassador.

Balfour meanwhile had heard from the Colonial Secretary, a coarser-grained and more self-confident statesman. "Am convinced message will do no good and will be bitterly resented," Chamberlain telegraphed. "America insists that Spain shall leave Cuba. Nothing less will satisfy them. Spain will rather fight. The message practically takes the part of Spain at a critical juncture and will be so understood in

America." Chamberlain, writing the next day to Balfour, feared Pauncefote's participation "will do harm," adding:

The American position may be right or wrong, but it is a very clear one—and to ask them in the name of the Concert of Europe (*absit omen!*) to alter it will probably be regarded by them as offensive. Hitherto, public opinion in the States has gratefully recognized that we have been more sympathetic than the other Great Powers. Now I fear that we shall be held to have thrown in our lot with them. However, what is done is done, and I only hope I am mistaken as to its effect.

Chamberlain's premonitions were not borne out. The incident did not become public until 1902 and by then so firmly fixed was the impression of British friendship in 1898 that the accusations of the Kaiser were heavily discounted where they were not actually disbelieved. Within a few months after the proceedings of April 14 had been bruited to the world by the German Emperor, Sir Julian, now Lord Pauncefote, died at his post in Washington without allowing his side of the story to become known. President Theodore Roosevelt took note of the German charges by pointedly calling on the British Ambassador. He also gave the London *Times* an interview avowing his complete faith in Pauncefote's goodwill toward America. He characterized the intimations, with usual Rooseveltian finality, as false. John Hay was then Secretary of State. To him, the Kaiser's behavior was as undignified as that of nursemaids "pulling caps" over the favors of a policeman. Hay instructed the Ambassador at Berlin to hand the Foreign Office, "without comment," the copy of a letter obtained from the insurgent forces in the Philippines, presumably incriminating the German Government in anti-American intrigues in 1898.

At the time, Chamberlain told Hay he would have resigned and published his reasons had Balfour endorsed Pauncefote's note. Elsewhere in Europe it was accepted without question that Pauncefote acted for his sovereign, if not for his Government. At St. Petersburg, Muraviev discerned in the move a British scheme to "drive a wedge between America and the monarchical powers of Europe."

Theodor von Holleben, Pauncefote's German colleague, considered it "very remarkable . . . that the British Ambassador today took the initiative in the fresh step. . . . We imagine that the Queen Regent has appealed to the Queen of England in that sense." Pauncefote, he said, had directed them to cable their governments. "Personally," the German Ambassador added, "I regard this demonstration rather coldly." Cambon dubiously advised the Quai d'Orsay that the note would have "sensational repercussions" in America. Only Pauncefote and the Austrians seemed to feel that American intervention should be arraigned on grounds of international morality.

No evidence appears, however, to bear out the suspicions in Berlin and St. Petersburg of a "British plot." Balfour was only too patently flabbergasted, Chamberlain too genuinely apprehensive. And on April 22, two days before Spain's declaration of war, Salisbury was again patiently cautioning the Queen that "even the very temperate and guarded note [of April 6] . . . was very much resented by a large portion of the community as an undue interference and had no other effect than to harden the war feeling." That was true. The *Review of Reviews* had warned Europe measuredly that "we in this country can never consent to have the Concert of Europe, as such, act diplomatically in any affair that concerns us." Such was the general burden of the press comment.

On the day before Salisbury wrote the Queen, April 21, she had entered in her diary: "War seems hopelessly declared . . . it is monstrous of the Americans."

5

The first diplomatic reaction to the Battle of Manila appeared before Dewey's victory had been reported in detail in either Europe or America. At the Wilhelmstrasse, Friedrich von Holstein, the subtle, conspiratorial Privy Councillor known to Bismarck as "the Lynx," prepared to reap an advantage by linking the Philippines, Hawaii, and Samoa, hoping to obtain European support for a scheme to require the United States to surrender one in order to gain title to the others. Cecil Spring-Rice, an attaché at the British Embassy in Berlin, got wind of the aspiration and wrote his friend Hay on May 3. That day Hay cabled the State Department: "Excellent authority in German matters suggests prompt action in annexation of Hawaii before war closes as otherwise Germany might seek to complicate question with Samoa or Philippine Islands."

McKinley's annexation treaty had been marking time in the Senate, unable to gain a two-thirds majority. Upon receipt of Hay's cable the President directed that a legislative detour be taken. The Administration leaders drew up a joint resolution (Texas had been annexed by joint resolution), which passed and was signed on July 8, 1898.

As a token of Anglo-American collaboration during the war with Spain, Spring-Rice—"Springie," Roosevelt's "gentle, pallid and polite" friend with whom he kept bachelor quarters one summer in the eighties in Washington, so relatively poor that they served domestic claret at dinner—had a better grasp of our interests in Berlin than did our own Ambassador. A few days after his valuable tip to Hay the British attaché again wrote the Ambassador in London, reporting the extent to which German colonial desires had been stimulated by the prospect of Spanish defeat, and ending with the admonition: "Therefore, I say again, let us try while we can to secure what we can for God's language."

The British made no secret of their desire to have the United States keep the Philippines as a means of enhancing Anglo-Saxon strength in the Far East, and also to prevent a struggle for their possession by other Powers, a contest in which Britain more than likely would have to take a hand. Rather than have the Philippines fall to Germany, the British would doubtless have pushed a claim of their own, and indeed when Salisbury conveyed to Hay the Ministry's wish that the United States hold them, the Prime Minister added the proviso that America give Britain the option of

purchase from Spain if for any reason she decided not to
absorb them.

Germany's avidity for possessions in the Pacific astonished
first the British Government, then the American Government. There seemed nothing the Germans would not do in
the way of intrigue and short of open hostility, in London,
Manila, Madrid, or Washington. To the German mind, Hay
came to believe, "there is something monstrous in the
thought that a war should take place anywhere and they not
profit by it." Even the Germanophile Ambassador White in
Berlin was moved to report that Germany "regarded the
emergency in the East as one from which she must gain something, or lose prestige with Europe, and even with her own
people." When Hatzfeldt went to Hay (as Spring-Rice had
foretold) to discuss what he termed the tripartite problem
of Hawaii, Samoa, and the Philippines, he conceded, under
quizzing, that his country was powerless to enforce a claim
in the Pacific. "We cannot remove our fleet from German
waters," he murmured, referring, of course, to Britain's over-
mastering power in the North Sea.

Henry Adams, a guest of the Hays' at Number 5 Carlton
Terrace, dined nightly with members of the governing elite.
The talk of the British, warmly pro-American, stimulated
the American historian to irony, remembering as he did the
bleak Civil War days when as secretary to the legation of his
father (Charles Francis Adams) he endured the slights of
these same persons or their elders. In the drawing-rooms of
Park Lane, Adams discovered everyone alight with the new
vistas opened for Anglo-Saxon authority in Asia and the
Pacific. All emphasis was placed on the conquest of the
Philippines, with its reaction on the "balance of power" in
China. The hegemony which the United States was acquiring over the Caribbean everyone took for granted, believing,
as Adams put it, that the duty of policing those islands fell
"to our lot."

The spectacle of England and America throwing in together moved the Yankee aristocrat out of his assumed

aridity. Referring to himself in the third person, as always in *The Education of Henry Adams,* he wrote:

After two hundred years of stupid and greedy blundering, which no argument and no violence affected, the people of England learned their lesson just at the moment when Hay would otherwise have faced a flood of the old anxieties. . . . To Adams, still living in the atmosphere of Palmerston and John Russell, the sudden appearance of Germany as the grizzly terror which . . . frightened England into America's arms seemed as melodramatic as any plot of Napoleon the Great. He could feel only a sense of satisfaction at seeing the diplomatic triumph of all his family . . . at last realized under his own eyes.

The moment, as Adams viewed it, represented the grand climax of the work by Adamses, himself and his ancestors, for a hundred and fifty years looking toward an imperial relationship between the politically severed nations. Discerning for the first time the operation of "law in history," he claimed a "personal proprietorship by inheritance in this proof of sequence and intelligence in the affairs of man . . . and this personal triumph left him a little cold toward the other diplomatic results of the war."

Likewise moved to utterance by the new pro-American climate was Chamberlain. A talk with Hay about the continuing reports of a Continental league against the United States, during which the Ambassador twittingly observed that the Ministry had not participated publicly in the post-Manila rapprochement, produced the Colonial Secretary's "startling speech" of May 13, an outgiving that rattled the windows at the Wilhelmstrasse. Chamberlain reverted to his chronic desire for a sealing of Anglo-Saxon unity in battle, a tribal ambition he would not live to see realized in 1917 and the true significance of which would escape his sons, Austen and Neville. Appealing for "closer . . . more cordial, fuller and more definite" arrangements with the United States, Chamberlain again ardently bespoke the day when the "Stars and Stripes and the Union Jack should wave together over an Anglo-Saxon alliance. . . . The union—the al-

liance if you please—the understanding between these two
great nations," said Chamberlain, "is indeed a guarantee of
the peace of the world."

The Chamberlain accents rolled across Europe and the
Atlantic alike. In Spain, Sir Henry reported, the speech was
taken as a fresh evidence of English hostility. In the United
States the *New York Times,* calling it the "most memorable
speech in a generation" and wondering if Chamberlain was
reporting a factual alliance, expressed a reservation that
the American people should have heard it first, perhaps,
from their own Government. Prophetically, the *Chicago
Tribune* doubted that an Anglo-American alliance would be
reduced to writing, but declared that the two "great branches
of the Anglo-Saxon race" were drawing nearer "for coöperation in peace, and, in logical sequence, in war as well."

William T. Stead, the famous English journalist, reported
that the Chamberlain speech had "discouraged" the Continental enemies of the United States and the British Press
generally supported the burgeoning American entente. On
May 1 the *New York Times* reported that "of all the newspapers in London only two, and they minor ones, in any
way suggest any pro-Spanish feeling." When the London
Times endorsed the American cause wholeheartedly on
April 21, the *Pall Mall Gazette* dubbed it a "tardy declaration," avowing that the time had come "when it is possible
to abolish the ancient grudge and stimulate in America those
feelings which have long been alive in England." The reconciling muse of Alfred Austin, the poet laureate, likewise was
put to the service of the accord. His "Voice from the West,"
published simultaneously in England and America a month
before the war, called for the mingling of the "Shamrock,
Thistle and Rose" with the "Star-Spangled Banner," the
concluding stanza reading:

> Yes, this voice on the bluff March gale,
>   We severed too long have been:
> But now we have done with a worn-out tale,
>   The tale of an ancient wrong,

> And our friendship shall last long as love doth last
> And be stronger than death is strong.

It remained for the retrogressive, cholerically anti-American *Saturday Review* to grumble that "the bulk of the English newspapers" were "calling on us to admire the attitude of the United States and accord our moral support to the Washington Government."

Chamberlain's speech acted as a prod to Bülow and Holstein in Berlin, and to Hatzfeldt in London. At once they undertook an attack on the Anglo-American accord. Dr. White, who had just assured the Foreign Office that his Government would welcome a sharing of its new Pacific holdings with a great "civilizing power" like Germany, was portentously warned that the Anglo-American tie would raise a Continental league against America. Quailing under the threat, White cabled the State Department that the "close relations and coöperation of the United States and Great Britain will certainly result in a Continental coalition against the United States." Assurances to Germany, he thought, would save "the United States later troublesome complications." White, already under State Department censure for his "untimely and embarrassing" proffers of collaboration in the Pacific, was informed that "nothing in the relationship between the United States and Great Britain need give any ground for apprehension on the part of the Continental Powers."

Hatzfeldt, holding that the accord could best be attacked in the United States, proposed to Holstein and Bülow that ways be found to persuade the Americans that (1) reports of German unfriendliness rested on English "invention," (2) German claims for a share of the fallen Spanish Empire would be more modest than English claims, and (3) the United States would have nothing to fear elsewhere if it made a deal with Berlin.

Fertile in supplying subject matter, Hatzfeldt was barren of suggestions as to how these concepts should be propagated in the United States. The American Ambassador, although perhaps willing, would be a poor vessel of communication.

"His personality and influence at home do not count for so much," Hatzfeldt adduced. As for Hay, his "intimate relations with President McKinley" would render him useful, but he was "obviously" pro-British, and on top of that Hay —once described by Henry Watterson as a "helter-skelter . . . man of the world, crossed on western stock"—was a "very silent man, even Lord Salisbury complaining of his reticence." Hatzfeldt need not have concerned himself at the moment. The news that Vice-Admiral von Diederichs had treated Dewey contemptuously at Manila inflamed American opinion that summer, creating a resentment that would militate against Germany for many years.

Otherwise, Hatzfeldt was kept busy submitting to Salisbury formulae for disposition of the Philippines, hatched in the minds of William and Holstein. The "fat spoils" of the Spanish South Seas appeared glitteringly before the Germans for weeks on end. Relying for a time on Dr. White's openhandedness, the Germans represented to Salisbury that under no circumstances would the Americans wish to retain the archipelago. There were proposals that Germany be given a protectorate on behalf of the Concert of Europe, or, failing that, that Britain and Germany accept joint responsibility. The Prime Minister was also sounded on a suggestion coming from Filipinos and Germans in Manila for the erection of the Philippines into an independent monarchy with a German prince as king. Germany, it was asserted, had grounds for interposing in the affairs of the islands because the Spanish Government had offered to make them over to Germany "in deposit." In their despair the Spanish had made the same offer to England. Salisbury terminated the importunities by observing that he feared the United States would "resent" any interference by Germany—or, for that matter, England—in the fate of the Philippines.

6

Convinced by midsummer of 1898 that the United States, backed by Britain, would have final say on the future of the

Philippines, the German Foreign Office industriously undertook to obtain its objectives—"maritime fulcra in East Asia"—
from Washington and London. The Kaiser bade Holleben
instruct the American Government as to the advantages of
assuring German friendliness by a "practical application of
the principle of 'live and let live.' " Hatzfeldt was ordered
to demand British support for a Philippine coaling station
"as the result of our participation in the protection of the
Philippines." And Jules Jusserand, the French diplomatist,
presenting a German viewpoint, cautioned Henry White
that the Germans were anxiously "stirring" in the Far East
and the United States might look for trouble unless it yielded
something.

In Germany the vials of wrath against the United States
were kept smoking, in the press, in the Reichstag, and in the
Wilhelmstrasse. Hay wrote Lodge that the "jealousy and
animosity felt toward us in Germany is something which
can scarcely be exaggerated." He went on:

> They hate us in France, but French hatred is a straw fire com-
> pared to the German. . . . The Vaterland is all on fire with greed
> and terror of us. They want the Philippine islands, the Carolines
> and Samoa—they want to get into our markets and keep us out
> of theirs. They have been flirting and intriguing with Spain ever
> since the war began and now they are trying to put the devil
> into the head of Aguinaldo.[1] I do not think they want to fight.
> . . . But they want by pressure, by threats, and by sulking and
> wheedling in turn, to get some thing out of us and Spain.

Andrew White had been Minister to Germany from 1879
to 1881. The tenor of German-American relations at that
time was unexceptionable. The Germans recalled American
sympathy in their war with France, the Americans were grate-
ful that German bankers had bought United States Civil
War bonds generously while they went begging in Paris and
London. Returning as Ambassador in 1897, White confessed
himself shocked to find a "generally adverse" feeling against
America, some classes being "bitterly hostile." White found

[1] Aguinaldo was then leading the Philippine insurrection against American occupation.

this feeling by no means confined to the "more ignorant," adding: "Men who stood high in the universities, men of the greatest amiability, who in former days had been the warmest friends of America, had now become our bitter opponents, and some of their expressions seemed to point to eventual war."

The reasons behind this shift of national sentiment were in the main economic, growing out of an acute realization that German-American trade relationships placed Germany at a disadvantage. This boiled down to the fact that Germany was dependent on the United States for raw materials while the United States needed little in the way of imports from Germany. Moreover, internal stresses were set up in relation to the United States, the agrarians wishing high duties on cheap American foodstuffs, low duties on manufactured goods, and the industrialists wishing the exact reverse. Moreover, in spite of German cartels, government assistance, and efficiency, the United States, with a higher wage level, was able to undersell German producers in certain lines—even in Germany.

Overriding all, through its succession of high tariff acts in the 1890's the United States had made it increasingly difficult for Germany to enter the huge American market. Hence trade between the countries remained always unbalanced. Dependence on American cotton, grain, and a host of other raw products prevented Germany from retaliating effectively. Thus in relationship to the English-speaking Powers at the end of the nineteenth century Germany felt herself inferior to the British on the seas and to America in commerce.

Envy of America's prodigious resources, her security behind her oceans, likewise played a part, for Germany was a country poor in raw materials and surrounded landward by potential enemies. There was also a psychological conflict in the German attitude toward this country, the product of ill-digested pride and envy. In one breath the press blackened America in toto, in the next boasted of the millions of "fine Germans" who formed the backbone of that country. So when Germany in 1898 ("in a perfect craze for colonial expansion," as Balfour reported to Henry White after a visit in October) found the United States, backed by Great Britain, blocking the way to a substantial share of the fallen Spanish Empire, German malevolence knew few bounds.

The Wilhelmstrasse's pertinacity did, however, gain a place in the Pacific sun. At the Paris peace conference ending the war with Spain the United States obtained Puerto Rico, accepted Cuba's independence in trust until a stable government could be formed, and agreed to reimburse Spain $20,-000,000 for the Philippines and the Ladrone island of Guam. Before the conference met, Hay, who had become Secretary of State in August, informed Holleben of the American decision, indicating that the United States Government had no objection to Germany's acquisition of the other Ladrones and the Caroline Islands. The German Ambassador received the concession with "joyous amazement." Although these atolls in the high Pacific had little or no economic value and scarcely any strategic use to Germany, their absorption (negotiated directly with Madrid) created a mood of imperialist elation in the Reich, replacing the black depression that had existed since Dewey had sunk the Spanish squadron at Manila. Parenthetically, Hay's easy renunciation, as a result of which these islands passed to Japan during the First World War, rises to plague the United States Navy nowadays, flanking as the islands do the sea road from Hawaii to the Philippines.

7

At the end of the war Victoria rested uneasily under a long indictment of British neutrality submitted by the Queen Regent, who charged that Britain, although withholding coal from Spain, allowed it to be supplied to the Americans, along with other materials from Hong Kong for the Americans and the Philippine insurrectos. She added that the British military attachés at Washington had co-operated with the Americans. Maria Christina also cheerlessly reminded the Queen that the British press had been far from neutral. Although the Queen Regent omitted mention of certain other matters, the Spanish Ministry bore a grudge over their belief that a British attaché in Washington had disclosed the arrival of Cervera's fleet at Santiago, the activities of an American secret agent against a Spanish agent in Montreal, and the fact that the Canadian Government had allowed the United States after war had begun to complete transfer of four revenue cutters from the Great Lakes to the sea by way of the St. Lawrence. One of the British attachés in Washington, Captain Arthur Hamilton Lee, observed the land war in Cuba, became an honorary Rough Rider, and in 1921, as Lord Lee of Fareham, First Lord of the Admiralty, would help to bring about the Washington Conference on the Reduction of Armaments.

Victoria referred the Spanish Queen's complaints to Lord Salisbury. As old age overtook the Queen, the task of clarifying the obvious in the many matters passing under her observation became one of the most wearisome of the Prime Minister's chores. Salisbury affirmed the strict neutrality of his Government on all points, though he was "painfully aware" that the press had lacked something of impartiality. Replying to the Spanish Queen Regent, Victoria impressively quoted Lord Salisbury's asseverations, bidding Maria Christina reflect that an adverse press did not necessarily connote an adverse public opinion.

At the end of 1898 the United States, as Mahan foresaw, had again betaken itself to the sea and external action. The experience, moreover, had disclosed an Anglo-Saxon identity of interest ranging from the China Sea to the North Sea. In both countries, even as the war was being fought partisans of collaboration sought means of retaining the mutual goodwill being demonstrated on all sides. One effort took the form of the Anglo-American League, a forerunner of the English-Speaking Union of World War days. The league was organized in London and New York in July. James Bryce, the Duke of Sutherland, R. C. Maxwell, and Sir Frederick Pollock took the lead in England. In America Whitelaw Reid, a later Ambassador to England, William C.

Whitney, Carl Schurz, and Daniel S. Lamont filled offices, the Church being represented by Monsignor Corrigan, the Roman Catholic Archbishop of New York, and the Right Reverend Henry C. Potter, the Protestant Episcopal Bishop of New York.

The dividends flowing out of improved Anglo-American relations were reciprocal. This country still had a major task to perform in the American seas, a task requiring British acquiescence. Soon Great Britain would be engaged in a stubborn colonial war and her friendlessness in Europe would duplicate America's isolation in 1898 from the sympathy of continental Europe.

IV. England Quits the American Seas: Concert in Samoa

JOHN HAY'S "splendid little war" left the United States with defense commitments exactly matching its strategical gains. Hawaii might be a sea bastion safeguarding the Pacific coast, and the Philippines a potential stronghold. Neither was self-defending. Senator Cushman K. Davis, chairman of the Foreign Relations Committee and a grave Shakespearean scholar, thanked God publicly that America had "ceased to be the China of the Western Hemisphere" but that desirable new status could be maintained only at the cost of constantly increasing naval appropriations.

The Pacific "frontiers," moreover, posed an immediate dilemma in 1898. Fifteen thousand miles of salt water and stormy Cape Horn lay between the Caribbean bases and Hawaii, and the Philippines were some thousands of miles beyond. It became suddenly apparent that we were a two-ocean Power with a navy scarcely sufficient for one. The new commitments required one of these alternatives: either fleets in both the Atlantic and the Pacific capable of coping with any likely enemy, or an isthmian canal contracting the distance between our coasts and magnifying the maneuverability of one strong fleet. The Government chose the second horn of the dilemma, electing to dig a canal.

There was, however, an obstacle. We had treaty rights to the transit of Nicaragua and the Isthmus of Panama; we had the strategical incentive, the means, and the will. Only the Clayton-Bulwer Treaty barred the way. That treaty, binding us since 1850 to an Anglo-American partnership in any Central American ship canal, inhibited an all-American canal. England still had the power of veto over our freedom of action in that respect, a strategical voice in Caribbean affairs that she had shown no willingness to relinquish. The treaty had been, as we have seen, steadily irksome. Nor were the British unaware of our attitude. In 1889, for example, Michael Herbert, the chargé d'affaires at Washington, reported that the Americans, "hating" the treaty, were "always inclined to pretend that it had lapsed." The half-century-old covenant stood as the last barrier to American ascendancy in the Caribbean. Now as the Administration reckoned the liabilities as well as the assets accruing from the Spanish War, it was plain that the Clayton-Bulwer Treaty stood also as a barrier to a proper defense of the Pacific possessions.

The situation confronting McKinley was not easy. On the one hand was the valuable Atlantic entente that had served us well during the recent war. As much as any other President, McKinley cherished the English-speaking tie. On the other hand, he faced the strategical necessities of his country —plus an urgent public sentiment in favor of an all-American canal. The desire for such a canal, growing chronic through the years, had been quickened by the voyage of the battleship *Oregon* (one of the 1890 class) from San Francisco to Key West to reinforce the North Atlantic squadron against Cervera—13,000 miles in sixty-eight days. Seldom has the exploit of a single man-of-war so engrossed the attention of a nation. The progress of the *Oregon* down the Pacific coast, around the Horn and north past the bulge of Brazil was daily measured in the press. Verse-makers celebrated the *Oregon's* journey, typical being the excellent Arthur Guiterman, who in a Kiplingesque strain depicted her swift passage south to the Horn, then brought her spankingly northward with these lines:

> Six thousand miles to the Indian isles!
>   And the Oregon rushed home,
> Her wake a swirl of jade and pearl,
>   Her bow a bend of foam.

The drama of the *Oregon's* race against time illuminated for the whole country our new responsibilities. Endlessly was the lesson of the *Oregon* iterated in the press, on the platform, and in Congress. We now had two coasts and thousands of miles of the Pacific Ocean to defend. A war might easily be lost while future *Oregons* were rounding the Horn into either ocean. There was, the public understood, no time to be wasted over the canal.

McKinley acted promptly. Without even waiting for the Treaty of Paris to end the war with Spain on December 10, 1898, he struck a glancing blow at the obstructive treaty. In his annual message on December 5 the President recommended that the United States, in the imperative name of "national policy," should dig its own canal. Pointedly ignoring the Clayton-Bulwer Treaty, he termed American control of such a waterway "indispensable" in view of the annexation of Hawaii and the developing situation in the Pacific.

The President was, of course, only bringing the policy of Hayes and Garfield up to date, but his declaration raised hackles in Europe, more so on the Continent than in England, who might have considered herself aggrieved. Although the unflaggingly Amerophobic *Saturday Review* demanded naval bases flanking any canal, and an unidentified Major General, writing in the *Outlook,* feared that England was about to lose a "key to the commerce of the world" through unwillingness to "irritate the United States," the British press generally did not rise above a mild querulousness. Since the dream of a passage to India via the Isthmus of Panama was older than English settlements in the Western Hemisphere, what, it asked, was McKinley's hurry? It was pointed out that ever since Alvarado de Saavedra noted for the benefit of Charles V early in the sixteenth century the providential proximity of the great oceans in that part of the world, bold minds (Jefferson, Goethe, and Henry Clay among them) had advocated such a waterway. The British, although they had backed our retention of the Philippines, had not followed the dash of the *Oregon* as closely as we had.

On the Continent, where it was now the fashion to regard the United States as an imperialistic "aggressor nation," McKinley's observations were taken as a blunt notice to

England to clear out of Central America. Continental chancelleries and the Foreign Office press were both gratified by
what they supposed would be a fissure in the Atlantic link
and annoyed by this fresh manifestation of American arrogance. While the Wilhelmstrasse was perversely discovering
new evidence of an Anglo-American entente, the Kaiser was
receiving the assurances of his cousin the Czar that Europe
need have no fear of such an Atlantic concentration, the two
countries being demonstrably unable to sink their differences.

A less comforting view was being taken at that moment by
the well-informed *Novoye Vremya* in the Czar's capital. Accepting America's friendship with its "traditional enemy" as
durable, that newspaper urged the Russian Government to
back France in a new attempt at a Central American canal
as a "counterweight" to the growth of "American power." In
Germany, on the contrary, the steadfastly anti-American press
affected to believe, in the words of the *Kölnische Zeitung,*
that "Uncle Sam's rampant jingoism" had estranged the
British. The "dear Anglo-Saxon cousins had best take note,"
that journal went on, lest "Yankee imperialism" gobble the
"rest of the world." It was clear to the *Vossische Zeitung* that
a lasting accord between the English-speaking Powers was
impossible because the boundless ambition of the Americans
"will not give to others even as much as Great Britain is willing to give."

The confusion of Continental observers was understand-
able. American foreign policy in the period immediately
following the Spanish War seemed, to a superficial view,
ambiguous. Calling for Britain's retirement from the Isthmus of Panama, the Government at the same time was
thwarting Canada's desire for a corridor from the Klondike
to the Pacific. By themselves these policies implied a settled
hostility toward the British Empire. But there was no such
hostility. Outside hemispheric waters, Anglo-American solidarity remained intact.

When England, absorbed by the Boer War, was vaguely
menaced by Continental diplomacy, Washington quietly re-
enforced her. Hay's diplomacy persuaded Bülow, the Boer

leaders, and a section of the American press ("England," said the *Kansas City Times,* "has committed the crime of the century—and this Government has been an accessory") that the United States was hand in glove with Britain. Concurrently also the English-speaking Powers followed similar policies in the Pacific. Hay led Lord Salisbury into a joint diplomatic and naval demonstration against an act of German usurpation in Samoa, British and American blood being "mingled" in a microscopic "war," chiefly interesting as a minute preview of 1917.

The German Foreign Minister, seeing in the Samoan affair an "undoubted rapprochement," in a talk with the Kaiser suspected that the "Anglo-Saxon Powers" would always be united against Germany. This was a disingenuous observation. Both Bülow and William were intimately familiar with the sustained efforts by Joseph Chamberlain and other influential Englishmen, who were in no way opposed by the United States Government, to bring Germany into better relations with England and America and attach her to the Atlantic System. The reluctance was more German than Anglo-Saxon.

Noting the European reactions to McKinley's canal declaration, Hay bade Henry White assure Salisbury that the President did not contemplate repudiating the treaty. As it happened, White was week-ending with the Prime Minister at Hatfield within a few days, and Salisbury, who often unbent with White, assured him in return that England had no desire to build or to share in the canal, a Central American canal being of "comparatively little importance to England now that [we] have the Suez Canal." The Prime Minister agreed that one Power, rather than two or more, should dig and operate the canal, and for his part he preferred that Power to be the United States. As for its military status, Salisbury supposed that it would be unfortified and neutralized in war as in peace, like Suez. White, unaware of the feeling back home concerning the terms of American proprietorship, saw no hindrance there. He found the rest of the Ministry also agreeable, Balfour seeming "quite sound."

To White, mending matters in London, as well as to Hay and Pauncefote the deed was as good as done. A treaty was hastily drafted by the Secretary of State and the British Ambassador, and signed on February 5, 1899. Hay, seeing the first Hay-Pauncefote Treaty off to London, was optimistic of an early settlement. He was to be disappointed. Few diplomatic undertakings ever set sail under more promising skies; few ever wallowed so pointlessly to a foreordained destination. The simple chore of removing Britain's veto over a canal in which she wished no part took three years, its course delayed by domestic politics in Canada, England, and the United States and complicated by an irrelevant dispute over glacial bays on the Alaskan coast.

After much backing and filling the British Government finally yielded, preferring to exchange the negligible and irritating partnership at the Isthmus of Panama for a larger association in Atlantic and world affairs. The free and orderly development of the Atlantic System was thereby advanced and Anglo-American friendship fundamentally strengthened. The cornerstone of the Atlantic System was mutual trust between the English-speaking Powers. That trust could be built only on a sense of equality, and not until Uncle Sam felt himself master in his own household and in command of his strategical necessities would the way be open to wholehearted, unprejudiced collaboration.

2

The Klondike gold rush in 1897 had found Canada—or so Canadians thought—at a geographical disadvantage. While nearly all the gold deposits lay within the Canadian boundaries, all ingress and egress were through the Alaskan ports of Skagway and Dyea, there being no railways or wagon roads into the Yukon. A glance at a map shows the Alaskan Panhandle curtaining Dominion territory from the Pacific for a stretch of 500 miles. After 1897 Canada claimed an outlet to the sea, centering her claim on Pyramid Harbor, near the American ports, with a corridor inland. This claim the United States rejected, resting its legal case on the treaty with Russia transferring Alaska in 1867, this in turn standing on a treaty between Russia and Great Britain in 1825 (a document admittedly hazy as to boundaries) and upon Admiralty maps which for two generations had mutely upheld the American contentions. A brisk, downright young nation, the Canadians pressed their argument on Washington, through London, with all vigor.

In 1898 a Joint High Commission had been set up to resolve an even dozen points at issue between the Dominion and the American republic. Of these, the boundary case was the most important and early in the life of the commission it became apparent that it would be the sticker. By February, 1899, the boundary question had become a fuse which set off tempers on both sides. Hay was convinced that the British chairman, Lord Herschell, recently Lord Chancellor of England, was seeking to intertwine the canal and boundary questions, hoping for a trade by means of which Canada would gain her port in exchange for abrogation of the treaty. "The slightest suggestion that his [Herschell's] claim is unfounded throws him into a fury," said Hay, who on his part would concede not an inch of Alaskan soil. "Pyramid Harbor," Hay told the London *Times,* "is as much our territory as Sitka or San Francisco," the Canadians having "never raised a tent or moored a canoe there."

Meanwhile, confirming Hay's suspicions of a trade, Chamberlain suggested that Canada be accorded a share in the canal, replacing Britain. The Canadians also, he argued, had two coasts to defend, and in the present stage of friction between the countries they feared that an all-American canal would "double" the United States Navy for hostile use against themselves. The Joint High Commission was wrecked on the boundary shoals in February, but not before it furnished Salisbury with an excuse for withholding action on the treaty. Sardonically, the Prime Minister contrasted the "precarious prospects and slowness of the negotiations which were being conducted by Lord Herschell with the rapidity of decision proposed in the matter of the [canal] convention." Whereupon, at the behest of Chamberlain and against the advice of Pauncefote, Salisbury pocketed the new treaty.

Hay stormed helplessly. Lodge, addressing Balfour through White, warned the Ministry that the "American people mean to have the canal and they mean to control it. . . . England does not care enough about it to go to war . . . and it would be ruinous if she did make war on us." Chamberlain conceded that the issues were "trumpery bits of irritation," but referred to a "certain feeling here of late that the United States had got the best of any arrangement" between the two countries. Canada was undergoing a hard-contested Dominion election. The Colonial Secretary reminded White that if the United States Government had to consider "tail-twisters" in Congress, the Ministry had to contend with "croakers in Parliament."

Not a wheel turned in the canal controversy during the remainder of 1899. One reason for British indifference was the onset and declaration of the Boer War. For several weeks before war began on October 11, 1899, when the Boers invaded Natal, efforts by the British Government to compose the differences with the Transvaal republic took precedence over all other matters. The tension between the British and the Boers was of long standing. It came down to the unwillingness of the English, who had a nominal protectorate, the largest economic stake, and the next most numerous group of European settlers in the Transvaal, to accept the rigorous rule of the ascendant Boers.

Determined to keep the republic Dutch in language, politics, and religion, the Pretoria Government, under Paul Kruger, refused to naturalize other Europeans, and the Uitlanders, predominantly British, had no voice in the Government, although they had developed the wealth of the republic in gold and diamonds. The Transvaal (South African Republic) and its sister republic, the Orange Free State, were virtually surrounded by the British at Cape Colony and in the other possessions to the west and north of them. The conflict between the static Boer state, agrarian and primitive, and the colonial dynamics of the British Empire was no doubt irrespressible. When in the summer of 1899 Kruger rejected Chamberlain's offer of a Joint High Commission, proposing instead an international arbitration, the die was cast and England began to ship reinforcements to the surrounding territories.

In the beginning and for eight months the war went against the British, who were bottled up in Ladysmith, Kimberley, and Mafeking. But as the Dominions rallied enthusiastically to the help of the mother country, as the numbers, equipment, and training of the British expeditionary forces began to tell, the Dutch armies were dispersed. In June, 1900, Pretoria fell to the British, and although the Boers maintained a guerrilla struggle for a year and a half, the issue was then as good as settled. The peace treaty, signed May 31, 1902, incorporated both the Boer republics in British South Africa.

In January, 1900, with the British stunned by their early reverses in South Africa, the Senate grew restless over the delay in the canal negotiations. Hay wrote Joseph Choate, the American Ambassador in London, concerning a resolution just introduced which, if passed, would take the question out of the hands of the executive branch and have the effect of denouncing the Clayton-Bulwer Treaty. The passage of this resolution, said Hay, would "place us in a most unenviable position before the world," but he added for the guidance of the Ministry: "the canal is going to be built. Nothing . . . in the Clayton-Bulwer prohibition will finally prevent [its] building. . . . As soon as Congress is convinced that the people . . . demand the canal it will be done." Hay felt that it would be "deplorable" for Britain to attempt a veto, especially in view of his conviction that the "veto would not be effective." It may be assumed from what follows that Hay's representation was effective.

Hay's letter was dated January 15. Just before midnight of February 3 he had a cablegram from Choate giving word that the Ministry had approved the treaty. Canada, it appeared, had receded, an exhibition of "magnanimity" that touched off tributes from both Salisbury and Hay. At this point began the final phase of Great Britain's surrender of a voice in the strategic affairs of the American seas. There were, however, other obstacles to overcome. The treaty now approved preserved all the elements of its predecessor except for the presence of Britain as a principal. Under the first Hay-Pauncefote Treaty the United States was forbidden to fortify the canal site. The waterway must be neutral, on the model of Suez, and its neutrality might be guaranteed by such other Powers, including England, as saw fit to adhere to the convention. This multilateral provision had never been operative under the Clayton-Bulwer agreement, because the envisaged canal had not come into being.

When the treaty reached the Senate in February a storm broke, astonishing Hay, who had not gathered the full content of the public demand for an all-American canal. The American people wanted a canal to be built, owned, operated, and controlled in war and peace (especially in war) by their own country. They wished no foreign interference, no shadow of such. Representative of the opposition, the *New York Sun,* asking Hay to correct a "stupendous blunder, honestly perpetrated," went on to say: "As if not satisfied with the gash made fifty years ago in the Monroe Doctrine, the negotiators of the new treaty actually ask the Senate to vote to go further and call over to this side of the Atlantic all the new powers of Europe to assist Great Britain in coercing us."

Theodore Roosevelt, Governor of New York and soon to be McKinley's running mate in the 1900 presidential campaign, arraigned the treaty forcefully in a letter to Hay (an intervention producing a faint spitefulness in their subsequent close relationship) wherein he asserted that it "strengthened against us every nation whose fleet is larger than ours." Roosevelt agreed with the *Sun* that the convention breached the Monroe Doctrine. Hay's friend Lodge led the revisionist forces in the Senate. McKinley and the powerful

Senator Nelson Aldrich might support the treaty without amendment; Admiral Dewey might throw his influence behind it by testifying that fortifications would merely make the canal a battle zone in case of war; and John Bassett Moore might learnedly argue that a neutralized canal was in harmony with "our great policy, the freedom of the seas"— but the public seemed dead-set to the contrary. The cooperative policy embodied in the Hay-Pauncefote Treaty had collided with another potent policy—supremacy in the Caribbean.

A House bill declaring the Clayton-Bulwer Treaty "obsolete" and calling for a fortified canal seemed certain of passage before the Senate could act. In the Senate it was being pointed out that the neutralization of Suez might suit England, with her naval base at Alexandria and military control of both ends of the canal in Egypt, but the United States had no foothold on the Isthmus of Panama and the treaty interdicted any attempt to gain one. Both parties in their national conventions took issue with the treaty. The Republicans discreetly called for "construction, ownership, control and *protection*" of the canal, but the Democrats let fly with both boots, branding the treaty a "surrender of American rights and interests."

The thunder from both right and left infuriated Hay. Minimizing the sound nationalistic reasons for wishing the treaty altered, he railed privately at the Irish and German politicians, writing White that they had "joined their several lunacies in one common attack against England, and incidentally against the Administration for being too friendly with England." No matter what sort of treaty had been drawn, he said elsewhere, the Bryan party would have "made us out the slaves of England." In a moment of exasperation Hay wrote White that he spent his whole time wringing "great concessions out of her [England] with no compensation, and yet these idiots say that I am not an American because I don't say 'to hell with the Queen.'" It was Hay's underlying "conviction that the one indispensable feature of our foreign policy should be a friendly understanding with England." His zeal for such understanding carried him in this situation into a rather extreme manifestation of Anglophilia. The first Hay-Pauncefote Treaty was amended by the Senate to permit fortification and exclude the sanction of other Powers. In transmitting the amended version to Choate, Hay suggested that "the amendments are not so fatally vicious as to justify the wreck of the treaty. Why should not Lord Salisbury say to us: 'Take your treaty, Brother Jonathan, and God send you better manners?' "

Salisbury failed to heed this advice. After the Boer War "khaki election" of 1900 triumphantly returning the Salisbury-Chamberlain Ministry, the Prime Minister surrendered the Foreign Office portfolio to the Marquis of Lansdowne, who helped usher out the policy of "Splendid isolation." In March, 1901, Lansdowne rejected the treaty. Hay promptly drafted another with Pauncefote, embodying the amendments and retaining the provision—which would embarrass subsequent Administrations—against discrimination in tolls in favor of the ships of any national, including, presumably, our own. The British accepted this treaty.

McKinley too had been re-elected, carrying all the states outside the Solid South and four Rocky Mountain silver states. Before the treaty returned from London he had been assassinated in September, 1901, Theodore Roosevelt succeeding. Two months later the second Hay-Pauncefote Treaty went to the Senate, being ratified on December 18, 1901, by a vote of 72 to 6. The Alaskan-boundary question would be sidetracked until October, 1903.

3

The twenty years of bickering among the representatives of Germany, England, and the United States in the Samoan condominium reached a crisis in the winter of 1898 (as it had ten years earlier) when the German officials overrode the treaty and attempted to seat their choice forcibly on the native throne. On January 27, 1899, Hay, safeguarding, as he said, "our Pacific work," addressed a sharp note to Count von Bülow. Sir Julian Pauncefote, a moderate, lawyerlike diplomat, described the message in a note urging Salisbury's adherence as a "scathing indictment of the German officials implicated in the disorders." Salisbury joined the protest, which was made to no purpose.

Diplomacy failing, in March a British and American naval force under command of an American admiral deposed the local German dictator and his king, unhappily shelling recalcitrant native villages, and landing forces into an ambush where two Americans and two Britons lost their lives. The incident at Samoa gained in importance as its repercussions promptly reached Berlin, London, and Washington, its effects proving surprisingly broad in the relationships of the three Powers. The Kaiser, expressing humiliation at Germany's enforced passivity in the presence of the Anglo-American naval concentration, fumed at the "blockheads of the Reichstag" for denying him ships. He was to use Germany's weakness there as an argument for the Naval Law of 1900, which by doubling Germany's naval force sharpened English apprehensions and helped to create the climate out of which came the First World War.

Taking his cue from Admiral von Tirpitz, William charged the Anglo-Saxons with plotting a "preventive" war before the German fleet could be, as the Admiral put it, "hatched out of its shell." Unless they had planned war, Tirpitz told Bülow and William, "one would have to assume that both John Bull and Brother Jonathan had gone mad." The full force of the Wilhelmstrasse was brought to bear against the "Anglo-American entente." In a spirited conversation with Sir Frank Cavendish Lascelles, the British Ambassador, the Kaiser belittled the power, consistency, and good faith of the United States as an ally and accused the British Government of "bribing the American press" to traduce Germany, adding that this "evil influence had not prevailed, as relations between Germany and the United States had now been put on a satisfactory footing. . . . All this being known in Germany increases the ill-feeling toward England."

Reversing its Spanish-American War policy, the Wilhelm-strasse was undertaking a full-scale courtship of Washington. Bülow, acknowledging in a memorandum that he had no leverage with which to pry this country away from England in the Samoan controversy, widened his American policy. Up to this time the German Government had placed its chief reliance in America on influencing the German-language press and the organized German vote toward bringing pressure on the State Department. In this enterprise the Pan-German movement played a considerable part. Now Bülow undertook to soothe American sensibilities. As a first step he announced in the Reichstag the withdrawal of a warship that had been guarding German interests in Manila. Here-after, he said, the Reich would entrust the protection of its nationals in the Philippines to the United States Government. He hoped this would put an end to the "canards" flying about Europe to the effect that the Germans were secretly helping the Aguinaldistas. At about that time Admiral von Diederichs was relieved of the naval command in the Far East, the Navy Office denying, however, that his recall was due to his unpopularity in America. Hay wrote Henry White in London that German diplomatic manners had lost their usual brusquerie, "the Emperor" being "nervously anxious to be on good terms with us, *bien entendu.*"

In the immediate wake of the naval demonstration, the German Government repudiated the conduct of its officials, but demanded an apology for a shell that struck the consulate. Hay replied with a note "blistering" the officials and justifying the shelling, but apologizing for damage done the consulate. On the ground that no English shell had struck that building, Salisbury ignored the demand for an apology, thereby provoking the Kaiser to an extraordinary complaint to Queen Victoria against her Prime Minister, who, said William, "despises Germany." He added that "Lord Salisbury cares no more for us than for Portugal, Chile, or the Patagonians." (On William's fortieth birthday, January 27, 1899, Victoria had noted in her journal: "I wish he were more prudent and less impulsive at such an age!") In her

reply, written a few days after her own eightieth birthday,
May 24, the Queen doubted "whether any sovereign ever
wrote in such terms to another sovereign, and that sovereign
his own grandmother, about her Prime Minister."

Salisbury's procrastinating methods with the Samoan negotiations enraged the Kaiser. By the following September
no apparent progress had been made. In that month it became apparent to the Germans that war was inevitable in
South Africa; thereupon German representations were revised. Bülow directed Hatzfeldt to warn Salisbury that
Anglo-German accord elsewhere would be impossible as long
as Samoa stood between the Powers. The Germans, who had
been willing to accept compensation in exchange for surrender of their interest in Samoa, now insisted that England get out. Hatzfeldt and Baron von Eckardstein, legation secretary, hinted to the Prime Minister and Chamberlain that German public opinion might compel their
Government to review the Anglo-Boer situation. After
lunching with Eckardstein on October 9, two days before
war began, the Colonial Secretary burst out in a fit of annoyance, declaring that "German policy since Bismarck has been
one of undisguised blackmail." In yielding, Salisbury ex-
acted a pledge of neutrality in the Boer War.

A treaty signed November 14, 1899, allotted all of Samoa
to Germany except Tutuila (containing the Pago Pago base)
and its neighboring atolls. These remained with the United
States. Great Britain obtained compensation in the Tongas,
the Solomons, and Togoland in Africa. William added the
title King of Samoa to his imperial honors, and Senator Pet-
tigrew of South Dakota gibed: "We blot out . . . a sovereign nation and divide the spoils."

Collaterally, the Samoan settlement plunged Chamberlain
into another attempt to gain a German alliance. For two
years, hope triumphing over experience, he had periodically
initiated negotiations to that end. The pessimistic Salisbury
viewed these efforts with "some dismay," expressing to Balfour a fear that the Germans would "blackmail us heavily."
This time Chamberlain, responding, as he said, to a sugges-

tion by Bülow, sought to include the United States in what Theodor Mommsen, the German historian, was to call "Chamberlain's three-cousin system."

A visit by the Kaiser and Bülow to London in November, 1899, afforded the Colonial Secretary his opportunity. Although gratified over his conversion of the "shame of Samoa" into a diplomatic victory, William carried to London a personal grievance inclining him against such overtures as Chamberlain's. For months before the Queen's eightieth birthday Bülow, a brazen flatterer, had been anticipating the Kaiser's role at that gathering of Europe's crowned heads and statesmen. William was there to appear as *arbiter mundi,* moderating the conflicts of Europe. But the invitation to the Queen's birthday had not come. Victoria and Salisbury had been annoyed at the Kaiser's behavior over Samoa and his encouragement of Boer emissaries. The November visit, taken by the British public as a pledge of neutrality, was therefore an anticlimax.

Chamberlain saw the Kaiser twice, Bülow repeatedly. At his first talk with Bülow, Chamberlain outlined conditions of alliance. First, said he, it must be borne in mind that good relations with the United States were "vital" to England and that the British Government would never agree to anything harmful to American interests. Bülow, remarking (as he noted in a memorandum) that the Spanish War had brought the United States into the front rank of World Powers to a degree unpredictable a year earlier, asked Chamberlain's help in "preventing further misunderstandings" with that country. "If you showed more friendliness to us," the Colonial Secretary replied, "it would be easier to intercede with the Americans." Bülow thereupon, according to Chamberlain, suggested that the Briton feel out sentiment in all three countries on a possible three-party accord by means of a "trial-balloon" speech. Whatever was said, on the day after the Germans departed for home Chamberlain exposed his aspiration to public view in an address at Leicester, vowing that "at bottom, the character . . . of the Teutonic race differs very slightly indeed from the character of the Anglo-Saxon.

. . . If union between England and America is a powerful factor in the cause of peace, a new triple alliance between the Teutonic and the two great branches of the Anglo-Saxon race will be a still more potent influence in the future of the world."

The seed fell on barren soil. Salisbury, who had warned Chamberlain that he was risking his personal reputation by the move, accepted the speech as another Chamberlain indiscretion. Sir Edward Grey, for the Opposition, declared Chamberlain must be kept out of foreign affairs, "or he will make impossible even our friendship with the United States." In America the Administration took no notice of the proposal, but Hay wrote White (no doubt for Chamberlain's eye) that "neither the President nor I saw anything but what was right and admirable in the speech—though, of course, I never use the word alliance."

In Berlin Bülow (as Salisbury had predicted) answered conciliation with defiance. His speech in the Reichstag on behalf of the Naval Bill of 1900 came during the "black week" of Boer successes in December. Predicting that "in the coming century the German people will be hammer or anvil," the Foreign Minister added that Germany would "allow no foreign Power to tread upon our feet or push us aside, either in trade or in politics."

His hopes dashed, his hands full with what the French press called "Chamberlain's war," the Colonial Secretary forswore further exertions toward Anglo-German rapprochement. "That was not the first time," he told Eckardstein later, "that Von Bülow has thrown me over in the Reichstag. There can be no more question of an association between Great Britain and Germany." To Lord Rothschild he lamented German shortsightedness in being unable to observe the "rise of a new constellation in the world." The Germans were, he felt, "beyond help."

A perusal of the Kaiser's so-called secret memorandum, written after similar negotiations undertaken in 1898, would have clarified Chamberlain's understanding of the reasons for his chronic failure. Therein the German Emperor wrote:

This proposal arises from anxiety with respect to the consequences of our navy law. In the beginning of the next century,
Germany will dispose of an armored fleet which, in conjunction
with similarly enlarged fleets, will bring England into real danger. Hence the intent either to force us into an alliance or to
annihilate us like Holland aforetime.

An alliance with England being undesirable, it was nevertheless, the Kaiser believed, "of great importance to keep
official sentiment in England favorable to us, and hopeful."
In his memoirs Bülow disclosed that the naval program
"would scarcely [have been] reconcilable with a really definite Anglo-German alliance based on mutual confidence."
The Germans, it was clear to themselves, desired a fleet, not
a pact.

4

During the "black week" the German Ambassador in
Washington called on John Hay. The Secretary of State,
preoccupied with the South African news, soberly remarked
that things looked bad. The German Ambassador felt
obliged to remind the Secretary that he was not the English
Ambassador. At the outbreak of the war, Hay bade Henry
White in London to "say many things for me to our friends
at the Foreign Office and to Mr. Balfour—in fact, many
more things than I have any business to say." Hay's pro-
British sympathies, President McKinley's also for that matter, were no secret to the diplomatic corps in Washington.

On January 2, 1900, Ambassador von Holleben, instructed
by Bülow, explored the prospects with Hay. He posed a
hypothetical question: In case England stripped the British
Isles of troops for South Africa, would she "always undoubtedly be able to count upon the United States as a friend?"
The British, Hay replied, could "count on the good offices
of the United States in every difficulty arising from the war,"
but he pointed out that "taking sides" or "armed intervention" would run "contrary to American tradition." Holleben probed further, supposing that this country had a natural interest in the fate of Great Britain. Hay quickly agreed,

amplifying his remarks by explaining: "If the existence of the British empire should be called in question there is no knowing what constellation might then make its appearance amongst the powers; the continued existence of the British empire, even though somewhat humbled, was a greater advantage to all the European powers than its downfall."

A majority of the Kaiser's military advisers (as was the case with American prospects in the war with Spain) assured him that England could not win. On a report from Hatzfeldt the Kaiser made a notation citing expert opinion that the end would be "England's complete defeat." On another report conveying word of rising British confidence the Emperor wrote that nobody in Berlin expected them ever to "reach Pretoria."

From St. Petersburg, and later from Paris, talk emanated of mediation, even of intervention on behalf of the Boers. A month after his first visit Holleben was sent back to sound Hay on this country's position in case of intervention. Upon Hay's appointment as Secretary of State, Holleben had cabled Holstein that the new man could not be "reckoned a friend of Germany." The renewed quizzing may have annoyed Hay. Holleben reported that he answered as before but in a "very excited manner." A few days earlier, Mark Twain had expressed substantially the Secretary's views, although in undiplomatic language, when, in a letter to William Dean Howells, he wrote:

England must not fall; it would mean an inundation of Russian and German political degradations which would envelop the globe and steep it in a sort of Middle-Age night and slavery which would last till Christ comes again. Even wrong—and she is wrong—England must be upheld. He is an enemy of the human race who shall speak against her now!

The United States Government unfailingly supported Great Britain on the diplomatic front. In March, 1900, the Boers besought intervention from the Great Powers of Europe, and the United States. Hay promptly asked the British Government if they would welcome our mediation, receiving the reply that the "intervention of any other Power" was unacceptable. When a Boer delegation visited this country in May, its members asserted that Hay had hurried to offer his good offices, publishing the negative reply to the world as a means of putting up a "fender" against them. "It was," one of the delegation told the journalist Walter Wellman, "a bit discouraging to see our answer lying on the table [Hay's] as we entered and before we had an opportunity to open our mouths." The Boer visitors, certain that the United States and Great Britain were "in league," declared that everyone in Europe believed that "the United States is ready to jump in and aid Great Britain in case of intervention."

When the Boers called on McKinley, he received them courteously, but when the spokesman began to recite their grievances against England, he walked to the window and called their attention to the beauty of the White House gardens and the Washington Monument beyond. A bit later, when President Kruger, having taken refuge in Holland, was invited by pro-Boer Americans to bring his cause personally to this country, Hay wrote the American Minister at The Hague, Stanford Newel, directing him to discourage Kruger's visit. Privately, Hay informed Newel that Boer sympathy was confined "almost entirely to opponents of the Administration." Upon thinking it over McKinley, fearful of the effect of a possible disclosure of the letter on his campaign for re-election, asked Hay to "recall" it. In a private note accompanying the "recall" the Secretary re-enforced his arguments against the coming of Kruger. The President of the South African Republic, whether for that or other reasons, disappointed the hopes of his would-be American hosts.

The British found their costly, disagreeable war against the bearded and bigoted Dutch farmers unpopular outside their empire, although within, in the Dominions, it lighted new and unexpected fires of loyalty. Volunteer armies from Canada and the antipodes sprang to the side of the mother country, producing intense gratification in England, foreshadowing empire solidarity in the World War and hastening the already discernible trend toward the Commonwealth. On the European continent, however, chancelleries, press, and public heaped scorn and mendacity on the British. Mommsen, who thought "every German was pro-Boer," called the war "not only a calamity but an infamy."

Chamberlain ("Joseph Africanus") drew the brunt of this, his heedless utterances making him a shining mark, but in Paris the press spared no one in British official life, the diatribes against Victoria finally growing so coarse that the British Ambassador was withdrawn in protest. The German press, duplicating its thorough and immitigable campaign against the Americans in the Spanish War, pushed the limits of decency, attacking the English as individuals and the valor and honor of British arms, and publishing every conceivable slur against British methods of making war. It was charged that the British used Boer women as shields in battle, and several hundred clergymen of the German Evangelical Church joined in a formal denunciation of the practice, only to be confounded later by evidence of the falsity of the charge. A few years later Dr. Hans Delbrück, the German savant, deploringly wrote: "The insults with which the English army and the English national character were at that time bespattered, not in the German press alone, but in the Reichstag were . . . so excessively gross that one could scarcely take it amiss if the English bore a grudge against us for them."

England had replaced Spanish War America as the butt of Continental censure, yet part of the American press, exhibiting our characteristic sensitiveness to Great Britain's international lapses, self-righteously joined the chorus of commination against the people who recently had stood between the United States and the Continent. The attitude of large sections of American opinion (excluding the Germans, who as usual echoed Berlin, and the Irish, deriving a bitter joy from any evil that befell England) was all the more remarkable because at the precise moment the United States was engaged in an overseas war at least as dubious morally as that of the British. A council of Church Fathers would be required to weigh the relative sinfulness of our Philippine expedition and the Boer War. The Filipinos, who had virtually won their war of independence when Dewey took Manila, were resisting our attempts at "pacification" with courage and hardihood; in South Africa the Boers, narrow, tenacious farmers, were fighting to keep a rich, expanding imperial domain within the bounds of an agrarian economy, a racial politic, and a Calvinistic sect.

In the flagrant anti-imperialist campaign of 1900 (a phenomenon to be examined later) the "chronic, slumbering animosity toward the mother country" deplored by Hay was revived for the benefit of Bryan and the German Foreign Office. There were, naturally, many Americans whose sympathies went out to the Dutch farmers in their fight for political ascendancy in the lands they had settled. Such was Andrew Carnegie, who financed a mass meeting in New York to protest the extinguishment of the Boer republics. But Carnegie also condemned the war on the Filipinos, as did the conscientious pro-Boers generally. There were likewise sincere voices on the other side. In a letter to Spring-Rice, Theodore Roosevelt labeled the Boers "belated Cromwellians." Proud of his own Dutch ancestry, Roosevelt considered that it was to the "advantage of mankind to have English spoken south of the Zambesi, just as in New York, as I told one of my fellow-Knickerbockers the other day: 'As we let the Uitlanders of old in here, I do not see why the same rule is not good enough in the Transvaal.' "

Few Americans supporting the English cared, as did the Yale professor Washburn Hopkins, to place their case on grounds of a "higher morality." Writing in the *Forum,* Hopkins averred that "wherever England has taken her stand, man has been bettered. . . . [This] will be proved again in Africa when Boer authority yields to her higher civilization." For the most part, the adherents of Britain applied only sound American pragmatism: England being our friend and constructively our ally, her downfall in South Africa would weaken the position in a hostile world of the English-speaking community, to our own detriment. Cap-

tain Mahan, receiving the first award of the Chesney Gold
Medal from the Royal United Service Institution in 1900,
expressed that point of view when he replied to the Duke
of Cambridge, a grandson of George III, who had conferred
the honor: "I value even more highly . . . the assurance
that . . . my works have contributed . . . to the welfare
of the British empire, the strength of which is so essential to
the cause of our English-speaking race."

The survival of the prestige of the "mother country"
likewise concerned the editor of *Harper's Weekly,* who at a
low point in British fortunes referred to the "stupendous
fact" that the British Empire's preponderance was in "mortal
danger." "Whether," he wrote, "we think the war against
the Boers . . . unjust or for the welfare of civilization,"
American "sympathies" should go to England, and "if we
have a proper pride of race, or a decent sense of gratitude,
[we should] mourn over their disasters." Undemonstratively,
this view prevailed with substantial portions of press and
public. Chamberlain complained to Hay about the clamor-
ous voices rising in America against the British Empire; he
was reminded of the fidelity of the Government to the debt
of 1898. At the Treasury there was gratitude to Wall Street,
where one shilling out of every five for prosecution of the
war was obtained, England electing to finance her major
requirements here rather than on the Continent. In all
British bonds for $223,000,000 were disposed of through
J. P. Morgan & Company. These were our first really large-
scale foreign loans and they prompted a speaker at the American Bankers Association meeting in 1900 to raise the entic-
ing question "whether the star of financial supremacy is not
to move westward from the precincts of Lombard Street to
our own chief city."

5

In the Continental, especially the German and Dutch,
press pro-Boer manifestations in America were eagerly hailed
as evidences of a loosening of the English-speaking link.

The English press, suggested the *Vossische Zeitung* complacently, is "inclined to underrate the power of the non-
English elements in the United States." This was at a moment when McKinley was being threatened with the loss of
a million votes if he allowed the British to buy mules for
South Africa. Amid the Boer victories the *Berliner Tageblatt*
doubted that the Americans could be "greatly impressed
with the military efficiency of the ally who was to join in
conquering the world." A report from a Mr. George Wilson
of Lexington, Kentucky, assured the *Amsterdam Handels-
blad* that French and German were as much spoken in the
United States as English. However, the German Ambassador, writing in 1899 after Bülow had launched the new
American course, found little evidence of a compensating
pro-German bias. To the contrary, Holleben wrote that the
"United States sees in Germany, next to itself, the only rising Power . . . on account of which a rising antagonism is
imminent . . . the smallest mutual misunderstanding can
light anew the coals and it is only too apparent that the heat
will be stronger then than before and that the Government
will then step ever oftener to the side of the war hawks, for
to give us a shove brings glory." Nor did such Anglo-American friction as could be discerned work to Germany's advantage in England.

A thoughtful German attaché in London, Count Paul von
Wolff Metternich (the Kaiser's "favorite diplomat" according to Spring-Rice) read into the stout American resistance
to Britain on the canal and Alaskan-boundary questions an
indication of "dislike" for the English, and "although the
English will not admit this fact to themselves or anyone else,
they know it perfectly well." The circumstance, however,
he reported to Bülow, was of no advantage to Germany because "England will stand far more from America than from
any other Power, and even in purely diplomatic issues it is
more difficult to make England take sides against America
than to make any other Power do so."

At about this time Richard Olney, writing in the *Atlantic,* called for a new realism in our international think-

ing. Having embarked on an external course, we must look to our defenses, not only in guns, ships, and bases, but in relationships with other Powers. England was, he felt, our natural friend; with her we virtually had an alliance, unwritten to be sure, but soundly rooted in mutual interest. "A nation is as much a member of society as an individual," said the former Secretary of State, and "we must shake off the spell of the Washington legend and cease to act the role of international recluse." Grover Cleveland mistakenly attributed to this article the chief responsibility for the "doctrine of expansion and consequent imperialism." Henry Adams, moralizing over the progression of Olney from the "20-inch gun" to his current Anglophilia, wrote: "We drift inevitably back to the British. . . . Economical and social interests are too strong." Olney's terms were strategic, not economic or social, and Adams might well have made reference also to his own Atlantic System as a cohering factor.

In retiring from the isthmus compact, Britain strengthened that system, as Mahan was to elucidate. In evidence of a good faith rare in history, the British gradually dismantled their great bases at Halifax, St. Lucia, and Esquimault, leaving them to decay under the watch of civilian employees. Garrisons were withdrawn from the Canadian army posts and the British West Indies. British evacuation from the American seas was soon complete. Gratifying to the United States, the shift of sea power benefited British naval policy as well, enabling the Admiralty to dispose of more strength in the home waters of the North Sea against the Power which was to stand disclosed as the archenemy of the Atlantic states.

In his book *The Problem of Asia,* published in 1900, Mahan remarked the "politic disposition to acquiesce in our naval predominance in the Caribbean . . . on the part of the greatest of naval States." The reasons he found to be three: our growing strength, England's desire to "unload herself" of responsibilities wherever possible, and the coincidence of Anglo-American world policies. It was therefore, said the power theorist, to England's "interest that we remain strong, and, since an essential element of our strength is in the Caribbean, we may prudently reckon upon the moral support of Great Britain in any political clash with other nations there, unless we take a stand morally indefensible."

In 1901 Lansdowne, casting about for buttresses of empire, held conversations with the German Ambassador looking to an offensive and defensive alliance. Like Chamberlain's efforts, this one came to naught, but covenants were drafted for mutual examination. Bülow, impressed by irresponsible war talk in Canada, stipulated that Germany be excluded from any war between the United States and Great Britain over the Dominion. In both drafts prepared by the British the special position of the United States was defined. The first agreed that the convention should not apply to "any questions arising in the American Continent or involving war with the United States"; the second comprehended the first, adding that the treaty should not bind "either high contracting party to join in hostilities against the United States."

Lansdowne and Francis Bertie, permanent Foreign Office official, filed memoranda of the negotiations. Lansdowne cited five objections to an alliance, Number 4 being the "risk of entangling ourselves in a policy which might be hostile to America. . . . With our knowledge of the German Emperor's views in regard to the United States, this, to my mind, is a formidable obstacle." Bertie enumerated German aspirations around the globe, some of them potential points of friction, adding: "I do not mention her ambitions in the American seas. They may safely be left to be dealt with by the United States."

The American seas were now American.

V. A "Great Part": Intimations of A Pacific System

THE UNITED STATES, John Hay remarked at Princeton in October, 1900, could "no longer cling to [an] isolated position amongst the nations." His conclusion evoked surprisingly little dissent except from the assorted ex-Populists, Free-silverites, Anglophobes, and habitual Democrats just then marching with William Jennings Bryan into the political wilderness under the banner of "anti-imperialism." The new century, it was apparent to almost everyone, was carrying our diplomacy into a new magnitude, one which pursued, moreover, the historic westward trend of American expansion.

Entrenched behind the Atlantic System of defense, feeling secure against British rivalry in the Caribbean (although the canal controversy still dragged along), the United States was turning toward its other great ocean, beyond which Hay, recruiting the Powers in behalf of the Open Door and taking command of the Boxer crisis, was making us an Asiatic Power. In the Boxer situation in 1900 Hay, in Henry Adams's exalted view, had "put Europe aside and set the Washington Government at the head of civilization." The Secretary of State, employing initiative and dash, was taking American foreign relations (as the *Mirrors of Washington* later described it) "on a grand Cook's Tour of the World." His enterprise pleased the nationalists as much as it nettled the anti-imperialists.

Hay's Asiatic course, in truth, grew out of a national spirit unabashedly robust. Many Americans, including Hay, Adams, Mahan, Theodore Roosevelt, and Lodge, believed the United States to be a success as a nation, its feet planted on the high road of destiny. The Russian Ambassador, Count

Cassini, might sputter to Hay over the Open Door notes: "You do not yourself see the vast *porteé* [import] of them!" The Secretary of State, chuckling with Adams over the Russian's vehemence, had no doubt of their import. He hoped to establish a new order of things in stricken China, prevent the further partition of that empire, and fortify the American trading position. (In midsummer of 1941, with the United States confronting Japan in concert with China, the British Empire, the Netherlands East Indies, and the Soviet Union, it seemed open to doubt whether Hay or Cassini had the better insight into the future.)

Adams, writing that Hay's diplomacy had "broken history in half," shared his confidence. The most engaging luminaries of their time in Washington, Hay and Adams dwelt side by side in the famous double mansion on Lafayette Square, opposite the White House. Two of Adams's ancestors had occupied the White House; Hay lived there as Lincoln's secretary during the dark Civil War days. The neighbors were in a sense collaborators also, Adams, who called himself the "stable companion" of statesmen, interpreting, relating, and reducing to literary form the daring patterns being traced by Hay at the State Department. Nor was Adams the only absorbed and notable observer of the diplomacy of the new century.

A more somber prophet, Mahan saw the United States undertaking a mission in the Orient on behalf of the Atlantic Powers, "the sphere," as he phrased it, "of our external action [being now] clearly indicated as the Pacific and the East." American "predominance in the Caribbean," wrote Mahan in 1900, was incidental to the cause of "permanent coöperation between the communities which speak the English tongue." He had in mind especially the English-speaking countries fronting on the Pacific: Canada, New Zealand, Australia, and the United States. Mistakenly, as it transpired, Mahan regarded British and American interests in the Far East as invariably identical. Often parallel, they would not follow identical lines until the latter 1930's, when the rise of Hitler as a threat to the Atlantic System coincided with Japan's all-

out war on China. It was only then that Mahan's estimate
would be fully confirmed.

Another prophet of that day, Brooks Adams, particularized
the Anglo-American future in terms not only of the Far East,
but of world power relations. A brother of Henry and himself
a historian, Brooks prefigured the future role of the English-
speaking Powers with astonishing prescience. In an article
published in 1900 Adams, who had charted a theory of imperial cycles in his work *The Law of Civilization and Decay,*
foresaw the United States becoming the center of Anglo-
Saxondom, with the British Isles a "fortified outpost" along
with Australia, the Philippines, and Hawaii. Within a few
years Spring-Rice would be terming the United States the
"stronghold of the English-speaking race," and forty years
thereafter the strategical concept of Brooks Adams and
Spring-Rice was to be widely acepted throughout the
English-speaking world.

In January, 1900, Albert J. Beveridge delivered his maiden
speech in the Senate. The world at the moment was discussing the Open Door démarche and England's setbacks in
South Africa while at home the "anti-imperialists" were demanding a policy of "scuttle" in the Philippines, where the
insurrection was still in progress. It was known that the prose
Kipling from Indiana would deal with foreign policy, so the
Senate galleries were crowded, the British and Japanese Ambassadors being conspicuously present. Beveridge did not dis-
appoint his audience. Glorifying our "imperial destiny" in
the Far East, the fledgling Senator proclaimed that God had
set His seal upon the Americans, not only as the "trustees of
civilization," but as His "chosen people, henceforth to lead
in the regeneration of the world." Moreover, God had "made
the English-speaking and Teutonic peoples the master organ-
izers of the world, to establish system where chaos reigns."
It was less than a month since Bülow had rejected Chamberlain's "three-cousin system."

Beveridge was to become a useful Senator and a scholarly
biographer, but to the present generation his mingling of
jingoism and piety seems a caricature of the expansionist

movement—a translation from the Pan-German. At the moment he struck a responsive chord. From Albany Governor
Roosevelt, impatiently awaiting a cue to step upon the national stage, telegraphed a "line to say how delighted I was
with your speech." In writing his friend George W. Perkins,
Beveridge vowed that isolation was "dead." Soon Roosevelt,
after surpassing Hay's interventionism and playing Far Eastern power politics to the hilt, would solemnly assure his
countrymen: "whether we wish it or not, we are a great people and must play a great part in the world . . . we have to
play it. All we can decide is whether we shall play it well or
ill." The sentiment was reminiscent of the categorical imperative uttered by Roosevelt's mentor Mahan in 1890: "Whether
they will or no, Americans must now begin to look outward."

More accurately than most Europeans, the Russians evalu-
ated Hay's new course as a break with our continental tradition. Cassini reported that the United States had "definitely
started on a policy . . . whose horizons are much broader."
Count Muraviev, the Russian Foreign Minister, opposed the
Open Door agreements, in part because the phrase was of
English origin, but he agreed that America had a larger view
of her "mission in the world." That was true. Yet Hay kept
the Asiatic policy in character. His Open Door structure, including both the notes asking for equal trade privileges in
foreign spheres and concessions and the circular addressed to
the Powers during the Boxer troubles, represented not so
much a departure in ideology as a widening, an extension of
principle from the Atlantic into the Pacific world. The
United States was merely suggesting for China what was accepted practice in the Americas—a guarantee of territorial
integrity and a ban on closed colonial trade areas. In a sense,
Hay was proposing a Monroe Doctrine for China.

2

The broad occasion for the Open Door notes which went
out to the Powers in the fall of 1899 (coincidentally with the
outbreak of the Boer War) was the fracturing of Chinese ter-

ritory that began in November, 1897, when Admiral von
Diederichs landed 600 men and seized the unresisting port
of Kiaochow. This cynical appropriation, rationalized if not
justified by the murder of two German missionaries, unloosed
the scramble for China that would reach its full flower in
1937 with Japan's all-out invasion and undeclared war. Immediately, Germany's occupation of the port of Kiaochow and
her demand for a 50-mile radius about it prompted Russia to
effectuate her desire for a warm-water port by seizing two
harbors in Manchuria—Port Arthur and Talienwan (Dairen).

Whereupon the British, not to be outdone, obtained a
lease of the negligible port of Weihaiwei on the tip of the
Shantung Peninsula, midway between Kiaochow and Port
Arthur. Salisbury grumblingly termed the acquisition a mere
"cartographic consolation." The British also gained from the
Peking Foreign Office, the Tsungli-Yamen, treaty recognition
of their oversight of the Imperial Maritime Customs—a sway
already theirs in fact—as well as the ceding of an area of 200
square miles on the mainland opposite the long-established
Crown Colony of Hong Kong. France likewise bettered her
position at China's expense, advancing from Indo-China to
make good rights to the bay of Kwangchow in the south.
These new leaseholds were all negotiated and ratified during
1898. Only the United States among the white Sea Powers
remained aloof from this dismemberment. It was not until
December, 1898, with the "purchase" of the Philippines, that
America became a Far Eastern Power, and although the
Peking Legation reported in August, 1898, that the Tsungli-
Yamen stood ready to cede us a port also, the prospect of a
Chinese concession struck no sparks in Washington.

The sudden appearance of Russia and Germany in North
China alarmed the English, who were fearful of a further
incursion that might carry one or both of these unfriendly
Powers into the fabulously profitable British trading pre-
serves in the Yangtze Valley. For reasons more limited, American commercial interests likewise grew uneasy. Half the foreign trade of the generally undeveloped north of China was
in American hands, a large part consisting of the sale of cot-

ton goods. Throughout 1898 the British agitated for a means of ensuring the Open Door in China, meaning, specifically, a guarantee from the Germans and the Russians that they would not exclude other foreign traders from their special holdings. Twice the British Foreign Office approached the United States Government without success. Failing to obtain joint action there, Salisbury negotiated with Russia a railway treaty fixing the Great Wall as the boundary of their respective spheres in the field of railway-building. Downing Street also made a treaty with Germany recognizing that country's claim to Shantung in exchange for a similar commitment respecting the Yangtze Valley.

By the time Hay issued the notes, Salisbury and Chamberlain had lost whatever interest they might once have had in such pious, unimplemented affirmations regarding trade privileges. Although the Prime Minister congratulated the Secretary of State on "accomplishing a work of great importance and utility . . . especially to our respective countries," he hedged on the terms of his acquiescence, seeking to exclude Hong Kong and Weihaiwei. Ambassador Choate, calling Salisbury's attitude "rather disappointing," persuaded him to give ground on Weihaiwei, but it was apparent that the latter had little real sympathy with or confidence in the restraining effect of the Open Door pledges.

Actually, Hay's motives for intervening in China are still unclear. Ostensibly he was asking the Powers to underwrite jointly the trade treaties the United States had enjoyed with China since clipper-ship days; since Daniel Webster, as Secretary of State, directed his commissioner, Caleb Cushing, in 1843 to insist upon most-favored-nation status for Americans in what came to be known as the Treaty of Whanghia. But Hay already had oral pledges from Germany and Russia and those Powers gave every present indication of honoring their promises. His objective was traditional enough. It was his request for a multilateral agreement binding the Powers in China to maintain the Open Door to all comers that marked the enterprise as a bold innovation in American foreign policy. Exceeding the routine safeguarding of American interests, the Secretary of State was plainly writing international law for the Powers in China, embarking this country on the co-operative course in the Far East foretold by Mahan.

So it was with the Boxer circular. Of all the leading Powers, the United States was least affected when in the early summer of 1900 the extreme nationalist movement known as the Fists of Righteous Peace, or Boxers, burst bounds in North China, murdering foreigners and Christianized Chinese and finally penning the diplomats and missionaries in the Legation compounds at Peking. Yet Hay, independently and without consultation with London—despite the current legend—took leadership. According to Adams, Hay acted because the European Powers, torn by mistrust, had shown their inability to co-operate even in the face of the tragic "drama of the Legations."

The Powers had bungled preparations for the military expedition to Peking. Russia had large forces in Manchuria, which she marched to Tientsin, where the expedition was being formed. Fearing the Russians and having only scant forces of his own in China, Salisbury offered to repay Japan's costs if she would send 30,000 troops as a makeweight against the Russians. Into this confused situation moved the American Secretary of State, announcing a policy that localized the Boxer uprising, averted what might have deteriorated into a long, general war, and saved China from punitive dismemberment. Hay insisted that the Powers treat the disorders locally and that they strengthen the viceroys of the unaffected provinces by courteous offers of assistance. In pursuit of that policy the United States Asiatic squadron conspicuously declined to fire on the forts at Taku, below Tientsin, when the Allied fleet shelled them for insufficient reasons but principally as a demonstration of force.

The siege was still unlifted when on July 3, 1900, Hay's circular went to the Powers. A definition of American policy only, it required no formal acknowledgment. None was forthcoming, although Salisbury hastily assured Choate of his approval. Yet Allied policy thereafter followed the outline contained in the statement. The American policy, Hay wrote, was to seek a "solution which may bring about permanent safety and peace to China, preserve Chinese territorial and administrative entity, protect all rights guaranteed to friendly powers by treaty and international law, and safeguard for the world the principle of equal and impartial trade with all parts of the Chinese empire."

Hay had enlarged upon the formula contained in the notes. This time he was seeking to advance the cause of China's political and territorial integrity; he had not ventured to touch on that desideratum in the notes. In informed circles here and in Europe he was credited with restricting the Boxer outrages, with moderating the opinion of the Chinese everywhere, and with quickening the Imperial Court's sense of responsibility. There seems little doubt that the Empress Dowager and her court had encouraged the Boxers, at least up to the point of wholesale pillage and murder. Adams termed Hay's coup the most "meteoric" accomplishment in the history of American diplomacy. All human "society," said Adams, "felt the force of the stroke through its fineness, and burst into almost tumultous applause."

There was, however, a minority opinion.

3

The Chinese policy, principally because of a widespread feeling that Hay was pursuing a parallel course with England, was a highly controversial issue in the presidential campaign of 1900. Not since Napoleon divided the infant republic into warring camps a century before had foreign considerations so played upon the political emotions of the American voter. The Democratic platform flatly denounced what it called the "ill-concealed Republican alliance with England." Behind Bryan, the "Boy Orator of the Platte," marched the Southern Democracy; recaptured elements of the Gold Democracy, disaffected in 1896; the Northern city machines, such as Tammany Hall; the professional Irish vote, reveling in the chance to strike an indirect blow for Irish freedom; and a large sec-

tion of the organized German community, swallowing its
thrifty dislike for free silver in order to damage Anglo-American understanding.

Hay's circular especially focused partisan attack. The opposition, he wrote Adams, called for his "impeachment because we are violating the Constitution," while the "pulpit"
was giving "us anathema because we're not doing it enough."
In the circular the *Washington Times* saw new evidence of
the "oft-denied, but nevertheless existent, McKinley-Salisbury
alliance." When St. Clair McKelway, editor of the *Brooklyn
Eagle,* published a widely current allegation that the British
had inspired the circular, Hay wrote him swearing that "no
power whatever was consulted as to the terms."

Josiah Quincy, writing in the *Contemporary Review,*
charged that Hay had committed the United States to the
concert of Powers in China, and as England's influence had
"sunk almost to zero," it behooved us to "maintain a strict
neutrality between England and Russia." On the other hand,
a writer in the *North American Review* interpreted the circular to mean that America had "crossed the Rubicon of imperial responsibility" and would hereafter be found in the
"Anglo-American sphere."

A partisan critic might have construed Choate's note transmitting the circular to Salisbury as referring to a prior understanding. Hay asked Choate to recall and revise the note.
Privately, he stormed against the expediency dictating such
craven behavior, lamenting to John W. Foster, a predecessor
in the State Department, the sad state of partisan affairs that
"compelled this Government to refuse the assistance of the
greatest power . . . in carrying out our own policies because
all Irishmen are Democrats and some Germans are fools."
Pauncefote, recently created a baron, retreated before the
partisan tempest, establishing his Embassy at Newport for
the summer and communicating with Hay on none but the
dreariest routine, an exhibition of reserve which baffled and
piqued Hay.

A preponderance of the German-language press attacked
England and "McKinley imperialism," apparently consider-

ing them interchangeable, echoing the mercurial Carl Schurz, who prophesied an "inevitable" revolution unless Bryan won. Throughout the campaign the well-knit German press threatened, scolded, and vilified McKinley, Hay, the "nativists," and the "Anglo-Saxons." This press, claiming to speak for 9,000,000 first- and second-generation Germans (the population being then 76,000,000), behaved as if it were completely alien, precisely as the German minority press conducted itself in non-German Europe. Scorn was poured on the institutions of democracy. American "corruption" was, as in the newspapers of Germany proper, a constant theme. To the *Chicago Freie Presse* McKinley was the "choice of the conceited Anglo-Saxon know-nothing, whose ignorance leads him to dream of world conquest." It was apparent to this journal that "McKinley is only the humble servant of England and will do nothing without orders from England." The *Davenport Demokrat* was certain that "McKinley, Hay, and the rest of them will only make the United States the tail of the British boa constrictor."

A study of the Anglo-American scene in 1900 discloses little or no objective reason for the "mad-dog hatred of England" which John Hay found animating many "newspapers and politicians." On the score of grievances between the English-speaking peoples, England and Canada seem to have had the worst of it. In recent times the United States had clamorously forced the British to give ground over Venezuela, it was in process of ushering Britain out of her ascendancy of three hundred years in the Caribbean and evicting her from her nominal share in the proposed isthmian canal. Nor had it shown an indulgent spirit toward Canada's desire for a corridor to the Pacific.

Much of the Anglophobia of 1900 was undeniably imported, and many thoughtful Americans, of Irish and German as well as British descent, challenged the encouragement of such grudges by responsible political leaders. Mahan sternly and pointedly deplored both super-Americanism and hyphenism, calling it a matter of patriotic duty to every citizen to consider whether he does well to cherish old animosities; to reflect whether the period in which, historically, these prejudices have their rise is not now as wholly past as the voyages of Columbus; or whether . . . they are simply transplanted to our soil from Europe by a process—in that case most misnamed—of naturalization. It is no true naturalization which grafts upon our politics sentiments drawn from abroad, and foreign to our interests and our duties.

The "melting-pot" was, however, simmering effectively in 1900, which was the peak year of German political activity in this country. The offspring of Pan-Germans were abandoning that narrow racism, conforming to the more civilized pattern of American life. German-language newspapers, which echoed their German contemporaries (even to the point of belittling Dewey's achievement at Manila out of loyalty to Admiral von Diederichs) when not intentionally serving the German Foreign Office, dwindled in numbers, prosperity, and influence. The owners and editors of such newspapers were of course courted by the German Foreign Office, steamship lines, and the Pan-German and German Navy League functionaries. Their survival depended upon keeping alive a sense of group superiority and a powerful attachment to the Vaterland. Fortunately theirs was a losing endeavor. Even in 1900 they spoke for only a minority of the Americans of German descent.

Up to the First World War the German Government used its Embassy, consulates, and German-American organizations as instruments of its drive for world power; but as it did so the "German vote" diminished, and when America entered that war the German-Americans supported the war effort with conspicuous devotion. By 1917 most German-stock Americans had ceased thinking of themselves as Germans. They were Americans, along with descendants of the numerous Germans who helped settle colonial America, the "blessed '48-ers," and the 200,000 Americans of German birth who fought for the Union in the Civil War.

In the Nazi attempt to establish a fifth column only the terminology is new. Before the last war the Pan-Germans, to whom the Nazis are indebted for a part of the nationalistic element in their ideology, fostered a politically conscious racial minority. The failure of this minority to retain its isolated character was due not only to the excellent judgment of the German-Americans themselves, but also to the underlying factor that the United States, unlike Switzerland, was not a federation, but a compound, of races. In 1900 the anti-English furor missed its desired effect in domestic affairs, McKinley and Roosevelt obtaining the largest electoral plurality up to that time. It did, however, enfeeble our foreign policy and, by a curious irony, at the expense of Kaiser William's ambition to cut a large figure at Peking.

The Kaiser, pulling wires in St. Petersburg, Paris, and London, gained assent to the appointment of Field Marshal Count von Waldersee as generalissimo of the Allied forces. In biding farewell to Waldersee and a sizable German force, William delivered the celebrated "Hun" speech, enjoining frightfulness and supplying the English-speaking world in 1914 *et seq*. with an epithet. When his men were to close with the enemy, the Kaiser bade them "remember this: spare nobody. Make no prisoners. Use your weapons so that for a thousand years no Chinaman will dare look askance at any German." An example of mischievous rhetoric, the Kaiser's injunction alarmed the American Government as well as the British. McKinley was already wincing under isolationist demands that he withdraw American troops. Salisbury in a talk with Henry White grumblingly hoped that means would be found to "exhaust Waldersee" before he could execute his instructions.

When the Legations had been relieved, McKinley carried his distrust to the point of threatening to withdraw from the Allied front at Peking to the coast, forming a momentary concert with Russia and leaving England to moderate the "much-prepared Waldersee" (Elihu Root's phrase). The suggestion of Russo-American retirement materially weakened the German position at Peking and it became Waldersee's task to placate the Americans and the Russians in order to preserve German prestige. The motives of the Russians, it was supposed, were wholly selfish, St. Petersburg wishing to draw the other European forces out of an area in which Russia claimed a special position, thereby gaining also the gratitude of the Imperial Chinese Court. McKinley's motives, it appears, were simpler. Although swept by the timidities that beset a President seeking re-election, McKinley did not propose to give up the field so long as American interests required the troops. But the last thing he wished before election was a revival of bloodshed in China, and in view of Waldersee's instructions McKinley imposed a condition on the German. He would stay, but only if Waldersee and his imperial master observed the policy of the Hay circular. Root, the able, ironical corporation lawyer from New York, was Secretary of War, but in Hay's absence while ill he was advising the President on foreign policy. Writing the Secretary of State, Root rejoiced at the opportunity to clarify the American position vis-à-vis Waldersee, recounting: "There was danger that after all the Emperor's windy eloquence, he might feel the necessity of kicking up a row to justify the appointment of Waldersee. I was very glad . . . that Russia gave us an opportunity to say that we would stay under definite understanding and not otherwise." Root believed that the incident had improved the position of the Open Door policy.

Using the incident as a pretext, the Kaiser, intent on discord between England and America, reported to British statesmen in January, 1901, that the United States and Russia were secretly linked in China. Queen Victoria's fatal illness had taken William to the Isle of Wight, where he improved the opportunity to talk politics. With the Prince of Wales, he enumerated the "symptoms" of Russo-American rapprochement. To Lansdowne, he reported (largely on the basis of the anti-imperialist campaign utterances) that America "hates England." Wall Street, he asserted, was financing Russian munitions purchases in the United States in exchange for Russian military support in an American drive on the English sphere in the Yangtze Valley. A bit earlier Hatzfeldt had sought to affright Salisbury by confiding "evidence" that the United States was "aiming at monopolistic trade in China and, in general, toward treating the Pacific as an American inland sea." Salisbury had not been impressed.

4

Whatever goodwill for Russia was generated by the joint stand at Peking had been dissipated by the time of the Kaiser's report. In the Boxer negotiations, opening early in 1901, the Russians flatly laid claim to all Manchuria for their services in policing those provinces. The demand, outraging the principles of the circular, overnight converted Russia in American eyes into the chief aggressive threat to the well-being of China—and the China trade. Unbrokenly thereafter until the Russo-Japanese War, the Czar's Government was regarded in Washington with dread and suspicion, and American policy was consistently shaped toward Japan.

Roosevelt was barely seated in the vice-presidential chair when Mahan wrote him lengthily on the Russian menace. If the United States and Great Britain so desired, said Mahan, they could check the Russian advance into China by the exercise of sea power alone. External assistance to China, however, he thought insufficient. Only if the "sea powers will require of China . . . liberty for the entrance of European thought as well as European commerce," the historian reasoned, could China actually be saved from partition and exploitation. Roosevelt agreed, holding Mahan's conclusion "eminently sound," but he despaired of America's taking an intelligent hand in the problem, since public opinion was "dull on the subject of China."

Early in 1902 England and Japan signed the Anglo-Japanese Alliance, destined in the words of a Nipponese statesman to be the "cornerstone of Japanese policy for twenty years." A military covenant, the alliance recognized special British and Japanese interests in China; gave Japan a free hand "politically, as well as commercially and industrially" in Korea; sanctioned Japanese intervention on the mainland in case of disturbances "arising in China or Korea";

and pledged the help of each party if engaged in war with more than one other Power. Dedicated, as by custom, to peace, the treaty nodded in Hay's direction by acknowledging the Open Door and the "independence and territorial integrity" of China and Korea. The aging Salisbury, author of "splendid isolation," had relaxed his grip; his successors, nervously in dread of adverse combinations in both Europe and Asia and regarding the United States as excluded from genuine alliance, had protected their Chinese flank at what seemed only the negligible expense of Korea. Japan, having the backing of the greatest Sea Power, was now free to challenge Russia and embark on her own mainland adventures.

Although Hay had not been taken into the confidence of Downing Street, he received news of the treaty without misgiving. When Russia and France hastily announced their own Far Eastern understanding, the Secretary of State blessed both undertakings, describing them as "renewed confirmation" of the Open Door and circular policies. The Anglo-Japanese Alliance, which in 1922 would be scrapped under pressure of American uneasiness, was actually welcomed in 1902 as a counterweight to Russia. What Holstein of the German Foreign Office feared had come to pass in a limited sense. In July, 1898, Holstein, noting reports that England was showing solicitude for Japan, advised Hatzfeldt of the profound consequences that would flow from a linking of English, Japanese, and American sea power. "For England," wrote Holstein, "an alliance with the United States and with Japan would create an absolutely ideal situation, ensuring this group for years the mastery of the seas, while the other partners would leave England a free hand in Africa."

It was at this time, parenthetically, that Holstein proposed "shattering" Britain's hope of an American alliance, setting "to work not in England, but in America."

Russia progressively closed the door to trade in Manchuria. As a consequence, the United States and Great Britain were drawn closer together. In April, 1903, President Roosevelt and Secretary Hay speculated about the possibility of concerted action with England and Japan, Hay voicing doubt that the public would "support" an "openly hostile" course. Roosevelt's ire rose during that year. In June, talking with Lyman Abbott, he called Russia's policy "very irritating." To Spring-Rice he wrote that Russia had engaged in a "consistent career of stupid mendacity." By mid-July the President announced to Hay that, being now "more confident that the country would back me in going to an extreme," he would not "give way" endlessly. On that same day Choate, under instructions from Hay, and Lord Lansdowne were formulating plans for mutual consultation and parallel action, Choate writing of the conversation: "I replied that I thought . . . you were disposed to have the two Governments keep step with each other. . . . He [Lansdowne] said he would be quite content to have you a little in advance, and to follow you." Hay agreed to that. In October he tried another tack, obtaining from Peking a commercial treaty providing for American consuls in Mukden and other leading Manchurian cities. But China was not master there, and the Russian press expressed annoyance at the presence of the consuls.

The United States Government was in a state of mind by no means impartial when in February, 1904, Japan attacked the Russian Asiatic fleet as it lay at Port Arthur, two days before declaring war. Roosevelt was delighted, "thoroughly well pleased," as he wrote Theodore, Jr., "for Japan is playing our game." In the ensuing war, as everyone is aware, England, Japan's nonbelligerent ally, and the benevolently neutral United States pursued parallel paths in support of the Nipponese, Wall Street joining with Lombard Street in financing them.

William II secretly backed Russia, encouraging Nicholas in a prewar belief that the Japanese would not fight and after war began encouraging the Czar's faith that the result was a "foregone conclusion." Addressing his cousin as "Admiral of the Pacific," signing himself "Admiral of the Atlantic," William portrayed the war as a struggle for the command of the "shores of the Pacific," which Russian sea power would assuredly win. The Kaiser's motives have been fre-

quently debated. He no doubt hoped for a quid pro quo in
North China if Russia won. He may have welcomed the ex-
penditure of Russian strength in the Far East, as has been
suggested, for its value in relieving pressure on his own borders; he may have hoped to "mire" the Czar in China to a
point where the Russian Emperor would become amenable
to a Russo-German alliance—that ignis fatuus of Kaiserlich
statecraft. Nor should his dread of the "yellow peril" be
ignored.

Whatever the motivation, two days after war began William undertook a diplomatic chore on Russia's behalf. Appealing to the champion of the Open Door through the German Ambassador Speck von Sternberg (Roosevelt's beloved
"Speckie"), the Kaiser urged the President to obtain from
the belligerents a declaration of respect for China's neutrality
"outside the sphere of military operations." Hay and Roosevelt detected a loophole, the President writing Root, in great
glee at having outwitted "Bill the Kaiser," that William
"wanted us to guarantee the integrity of China south of the
Great Wall, which would have left Russia free to gobble up
what she really wanted."

Hay redrafted the German note to cover the "neutrality
of China and, in all practicable ways, her administrative
entity." Although neither belligerent subscribed to the note,
Germany, to use Roosevelt's words, "cheerfully acceded." Un-
mindful of William's double game and wholly unsuspicious,
the President conveyed to him his appreciation for "generous
initiative and powerful co-operation." Had Roosevelt been
privy to the diplomatic correspondence between Berlin and
St. Petersburg, he might have withheld his thanks. The Russians, justifiably annoyed at the amended note, complained
to Bülow, who thereupon denied responsibility, charging
that the initiative had come from France! The note had ignored the status of Korea, which bore the same relationship
to Japan that Manchuria did to Russia, a circumstance confirming to the Russians their conviction of Roosevelt's enmity. Thereafter the President attracted the virulent notice
of the Muscovite press, already aggrieved by his repeated
protests over Manchuria. Spring-Rice, then serving in St.

Petersburg, wrote Roosevelt that he was "feared here as much as Napoleon was"—surely a flattering exaggeration.

Roosevelt, indeed, made no pretense of neutrality. In July, 1904, he wrote Spring-Rice with enthusiasm of his exertions in the common cause:

As soon as war broke out, I notified Germany and France in the most polite and discreet fashion that, in the event of a combination of powers against Japan to try to do what Russia, Germany and France did to her in 1894 [it actually was '95], I should promptly side with Japan and proceed to whatever length was necessary on her behalf. I, of course, knew that your government would act in the same way, and thought it best that I should have no consultation with your people before announcing my own purpose.

A truly amazing commitment, but it is said that searches of the German and French archives disclose no evidence that Roosevelt swung the "big stick" as related. The story may, or may not, be apocryphal. There can be do doubt that it conformed to the President's bent. Since July, 1898, when he remarked to Sternberg his gratification at Japan's growth into a "formidable counterpoise to Russia in the Far East," Roosevelt had steadily expressed a pro-Japanese bias. Suspecting the straightforwardness of the Russians, attributing to them a detestation of Americans and American civilization, and disapproving the reactionary character of Russian despotism, Roosevelt found his antipathy replenished at this period by Spring-Rice's letters. In the same month in which he reported his caveat to France and Germany the President discussed with Hay a project that would have amounted to a naval intervention against Russia.

In attempting to blockade Japan the Russians were halting, visiting, and detaining ships suspected of bearing contraband, notably cotton, to Japan. If the Russians dared seize an American merchantman, Roosevelt told his Secretary of State, he would like nothing better than to "move our Asiatic squadron northward . . . with the intention of having our squadron bottle up the Vladivostok fleet." Indeed, he ordered the Bureau of Navigation to plot such a maneuver. The country was spared the risk of war seemingly only because no American vessel fell into Russian toils. Roosevelt's words, however, even the naval order, were no warranty of corresponding action. His moods were changeable, his opinions in conversation and correspondence impulsive and contradictory, but he actually acted in state matters, as he was himself to point out, only after the "most careful deliberation."

5

What might be termed Roosevelt's conversational instability found graphic illustration during this period. With apparently no thought of duplicity, he contrived to convince Sternberg of a pro-German orientation at the same time that his acts followed an unfailingly pro-British course. The Kaiser seems not to have shared his Ambassador's confidence, remaining generally skeptical of Roosevelt's friendship, as he was unimpressed by the realism of his diplomacy. William's scribbled comments on Sternberg's reports often took a satirical tone. In August, 1904, the President suggested to Sternberg a German-American agreement at the end of the Russo-Japanese War under which Korea should be allotted to Japan as a protectorate and Manchuria ruled by a Chinese viceroy "to be appointed by Germany, not England." On the margin the Kaiser wrote: "The noble gentleman seems to intend to horn in on world politics." Regarding Roosevelt as a "dilettante," William complacently thought he understood the state of the public mind in America better than the President did.

Sternberg wrote of long, amiable talks at the White House, of Roosevelt assuring him that he would "like to go hand in hand with Germany in Eastern Asia," and of the President, in a mood petulant to the point of indiscretion, belittling Chamberlain, Balfour, Lansdowne, and Sir Mortimer Durand (Pauncefote's successor), "this creature of an Ambassador," finally declaring, "The only man I understand and who understands me is the Kaiser." To this avowal the Kaiser added a footnote: "Very flattering!" But with others than his friend Speckie the President was often drastically unflattering, terming the Kaiser an "autocratic zigzag," a "grizzly bear" who was "very jumpy and nervous," a man given to "sudden vagaries" and "wholly irrational zigzags," and, above all, untrustworthy. In reply to a reproach from Spring-Rice, Theodore wrote: "You might as well talk about my being under the influence of Bryan."

So it was with Roosevelt's attitude toward the British. He could write one day that while "friendly to England . . . I do not at all believe in being over-effusive." This to Lodge. And to Finley Peter Dunne he could decry Englishmen as dull and uncongenial, wishing them well "at a distance," attributing England's recent friendship to the growth of our fleet. While with English correspondents he was capable of ecstatic "race patriotism," as in this letter to Spring-Rice: "I feel so perfectly healthy myself and the Americans and Englishmen for whom I care . . . seem so healthy, so vigorous and on the whole so decent that I rather incline to the view of my beloved friend, Lieutenant Parker . . . whom I overheard telling the Russian naval attaché at Santiago that the two branches of Anglo-Saxons had come together, 'and together, we can whip the world, Prince.'" He had, in truth, numerous lifelong friends in England with whom he corresponded, such as Bryce, George Trevelyan, and St. Loe Strachey; he had scarcely any such intimates in Germany.

If he ever reflected on his inconsistencies, Roosevelt must have hoped that his correspondents would never meet and compare notes. The fickleness of his attitude toward the Great Powers, the eupeptic ease with which he disposed of the grim, complex, and deep-seated rivalries hurrying Europe toward cataclysm, proved a severe trial to the responsible statesmen in Great Britain. Downing Street, in one of the British Empire's complicated hours, with danger threatening on a score of fronts, viewed the first Roosevelt with perplexity. Unaware of the impression he created abroad, Roosevelt found time between lecturing the British, the Germans, the Japanese, and the French to take up jiu-jitsu and have

Pastor Wagner, apostle of the "simple life," at the White House for luncheon.

The British courted the unpredictable Teddy (as did the Kaiser), King Edward sending him a treasured miniature of John Hampden, the Roundhead, as an inauguration present in 1905, over protests of the Windsor librarian. Roosevelt fascinated the King, who thought the Rough Rider personally as brave as a "tiger." When Durand gave him the King's present, the President bade him keep it a secret for fear the Anglophobes might make a point of it; but the next day, while the Durands were entertaining the Baroness von Sternberg at tea, another guest, fresh from the White House, reported that Roosevelt was showing the miniature with gratified comment on Edward's thoughtfulness. The Ambassador thought it somehow pathetic that the chief of a great state should conceal a present from the chief of another state. To Durand, Roosevelt said: "So far as my descent goes, I suppose I am hardly an Anglo-Saxon, but I firmly believe that our two countries must stand together." When the Kaiser sent him an etching of Frederick the Great reviewing his troops, Roosevelt was pleased; amused also by William's note, which called Frederick his ancestor. "Frederick left no issue," the President chuckled.

Spring-Rice, having a tender affection for the whole Roosevelt family, might exclaim upon word of McKinley's assassination that the United States was "awfully lucky to get the best man possible by a fluke." He would also wearily liken his friend's scattering enthusiasms to those of a boy of six. Although Roosevelt's utterances imply that he saw himself as a wholly independent ruler, moderating the affairs of Europe and Asia with unfettered hand, in reality he conducted this country's foreign affairs as if guided by an Anglo-American entente. By some polar attraction, he inevitably pursued in both Asia and Europe the line of British interest. No President ever maintained a closer identity in action with London; few Presidents since the United States became a potential Sea Power in 1890 (and hence to be reckoned with) have had, however, a slighter influence on British policy.

Roosevelt's personalized, subjective diplomacy, his brusque unwillingness to sort out the roots of profoundly tangled international problems, puzzled the uninspired young men at the Foreign Office in London. The British paid him in the coin of flattery rather than of respect, treating him much as he handled the Kaiser, with mingled homage and neglect. Although the President's "hair-trigger" diplomacy complemented British policy in almost every detail from 1901 to 1909, the United States gained little in exchange for pulling English chestnuts out of the fire in Asia and Europe. His deeds, as we shall see, enhanced the Atlantic System, but his contradictory and unco-operative protestations failed to advance the cause of Anglo-American understanding. The fact is that Roosevelt was emotionally pro-English, anti-German, fond of France, and indifferent to the other Continental Powers. While still Governor of New York he assured Spring-Rice by letter that Anglophobia was a waning influence in American political life, vowing with his usual dogmatism: "Americans who are Anglo-Saxon by adoption are . . . quite as strong about the unity of the two peoples as any others. . . . The Navy is a unit in wanting to smash Germany. . . . The professional Irishman is losing his grip and the bulk of the Irish are becoming American. . . . The feeling of hostility to England is continually softening." Yet publicly, in his role as politician and despite his familiarity with Mahan and his grasp of strategical concepts, the President could not bring himself to acknowledge the interdependence of the English-speaking Powers.

Early in 1905, as Roosevelt began to play power politics with the Far Eastern war, Adams wrote from Lafayette Square to a mutual friend: "The twelfth century still rages wildly here in the shape of a fiend with tusks and eye-glasses across the way. The wild boar of Cubia [sic] I love him. He is almost sane beside his German and Russian cousins. . . . What is man that he should have tusks and grin?"

6

The motive for the "great part" which the President now proposed to play was preservation of the balance of power in East Asia in the general interest of American security. Welcoming the war as a check on Russia's looming ascendancy in North China, Roosevelt interposed to halt it when Japan's overwhelming victory appeared probable. A wholly triumphant Japan was no more to his liking than a dominant Russia. As realistic as the protagonists of Realpolitik at the Wilhelmstrasse, Roosevelt had begun to consider the consequences of a Japanese victory as early as June 13, 1904, when he supposed in a letter to Spring-Rice that "if they [the Japanese] win out, it may possibly mean a struggle between us and them in the future."

In January, 1905, with the Russian land forces falling back in the interior of Manchuria and only the Asia-bound Baltic fleet between the Czarist Empire and humiliating defeat, Roosevelt put out feelers for mediation through his confidants in the diplomatic service of other Powers—Spring-Rice at St. Petersburg, Sternberg and Jules Jusserand (the new French Ambassador) in Washington. Relying on these diplomats more than on his own (with a few exceptions) and lacking a reliable intelligence service, the President was not aware that in that same month the British had proposed a revision of the Anglo-Japanese Alliance. The British were moving with Tokyo before the Japanese could be sure of the outcome of their war. The new draft extended the protection of the alliance to the boundaries of India, strengthened Japan's position in Korea as a quid pro quo, and fortified the defensive clauses by bringing either signatory to the side of the other in case of aggression by a single outside Power instead of two, as before. These negotiations may have accounted for the reserve which greeted Roosevelt's feelers in Downing Street.

By April France, alarmed over a challenging visit by the Kaiser to the Sultan of Morocco (an incident to be examined in the next chapter), wished the war in the Far East at an end. Moreover, the money of French *petits rentiers,* which was financing the Czar's war effort, was sensitive. Mukden had fallen in March, and realistic French analysts thought only a miracle could save Russia in Manchuria. Discussing peace with the Japanese Ambassador, the French Foreign Minister, Théophile Delcassé, discovered that the Mikado's Government was now confident of a crushing victory and had in mind a sizable cash indemnity. Hope, however, still lingered in St. Petersburg. George von L. Meyer, who had been transferred from Rome to be Ambassador at the Russian capital on a hint from Spring-Rice to Roosevelt that a "stronger man" would be useful there, discovered this when on April 12 he sounded the Czar on peace. The Czarina, Meyer noted, "watched him [the Czar] like a cat," indicating otherwise also that she wished the fighting to continue. Like other influential persons in St. Petersburg, the Czarina still pinned faith to the Baltic fleet under Admiral Rozhdestvensky.

But on May 27, 1905, the Baltic fleet, which rated in battle efficiency about with the Spanish fleet of 1898, was destroyed in the Battle of Tsushima. Russia had lost the war. Japan, too, her lines extended, and pinched by the English and American bankers, was quite ready for peace. On May 31 the President congratulated Baron Kaneko, a Japanese journalist and diplomatist, that "neither Trafalgar nor the defeat of the Spanish Armada was as complete—as overwhelming." That day also the Japanese Minister, Baron Takahira, received instructions from Tokyo to the effect that Japan hoped that Roosevelt, "of his own motion and initiative," would invite the belligerents to down arms and discuss peace. The Japanese notion of spontaneity amused the President.

Defeated in the Far East, Russia was also riven by internal strife. The rifle fire that had felled Father Gapon's petitioners before the Winter Palace still echoed. The Duma, ineffectual but articulate, stimulated the radical intelligentsia to revolt, and the Okhrana contrived jacqueries among the peasants against liberal landlords. There were uprisings and the revolution—which would be deferred until 1917—was expected hourly. Under those circumstances the Czar, a "preposterous little creature," in Roosevelt's phrase, lost his aversion to peace. William II busied himself for Roosevelt's peace project also, indulging, as Spring-Rice reported after a visit to Berlin, in a "violent love-making to Tower and Meyer," persuading them of his support. Charlemagne Tower, formerly at St. Petersburg, was now Ambassador to Berlin, and Meyer had also been in the German capital on a visit. The Kaiser, it was suspected, trembled at the prospect of a revolution destroying the autocracy in Russia and possibly lapping over the border into Germany.

In a telegram to "Nicky" signed "Willy," the Kaiser advised his cousin that Roosevelt, if anyone, could bring the Japanese to moderate terms. "Should it meet with your approval," he added, "I could easily place myself privately en rapport with him [Roosevelt], as we are very intimate." This was on June 3. The next day William told Tower that he was pressing the Czar for peace. On June 6, the Czarina's birthday, an occasion which impeded Meyer's effort to take up affairs of state with the Czar, Nicholas agreed to Roosevelt's intermediation. Roosevelt was now the arbiter of the Far East. His selection suited both sides, he being the only head of a Great Power who was acceptable to both. The negotiations ("playing with kings," Adams called it) exhilarated Roosevelt, although in writing to Lodge he reflected that the "more I see of the Czar, the Kaiser and the Mikado, the better I am content with democracy, even if we have to include the American newspaper as one of its assets— liability would be a better term."

The war having ended, there remained the peace settlement. Japan, mindful of the money prize gained from China in 1895, flatly demanded a large indemnity, although experienced European diplomats were certain that the project was futile. Russia had never paid an idemnity, the Treasury was empty, and few authorities believed that Japan could collect without reducing St. Petersburg by arms. In vain Roosevelt besought England's help in bringing her ally to reason. "Every true friend of Japan should tell it," he expostulated to Durand, "that the . . . civilized world will not support it in continuing the war merely for the purpose of extorting money from Russia."

Durand cabled Lansdowne that he had sidestepped Roosevelt's request, "supposing that His Majesty's Government would probably be reluctant to take any step which could embarrass Japan." Lansdowne approved his course. When the President again asked for help, the Foreign Secretary commented that "our advice [to Japan] would not be taken and would be resented." At the peace conference opening on August 10, 1905, at Portsmouth, New Hampshire, Korea was handed over to Japanese "protection" (in line with the renewed alliance); Japan took the Port Arthur leasehold and rights in southern Manchuria, leaving Russia the sphere along her railway in the north; the island of Sakhalin was divided, Japan obtaining the southern portion—but there was no cash indemnity.

For his efforts the President won the Nobel Peace Prize and the plaudits of Henry Adams, who declared in a letter from Paris that his friend had "established a record as the best herder of emperors since Napoleon. . . . I need your views about the relative docility of Kings, Presidents of South American republics, railway presidents and Senators." In addition to the plaudits, the President had also saved the letter of the Open Door policy, Japan and Russia agreeing that Manchuria should return to the sovereignty of China. Korea, of course, was irreversibly Japan's.

Roosevelt had not waited for the peace conference to add his own sanction to the Korean protectorate. In May, 1905, he sent William Howard Taft, who had pacified the Philippines, on another placating journey to the Far East. So far as the public knew, the Secretary of War was returning to the scene of his proconsular triumphs to anneal certain minor rifts in the accord between the Filipinos and the colonial administration. Taft suggested that he carry along a party of Congressmen for a look at the archipelago. A romantic flair was given the junket by the presence of Miss

Alice Roosevelt and Nicholas Longworth, a Representative from Ohio, who were soon to be married.

Privately, Taft was under instructions to conduct negotiations during a visit to Japan. Scenting this fact, Roosevelt wrote Hay, "Cassini is now having a fit." Roosevelt, who more than any other American contrived the American acquisition of the Philippines, was now in a renunciatory mood. Before Taft departed he suggested that his emissary hint to the Filipinos that they might soon have their freedom, a proposal that Taft negatived. The islands, Roosevelt was convinced, were our "Achilles heel" in the Far East. At about that time Sternberg reported that the President was sick of the Philippines, considered them a strategical liability, and would like to cut them loose if he could do so honorably.

For the sake of the Philippines, Roosevelt and Taft now extended approval of Japan's advance into Korea, swinging unmistakably into the orbit of the Anglo-Japanese Alliance. Taft saw the Japanese Prime Minister, Count (later Prince) Katsura, on July 27, cabling an extended memorandum on the conversation two days later. The "agreed memorandum" came close to being a secret understanding, in which Japan renounced "aggressive designs" on the Philippines and the United States agreed that Japan should "establish a suzerainty over Korea," forbidding Korea to "enter upon [any] treaties without the consent of Japan." Roosevelt's cabled reply, received in forty-eight hours, read: "Your conversation with Count Katsura absolutely correct in every respect. Wish you would state to Katsura that I confirm every word you have said."

Five months later, Korea was declared a protectorate; in August, 1910, it was annexed to Japan.

7

The United States, following a path parallel to that of Britain in the Russo-Japanese War and in respect to Japan's ambitions, was by now inextricably involved in the Far East. Ironically, the first consequence was that Japan, emerging as the overshadowing power of East Asia, scarcely waited to catch her breath before exhibiting a lively ingratitude toward the American friend. Public cupidity in Japan, whetted by political promises of a large cash indemnity, vented its disappointment on Roosevelt. Martial law had to be invoked in Tokyo to repress rioters, who fired police stations, burned four American churches, menaced the American Legation, and inflicted a thousand casualties. In vast numbers of Japanese homes lithographs of Roosevelt were turned to the wall.

The President, who had rushed in where the English feared to tread, was reaping the all too common reward of the peacemaker. "The attacks by the Tokyo mob," he wrote St. Loe Strachey, editor of the *Spectator,* "have an ominous side and reconcile me to her failure to get a great sum of money." To Colonel George Harvey, a later Ambassador to England, Roosevelt blamed the politicians for "letting everybody talk as if they had gotten the worst of it," when, as a matter of fact, Japan had benefited enormously, being now a "formidable sea power," a match in the Pacific "for any nation save England."

The sea-power aspects of Japan's victory had not escaped American navalists. In March, 1904, Cabot Lodge launched a campaign in the Senate for a "navy second only to Great Britain's"—the first time America had considered that yardstick. Increasingly the Nipponese were to be disclosed as a potential enemy. During the next generation immigration and naturalization disputes, provoked in part by a heightened racial self-esteem in Japan, in part by the intransigeance of California, were periodically to roil relations between the countries. At a time of acute tension Roosevelt, his trepidations fed by alarmist reports of Japanese naval strength from Berlin and inflammatory talk by the Kaiser about Japanese "reservists" in Mexico, was to send the Great White Fleet on a cruise around the world. The President hoped thereby to allay Japanese pugnacity. From Tokyo the British Ambassador informed London that the visit of the fleet to Japan "has had all the effect our allies wanted it to and has put an end to all nonsensical war talk." The British Ambassador seems to have forgotten with which country Britain was allied. The formidable armada called at New Zealand and Australia, suggesting the existence of an English-speaking solidarity in the Pacific as well as the Atlantic. Canada applauded the progress of the fleet almost equally with this country, and among Canadians calling at the White House to express approval of the gesture was W. L. MacKenzie King, who was then the Dominion Commissioner of Labor.

The mild co-operative policy initiated by Hay was to grow gradually out of all semblance as each Administration strengthened the American claim to a decisive voice in the Far East. The United States, however, was going it alone. America constantly claimed an interest in the disposition of Far Eastern affairs, and reserved the right to intervene morally, to pass judgment on other Powers—yet, by reason of that strange dualism afflicting and enfeebling American foreign affairs, the Government was unable or unwilling to enter into the specific power relationships that might implement its will. Consciously neglecting its defenses, shrinking from express commitments with its "natural ally," nevertheless for a generation the United States blocked Japan's ambitions at almost every turn. In 1905 Balfour, commenting to Spring-Rice in a memorandum intended for Roosevelt's eye, proposed an Anglo-American alliance covering the Far East in these words:

If America and ourselves were to enter into a treaty, binding us jointly to resist . . . aggression, it would never, I believe, be attempted. Together we are too strong for any combination of powers to fight us. I believe there would be no difficulty on this side of the Atlantic. The difficulty, I imagine, would be rather with the United States, whose traditions and whose Constitution conspire to make such arrangements hard to conclude.

In the polite terms of diplomacy Balfour was putting his finger on the flaw in the American Far Eastern policy. The United States would interfere, exercise moral suasion, or scold; it would not accept the logical responsibility of its interference. At home in the Atlantic world, the United States behaved there with realism and consistency. Not so in the Pacific. In the end, of course, under the rigorous pressure of war waged by a world-wide Axis, America was to draw together with the English-speaking peoples bordering the Pacific, with the British, and with the Dutch and the Chinese, in a Pacific concert also. The steps, slow and halting, were beset by the contradictions, the indecisiveness, the soft refusal to take responsibility that grew, in part, out of the "dull" understanding noted by Roosevelt. It seemed likely that it would take the fires of war finally to disclose to America her vital interest in her other ocean. Yet even in the uncertain days of 1941 signs were not lacking that the English-speaking Powers proposed to enlarge and solidify their Atlantic System into a new era for the Pacific world as well. For one thing, the New Zealanders, Australians, and Canadians were beginning to demand that Britain and America formulate a policy based on something more substantial than expediency.

VI. Fortifying the Atlantic System

THEODORE ROOSEVELT'S FAR EASTERN labors by no means exhausted his capacity for the strenuous life in the crowded years 1902-06. Events on the Atlantic side of the earth likewise challenged Henry Adams's "Tsar Rooseveltoffsky" to "play a great part"; events which were to confirm and reenforce the Atlantic System.

In November, 1902, the Kaiser crossed to Sandringham for some pheasant-shooting with his Uncle Edward, amid a healthy British suspicion that he was after larger game than the birds of Norfolk. While in England William involved the Balfour Ministry—and Roosevelt—in a tempest over Venezuela that in the end bolstered Anglo-American relations, repairing such breaches as were made by the 1900 presidential campaign and the canal and Alaskan-boundary disputes. Soon the Rough Rider President was taking a hand in the European balance of power over some obscure matters concerning Morocco. Although not altogether aware of it, he acted in the interest of the Atlantic Powers. Conforming as usual to a major line of British diplomatic strategy while thinking of himself as a wholly independent force, the world-traipsing President bewildered the British Foreign Office by contradictions between word and deed typically Rooseveltian. Downing Street (the ogre of American isolationists) was not at its most acute during this period, a time in which the Concert of Europe was tuning up for the World War with a President of the United States pitching the tune.

English skepticism over William's sporting junket was fed by hints in the official German press that the Wilhelmstrasse counted on this visit to restore Anglo-German relations to their "unprejudiced Bismarckian basis." It was justified within a month when an allied English and German squadron shelled La Guaira, the port of Caracas, Venezuela, as the opening gun in a debt-collecting expedition. The bombardment loosed on the British Ministry a wave of recrimination, during which it was assumed, most pointedly by Strachey's *Spectator* and the Liberal *Daily News,* that Balfour and his Foreign Minister, Lord Lansdowne, had foolishly fallen into a trap of the Kaiser's baiting.

In the anger of the Opposition at the German "alliance," described by the *Spectator* as "one of the most amazingly indiscreet ever made," even the throne did not escape. It was charged that King Edward, being the host at Sandringham, must have been a party to the obnoxious negotiations and hence had overstepped the bounds set upon the constitutional monarchy. Edward's subsequent irritation over the Venezuelan adventure and the mistrust that gave rise to his celebrated mot that his nephew was the "most brilliant failure in history" shake credence in the charge of royal complicity. The Caribbean concert was, however, consummated at Sandringham at a two-hour conference between William and Lansdowne, and it seemed unlikely to the Liberal statesmen that the King was wholly in the dark concerning it, although the agreement had been in the making since July.

The aging Lord Salisbury (Hay's "great Cecil") had finally passed the Premiership to his nephew Arthur Balfour. Salisbury would be dead within the year, and the equivocal Balfour already missed the unhurried, rocklike judgment of the pessimistic squire of Hatfield. Although always dubious of America's political steadfastness, Salisbury was a better friend of the United States than more demonstrative Ministers such as Balfour. The new Prime Minister and Lansdowne had taken a short view of the Kaiser's proposals. They had a grievance against the Venezuelan dictator, Don Cipriano Castro—Roosevelt's "unspeakably villainous little monkey"—growing out of the seizure of some British vessels suspected of running guns to forces in revolt against Castro.

During his eight years as President, Castro's rule was frequently under fire. He was, moreover, notoriously casual about meeting foreign obligations. Both London and Berlin had counts against him on that score. On top of the Ministry's annoyance with the Castro regime, Balfour and Lansdowne were apprehensively scouting for more diplomatic anchors to windward, although the Anglo-Japanese Alliance was fresh in the locker. Later Lansdowne would explain that he did not wish to offend the Kaiser by repulsing his suggestion of a joint expedition to discipline Castro.

Whatever the motivation in each country, the pecuniary stake scarcely justified forcible action against Venezuela in consideration of the risk involved. When the British and German claims were finally submitted to The Hague for arbitration, England's claim was found to involve only $20,000,000, Germany's only $2,000,000. For those sums the two Powers invaded a sea which the United States had marked for its own, setting in train military operations that might have got out of hand to the extent of calling for American intervention. Both governments sounded the State Department in advance, it is true. In his first annual message of December, 1901, Roosevelt had gratuitously opened the way for such action by European states, disavowing any right on the part of the United States under the Monroe Doctrine to stand between a delinquent Latin American government and its creditors. Bound by Roosevelt's renunciatory doctrine, Hay stiffly informed the British and German Ambassadors that while the United States regretted a show of force to such ends, he could not advise them against proceeding.

2

The way being open at Washington, the allied naval command bombarded La Guaira on December 10, 1902, captured Venezuelan gunboats, imposed a disproportionately imposing "pacific blockade," and subsequently shelled other ports. Castro yielded two days later, begging the United States Government for mediation, the Allied Powers for arbitration. Hay transmitted the note to London and Berlin without comment, although Holleben, the German Ambassador, reported him "bitterly displeased."

So far the American reaction generally had been one of puzzled alarm. Roosevelt and Hay, poring over the dispatches, refrained from public comment. Admiral Dewey was at Culebra, Puerto Rico, with more than fifty men-of-war, ready to sail "at a moment's notice," as he later told Henry A. Wise Wood. His orders were then secret, the presence of the fleet in those waters being supposedly only for winter maneuvers. American wrath was not yet aroused by the intrusive appearance of a European squadron in "mare nostrum," although here and there newspapers, notably the *Baltimore American* and the *Chicago Inter-Ocean,* demanded that Dewey be sent to the scene, and the *Norfolk Virginian-Pilot* called the attack on La Guaira an "insolent and defiant challenge of the Monroe Doctrine—a cut across the face with a whip." At the other pole, Colonel Henry Watterson's *Courier-Journal* cynically suggested jettisoning the Monroe Doctrine at this point, taking the Caribbean region for ourselves, and standing aside from whatever ambitions Germany and England might have elsewhere in Latin America.

But Ambassador von Holleben, who would be recalled in disgrace during the Venezuela episode, early detected symptoms of annoyance with Germany. On the day Castro's note reached Berlin he advised the German Foreign Office against further military demonstrations in view of a "renewed attempt to revive anti-German agitation in the United States." His advice was discounted, Wolff Metternich, now the German Ambassador at London, being ordered to remind Lansdowne that Washington had not sponsored the note, but merely passed it on—a sign to the Wilhelmstrasse that America was holding aloof. On December 15, therefore, Metternich urged Lansdowne to reject arbitration and proceed to the blockade. But that day Henry White, after seeing Balfour in his private room at the House of Commons, cabled Hay that British sentiment was rapidly coalescing against the Ministry on the Venezuelan issue, adding:

"The whole . . . matter, especially Britain acting with Germany, unpopular . . . the sinking of ships certainly is."

The truth was that the reports of Allied naval guns in the Caribbean echoed more loudly in Balfour's ears than in Don Castro's. A storm of Teutophobia swept England, shaking the Ministry, which lost a seat in a bye-election on the question. A terrific barrage was being laid down in the Liberal press, going unanswered for the most part by the journalistic supporters of the Government. Balfour apprised White that the Cabinet would oppose landing any troops in Venezuela, a step which might lead to an indefinite occupation, and hastened to assure the House of Commons on that point. Responding to questions in both houses, Lord Lansdowne and Lord Cranborne—Foreign Affairs Under-Secretary and a Cecil—affirmed British recognition of the Monroe Doctrine, which had not been called into question by Washington. The Duke of Devonshire and Sir Charles Dilke likewise made speeches denying any British desire to override that doctrine.

Carnegie cabled John Morley that in linking herself with the "most dangerous Power" Britain was "playing with fire." Morley, passing the cablegram to the Cabinet and also to the powerful Opposition leaders—Bryce, Harcourt, and Sir Henry Campbell-Bannerman—replied that "people here loathe the German alliance. The main thing is to get rid of the wretched mess. Balfour has a thousand gifts, but he is not really a sound man to be the chief ruler of this country." White reported the Ministry "taken aback by the great unpopularity of their agreement with Germany," and the Prime Minister hurriedly wrote Carnegie of his heartfelt desire to "preserve the warmest and most friendly feelings" between their two countries. He hoped the Americans would see that nothing done in Venezuela "can in the smallest degree touch their susceptibilities," and as for the Monroe Doctrine, the Ministry had "not the smallest objection (rather the reverse!)." Carnegie promptly placed his English correspondence in the hands of the President and the Secretary of State.

Admiral Lord Charles Beresford, commanding the Mediterranean fleet, announced his suspicion that the Germans were "testing" the Monroe Doctrine, with unintentional British help. Playing upon England's deep resentment of Germany's abusive attitude during the Boer War, Kipling published mordantly anti-German verses, "The Rowers," replete with such epithets as "cheated crew," "Goth," and "shameless Hun." Only a little while before the Kaiser had telegraphed his sympathy to the poet during an illness.

3

On December 16, Lansdowne told Metternich that the British would arbitrate. Metternich counseled Bülow to agree. From Holleben came similar word. Wall Street, the Ambassador had learned, favored a ready settlement, and he raised doubts of the effect on trade if Germany stood out. On the Metternich dispatch William made this minute: "His Royal Majesty has lost his nerve. Grandmamma would never have said that!"—an allusion which, taken alone, would assign more responsibility to the King than otherwise appears. At this time the Germans also had before them a report by Sternberg, not yet the Ambassador, of a recent visit to Washington, where he had enjoyed a confidential talk with the President. "That," Sternberg wrote Roosevelt, "gave me a chance to tell them the truth. I've told them every bit of it, and have used rather plain talk."

While the Kaiser and the Chancellor pondered their decision, a note of urgency entered the deliberations, arising, it appears, from some occurrence in the United States. Concurrently, Lansdowne telegraphed Ambassador Lascelles in Berlin that "action should be taken . . . at once, without waiting until Washington exchanges the role of postmaster for one of a more active character." London, it seemed, was also in receipt of disturbing news from overseas. The next day, December 17, Chancellor von Bülow telegraphed Metternich to close at once with the British in order to forestall the possible arrival of a "ready-made solution" from Washington.

What had happened to persuade both Powers that the United States was likely to take a hand? The question leads into a famous historical enigma. Had Roosevelt, as he circumstantially maintained thirteen years afterward, sent for the German Ambassador, informed him that Dewey had steam up, and suggested that he caution his Government to accept arbitration at once? Historians have taken sides in the dispute, and recently an authority on the Monroe Doctrine, Dexter Perkins,[1] concluded in print that the President had falsified his memory. As Roosevelt told it, when the Ambassador failed to grasp the gravity of his remarks, he served him with an oral thirty-six-hour ultimatum to arbitrate or risk an encounter. The Ambassador, retiring in agitation, returned within twenty-four hours bearing word that his Government would accept arbitration.

This melodramatic version, appearing in William Roscoe Thayer's *Life and Letters of John Hay* in 1915, was at once sifted by historians, some of whom, notably John Bassett Moore, pronouncing it implausible. Whereupon Roosevelt confirmed the passage in a letter to Thayer, ascribing the reason for his blunt action to a conviction that "Germany intended to seize some Venezuelan harbor and turn it into a strongly fortified place of arms on the model of Kiao-Chow."

When the German archives were opened after Versailles, a search was made for dispatches bearing on the incident. None of that tenor was found from Holleben. The records show Holleben to have been absent from Washington December 14-16 and the White House visiting-lists put him down for only one call in December, on the sixth. Yet the late William Loeb, Roosevelt's secretary, recalled for Henry Pringle, biographer of the President, two visits by Holleben in December within a few days of each other. He remembered remarking to the President after the first call: "You gave that Dutchman something to think about. The trouble

[1] In *Hands Off: A History of the Monroe Doctrine,* Little, Brown, 1941.

is . . . [he] is so afraid of the Kaiser that I don't think he will give a correct picture of your attitude."

If Holleben made one of these visits on December 16, it is not impossible that he received a forcible expression of the President's desire for arbitration. There is also a possibility of his sending a highly confidential dispatch direct to Hol-stein, the message being withheld from the files, as some-times happened. That is wholly speculative. Of clearer value were letters written in 1906 to Whitelaw Reid, Ambassador at London, and to Henry White. To the former Roosevelt said: "I finally told the German Ambassador that . . . the Kaiser ought to know that unless an agreement for arbitra-tion was reached . . . I would . . . move Dewey's ships south." In the White letter he said he "saw the German Ambassador privately myself," asking him to tell the Kaiser he had put Dewey in charge of fleet maneuvers in the West Indies. These letters, of course, antedated the First World War, in which Roosevelt emphatically backed the Allies. It has long been suggested that wartime aversion might have height-ened his recollections to Thayer.

During that war Roosevelt told the story to Stéphane Lauzanne, who published it both in France and in the Eng-lish-speaking countries. The Lauzanne version adds a new complication. Therein Roosevelt portrayed the incredulous German Ambassador obtaining confirmation from Dewey. But Holleben hastily departed this country in January, 1903, and presumably the Admiral remained constantly with the fleet in the West Indies until the Powers lifted the Vene-zuelan blockade in mid-February. The simplest construction to place on this evidence, beginning with the sudden belief in London and Berlin that intervention was imminent from the United States, is to suppose that Roosevelt did indicate to one or more diplomats on December 16 that his patience was wearing thin and that further delay would provoke action by him. Such a hypothesis, based on the objective probabilities, gives due weight to the President's often re-peated, if perhaps romanticized, story.

The Powers agreed to arbitration in principle on Decem-

ber 18, requesting Roosevelt to serve as arbitrator. Through
John Hay's instrumentality and without the President's
knowledge, that thankless chore was shifted to The Hague
Tribunal, where the Germans had offered to refer it as
early as July, 1901, Castro declining. The agreement to arbitrate failed, however, to end the "wretched . . . business."
Mistrusting Castro's bona fides, the Powers imposed their
"pacific blockade" on Christmas Day—seven years to the day
after a Caracas multitude almost wrecked the American
Legation in exuberance over Cleveland's message.

As the blockade lengthened week by week, the American
temper shortened. England's part, never greatly resented,
passed from view, and it was Germany which attracted the
country's rising ire. At the end of December the British Ambassador reported that the "outburst in this country against
Germany is truly remarkable and suspicion of the German
Emperor's designs in the Caribbean are shared by Administration, press ,and public alike." Six weeks later he was less
disinterested, observing that England's good relations with
this country would be "seriously impaired" by further co-
operation with Germany. The British Ambassador professed
to see as a factor in the growing truculence the fine hand of
the big-navy men and the shipbuilders.

On January 17, 1903, fuel was sprayed on the flames by a
German shelling of San Carlos, a fort at Maracaibo. The
British had bombarded Puerto Bello in December with little
comment. Both measures had the stamp of legality. Yet the
German action (perhaps because the controversy was believed near its end) aroused the United States. Similar repercussions were felt in London. The Germans had scuttled
gunboats, arousing the Admiralty to condemnation of such
"absurdity and wilfulness." Germany now became to the
Spectator the "mischief-maker of the world" and to the
Daily Mail Germany's naval strength was a "grave peril
to the world."

Count Metternich, dining in the royal presence, found
King Edward "grumpy," irritated because the blockade was
dragging out, and more eager for an abatement of the nui-

sance than for collection of money due. White, arriving late at a court, was told the King wished to see him. "He talked," White wrote Mrs. White, "about Venezuela and was generally rather hostile to the 'ally,' but most friendly to us. . . . His Majesty was really very outspoken." In a report to Hay, the legation secretary described "strong representations to the Prime Minister from influential quarters inside the Cabinet as to the necessity for immediate termination of the situation by raising the blockade, even if severance from Germany is necessary. Popular discontent and pressure are increasing."

Balfour, writing Carnegie again, assured him that Anglo-American accord had been his "most fondly cherished hope . . . through all my political life," adding that while "the parties are divided upon most subjects . . . *one thing*" on which they were agreed was "the desirability of good Anglo-American relations." In public also, Balfour extended the olive branch, declaring in a speech at Liverpool that the Monroe Doctrine had "no enemies in this country that I know of," continuing:

We welcome any increase of influence of the United States . . . upon the great Western Hemisphere. We desire no colonization. We desire no alteration in the balance of power. We desire no acquisition of territory. We have not the slightest intention of interfering with the government of any portion of that Continent.

From a German source came likewise in January a genial reference to the Monroe Doctrine. Sternberg had just been appointed Ambassador to the United States. A little soldier with many afflictions who hated writing reports and was cherished by Roosevelt, he met interviewers in New York on his way to his new post. Cheerily he said: "The Emperor understands the Monroe Doctrine thoroughly. . . . He appreciates the feeling for the Monroe Doctrine and would not think of occupying a coaling station or territory. He would no more think of violating that Doctrine than he would of colonizing the moon." The statement drew down on the new Ambassador a reprimand from Berlin; he was told to take more account of German sentiments, which, from Bismarck to Bülow, regarded the American assertion of the Monroe Doctrine with undeviating aversion.

Throughout January, 1903, the American press predominantly echoed a privately expressed judgment of Roosevelt's on the San Carlos incident: "Are the people in Berlin crazy? Don't they know they are inflaming public opinion more and more? Don't they know they'll be left alone without England?" Except for the German-language press, which generally upheld Germany's conduct, shared the opinion of the German journals that England was a "bad ally," and exhibited lack of sympathy for American alarm and concern, the American newspapers condemned the bombardment as "brutal" and "unwarranted." The *New York Times* summed up a prevailing view when it doubted if "worse international manners" had ever "come under the observation of civilized men."

4

Confronted by American disapproval and Britain's obvious dislike for the punitive yoke in Venezuela, as 1903 opened the German Government knew itself again to be isolated from the English-speaking community. The German official press, reacting characteristically, reversed itself and returned to the attack on America. During 1902 the German press had sought to woo this country in line with the Wilhelmstrasse's placatory policy. This was the year of Prince Henry's state visit, an inspiration of his brother the Kaiser, who gave other evidences of his gracious interest in the United States as well. As a gift to the nation William inappropriately sent a statue of the militaristic despot Frederick the Great. He gave manuscripts to Harvard University, and he contracted for the building of his yacht *Meteor* in an American shipyard. Prince Henry's visit suffered from its sectarian nature. In reality it was a mission to the German-Americans, and the United States Government only half-heartedly acknowledged its official character. (Misled by crowds, German banners, and sycophants, Henry informed the Kaiser that a third of the

American population was German and loyal to the Hohenzollern dynasty.) Frederick's statue embarrassed the Government for several years, being finally installed at the Army
War College in Washington. The Kaiser insisted that Miss
Alice Roosevelt, as the "Princess Royal," should christen his
yacht. When the President heard that a brief speech would
be required of her, he confessed to Hay that the only "motto
sufficiently epigrammatic that came to my mind was 'Damn
the Dutch.' "

All that goodwill policy was forgotten by the Pan-German
organs in January, 1903. A journal named *Gegenwart* rated
the Government severely for having "humbly" asked permission from the "big-mouthed Yankees" before striking at Venezuela. The Monroe Doctrine came under renewed fire from
the right and the center. It was, of course, a "nonbinding
monologue" *(Berliner Post)*, merely the "personal opinion of
the Chief Magistrate of the United States in 1823" *(Ham-
burger Nachrichten)*, and the *Berliner Vossische Zeitung* was
certain no European state would ever recognize it.

The exasperated tone of these strictures arose, no doubt,
from a realization that the United States and Great Britain
had again been drawn together in an Atlantic matter. Germany was again forced to observe that the Monroe Doctrine
lay behind the guns of the British fleet. Together, the English-speaking Powers presumably would bar Germany, as in
the past, from Latin America. The Kaiser, Bülow, and Tirpitz, practioners of Realpolitik, had, it is apparent, a material
motive for attempting to breach the Atlantic System. They
failed to reckon with one formidable factor: Apart from its
sincerity in wishing to safeguard Latin America from European conquest, the United States preferred not to have Germany as a neighbor. England agreed. Being pragmatists, the
English-speaking peoples were uneasy in the presence of the
neo-Prussian *mystique*. The aims of the Pan-Germans were
disturbingly nebulous; there was a harsh frenzy in their talk
of race and war. On the part of America, there was no desire
to conquer the rest of the hemisphere; equally was she cer-

tain that she wished no avid European Power attempting
that task.

In exonerating England and ascribing to Germany imperialistic ambitions in the second Venezuelan crisis, the
American public reasoned from known facts. Since 1898 Germany had been exerting pressure to the south. As England
retired from the Caribbean, the Germans had been giving
every indication of a will to move in. During the Spanish
War, when it was briefly assumed that the United States
might be too heavily engaged to resist encroachments, there
was strong agitation in Germany for the acquisition of a foothold in the West Indies. The Danish West Indies (Virgin
Islands) and Santo Domingo were first choice. Then and
thereafter Tirpitz and the navalists also coveted the Galá-
pagos Islands (600 miles southwest of the Isthmus of Panama), a harbor in Venezuela, and the Dutch possessions Cura-
çao, St. Eustatius, and Dutch Guiana. There was also a steady
drumbeat in the Pan-German press on behalf of German
destiny in Brazil, the professors writing provocatively about
secession of the southern Brazilian states, with their large
German population. Early in 1900 Tirpitz recommended to
the Reichstag budget commission an appropriation for a naval base in South Brazil.

Taking cognizance of this and other developments, the
United States Government thought the time ripe to remind
Germany of its unremitting interest in South America. Secretary Root accordingly observed amidst cheers at a public
dinner in New York City: "No man who carefully watches
the signs of the times can fail to see that the American people
will within a few years have either to abandon the Monroe
Doctrine or fight for it." The Secretary concluded that "we
are not going to abandon it." A bit later, Lodge uttered a
grave warning in the Senate regarding German interest in
the Virgin Islands, saying: "A nation of Europe which dares
to take possession of those islands . . . there on the road to
the canal . . . would be, by that very act, an enemy of the
United States. Such an act . . . would mean war." Omitting

to name Germany, Lodge suggested that a certain European Power with a rapidly growing navy might "want to test the Monroe Doctrine." The United States, he added, was ready for the test.

Holleben, reporting these utterances, ascribed them to a "truly hysterical irritation" against Germany. At this time also Roosevelt wrote Spring-Rice that the United States Navy should be kept "at a pitch that will enable us to interfere promptly if Germany ventures to touch a foot of American soil."

The surface of German-American relations was periodically ruffled by "incidents" during the years at the turn of the century. An American naval commander found a German warship sounding the waters off Margarita, a Venezuelan island suitable for a naval station. Inasmuch as the "Germans are not much given to unselfish work for the benefit of mariners," the commander reported his finding. Hay had the Berlin Embassy state "discreetly and informally, but decisively," that such curiosity might lead to diplomatic measures. There was also the circumstantial report that the Kaiser was negotiating personally for purchase from Mexico of a strip of Lower California containing two good harbors. Ambassador Choate, in private life a leader of the American bar, thought sufficiently well of his information to order a thorough report. "Discreet" inquiries in Berlin brought denials. Queen Wilhelmina's marriage to Duke Henry of Mecklenburg-Schwerin was followed by reports of new German designs on Holland and her colonies. Henry White was instructed to sound the British Government on its attitude toward German infiltration into the Netherlands. Dining with Balfour, White was told that England would resist any step toward the absorption of Holland.

In 1902 the United States tried to buy the Danish West Indies, bidding $5,000,000. The Landsthing (upper house) rejected the offer in October by one vote. White, who had been active in the matter, had "little doubt the result is due largely to German intrigue." This view was generally credited in Washington and London. Lunching with the

King and Queen of England soon after the Danish vote,
White found Alexandra pleased that her native land had not
alienated a colony. "I hope," she added, "that you will never
let Germany have the islands; that is what we Danes would
dread above all." Edward, expressing his regret, predicted
"you will have them yet." Not until 1916 was the purchase
consumated. The price then was $25,000,000.

Anglo-American relations, scarcely disturbed during the
Venezuelan crisis, emerged from it stronger than before.
Carnegie reflected the general view in this country when in
writing Balfour in July, 1903, he asserted that "in the Venezuelan invasion Britain was all right, Germany the real
enemy. . . . Britain is today our only real friend, even with
the masses, something unknown before," adding that "were
Britain in serious trouble today—I mean in extremis—
America could not be held."

Anglo-German relations, on the other hand, were
worsened. The Venezuelan fleet actions were the last use
of force by overseas Powers in the Americas. They likewise
represented the last joint action by Germany and England
until the First World War found them enemies. "The German connection," White reported, "has been a tremendous
lesson for them [the British]." The public had given a positive sign that they wished no more undertakings with the
North Sea cousins. About 1902 England began to turn toward
France. In the spring of 1903 Edward visited Paris in state,
a call promptly returned by President Loubet. From that
exchange, it has been popularly thought, dates the beginning
of Franco-British rapprochement.

5

Once the Venezuelan matter had been lodged at The
Hague, the German Government resumed its efforts to gain
American goodwill. Ambassador von Sternberg's appointment had been favorably received, the press treating it as a
good augury. Henry Adams magnified the importance of the
gesture, writing in *The Education of Henry Adams* that he

had "seen Hay, in 1898, bring England into his combine; he had seen the steady movement which was to bring France into an Atlantic System; and now he saw the sudden dramatic swing of Germany toward the West." If Germany might only be "held there," Adams calculated, "a century of friction would be saved."

That was not to be. A system supposes collaboration, not Machtpolitik. The Kaiser, Chancellor von Bülow, and Admiral von Tirpitz proposed on the seas mastery, not co-operation, and in Europe, continental hegemony. Momentarily, however, Bülow showed an accommodating spirit toward America. Twice he denied in the Reichstag the reports of German ambitions in the Americas, calling them a "mare's nest" and the "most unfortunate and conscienceless rumors." The United States Government was not unduly impressed. The Chancellor followed the main line of German strategy from Bismarck to Hitler regarding the Monroe Doctrine, that line being either to denounce or to ignore it. Bülow ignored it. He did, however, curb aggravating outreaches of Pan-German policy toward the Western Hemisphere, refusing support to the *Berliner Tageblatt* for a special bureau in Rio de Janeiro and censuring the *Grenzboten* for advocating political migration to Brazil. In July, 1903, he again denied secret designs against Latin American states in an interview published in the *Berliner Lokal Anzeiger,* simultaneously directing Tirpitz to moderate the arrogant behavior of German naval commanders in Caribbean ports.

The United States Government and people were by no means vengefully inclined toward Germany. As the *New York Sun* accurately put it, "the future of German-American friendship . . . rests with Germany." Delighted by Sternberg's presence, Roosevelt exuded racial flattery to Professor Hugo Münsterberg, a distinguished bearer of Kultur to Harvard University. "Germany, England and the United States," Roosevelt prophesied to the Pan-German Münsterberg, "are the three great nations of the future. The Slavs need a hundred years and the Latin races are played out. And the coöperation of these three peoples need have no limit—the Monroe Doctrine is no rigid article of faith."

Irresponsibly, the President toyed with the idea of German acquisition of territory in Latin America while on a famous horseback ride with Sternberg in February, 1902, just after the Venezuelan blockade had been lifted. Although the United States Navy, as Roosevelt said, saw Germany as their next enemy, he himself was not at all certain that a German state carved out of Brazil might not be the best hope for South America. In a generous mood, the President yet withheld his full trust. Sternberg wrote Bülow of his feeling that "the President does not treat with absolute confidence Germany's assurance regarding the respecting of the Monroe Doctrine. I took the opportunity to assure him emphatically that Germany does not think of territorial acquisition in South and Central America."

The Ambassador realistically informed Chancellor von Bülow that the Venezuelan matter had reacted favorably on American prestige below the Rio Grande, at the same time diminishing Germany's standing in this country. And Dewey —he gave Roosevelt as his authority—really had been under "secret orders" at Puerto Rico.

Reflecting the Government's pro-American bias, in the spring of 1903 the German press took a less exigent line. Answering suggestions that the aim of Wilhelmstrasse diplomacy was the severing of the Anglo-American tie, the *Vossische Zeitung* declared that the Kaiser's "desire for closer relations with both Great Britain and the United States" was greater than his desire "for any discord between the two great Anglo-Saxon Powers." Agreeing, the German *Nation* felt, however, that "in the United States as well as in Great Britain powerful interests are at work to cast suspicion upon German diplomacy." From this hypothesis the Social-Democratic *Berliner Vorwärts* dissented, declaring that the "Kaiser's great aim" had been to sunder the English-speaking Powers, an effort enjoying in Washington the "adroit" support of Count Cassini, the Russian diplomat. (Cassini's pro-German machinations were well known to

Hay.) This newspaper concluded that the Kaiser would fail because of American self-interest, since the United States regarded itself as "the heir of the British Empire." It "will not," the editor added, "let this asset go to waste."

Out of the Venezuelan crisis came a new American naval orientation. Five battleships were authorized by the Naval Act of March, 1903, and in the arguments for the huge appropriation Germany was declared to be the enemy. William H. Moody, the Secretary of the Navy, admitted to Sternberg that Germany had "definitely become the measure for us." This country had joined the Anglo-German naval race. Roosevelt confirmed Moody's assertion when in talking with Hay six weeks later he asserted that "both the Dutch and Danish West Indies will be a constant temptation to Germany unless or until we take them. The way to deliver Germany from temptation is to keep on with the upbuilding of our Navy." From the Venezuelan incident to the First World War, Germany did not again yield to temptation in the Americas.

A casualty of the Venezuelan matter was Canada, in the disgruntled opinion of the Dominion. The Alaskan-boundary dispute finally came to a head in January, 1903. Unwilling to accept arbitration, Roosevelt offered instead a joint commission to consist of three Britons and three Americans, all to be "impartial jurists." At this solution the Canadian press railed, but Balfour and Chamberlain agreed with Roosevelt. Thereupon it was said in the Dominion that the British Ministry was expiating the Venezuelan blunder at Canada's expense. The President's methods in the controversy could not be commended by objective Americans. He blustered and bullied, he secretly and a bit ridiculously reinforced the garrison in southern Alaska, and his choice of "impartial jurists" moved responsible Americans to uneasy laughter, England to "dismay and surprise," and Canada to fresh animosity. Roosevelt's nominees (after the Supreme Court bench had declined to furnish the commissioners) were Root, Lodge, and Senator George Turner of Washington State. Although a great jurist, as Secretary of War Root was a

member of the Administration, one of the litigants; Lodge
was publicly committed to the Government's cause; and
Turner came from a state where feeling against Canada's
contentions ran high.

The matter had been reopened in June, 1902, when Sir
Wilfrid Laurier, the Dominion Prime Minister, appealed
to Henry White while in London for assistance in disposing
of it with honor. Sir Wilfrid, having no hope of satisfaction
for Canada's claims to a port and a corridor in the Alaskan
Panhandle, suggested territorial compensation elsewhere or
a money award. His proposal stirred Roosevelt to strong
language: "to pay them anything," he told Hay, "would
come dangerously near blackmail." The President regarded
Canada's case as "false," its presentation as "an outrage, pure
and simple." Lord Minto, the Canadian Governor-General,
was in London at that time. He indicated to White his lack
of confidence in the claim and his desire to see it out of the
way. From those talks arose the commission.

The British, appointing Lord Alverstone, the Chief Justice
of England, to head their commissioners, allowed the proceedings to lag. Whereupon Roosevelt declared to Lodge that
England "must be kept right up on the mark," threatening
to emulate Cleveland, send a message to Congress, and "run
the boundary as we deem it should be run." To Hay he
talked lightly of acting "in a way that would wound British
pride." In London White patiently set the wheels in motion
once more.

Under the award, Canada obtained the Portland Canal,
an inlet at the southern extremity of the Panhandle where
the Alaskan coast joins that of British Columbia, and two
of four small islands offshore. This "compensation" was far
from the Klondike and nearly 500 miles from the port sought
by the Canadians. The two Canadian commissioners declined to sign the award. Lord Alverstone, heatedly condemned in the Dominion for having "truckled to the
Yankees," observed good-humoredly at a public dinner in
London that "if . . . they don't want a decision based on the
law and the evidence, they must not put a British judge on

the commission." Roosevelt rather shamelessly cited the award as "signal proof of the fairness and good-will with which two friendly nations can approach and determine issues."

The Venezuelan episode produced new attitudes toward the use of outside force in the Americas. Roosevelt enunciated one, which came to be known as the Roosevelt Corollary to the Monroe Doctrine. Dr. Luis Drago, an eminent international lawyer of the Argentine, contributed the second, the Drago Corollary. Chagrined over the passive role the United States had been required, through his own statement of policy, to play in Venezuela, the President announced that hereafter this country would, in effect, police Latin America, standing between those republics and European claimants but collecting bills and preserving order with its own means. For years English publicists had been proposing that this country accept responsibilities of that character. The Roosevelt Corollary, which let this country in for more than two decades of friction with our neighbors, was proclaimed by Root in a speech on May 20, 1904, in New York City. After professing friendship to Latin America, Root continued:

If a nation shows that it knows how to act with decision in industrial and political matters, if it keeps order and pays its obligations, then it need fear no interference from the United States. Brutal wrongdoing, or an impotence which results in a general loosening of the ties of civilized society, may finally require intervention by some civilized nation, and in the Western Hemisphere, the United States cannot ignore this duty.

A span of oxen could have been driven through the Roosevelt Corollary by a truly imperialistic government. In effect, it declared a protectorate over the entire hemisphere. When criticism arose from all three Americas, the President expressed new satisfaction with his work. He told Hay it was "only the simplest common sense, and only a fool or a coward can treat it as aught else." Authority was added to the Roosevelt Corollary when rephrased in the annual message for 1904. A few months later Henry Adams, who never rated the first Roosevelt's diplomatic capabilities too extravagantly, remarked that "Root has to carry the Monroe Doctrine. . . . Roosevelt is already wabbling over the whole hemisphere to find a foothold for any doctrine at all." The Roosevelt Corollary remained, of course, a unilateral assertion.

Dr. Drago's formula became international law in 1907 when adopted by the Second Hague Conference, binding signatory powers not to use force in collecting defaulted obligations unless the debtor states refused to arbitrate, blocked a settlement, or failed to honor an award.

6

The eyes of Washington and the European capitals, focused, as we have seen, on the Russo-Japanese War, were diverted in the early months of 1904 to Morocco by minor events that foreshadowed the world's concentration on that hot, decayed land of mountain and desert in Northwest Africa. The kidnapping of an American, Perdicaris, by a bandit chieftain and the signing of an Anglo-French treaty covering the status of Morocco and Egypt held the shifting rays of the international spotlight only briefly. Yet the second put in sequence the so-called Moroccan crisis, a struggle for dominance amongst the European Powers setting the stage for 1914 and bringing the New World in the person of Roosevelt into the scale to "redress the balance of the Old"—as in 1823. The President, influencing power relationships in Asia, found time also to cast the decisive voice in the diplomatic cockpit at Algeciras, whither the Powers repaired ostensibly to settle the fate of Morocco but actually to confirm their adherence to the rival forces being aligned in Europe.

France and England signed the Mediterranean Pact on April 8, 1904. Its broad effect was to guarantee England a free hand in Egypt, France a free hand in her Moroccan protectorate. France and England had shared a nominal protectorate over Egypt from 1879 to 1882, when a change of Ministry in Paris caused France's withdrawal. England thereupon strengthened her grip on Egypt. In 1904 the French were still unreconciled to their loss. The French claim to a special interest in the remnants of the old Sheriffian Empire in Morocco reached back at least to 1778, in which year a treaty between Louis XVI and the infant American republic had pledged French good offices with the "King or Emperor of Morocco or Fez and neighboring regencies" on behalf of the citizens, trade, and shipping of the United States. France had held Algiers, to the eastward of Morocco, since 1830. In 1844 the French conquered parts of Morocco, gradually thereafter extending their sway from Algiers. French Morocco fronted on the Atlantic, Spanish Morocco, a corner north of the Riff Mountains, on the Mediterranean. By 1904 French trade and influence held first place in Morocco, Britain's was second, and Germany's interest negligible. The German activities were confined largely to the Atlantic seaport of Casablanca.

News of the treaty created no ripple in the greater affairs of the Powers. Delcassé, the French Foreign Minister, informed Prince Radolin, an able Pole who was German Ambassador to Paris, of the terms of the treaty seventeen days before it was signed. Five days after its announcement Bülow said in the Reichstag that he saw "no reason to suppose that the Anglo-French agreement [was] aimed at any other Power." The Chancellor had "no cause to think that our interests in Morocco will be disregarded or injured." Although the Kaiser later was to hint that the treaty contained secret clauses dealing with France's aspirations on the Rhine, he showed no concern at the moment. As a matter of fact, the covenant contained no reference to any matters outside the Mediterranean basin.

Throughout 1904, in truth, the German Government, accepting the treaty as a mere mutual validation of the French and English spheres, signified no displeasure with it. However, the Pan-German League convention of 1904 denounced it as a "humiliation for Germany," urging the Government to demand an Atlantic seaport (preferably Casablanca) in "compensation." But in October Baron von Richtofen, who had succeeded Bülow as Foreign Minister, asserted in the Reichstag that Germany's interest in Morocco was "exclusively economic." Bülow too had taken a mollifying line in answer to questions from Pan-German Deputies, disavowing any desire to "overthrow rivals"—a moderation that failed to lull the *London Times;* the Thunderer accused the Chancellor of uttering "timely 'anti-Machiavels' " calculated to quiet suspicion abroad.

The abduction of Ion Perdicaris on May 18, 1904, served alike to acquaint the European world with unsettled conditions in Morocco and to remind the Americans of the existence of that country. Roosevelt found it politically useful as well. Perdicaris, who lived with his wife, his foster-daughter, and her husband Mr. Varney, a British subject, was kidnapped with Varney as they were taking their after-dinner coffee in the garden of the Perdicaris villa, Place of the Nightingales, on a hill above Tangier. The kidnapper was one Raisuli, a revolted sheik, who wished only, it appeared, to use Perdicaris and Varney as hostages to compel certain tribute and concessions from the Sultan. Roosevelt and Hay acted with vigor, ordering the European squadron to Tangier.

The exotic names and picturesque circumstances of the abduction entranced American newspaper-readers. Roosevelt's swift action and bold words stimulated patriotic emotion. Perdicaris had not been returned when the Republican National Convention, slated to renominate Roosevelt, met at Chicago. In that juncture Hay couched a new demand for Perdicaris' release in a phrase that swept the Republican gathering to riotous applause: "We want Perdicaris alive or Raisuli dead." The phrase, attributed to Roosevelt, was taken as graphic evidence of the solicitude of the Administration for American interests in any quarter of the globe, and Hay sardonically reflected on the value of a "concise impropriety" in whipping up political fervor. In due time the Sultan yielded to Raisuli, and Perdicaris and Varney were restored to their home. A gentle dilettante and amateur painter, Perdicaris returned with lavish praise for the kindness of his captor.

Between October, 1904, and March, 1905, Germany's attitude toward the Mediterranean Pact underwent a profound change. The Pan-German organs and Deputies kept up their attack, construing the treaty as a slight to German prestige. Holstein persuaded Bülow to see in the treaty a step toward an Anglo-French entente, which in fact it was. The Wilhelmstrasse was already exhibiting signs of that morbid fear of "encirclement" which was steadily to grow more fixed up to 1914, and continues today. Post-Bismarckian diplomacy pursued in the main a destructive course, aimed rather at preventing combinations of power than linking other Powers to Germany. Whereas the Iron Chancellor had woven a system of alliances across Europe, buttressing the German Empire's security and enhancing its authority, William II, guided by Bülow and Holstein, seemed unable to make effective covenants with anyone. The duality of the German aim —a desire for both command of the seas and Continental hegemony—negatived a strong, coherent policy at Berlin. Hence the Kaiser frittered away his energies and Germany's good repute by striving against accords existing elsewhere, as in the case of Anglo-American understanding, now with the Mediterranean Pact, and presently in the effort to divide France and Russia through the Czar at Björkö.

By March, 1905, the Wilhelmstrasse was ready to strike at the Anglo-French treaty by way of France. Mukden fell on the tenth. Russia was evidently "mired" in Manchuria. France, torn by her recurrent clerical strife and an outburst of anti-Semitism, had just been shown to be deficient in military equipment. The French were unprepared for war and their rapprochement with England was still in an incipient stage, Holstein assuring Bülow that Britain's attachment to France was merely "platonic" in any case.

On the day of Mukden's fall, the Kaiser undertook to recruit Roosevelt for his campaign. Through Sternberg (a medium regularly used by the two chiefs of state to carry on chatty, informal intercourse) the Emperor asked the President to join him in a declaration to the Sultan of Morocco. The United States, as William pointed out, had an interest in the status of Morocco, being a signatory to a convention covering extraterritorial privileges in that country drawn by the Powers in 1880. His argument was directed to the principle of the Open Door. France, he said, was asserting ascendancy prejudicial to the commercial opportunities of the other Powers. What he proposed specifically was a joint declaration binding the United States and Germany to uphold the Sultan's independence. Nothing was said of the Mediterranean Pact. It is by no means certain that Roosevelt understood the Kaiser's real bent. He replied that American interest in Morocco was "too slight" to warrant such an intervention, adding didactically that he never took a step in foreign affairs "unless I am assured that I shall be able eventually to carry out my will by force." He had in mind the dispatch of warships in the Perdicaris case.

Three weeks later, on March 31, the All Highest paid his spectacular visit to the Sultan. Mounted on a "strange horse," trembling alike at his political audacity and the news that the lawless Moors had "shot an Englishman yesterday," William greeted the Sultan at Tangier as an independent sovereign beholden to no European Power. The gesture, engineered by Bülow and Holstein over the Kaiser's own judgment, was calculated to strike the Anglo-French agreement between wind and water. Instead of a solid shot the Wilhelmstrasse bolt was to turn into a boomerang.

The immediate impact on Europe was, however, great. War talk flared in the press, and the chancelleries, awaiting the arrival of the Baltic fleet in the Sea of Japan, interpreted the visit as a storm signal. King Edward fumed at the "theatrical fiasco," but his Ministry took counsel with the French. Delcassé poured irony on the occasion, but the timid French Prime Minister, Maurice Rouvier, feared the worst. In the United States Roosevelt, who chronically underestimated the depth and rigor of the European power conflict, remarked lightly to Hay that "this was as funny a case as I have ever seen of mutual distrust and fear bringing two peoples to the verge of war." It would be several weeks before Roosevelt saw in the Kaiser's maneuvers a real threat to the peace of Europe.

Five days after the Kaiser's Tangier exploit he renewed his solicitation of Roosevelt. This time he dropped pretexts and made a frontal attack on the Anglo-French treaty. On the day before, William, encouraged by reports from Stern-berg, had assured Bülow that they could count on America's help. This would, he exulted, weaken England's position, since the British, he said, were "afraid to oppose America too openly." The second attempt to ensnare the President only convinced him that delusions were rampant in the Euro-pean chancelleries. On his way to Colorado for a bear hunt he dropped off a letter in Texas to his Secretary of War, William Howard Taft, who had been left "sitting on the lid" in Washington. "I wish to Heaven," he wrote, "that our excellent friend the Kaiser was not so jumpy and did not have so many pipe dreams."

This was on April 8. Six days later Sternberg appeared with a new proposal. Prince Radolin had encountered a stone wall in Delcassé, who resisted pressure for either re-vision or denunciation of the Mediterranean Pact. The Wil-helmstrasse turned now to an international conference as a means of undermining the Moroccan arrangement. Sternberg asked Taft to drop a "confidential hint" in behalf of the con-ference proposal to the British, who had displayed no inter-est. Taft gave Sternberg his offhand opinion that the Presi-dent would be disinclined to encourage a conference unless France agreed, repeating the conversation to the French Ambassador, Jules Jusserand. The German plan as related by Sternberg was for a conference of the 1880 treaty Powers to conduct a thorough examination of the Open Door in Morocco.

Taft shrewdly gathered, as he explained to Jusserand, that Germany's meddling arose from "sentiments of their dig-nity." At about this time Chancellor von Bülow dropped the mask in the Reichstag, attributing Germany's concern with Morocco to "our dignity and our authority as a World Power." The note of prestige was being openly avowed in the

German press. For a month longer the situation hung fire. When the conference finally came, it was the American President who brought it to pass.

7

The destruction of the Russian fleet at Tsushima on May 27, 1905, threw the cogs at the Wilhelmstrasse into high gear. Pressure on Washington, Paris, and London was intensified. The Kaiser and Bülow privately began the draft of a mutual defense treaty designed to wean the defeated Czar away from France as a complement to the attempt to disrupt the Anglo-French accord. An ultimatum was served on Rouvier: Franco-German relations could not hope for betterment as long as Delcassé remained in the Foreign Office. Delcassé resigned after a torrid session of the Ministry, warning his colleagues: "Germany is not a country that can be appeased by concessions. Stretch out your little finger to her and she grabs your hand, then your arm, then your shoulder, and soon your whole body passes into her grip."

The day before Delcassé's retirement (Germany's only victory during the whole Moroccan episode) William placed in Roosevelt's hands an instrument that would return to plague Germany at the forthcoming conference. He promised that in exchange for the President's assistance with the French and the British he would "in every case be ready to back up the decision which you consider to be most fair and most practicable." The pledge gave Roosevelt a leverage which he was by no means backward in applying.

Roosevelt still held back. Reporting the rise in German exigence to Jusserand on June 14, he declared himself unwilling to be the Kaiser's "decoy duck." The President and the French Ambassador had gradually moved into the relationship of collaborators—not to say conspirators. The extent of their collaboration was only disclosed with the publication of Jusserand's memoirs and the opening in 1937 of the French archives for the period. In later justification for the robust part he played in this European quarrel, Roosevelt always ascribed it to his belief that France was right, Germany wrong, never troubling to relate his acts to American (or Atlantic) interest. In talking things over with Jusserand he had assumed that France would resist yielding territorial compensation to Germany in Morocco, since she was, he supposed, reluctant to have the Germans as neighbors there. Jusserand agreed that Germany's proximity in North Africa was the last thing France wished.

Roosevelt wondered if a conference would not be the easiest way out. The Ambassador objected that the Germans insisted on a wide-open program, a conference admitting all questions concerning Morocco, past, present, and future. This meant that all international commitments would have to go into the hopper. Apart from the English pact, the French had treaties with Spain and Italy, the first recognizing Spain's claim to Spanish Morocco, the second sanctioning an Italian protectorate in Tripoli in exchange for a like commitment regarding the French in Morocco. France could not agree to such a conference without destroying her whole Mediterranean position.

The Kaiser's gorge was steadily rising. On June 15 he threatened war on France, blaming England for French recalcitrance. Taking the War Lord at his word, Roosevelt weakened on June 16. A war between France and Germany, he told Jusserand, would widen until it became "literally a world conflagration." He therefore advised that "some satisfaction must be granted to the limitless vanity of Wilhelm, and it would be wise to help him save his face if war can thereby be avoided." Roosevelt even had a solution for the agenda obstacle, dictating to the Ambassador an agreement under which the two Powers were to "consent to go to the conference with no program and to discuss there questions in regard to Morocco save, of course, where either is in honor bound by a previous agreement to another power."

An ingenious by-pass, the Roosevelt formula was acceptable in Paris. The Germans, beginning to grasp at straws in the face of British impassivity, likewise agreed. Throughout the controversy London had been profoundly reserved, insisting that the problem concerned France alone, an attitude that provoked Roosevelt into a number of picturesque flings at the British Government—barbs which, joyously reported to Berlin by Sternberg, helped assure the Emperor of Roosevelt's malleability. Roosevelt found no difficulty in maintaining his intimate relations with the German Ambassador during the running intrigue with Jusserand. It was the Frenchman, however, to whom the President showed his correspondence with the Kaiser, giving him leave to "modify" the replies and adopting "without hesitation divers suggestions." Sternberg had no such private access to the White House negotiations with the French.

Jusserand's reports to the Quai d'Orsay revealed in daily detail the developments in the game of outwitting the Kaiser. The concealment was perfect, the German Foreign Office no more suspecting double play than had Roosevelt penetrated the Kaiser's duplicity in the exchanges over Chinese neutrality at the beginning of the Russo-Japanese War. The President believed that he was engaged in extricating France from an awkward situation and improving, in some rather indistinct way, Anglo-German relations. He repeatedly informed Sternberg that he disapproved of the mistrust and hauteur existing between London and Berlin, he scolded Spring-Rice, still in St. Petersburg, also in that vein. Summing up the President's conduct toward France, Jusserand confided to his Foreign Office that "the President has certainly sought as best he could and with the sincerest friendship, the most practicable means in his judgment for avoiding the calamity of war. He has in any case, despite the solicitations and advances of Wilhelm II, refused to do or say anything that might range him on the side of Germany. . . . On the contrary, it is our cause that he has wished to defend."

The French accepted the Roosevelt formula on June 25, whereupon the President allowed Sternberg to learn that Paris was in an acquiescent mood. When the Kaiser promptly assented, Roosevelt congratulated him on a "genuine triumph for the Emperor's diplomacy." He grinned as he recited the message to Jusserand, hoping that the French people would not "take it amiss if I am found particularly flattering toward the Emperor." On July 8 the conference was set for Algeciras, Spain, a seaport opposite Gibraltar, in January, 1906. Henry White, by now Ambassador to Italy, was selected as the chief American delegate.

8

Roosevelt's Algeciras diplomacy may or may not have forestalled a general war. In common with many authorities on the period, the President thought that it had. On April 25, 1906, Theodore the Peacemaker, having in the year of 1905 "ended" the Russo-Japanese War and brought the European Powers to the council table, preened himself in a remarkable letter to Jusserand on their joint labors in conciliating Berlin and Paris. This letter, curiously neglected by historians of the Algeciras episode, began by bestowing rather stilted and un-Rooseveltian praise on the French Ambassador, a modest and gifted critic, historian, and man of letters who represented his country in Washington for so many years that he became a gracious institution. The President asserted it as "the simple and literal truth . . . [that] in my judgment we owe it to you more than any other one man that the year which has closed has not seen war between France and Germany, which, had it begun, would probably have extended to take in a considerable portion of the world." The President "came into the matter most unwillingly" and only then because of his confidence in Jusserand's "high integrity."

So far Roosevelt pays tribute to the Ambassador's reliability as a fellow conspirator. Then the tenor of the letter changes. The magnificently untrammeled Rooseveltian ego delivers a thrust; Jusserand is relegated to a secondary role as the letter continues: "If in the delicate Morocco negotiations [I had not] been able to treat you with absolute frankness and confidence . . . no good result could possibly have been obtained." It was, then, Roosevelt who obtained the good result, Jusserand who contributed. The facts, examined

impartially, bear out the second construction. Undoubtedly
it was Roosevelt's intercession that rescued the Franco-German negotiations, inducing France to yield to Germany's
threatening importunities and evolving the formula that resolved the agenda impasse.

The evidence on the question of war and peace in 1905 is
less clear. There was a strong war party in Germany, in which
were active Friedrich von Holstein (whose brain-child the
attack on the Mediterranean alliance seems to have been)
and elements in the General Staff. Count von Schlieffen,
chief of the General Staff and author of the "Schlieffen
plan" for war in the west, believed the "present moment
favorable." But while the German Army was ready to try
conclusions with France, the Kaiser, Admiral von Tirpitz,
and the naval party approached the matter with less confidence.

It could not have escaped the notice of the German navalists that Sir John Fisher, First Sea Lord, had recently
concentrated new battle strength in the North Sea. The
Anglo-American understanding, confirmed anew after the
second Venezuelan crisis, had enabled him to withdraw his
forces from the American seas. The British North American
squadron was now based in England, visiting the Dominion
of Canada, the Caribbean, and the American offshore possessions only once a year "to show the flag." Furthermore,
the Anglo-Japanese Alliance had freed Britain's hands in the
Far East to some extent. Under the Mediterranean Pact also
the home fleet had benefited, the decline of Anglo-French
rivalry in that sea making it possible to reduce the fleet based
there. Thanks to the Balfour-Lansdowne "diplomatic revolution," which was rapidly obliterating "splendid isolation,"
and to Fisher's bold strategic dispositions, the British fleet
ready for action in the North Sea was overwhelmingly superior to anything Tirpitz could bring to bear.

During the interminable negotiations leading up to the
Algeciras Conference the Kaiser and Tirpitz gave Roosevelt
to understand that they had supreme faith in a naval victory.
It was during this period that the German theoreticians

worked out an optimistic doctrine of German tactical ascendancy. Although the British fleet outmatched the German in
tonnage and other elements of size, it was held that the
British command personnel had declined from the great days
of Drake, Hood, and Nelson. German navalists maintained
that German naval wits were sharper, and hence would prevail in sea warfare with the decadent British. These suppo-
sitions scarcely reached the dignity of discussion in British
naval circles. Roosevelt, always acute in matters of sea power,
gave little weight to the German assertions, writing the
Kaiser in June, 1905, in a warning vein: "Without mention-
ing the certain loss of your colonies and your fleet, which
England will bring about, suppose that you triumph over
France . . . the addition to your State of a new French province would only increase the number of your enemies within
your frontiers: it would be like a poison to you."

In England there were signs that war at the existing naval
ratios might not be unwelcome. Writers in the *Army and
Navy Gazette* and *Vanity Fair* spoke approvingly of a "preventive war." Privately, navy officers wondered if the German Navy should not be "Copenhagened," that is, destroyed
as was that of the Danes by Nelson in 1801 as a preventive
measure. But when Admiral C. C. F. Fitzgerald published
such sentiments in a service journal, Fisher called it a "mischievous and unpatriotic act." Fitzgerald nevertheless escaped official rebuke. Of a lay writer who gave vent to like
opinions, Balfour said he "should be hanged."

Arthur Lee (Roosevelt's "trump") was a Civil Lord of the
Admiralty. In a routine speech delivered to his parliamentary
constituency at Eastleigh, Colonel Lee spoke with satisfaction
of the readiness of the fleet, saying that "if war should unhappily be declared, the British Navy will get its blow in
first, before the other side had time even to read in the papers
that war had been declared." Lee's words struck instant fire
in Berlin. The Kaiser and the *Berliner Tageblatt* construed
them identically as a "threat of war." The Emperor vainly
demanded of Sir Frank Lascelles, the British Ambassador,
that the Government discipline the "corsair" Lee on penalty

of a "storm" in the German press and a new and "colossal
program" of naval construction.

Chancellor von Bülow, to whom the British were "over-
mighty Spartans" whose downfall must be accomplished by
patience and guile, sought to persuade Roosevelt, via Sternberg, that the British plotted destruction of the German
fleet "for reasons affecting [their] Far Eastern policy." As
Bülow presented the matter, "if the German fleet was out
of the way, America could do nothing to oppose the partition
of China." The President doubted that the German fleet
could be regarded as a disinterested champion of the Open
Door in China. This appeal to American solicitude for China
came on June 10, 1905, an aspect of the "shock diplomacy"
then being employed on Roosevelt that was obviously based
on a belief that the United States Government feared and
suspected the British. Such was not the case.

On balance, in 1905 the British seem to have been better
prepared to fight at sea than were the Germans. Psychologically, the British were readier than they would be in 1914.
Germany's fleet ranked second in 1905, but it was a far second, and the Anglo-French naval strength combined would
have rendered a sea conflict hopeless for Germany from the
start. On land the Germans had, no doubt, a corresponding
advantage over the Anglo-French coalition, with the French
forces enfeebled, French morale at one of its periodically
low ebbs, and the British Army, as usual, scattered over the
empire and weak. The French, moreover, would have been
deprived in 1905 of Russia's full assistance, and in 1914 the
diversion created by the Czar's vast if poorly equipped armies
in the East saved Paris. To the extent that the intervening
years allowed for some military recovery in Russia the English and French were better off in 1914 than they had been
in 1905.

Whether Roosevelt's intercessions actually averted war in
the earlier year, the central fact—for our purposes—remains
that an American President was willing to accept a certain
international responsibility. Roosevelt was a vigorous nationalist, suspicious of rigid commitments abroad. His

policies were improvised and often based on superficial information, his zest for diplomacy seemed boyish and irresponsible—yet he correctly reasoned that the United States could not escape altogether the obligations of its power and wealth. The thought is, of course, purely conjectural, but one cannot avoid speculating on what the probable course of events might have been in 1914 had there been in the White House a daring nationalist instead of an indecisive internationalist.

A little more than two weeks after the Powers had agreed to meet at Algeciras, the Kaiser attacked France diplomatically through her other ally. Hopeful of separating England and France at the conference, he attempted a prior severance of France and Russia at Björkö, an island in the Gulf of Finland where the yachts of the Emperors met by prearrangement. William and Nicholas met as "simple tourists." On the first evening the German handed his cousin the proposed treaty, which had been drawn so secretly that only William and Bülow knew of its existence.

The Emperors, sitting in a salon on the Czar's *Polar Star,* discussed the treaty alone, first putting down their kinsman Edward VII as the "greatest mischief-maker and most dangerous and deceptive intriguer in the world." Slow-witted and dazed though he was by the unaccountable blows of fate in the Far East, Nicholas nevertheless was saved from his dazzling companion. The treaty as drafted bound each Power to go to the aid of the other if attacked, but somehow the clause "in Europe" had been inserted into the pledge. William failed to see the materiality of the reservation, which he himself accepted responsibility for, to Bülow's amazement. "This," he remarked as he pocketed his signed copy, "should cool down British self-assertiveness and impertinence. It is God who has willed it!"

The treaty as amended, however, fell short of Germany's objectives respecting the British. The Germans and the Russians were linked in Europe but not in the Middle and Far East. Back in Berlin, Bülow informed the Kaiser that the reservation made the treaty "valueless," threatening to resign.

William begged the Chancellor to stand by, pleading that his departure would throw his sovereign into a breakdown, during which anything, including self-destruction, might occur. Bülow remained. In October Count Lamsdorff, the Russian Foreign Minister, persuaded the Czar that he had been disloyal to his ally France. The Czar thereupon asked William to amend the covenant, excluding France from its provisions. The Kaiser stiffly declined, replying that "what was signed was signed, and God was our witness." The treaty, unratified, perished of inanition.

9

At Algeciras, Germany's diplomatic luck was no better. It was early apparent that the Reich was all but isolated, being able to count only on Austria among the Powers. In the sole test vote of the conference France mustered ten votes, Germany only three. Russia, represented by Cassini, generally supported her ally. The British, bound by a generalized loyalty as well as Article IX of the Mediterranean Pact, backed the French. That article pledged mutual diplomatic support in maintaining the North African position of each Power. Edward VII, indicating British solidarity, bade the French Ambassador "tell us what you wish on each point and we shall support you to the letter." A Liberal Ministry under Herbert Henry Asquith had won a heavy majority in the House of Commons in January, 1906, and the Prime Minister and Sir Edward Grey, the new Foreign Secretary, were no less Francophile than Balfour and Lansdowne. Sir Arthur Nicolson, veteran diplomatist and the British delegate to Algeciras, had explicit instructions to accept the French representations. For his own guidance Sir Edward Grey prepared a private memorandum on England's position vis-à-vis war if it should come over Morocco, pointing out the penalties that would fall upon his country should it leave France in the lurch. He wrote that in such an event: "The United States would despise us, Russia [Downing Street was at the moment contemplating an Anglo-Russian entente] would not think it worth while to make friendly arrangements with us about Asia; Japan would prepare to re-insure herself elsewhere, and we should be left without a friend, or the power of making a friend."

As for the other English-speaking Power, White had instructions to stand with France. In July, 1905, the experienced, witty, and conscientious Hay had laid down his earthly cares. Elihu Root succeeded him. Root, calling White's attention to a State Department suspicion that Samuel Gummere, the Minister to Morocco and White's associate at Algeciras, was pro-German, cautioned the senior delegate: "This, if true, must not be allowed to throw us over into even apparent antagonism to the Anglo-French alliance, or to make us a means to breaking that up. It is useful to us, as well as agreeable."

The Secretary of State related these instructions to Jusserand, adding that the American delegate had been told to stand with the "liberal nations," and "you can imagine whether he will conform with pleasure to such instructions." Root, usually sharper in his definitions than Roosevelt, understood that at Algeciras the United States was supporting a complex of which it was a part.

The chief issue at the conference arose over the question of who should police Morocco. The French regarded this job as falling logically to them. Germany sought to weaken French control by providing for a neutral force, with inspectors and officers chosen from Switzerland, the Netherlands, or another small, disinterested state. France conceded only that the Spanish should police Spanish Morocco, the commanding officers of the French and Spanish forces reporting nominally to the Sultan. The conference hung for weeks on that point, deadlocked, with the delegates irritated, with no categorical threat of war but with its possibility always latent. In mid-February Roosevelt asked White to submit a "fair" solution, White responding with a three-part formula: (1) the police to be under the nominal authority of the Sultan, (2) officers and noncommissioned personnel to be French in French Morocco, Spanish in Spanish Morocco, (3) the Inspector General to make his yearly report to the

Italian Government as well as the Sultan. Italy's presence
in the latter capacity gave an international flavor to the
arrangements and brought the third Mediterranean Power
into the picture. This was, of course, substantially the
French position.

Roosevelt accepted White's program with unimportant
modifications, transmitting it to the Kaiser. There ensued
another spirited exchange of dispatches between the Kaiser
and the President through Sternberg. In effect, the decision
was being tranferred from Algeciras to Berlin and Washington. Roosevelt clung to the White proposal immovably.
Meanwhile his attitude and his utterances were cabled to
White, who relayed them to the chief French delegate,
Amédée Revoil, who, in receipt of similar word from
Jusserand via Paris, rejected any compromise, giving ground
here and there only in detail.

On March 7, 1906, the President informed his "excellent
friend" William II that he would ask "no more concessions
from France." Soon thereafter the Austrians introduced an
alternative, under which France should police four ports,
Spain three, and Casablanca be placed under a neutral
officer also serving as Inspector General. German interests,
it will be recalled, were centered at Casablanca. The British,
fatigued and willing to give and take, advised France to
yield, as did Cassini. Whereupon the Germans allowed the
press to know of their Anglo-Russian triumph, predicting
early acceptance of the Austrian plan. Sir Arthur Nicolson
thought the matter settled, telegraphing Grey that the "Germans have been wonderfully conciliatory." Grey replied
that "Germany has conceded the substance and it would be
too bad if France sacrificed the substance to the shadow."

However, the friendly Powers were reckoning without
Roosevelt. In remote Washington there would be no yielding to expediency. By now the President had come to regard
the White formula as the "American plan." The Austrian
proposal he deemed "absurd"; to him it smacked of the
very spheres of influence which the Kaiser had seemed at
the outset so bent on avoiding. It is possible that Roosevelt

had taken the German appeals to the Open Door seriously. "The proposition I suggest is better and safer and the only one I can support," Roosevelt told the Kaiser. Jusserand saw a copy of this note and hurried off a tip to Revoil, who stood pat. As a clincher, the President reminded William of his promise to accept the President's judgment on any issue. Jocosely, he hinted to Sternberg that he might publish the Algeciras correspondence, wherein the Kaiser had been quite candid. In his search for a quid pro quo the Kaiser, heartily sick of what he soon was to dub "that idiotic conference," asked the President to receive at the White House a delegation of Old German Warriors, making the reception the occasion of a tribute to William's statesmanship. Roosevelt agreed.

The German delegates were instructed on March 21 to withdraw their opposition to the "American plan." "The immediate removal of all misunderstanding is of far more importance to Germany than the whole Moroccan affair," said the Emperor. Upon receipt of word that agreement had been reached on all points, he telegraphed "Bravo" to his representatives. White advised the German Ambassador at Rome of his belief that "the victor at Algeciras was England." On the margin of this dispatch William scribbled: "Correct!" Bülow was made a prince, Holstein was forced to resign. His going was taken as a sign that he bore the blame for the failure over Morocco. In Europe generally it was said that "Germany had her conference but France had Morocco."

Anglo-French understanding, having withstood its first external assault, emerged from the Moroccan crisis immeasurably strengthened. Grey had sanctioned conversations between the French military attachés and the English General Staff. Naval consultations followed. The military plans for 1914 were in the making. Soon Russia was to be added to the Anglo-French Entente, opposing to Bismarck's Triple Alliance the new Triple Entente. Another by-product of Algeciras was the realization that where Britain was in-

volved Italy could not be considered a reliable member of
the Triple Alliance.

Roosevelt, eulogizing the Kaiser before the Old German
Warriors, could reflect on no direct gains for his country.
He had demonstrated for the world to read the solidarity
of the great Atlantic Powers vis-à-vis Central Europe, but it
seems unlikely that he saw his activities in such terms. The
President narrowed his interest to support of the French—
as did the English also, for that matter. Grey apprehended
Roosevelt's part only dimly, writing him on December 2,
1906, that it "was felt all through the Algeciras conference
that American influence was not being used against France
and us."

In 1910, when Grey entertained Roosevelt in England
on his way home from the African big-game hunt, the Foreign Secretary heard for the first time of the President's
collaboration with Jusserand in circumventing the Germans.
Such a state of ignorance testified both to the unwisdom
of keeping Ambassador Durand in Washington and to the
fallibility of the English intelligence service. Nor was Sir
Arthur Nicolson better advised. In Harold Nicolson's biography of his father, *Portrait of a Diplomatist,* there is no
indication that the British delegate was aware of the powerful influence placed at the disposal of the English interest.
The Nicolson version was, it is fair to say, incidental to
biography, and the more recent French sources were not
open to the author.

In reality, the Britsh half suspected Roosevelt of being
under the Kaiser's sway as to the Moroccan matter. Whitelaw Reid wrote the President from London in this vein
on June 19, ten weeks after the conference adjourned, that
"the Emperor's assiduous efforts to cultivate the most intimate relations with you have attracted the attention of all
the chancelleries in Europe," adding that "a common comment on it is that the Emperor overdoes his lovemaking as
he does his diplomacy, with a certain German confidence
in the value of brute vigor in either pursuit."

Roosevelt replied in high spirits, pointing out that while

he had handled the Kaiser suavely and pleasantly in the Algeciras matter, "at the end I stood him on his head with great decision." He continued: "As for Germany, I really treat them much more cavalierly than I do England, and I am immensely amused at the European theory (which cannot, however, be the theory of the French Government) that I am taken in by the Kaiser. I am very polite to him, but I am ready at an instant's notice to hold my own."

It remained for Root to identify a tangible gain obtained at Algeciras. The Germans had been denied control over an Atlantic seaport, Casablanca. It had been understood at the conference that the Austrian proposal for the neutralization of that port included a German aspiration that it be assigned to a state within the German sphere in Europe. The American Secretary of State, in a casual chat with Durand, remarked that Great Britain had not "seemed to mind" having Germany for an Atlantic neighbor established near Gibraltar, and that the situation really had been "saved" by the President.

It was, however, the incisive, worldly, and far-reaching understanding of Henry Adams that best apprehended America's underlying stake in the Moroccan crisis. Writing a friend in late January, 1906, at a time when it appeared the conference might adjourn in disagreement, Adams held: "We have got to support France against Germany and fortify the Atlantic System beyond attack; for if Germany breaks down England or France, she becomes the center of a military world, and we are lost." The historian saw the conflict as irrepressible. "The course of concentration," he went on, "must be decided by force—whether military or industrial matters not much to the end." By 1906 Adams had lost faith that Germany could be attached to the Atlantic world.

10

The year 1906 had its own significance in terms of American sea power. Mahan obtained a belated and routine recognition from his Government, being promoted Rear

Admiral as the time came for his retirement. By a pertinent coincidence, in that same year Jane's *Fighting Ships,* the naval record, first ranked the United States Navy second to the British. The German Navy was third by a close margin. Only sixteen years had passed since the Secretary of the Navy and the Naval Policy Board had sensationally transferred Mahan's "fighting-force" concept from the lecture room and the printed page to the field of national policy. That year likewise saw a controversy between Mahan and Roosevelt over the freedom of the seas, a historic phrase infrequently defined and of changing content.

In 1906 freedom of the seas meant the immunity of private property, ship and cargo, both belligerent and neutral, from seizure in time of war. A rallying cry for pacifists, the phrase was being used as a lever toward restricting war. It provided, as then understood, a revolutionary alteration in the rules of war at sea. The hope of the pacifists was to minimize the scope of navies and extinguish the blockade. Roosevelt, whose inconsistencies shone as magnificently as his self-assurance, had been attracted by the noble implications of the phrase, finding it easy to embrace the new doctrine while at the same time advocating a larger navy.

The Czar had called the Second Hague Conference to meet in 1907, and Grey and Lord Haldane, then Secretary for War, had asked Roosevelt to use his good offices with the Kaiser toward naval limitation, a request which the President felt might tax his influence with his friend at Potsdam. "That I can work with France and England I have no doubt," he wrote White. Of Germany he had doubts. He felt it would be a mistake for the "free peoples" to do anything that might weaken their force against "military despotism and military barbarism."

Mahan, venturing his advice on the sea-power problems likely to be raised at The Hague, exemplified that view. Opposing freedom of the seas, the Admiral cited German hostility toward the "English-speaking communities," pointed out what a boon an unmolested seaborne trade would be to Germany in wartime, and declared that exemption from blockade would "remove the strongest hook in the jaw of Germany that the English-speaking people have—a principal gage for peace." Referring to American experience, Mahan thought it possible that "our Government, a century ago, would have signed away the right of commercial blockade, which so helped us in the Civil War." In Napoleonic times the infant American states were demanding the right to send their merchant vessels wherever they chose. In the Civil War the shoe was on the other foot, the Federal forces using the blockade for slow strangulation of the economy of the Confederacy. Again in 1898 the United States applied the law of blockade. On both occasions neutral rights were what the blockading authorities said them to be.

The Admiral closed on a dark note. The "political future" to him was "without form and void" in both the Atlantic and the Pacific worlds. "We will have to walk very warily," said Mahan, "in matters affecting our future ability to employ our national force." Impressed by Mahan's hostage argument and his appeal to historic naval policies, Root asked the Navy Department for an opinion from the General Board of the Navy, at the same time begging Roosevelt to make a most thoughtful study of the whole situation before instructing our delegates to The Hague. The General Board summed up its comprehensive report with the assertion: "Should private property at sea be immune in time of war, this great advantage would be lost to Great Britain, as well as to the United States, and the immense assistance we might expect to receive from Great Britain would be tremendously decreased."

The President replied coolly to Mahan, noting a contemporary "tendency to protect private property on sea and on land," and observing with what seemed a hint of reproof that "earlier races killed or enslaved every private citizen of a hostile nation whom they could get at or destroy and took his property as a matter of course." At The Hague the American delegation, making common cause with the gratified Germans, spoke, argued, and lobbied for freedom of the seas. They failed, however, to seek its land-war equivalent, which would forbid armies to attack unfortified places, seize or destroy factories, railroads, power plants, or homes, or otherwise disturb civilians and private property. America and England, insular Powers, were dependent on the seas for defense. Germany was not. For once Roosevelt was veering from the line of British interest. In so doing he harmed American interest as well, the effect of his stand being to weaken the "free peoples" as against the Powers he described as despotic and barbarous. Fortunately for the Sea Powers, the conference did not follow the lead of Roosevelt and the Germans.

Unlike Roosevelt, the United States Navy in 1906 supported the solidarity of the English-speaking Powers. In the report of the General Board, England was identified as the friend, Germany as the enemy—a supposition reminiscent of Dewey's oracular statement when interviewed at Trieste in 1899 on his return journey from Manila that "our next war would be with Germany." The board held that the "welfare of the United States, and its immunity from entanglements with other powers, is greatly strengthened by strong ties of friendship and by unanimity of action with Great Britain." As for Germany, the board had no doubt that when her fleet was considered "ready" she would "test the Monroe Doctrine by annexation or a protectorate" on this side of the water, "many things" having indicated that "she has her eye on localities in the West Indies, on the shores of the Caribbean, and in parts of South America."

The General Board of the United States Navy anticipated war with Germany. It expected, in that event, at least the "passive friendship of England."

VII. The First Battle of the Atlantic

WHEN WAR CAME in 1914, the expectations of the General Board were reversed. It found England, not America, hoping for "passive friendship" against the mightiest Continental Power. The forereaching shadows of that war, a conflict which thoughtful men suspected would bring the first general upheaval in the West since Napoleon, were visible in 1910, coloring the thought of the Atlantic world. In May Theodore Roosevelt, accepting the Nobel Peace Prize at Christiania for "ending" the Russo-Japanese War, advocated establishment of a "league of peace" employing force "if necessary." Such a benevolent concert of the Powers Roosevelt felt would be a "master stroke." Only a week later, after reviewing with the Kaiser the Potsdam Guards, the former President left Germany with the distinct impression, as he wrote President Taft, that when war came the Germans would "inevitably" violate the neutrality of Belgium. Thus within one week were the hopes of peace and the anticipation of war dramatized in Roosevelt's experience.

In 1910 Admiral Mahan took a grimly practical view of the prospects. Concerned for the security of the Atlantic System, he looked ahead to America's stake in any general war. The clatter of the rival riveters in the shipyards on the Elbe and along the Clyde suggested that the next war was to be fought in part on the Atlantic. In that case—the British Navy being to Mahan the "sole military force anywhere in the world superior to anything that Germany can as yet bring into action"—it behooved the United States to strengthen its ties with the British Empire.

Of the prophets of war in 1910, Admiral Sir John Fisher was among the most explicit, Commodore William S. Sims, U.S.N., the most impulsive, and Spring-Rice as despairing as any. From the backwater of Stockholm, where the diplomat awaited promotion to Washington, he gloomily reported to American friends the advance of the "Red Man" on Europe. Fisher, noting that the Kiel Canal would be enlarged to admit dreadnoughts by the summer of 1914, specified that season as the one in which Germany would strike for command of the seas. At a Guildhall banquet Sims promised that if and when England was menaced by a Continental force she could "rely upon the last ship, the last dollar, the last man and the last drop of blood of her kindred beyond the seas." Seven years after that Admiral Sims would be commanding a World War fleet in European waters, but at the moment President Taft thought it well to reprimand such farfetched imprudence. Sims's comradely sentiments had graveled the German press, in America and in Germany; and the Anglophobes, their patriotic sensibilities affronted, were demanding his court-martial.

The rising sense of apprehension produced in 1910 an impressive peace movement. As if responding to a subconscious desire for the warding-off of destruction, numerous societies for the discouragement of war sprang up in England and America. Roosevelt's speech at Christiania gave impetus to the movement, a drive not sustained by Roosevelt himself. Taft was convinced that Theodore, for all his peacemaking, was "obsessed with his love of war and its glory." The President, midway of his ill-starred term, lacked the imagination, the daring, or the aptitude to "play a great part," his foreign relations being entrusted to the inexpert and conventional Philander C. Knox.

Taft, however, entered into the peace cause wholeheartedly. It was his pacific labors, his negotiation of arbitration treaties with England and France—Germany characteristically declining—that inspired Carnegie (Mark Twain's "St. Andrew") to endow peace with $10,000,000 in 1910. "Your noble . . . leadership amongst rulers," the flushed little

Utopian wrote Taft, "prompted me to create the fund." Carnegie "saw clearly that peace was within our grasp because the other branch of our race was ready to follow you." Instructing the trustees of the Carnegie Endowment for International Peace and its first president, Elihu Root, the donor declared the day at hand for war to be "discarded as disgraceful to civilized man."

In later years, certain friends of Theodore Roosevelt were to assign him prior rights to the League of Nations concept because of his Christiania address. A clearer title ran to the movement begun in February, 1910, by Theodore Marburg, a wealthy Baltimore peace reformer and self-styled "publicist." Marburg launched his American Society for the Judicial Settlement of International Disputes with the endorsement of Taft and Woodrow Wilson, then president of Princeton University and soon to be Governor of New Jersey. This society actively supported Taft's unfruitful endeavors toward international arbitration (the isolationist minority in the Senate shredded the treaties with England and France beyond hope of ratification) and Taft returned the compliment by taking leadership in Marburg's enterprise when in 1915 it was converted into the League to Enforce Peace. The League to Enforce Peace, sponsored also by John Hays Hammond, Hamilton Holt, and President A. Lawrence Lowell of Harvard, gained influential adherents and helped prepare a receptive public opinion for Wilson's crusade, although the First World War President was to make little use of Marburg's mechanism or its leaders.

A note of optimism so unrealistic as to approach frivolity ran through much of the peace fervor of that year. In June Congress by joint resolution authorized a Peace Commission of five members to consider means for reducing land armaments and combining the "navies of the world" into "an international force for the preservation of universal peace." Theodore Roosevelt refused appointment as chairman, all the Foreign Offices sounded on the matter except Britain's returned definitely discouraging answers, and the Administration allowed the enterprise to drop from sight. Norman

Angell proved in his enormously popular book *The Great Illusion* that a general war was impossible because too costly. David Starr Jordan was equally certain that "great international wars are already practically at an end."

The movement bathed pulpit, platform, and press in a moral glow. The magazines, typically Walter Hines Page's *World's Work,* published "universal peace numbers" containing large assortments of wishful prose. Such escapist literature worked mischief, blinding Americans to the realities, seeming to free them from the obligation to understand the world relationships of their country. By stressing the abstract wickedness of organized human slaughter and the pitiful role of the individual caught in its toils, the subjective wing of the peace movement likewise impaired the American will to maintain this country's status in a world where war was still a firmly entrenched instrument of national policy.

Mahan's clear, unemotional voice rose above the chorus of the "peace cranks" (Taft's words) as he bade the United States realize that it could "no longer stand apart" from the forces moving toward conflict. Dealing in the stark terms of strategy and power, he found the time at hand for this country to choose its orientation consciously, not waiting, as in the Napoleonic Wars, until exasperation blurred judgment. In any general war Mahan assumed that the United States would be forced to bear a part, as it had been in the Napoleonic struggle.

In 1812, although the United States was young, weak, torn by faction and by section, its frigates fought gallantly if ineffectually for the freedom of the seas and to impose respect for the flag on the Atlantic and in the Caribbean. The enemy then was England, but it was a hard choice for President Madison, a Virginian, a Princetonian, angular, conscientious, and iron-willed. Both the English and Napoleon were treating America with contempt. Inferior at sea, the "monster Bonaparte" hastily burned American merchantmen to the water line wherever he found their destruction to his liking. The British, having command of the seas and hence more time and assurance, hauled American ships into prize courts.

As the Emperor's star began to wane Madison threw in his lot with him, obtaining a declaration of war as Napoleon rode for Moscow. By an ironical circumstance it was the day after the English Parliament had repealed its provocative Orders in Council.

A century later Mahan in his book *The Interest of America in International Conditions* (1910) was portraying the strategical approximation of Anglo-American relations, patiently generalizing that

in the horoscope of every nation there is usually one other power, accordant relations with which are of primary importance. . . . Having in view not the British Isles only, but the other constituent parts of the empire, Australia, Canada, New Zealand —all with Pacific frontiers and cherishing political incentives commonly with our Pacific States—and especially in view of the British Navy, there is strong reason to believe that international considerations should assign to the British Empire this prominent place in the understanding of America.

Mahan thought we might prefer the British Empire as our partner because of its "far more liberal institutions and consequently weaker organization of force," because also, "being replete to satiety with colonial possessions, [it] has no adequate stimulus to aggression, least of all against the United States." As always, the Admiral placed his argument on solid ground. His conclusion rested upon a "cool calculation of possibilities, an estimate of balances, a recognition that the United States can no longer . . . proceed safely without a . . . formulated concept of the particular, as well as the general, relationship amongst States."

The contrasted doctrines of the Mahan and Marburg schools, nationalist and internationalist, were to dominate foreign policy during the eight years of the Wilson Administration. First Mahan, in the seventeen months from Wilson's first inauguration in 1913 to the outbreak of the First World War in 1914. Then Marburg, as Wilson, Spring-Rice's "hardened saint," sought to equip himself for the role of *arbiter mundi* by adopting a judicial attitude toward the belligerents. Then in April, 1917, when Wilson was compelled by clear national interest to abandon his detachment, the two streams of policy merged for a time. Mahan's limited, rational program gave way again at the Armistice of 1918 to the powerful dream of a world state organized to preserve the status quo.

2

Not since the heyday of the "McKinley-Salisbury alliance" had Anglo-American relations been so felicitous as in the first phase of the Wilson term. The President stood nearer to Britain in actual parentage than most of his predecessors, including Washington, his mother having been born in England. In the Presbyterian manse of his Virginia boyhood British cultural influences ran strong and deep. The Lake poets, especially Wordsworth, touched tender chords in Wilson (Spring-Rice noted that his eyes grew misty as he quoted Wordsworth), and on his yearly holidays abroad he preferred England, regarding the rest of Europe as somehow alien. Likewise drawn sentimentally to England were the President's most creative coadjutors in foreign affairs: Colonel Edward M. House, the suave Texan with the gift for benign intrigue, and Walter Hines Page, the ardent, impressionable journalist and publisher.

Bryan, who brought to the State Department the worthy talents of a county chairman, a popular evangelist, and a temperance lecturer, maintained toward England a detached and suspicious attitude. His cultural ties ran nowhere but to Nebraska—the Nebraska of the square frame farmhouse, the King James version, and the mail-order catalogue. Bryan scarcely counted as a policy-maker. The President was preeminently his own Foreign Minister. Of the three men who most intimately shaped policy—Wilson, House, and Page—the President, one gathers in retrospect, had less of cognate background than the others, less facility at understanding the racial, economic, and strategic elements flowing into the relationships of the Powers. Wilson was disposed, moreover, to equate international problems to a transcendental scale of values—the good, the true, the beautiful—when not taking refuge behind a professorial cynicism.

Both House and Page, essentially more sophisticated than their chief, were fascinated by power problems. In his apocalyptic novel *Philip Dru, Administrator,* published anonymously in 1912, House exhibited that bent elaborately. His pre-Fascist hero seized the state by revolution, imposed a reformist, single-tax regime, a sort of kindly totalitarianism, and organized a league of the Western Powers. House had insinuating gifts for mediation and a sure skill at manipulating the state mechanism. As for Page, he had gone to school directly to Mahan, publishing the historian's measured essays on national destiny regularly for twenty years before he was plunged into the heart of world affairs by becoming Ambassador to London in 1913.

The case of Page deserves particular attention. Wilson told Taft in 1917; "Page is really an Englishman." A favorite quip of the Anglophobic isolationists in the disillusioned postwar years was that Page had been the "best American Ambassador England ever had." In those years Page became the rhetorical butt of those who believed we had been gulled into the war by the Foreign Office, Wall Street bankers, and English propagandists. The objective fact seems to be that Page believed, as implicitly as John Hay, Henry Adams, Mahan, or Carnegie, in the virtue of the Anglo-American tie, that he was a nationalist—in contrast to Wilson's internationalism, House's opportunism—and a sound American seeing a dynamic future in terms of an English-speaking world bloc, with America calling the turn.

In the months before the war dulled his interest in power speculations Page's letters from London demonstrated his zest for the cause of Anglo-American hegemony. To House he wrote late in 1913 that the "English-speaking peoples now rule the world in all essential facts. . . . Only the British lands and the United States have secure liberty. They also have the most treasure, the best fighters, the most land, the most ships—the future in fact." Even more exuberantly, the Ambassador wrote David F. Houston, the Secretary of Agriculture: "England and the whole English world are ours, if we have the courtesy to take them—fleet, trade and all; and we go on pretending we are afraid of entangling alliances. We're in the game. There's no use letting a few wild Irishmen or cocky Germans scare us. We need courtesy and frankness, and the destiny of the world will be in our hands."

In those first months Page was sure there was "more enthuiasm for the United States here, by far, than for England in the United States." He wrote the President that the English would "hold fast to our favor for reasons of prudence as well as for reasons of kinship. And whenever we choose to assume leadership of the world, they'll grant it—gradually—and follow loyally. They cannot become Frenchmen and they dislike the Germans. They must keep in our boat, for safety as well as comfort."

Page's fault, if fault he had, seems to have been that his head whirled too dizzily with notions of American ascendancy in a world of power arrangements that aroused only the distrust of his less adventurous countrymen. In 1898, as editor of the *Atlantic* Page startled the thin-blooded anti-imperialists of Back Bay by flaunting the American flag in colors on the austere cover of that magazine. Again in 1913 he was being the dilettante imperialist. Twice Page's outspoken Anglophilia stirred angry outcries in the Senate, the German press, and the Hibernian lodge halls. Each time the President publicly supported him without reproof.

Wilson inherited from Taft two issues disturbing to Anglo-Amercian relations. One, the question of the Mexican presidential succession, arose within the last month of the Taft Administration. In February of 1913 Victoriano Huerta, a general called to Mexico City to protect President Francisco Madero, accomplished or permitted his murder instead. The assassination brought on widespread disorders, imperiling the large American population in Mexico. Besieged by appeals for protection, Taft withheld it, casually advising Americans to quit Mexico, their livelihoods, and their investments.

So matters stood when Wilson took the inaugural oath. The incoming President projected Taft's negative, hands-off policy into one of active intervention. He declined to recognize Huerta and erected his refusal into a general policy of withholding American recognition from any regime in Latin-America "founded on violence." With his customary readiness to lapse into elevated generalization, the President hailed his policy as "closing one chapter in the history of the world and opening another of unimaginable significance."

Taft's part had not been merely passive in the other situation, which dealt with discriminations in Panama Canal tolls. In 1912 Taft signed a bill exempting American coastwise shipping from tolls when the canal should be finished in 1914, justifying on debatable legal grounds what the British called a breach of the Hay-Pauncefote Treaty. The President had not minced words about this delicate international question, reminding the British that "we own the canal. It was our money that built it."

The British, standing on what they conceived to be their treaty rights, protested with all vigor. Whitelaw Reid, an exemplary Ambassador who in Sir Edward Grey's phrase had "lived as a friend amongst us," reported that not in all his time in London had the United States endured such a "bad press." Representative of English journalistic opinion, the *Outlook* characterized the tolls act as "barefaced robbery," to say nothing of "grand larceny." In diplomatic phraseology the Foreign Secretary allowed the Ambassador to know that the British Government believed that the United States Government had welshed on a solemn undertaking.

On this side of the Atlantic a strong group in the President's party, including Root and Lodge, opposed discrimination. Their words carried weight because both had been in John Hay's confidence when he negotiated the treaty by which Britain retired from her joint interest in an isthmian canal. The issue, which was of course political and diplomatic, not legal, was restricted by the party upholding discrimination to an interpretation of the clause guaranteeing equal treatment, in tolls and otherwise, to the merchant shipping of "all nations." Taft and his advisers construed the words to mean "all other nations," holding with Roosevelt during his 1912 campaign as a Progressive candidate for the Presidency that we had a "perfect right to permit our coast-wise traffic . . . to pass through the canal on any terms we choose, and I personally think that no toll should be charged on such traffic."

The remission was, of course, a concealed subsidy, working to the minor disadvantage of the British and other shipping interests. Wilson too had guardedly favored discrimination in his 1912 campaign. His mind was open, however, and strong doubts arose when in January, 1913, his close friend Dr. John Latané of Johns Hopkins University published a scholarly treatise in the *American Journal of International Law* declaring the tolls act an indisputable infraction of the Hay-Pauncefote Treaty. Soon Wilson agreed that the tolls act violated our plighted word, a change of front to which we shall return.

On inauguration day, 1913, the British had us constructively in the wrong in a question related to that familiar bone of contention, the canal, but before long the British Government was to transgress the Wilson doctrine of nonrecognition —evening the score. Page's first duty in London had been to explore the Mexican situation. He reported that Grey would follow the President's line. A month later the British recognized Huerta without notice to the United States, at once convincing the Administration that oil, personified by Lord Cowdray, was at the bottom of the reversal. Cowdray had a contract to supply the British Navy with Mexican oil. There seems no doubt that he had made his peace with the usurping President to avoid a default on the navy contract, persuading the Foreign Office to follow suit. In this country the Standard Oil interests, with large Mexican holdings, disapproved of Huerta, giving some color to the British retort that in Mexican oil it apparently mattered whose ox was gored.

Meanwhile, Grey compounded his offense, from the American point of view, by transferring to Mexico as Minister Lionel Carden, a stiff-necked, anti-American diplomat who had made himself persona non grata to the State Department while Minister to Cuba. The British Foreign Office, with what seems to have been a mixture of hauteur and loyalty to a zealous servant, had rejected the protests of the Taft Administration, and now Carden, knighted and promoted, gave an interview in New York on his way to his new post, endorsing Huerta and advising the President that the latter "knew nothing about Mexico." Arrived in Mexico City, Sir Lionel, who seems to have been scarcely a reconciling agent, talked freely to the press, bestowing his approval, and by implication London's, on Huerta. He presented his credentials on the day the President imprisoned all dissident members of the Mexican Congress and announced a rule by decree. The situation, exhibiting the British Foreign Office at its cynical worst, called for skillful diplomacy.

Page's task was twofold: first, to obtain an about-face in Mexico from the Asquith Ministry; second, to procure the removal of the obnoxious Sir Lionel. The British Minister had, among other things, organized a solid European front behind Huerta and against Wilson. Working with Page was the reputed Salisbury dictum that no dispute with America should be permitted to get out of hand. The precarious balance of power in Europe and the Anglo-German naval race likewise contributed to the prospects of British accommodation, as did the mollifying fact that the President now favored repeal of the tolls act.

In July, 1913, Colonel House, making the first of his pilgrimages to European chancelleries, asked Grey to avoid agitating the tolls question for fear of arousing the resistance of the Anglophobes, meanwhile putting his case in Wilson's hands. Page, with admirable persistence, was at the same time exerting steady pressure on Grey, on Asquith, on the influential Lord Chancellor Haldane, on the press, through certain leading editors, and even on Lord Cowdray. Himself an enthusiastic convert to the nonrecognition policy, Page earnestly sought to spread the light in England. His most eloquent homilies failed, however, to move the British to repentance until they became convinced that their intransi-

geance was hurtful to larger ends. In letters and dispatches of
the period Page roundly scolded the British for their insistence on sheer order in Mexico in preference to the Wilson policy. The Ministry, it is fair to say, was perplexed by
Wilson's unwillingness to back his moral intervention with
force, and by his abandonment of the American population
and interests in Mexico to the hazards of civil war and ban-
ditry. Plainly they thought the policy irresponsible, an impression confirmed when the President, asked by Sir William
Tyrrell in Washington for an outline of his principle, replied: "I am going to teach the South Americans to elect
good men to office."

Tyrrell, Grey's parliamentary secretary, visited Washington unofficially in the fall of 1913. It was given out that he
came to see his friend Sir Cecil Spring-Rice, who was ill. It
was Sir Cecil's misfortune that he reached the Washington
Embassy too late, his friendships with Roosevelt and Lodge
standing him in no stead, gaining him rather the suspicion of
White House circles. Tyrrell saw the President and Colonel
House and, whether as a result of the talks or not, Anglo-
American relations thereafter rapidly recovered their amiability. Soon Sir Lionel waited on Huerta at the head of the
European wing of the diplomatic corps, and advised him to
resign, as there would be no further European support. Carden was shifted to Brazil. At the Lord Mayor's banquet in
November Asquith denied there was any ground for believing that the Ministry had carried out a Mexican policy "deliberately opposed to the United States." In March, 1914,
Wilson asked Congress for repeal of the tolls act, saying: "We
are too big, too powerful, too self-respecting a nation to interpret with too strained or refined a reading the words of
our own promises just because we have power enough to read
them as we please."

The President expected only perfunctory opposition. He
was disappointed. The fight for repeal furnished the first
genuine test of his sway over Congress, and a vituperative debate raged in Senate and press. Wilson was deserted by numerous party leaders in the Senate, including James A. Reed

of Missouri, James K. Vardaman of Mississippi, and James A. O'Gorman of New York, voice of the Irish separatist junta in this country. To Wilson's aid, however, went allies from the other side of the aisle, such as Lodge, Root, the erudite Theodore E. Burton of Ohio, William S. Kenyon, and Porter J. McCumber. The opposition followed the time-tried pattern of arraigning English transgressions from the days of Clive and Lord North while neglecting the merits of the issue under debate. Petitions from the Irish-American societies flooded Congress, the German propagandists took a hand, the Hearst press twisted the lion's tail with practiced dexterity, and Wilson was accused, as McKinley and Roosevelt had been before him, of "truckling" to Great Britain, if not being actually hand in hand with King George.

When Wilson won, the Senate voting repeal 50 to 35, American prestige bounded above par in London. The Pages were at a ball at Buckingham Palace the night the news crossed the Atlantic. Page's biographer, Burton J. Hendrick, describes the acclaim bestowed upon the Ambassador by a procession of public men, adding that the "King and the Prime Minister were especially affected by this display of fair dealing in Washington." Wilson's high-minded leadership, Grey wrote Spring-Rice, contributed "something to the good of public life, for it helped to lift [it] to a higher plane and to strengthen its morale."

3

Tyrrell's visit revived the vision that had tantalized Mahan, Rhodes, Carnegie, Chamberlain, Hay, Henry Adams, Henry White, Olney, Bryce, and Harcourt. House wrote Page: "I told him [Tyrrell] that you and I had dreamed of a sympathetic alliance between the two countries and that it seemed to me that this dream might come true very quickly because of the President and Sir Edward Grey." To which Page replied: "Suppose there were . . . the tightest sort of an alliance, offensive and defensive, between all Britain, the colonies and all, and the United States—what would happen?

Anything we'd say would go, whether we should say, 'Come in out of the wet,' or 'Disarm.' That might be the beginning of a real world alliance and union to accomplish certain large results—disarmament, for instance, or arbitration—dozens of good things."

The President, his enthusiasm held in tighter check, wrote Page that he too longed "for an opportunity to do constructive work all along the line in our foreign relations, particularly with Great Britain and the Latin American States." Page propagandized zealously for Anglo-American accord, gaining as an adherent Cowdray, who had promised Grey to be good in Mexico and had surrendered an oil concession in Bolivia in token of repentance. "Whatever the United States and Great Britain agree on, the world must do," the oil Baron exclaimed, whereupon Page in reporting his views added his conviction that "these two Governments must enter a compact for peace and for gradual disarmament . . . then we can go about our business for (say) a hundred years."

Grey, a conciliatory nature-lover with a tinge of faint melancholy over the state of the world, humored Page's optimism. The Foreign Secretary and the Ambassador enjoyed an intimate personal understanding, based on similarity of tastes in the library and outdoors. Grey perhaps had a clearer view of the import of the Anglo-American aspiration as an attempt to freeze the status quo against the thrust of such virile peoples as the Germans, warlike, technically proficient, and wishing also to enjoy the fruits of empire and the command of the seas. Nor had the Foreign Secretary, hurt by the surge of Anglophobia over the tolls issue, any illusions about the obstacles to full concert. In his memoirs, published in 1925 under the title *Twenty-five Years,* Grey (then Viscount Grey of Fallodon) remarked on that "certain intimacy . . . of attraction and repulsion, which has made the relations between Britain and the United States at once more easy and more difficult, more cordial and more intractable than those between any two other countries."

It was during Tyrrell's visit also that a project took shape in Washington at once more definitive than the hope for alliance and larger in immediate scope. Colonel House, personally desirous of "playing a great part," eager to put the influence of the Western republic and its scholar-President to the test, gained Wilson's approval for a grand intervention in Europe, the first in a sequential chain leading to Versailles. Specifically, the plausible, soft-spoken little "Assistant President" and peripatetic Ambassador-at-large, proposed laying, if possible, a restraining hand on the naval race which at the moment was plunging Britain into a new spasm of alarm.

England had repeatedly sought Berlin's agreement to what in March, 1913, Winston Churchill, First Lord of the Admiralty, termed a "naval holiday." In 1912 Haldane (Page's "foxy Scot") made a genuine effort, going on an unofficial mission to Berlin, where he interviewed the Kaiser, Tirpitz, and the ranking figures in the civil Government. He found William evasive, Tirpitz frankly implacable against England. Coinciding with Tyrrell's American sojourn, in October, 1913, Asquith and Churchill renewed their attempt to conciliate the German navalists. Churchill brought the matter into the open in a speech at Manchester that aroused worldwide notice: "Now, we say to our great neighbor, Germany, 'If you will put off beginning your two ships for twelve months from the ordinary date when you would have begun them, we will put off beginning our four ships, in absolutely good faith, for exactly the same period.' "

The Prime Minister publicly approved the proposal. In reply the Germans coldly cited the ironclad nature of their Naval Law; the German Government could not depart from its schedule. The tone of the official and semiofficial German press was derisive. In answering the German repulse the British Government reaffirmed its policy of laying down two capital ships to Germany's one. Yet in January, 1914, David Lloyd George, Chancellor of the Exchequer, undertook on his own a mollifying gesture, implying in an interview the desirability of reducing the cost of the naval program. A burst of indignant protest arose both in England and across the Channel. Churchill hastened to Paris to soothe the fears of the French Allies, closely followed by Asquith, who pleaded that he was merely seeing his daughter off to the Riviera but who nevertheless found time to reassure the French Ministry. Matters seemed to be at an impasse.

In Washington Colonel House, canvassing the British case with Sir William, was lightheartedly proposing to move into this vortex of suspicion and dread. He accepted Tyrrell's representations that Britain's efforts to abate the sea-power rivalry had been sincerely wholehearted. Tyrrell offered to show him in London the Foreign Office file on the subject. To the President, House reported that England's position had been "entirely right." Tyrrell suggested that House, allowing the Germans to know that he was the "power behind the throne" in America, proceed directly to Berlin, there informing the Emperor confidentially that England and America had "buried the hatchet," and seeking from him assurances that he could take to Paris and London. This advice accorded with House's own inclinations.

Wilson's assent was unreserved. In laying the tolls question before Congress in March the President spoke mysteriously of "matters of even greater delicacy and nearer consequence," asking Congress to "grant" him its confidence in "ungrudging measure." It was only when the details of House's preparations for his errand became known that light was shed on the President's reasons for asking a free hand in foreign policy. In January, maturing his plans, House invited to luncheon Benjamin Ide Wheeler, former president of the University of California and a one-time Roosevelt lecturer at the University of Berlin. Wheeler and the Kaiser had struck up a personal friendship, the American dining informally now and again in Berlin with the royal family. House's designs at this time included Japan, his power-avid mind toying with the outlines of a league of Powers to include not only Britain and the United States, but Germany and Japan as well. Wheeler warned him against approaching the Kaiser with regard to the Japanese. The Emperor felt, he said, "very strongly upon the question of Asiatics," thinking that the "contest of the future will be between Eastern and Western civilizations."

In May House sailed for Hamburg on the Hamburg-American liner *Imperator*. His experience in Germany was alarmingly revealing. Tirpitz demonstrated a hatred of England approaching the pathological. General Erich von Falkenhayn of the General Staff was politely noncommittal. The civil Ministers, Gottlieb von Jagow at the Foreign Office and Solf the Colonial Secretary, treated House kindly, but he concluded they had no power. As Chancellor von Bethmann-Hollweg's wife died just as House reached Germany, he was deprived of a conference with the Chancellor. His audience with the Kaiser was delayed, House and James W. Gerard, the American Ambassador, believing that the delay was by intent of the military circle surrounding the throne.

On June 1 House traveled with Gerard out to the New Palace at Potsdam for a ceremonial occasion, the Schrippenfest, at which the picked battalions stationed in Potsdam once a year enjoyed a sermon, white bread, and beer in the royal presence. This was the last of the Schrippenfests. After luncheon the Kaiser and House walked on a terrace, the Emperor monopolizing the talk. Expressing contempt for the military prowess of England and France, William avowed his fears of Russia. How, he asked, could Germany reduce her armaments with 175,000,000 Slavs on the eastern frontier? He was amusingly contemptuous of Bryan's "cooling-off" treaties, agreements to wait a year before beginning hostilities which the Secretary of State was hopefully negotiating with thirty-four nations. The Germans, said William, would sign no such self-denying ordinance. House recalled this part of the conversation in 1917, when, if a Bryan treaty between Germany and the United States had existed, it might have deferred the American declaration of war for a year.

"We white nations should join hands to oppose Japan and the other yellow races," cried the Emperor, "or some day they will destroy us." House managed to break in with a mention of the desirability of a tripartite agreement among England, Germany, and the United States, without impeding the flow of imperial opinion. He was unable to bring the talk around to the naval competition. "The last thing," the Kaiser finally said, "that Germany wants is war. . . . In a few years Germany will be a rich country like England and the United States. We don't want war to interfere with our progress." Then as the Kaiser was dismissing House he trumpeted his belief that "Every nation in Europe has its bayonets pointed at Germany—but we are ready!"

Discouraged, House wrote home that he saw in Germany the possibility of "an awful cataclysm," with "militarism running stark mad," with the army and navy by far the most potent factors in the German Empire, even transcending the dynasty itself in genuine power. "If Germany insists upon an ever-increasing navy, England will have no choice," House felt. "The best chance for peace is in an understanding between England and Germany in regard to naval armament, and yet there is some disadvantage to us by these two nations getting too close." Hurrying to Paris, House found conversations impossible with a distracted Government. There had been three Ministries within two weeks.

The British also were rent domestically, with Sir Edward Carson at the head of his Ulster Volunteers threatening revolt in Ireland, and the suffragettes promising to dynamite the Houses of Parliament any day. House appeared to Grey, Asquith, and Lloyd George as an innocent Cassandra from overseas. At a luncheon given by Page they showed themselves unimpressed by the American emissary's findings in Germany. The English statesmen relied on the pacific nature of Bethmann-Hollweg and the presence of Prince Lichnowsky, a Pole, an Anglophile, and an ingratiating gentleman who had been recalled by the Wilhelmstrasse from retirement on his estates to take over the German Embassy in London.

To House's warning that the military were in complete control of German policy they remained graciously deaf. At luncheon with Tyrrell and Page, House observed that in Germany he felt that he was "living near a mighty electric dynamo. The whole of Germany is charged with electricity. Everybody's nerves are tense. It needs only a spark to set the whole thing off." Grey, who believed that the Kaiser would not have sent Lichnowsky to London if he intended war, explained to House why he could not accept his suggestion that they both travel into Germany for a last-minute conference with the Kaiser during Kiel week late in June. The French and Russian Allies, said Grey, would take fright if he went to Germany.

Early in July the Colonel sailed for home, convinced that the cataclysm would not be long deferred. Within a month the war (Page's "grand smash") was overwhelming Europe. The British fleet was at battle stations in the North Sea, the Uhlans were moving through Belgium as a gray-green tide, Russia's peasants and England's "Contemptibles" alike were exposing themselves to the might of the strongest military machine on earth.

4

The war, although long anticipated, struck many persons with the force of doom. A stunned Carnegie concluded his autobiography with these sentences: "The world is convulsed by war as never before. Men slay each other like wild beasts." Yet Carnegie, a guest of the Kaiser on his yacht during the Kiel week of 1907, had heard from the imperial lips: "I will not allow John Bull to give me orders on how many ships I am to build." Carnegie had been urging William to come to terms with England on the naval limitation England dearly wished—and was prepared to pay for. Page, taking over the German Embassy, found Prince Lichnowsky wandering about in pajamas, unable to collect his faculties.

Wilson and Theodore Roosevelt, later poles apart, agreed emphatically at the outset that the war was none of our business. The President's injunction on Americans to be "neutral in fact as well as name, impartial in thought as well as in deed," was matched by Roosevelt's early indifference to the plight of Belgium, expressed in the *Outlook* in August: "When giants are engaged in a death wrestle, as they reel to and fro they are certain to trample on whomever gets in the way of either of the huge, straining combatants." At the same juncture, Mahan could not be so certain that we would re-

main aloof if it appeared that Germany might command the
seas.

In a general interview with the American press on the day
before England declared war (August 4, 1914), the Admiral
exhibited the clairvoyance usual with him in anything relating to the aspect of force known as war. The issue would be
decided eventually by sea power; Britain's capacity to con-
centrate strength in the North Sea and impose a blockade
would finally beat Germany to her knees. The Zeppelin he
believed an overrated striking weapon. He minimized the
power of the submarine, holding truly that it would not (as
some naval authorities were prophesying) shelve the battleship, but failing to give it its true value as a commerce-
raider. Italy, he felt, would fight with England rather than
Germany; Russia, like the Zeppelin, would not provide the
military power expected of her.

"Germany's procedure is to overwhelm at once by concentrated preparation and impetuous momentum," said
Mahan. "If she fails in this, she is less able to sustain a prolonged aggressiveness, as was indicated in the Franco-Prus-
sian war during and after the siege of Paris." Should the
Germans defeat both France and Russia on land, they would
gain a "respite," which might enable them to build sea
power measurable with England's. "In that case," the Admiral continued, "the world would be confronted by the
naval power of a State, not like Great Britain, sated with territory, but one eager and ambitious for expansion. . . . This
consideration may well affect American sympathies." Mahan
had gone astray technically, but not as a power theoretician.
He expected the United States to be drawn to Britain's side
if the sea supremacy of the latter was endangered—but it was
the submarine, not surface power, that threatened Britannia's
rule in 1917.

The idea of a preventive war to keep Germany from control of the Atlantic was by no means unique with Mahan.
His expression on August 3, 1914, however, was no doubt the
earliest in actual wartime. To him, Britain was a "fortified
outpost" (Brooks Adams's phrase) of American sea power.

In German hands, the British Isles would be an advanced base usable against the United States. Unfortunately for American understanding of the strategic problems of the First World War, Admiral Mahan was twice silenced, first by a presidential order on August 6 muzzling all United States Army and Navy officers, active, reserve, and retired; and finally by death four months later. Wilson would not except the great Admiral from his order, nor was there any indication that he desired to avail himself of Mahan's counsel. It may be doubted that Wilson, who was unfamiliar with strategy, warfare, and power relationships, understood Mahan's usefulness to those formulating America's course in a world at war.

Mahan died at the age of seventy-four on December 1, 1914, in the Naval Hospital at Washington. The press of the world, lifting its gaze from trench warfare for an instant, recalled that Mahan's teachings had instructed the Kaiser that dominion depended upon sea power. (In 1939 Grand Admiral Erich Raeder said: "All wars will be settled by sea power.") A world-famous Admiral who never had commanded a ship in battle, Mahan was accorded high honors. Franklin D. Roosevelt, Assistant Secretary of the Navy, represented the Government in arranging the ceremonial. If the President was unaware of Mahan's sagacity and worth as an interpretative historian, the Assistant Secretary of the Navy was in no such darkness. Franklin Roosevelt, an amateur of sea power, had studied Mahan to good purpose.

The modified Mahanite Page quickly and accurately rationalized the American stake in defeat of Germany, writing House: "If German . . . brute force could conquer Europe, presently it would try to conquer the United States; and we should all go back to the era of war as man's chief industry . . . our Monroe Doctrine would at once be shot in two, and we should have to 'get out of the sun.' " In a mood clearly prescient, Page presented the alternative. "If England wins . . . [she] will not need our friendship as much as she now needs it; and there may come Governments here that will show they do not." House too recog-

nized our strategical concern in the outcome, reporting to
the President early in August: "If the Allies win, it means
largely the domination of Russia on the Continent of
Europe; and if Germany wins, it means the unspeakable
tyranny of militarism for generations to come. . . . Germany's success will ultimately mean trouble for us."

Page's perception of the sea-power aspects of the issue was
incomplete; House's understanding was even dimmer. Both
men instinctively chose sides with England, Page with undeviating openness, but their sympathy was largely ideological or sentimental. The Ambassador, according to Sir Edward Grey's compact analysis, saw in the war a "struggle
to the death between the forces in Europe that made for
American idealism, and the forces that would destroy and
replace it by something that was to him detestable."

In the first sixty days of war Wilson, not yet impelled by
a desire to bestride the world as a moral Colossus, leaned in
private toward the English synthesis. The "strange, impeded,
self-absorbed" professor (in the *Mirrors of Washington* appraisal) agreed, moreover, with House and Page that German victory would shake America rudely out of her pacific
lethargy. On August 30 Wilson replied to House's size-up
of the War's consequences, affirming that "if Germany won,
it would change the course of our civilization and make the
United States a militaristic nation." In mid-September, talking with his fidus Achates, the President inquired: "Shall we
ever get out of the labyrinth made for us all by this German
frightfulness?" adding that "he never had been sure that we
ought not to take part in the conflict; and, if it seemed evident that Germany and her militaristic ideas were to win,
the obligation upon us would be greater than ever." At
various times in conversations with Joseph P. Tumulty, his
secretary, the President gave rein to a pro-English bias, observing once, in the first stages of the controversy over neutral rights at sea, that he doubted whether he should do anything to embarrass England "when she is fighting for her
life, and the life of the world." At another time he expressed
the belief that England was "fighting our fight."

Soon, however, the Allies held on the Marne, Paris and France were saved, the British fleet asserted control of the seas, the threat to the United States of a triumphant Junkerdom seemed remote, and the President settled into cynicism regarding the conflicting claims of the belligerents. Unmoved by the German reduction of Belgium, although the United States Government also was signatory to the Hague Convention guaranteeing the neutrality of that country, in the fall of 1914 Wilson began to accept the German interpretation of the causes of the war (anticipating the war-guilt "revisionists" by several years), ascribing the war exclusively to imperialistic rivalry between England and Germany.

A legend sedulously cultivated in the postwar years attributed the entrance of the United States into the war to the effectiveness of English propaganda, at the same time deprecating Germany's efforts to influence American opinion as naïve, maladroit, and futile. Futile they were not. The British appeal was overtly addressed to the whole nation, the German appeal to racial blocs and pressure groups. The German and Austrian Embassies and consulates, expending millions of dollars, carried on what Theodore Roosevelt called a "great alien conspiracy," intriguing, threatening politicians, and indulging in "propaganda of the deed" by blowing up factories and attempting to disrupt railways.

The effect of German forcefulness was not lost on the White House. In the November election the Democratic congressional majorities declined under the 1912 mark. Although this was attributable to the reconciliation of Republicans and Progressives in many districts, Dr. Hugo Münsterberg, writing the President, laid it to another cause, a defection of the "German-American vote." Moreover, the German psychologist warned the President of a further desertion to be made up of the "very large and influential group" comprising the "German, Swedish, Jewish and Irish vote." The "friends of Germany," Münsterberg went on, proposed to organize a "systematic campaign"—unless Wilson mended his ways—"to take care that the Democratic party

become tabooed as the one which has made America practically an ally of England."

Wilson replied placatingly to this gross insult, expressing
"a great deal of surprise" at the tone, but answering points
raised with circumstantiality. Robert W. Lansing, then the
Counselor of the State Department, gave the President a
spirited memorandum properly characterizing Münsterberg
as an alien agent and urging that the correspondence be
made public. Wilson, a stanch party man, rejected the advice. Spring-Rice, unwelcome at the White House, was to insist that the German Embassy under Count von Bernstorff
enjoyed far freer access than his to the President, a disadvantage that might have been overcome by House's pro-Ally
leanings.

In his annual message in December, 1914, the President
announced a lofty impartiality. The United States being "untouched" by the "causes or objects" of the war, he saw no
need for Americans to arm or otherwise disturb themselves.
Wilson subscribed to the pacifist thesis that armaments of
themselves promote war, the lack of armaments warding off
war. He was willing, he indicated, to mediate the struggle in
the name of humanity. The President's assumption of unique
virtue seldom failed to annoy the consciously fallible. Theodore Roosevelt, who had reversed himself on Belgium in October, stormed now that Wilson was leaving the country
defenseless to improve his qualifications as a peacemaker,
hoping that "he would be employed as a go-between, as the
man to fetch and carry amongst the warring powers when the
time for peace negotiations arrived." Roosevelt had not held
the role of peacemaker so lightly in 1905.

5

The gaunt-souled perfectionist in the White House (like
Madison "a Virginian, a Princetonian, angular, conscientious, and iron-willed") was being introduced to destiny. Of
all those bringing him face to face with fate, Colonel House
was the most insistent, as he was the adviser nearest the

throne. Late in September House, questing for vicarious power, had vowed in his diary to "get him [Wilson] absorbed in the greatest problem of worldwide interest that has ever come, or may ever come, before a President of the United States." By virtue of his place at the head of the most powerful neutral nation Wilson qualified, almost without asking for it, for a supreme niche in history. He could, wrote House, dictate the "greatest peace the world has ever seen." His opportunities, "if properly followed," would "bring him worldwide recognition." There were others tempting Wilson with this heady wine—Page, Lord Bryce, and many minor individuals who perceived the Providential chance for making the world over in Wilson's image.

Soon after his annual message of 1914 the President and his "Grey Eminence" House prepared their first "unofficial" intervention. House, who liked nothing better than to patter down palace corridors, went to Europe early in February, 1915, charged with seeing whether the time was ripe to propose a "general convention of all neutral and belligerent nations." Wilson was of course to preside; the call would come from him if the powder-grimed belligerents were agreeable. The mission, carrying House to London and Berlin, came to naught.

Before House reached Berlin in March, the general situation had altered. A proclamation by the Germans of a counterblockade of the British Isles by submarine had brought from Wilson on February 10 a note insisting that the United States Government would hold Germany to "strict accountability" for the loss of life or property at sea. Meanwhile it had become apparent to the Germans that this huge industrial country was to become what Grey called the "reserve arsenal of the Allies." Shut off from the seas themselves, the Germans could look for no substantial help from American raw materials except through the neutrals—and Britain was methodically plugging those leaks. The United States had, of course, an incontestable right to purvey goods of any sort to any belligerent, the Hague Convention of 1907 expressly granting that privilege to neutrals. Ironically, it was the German delegates who had pressed for the provision, the Krupps, and the German Government as well, wishing no hindrance to their sale of munitions abroad in war or peace.

In May the *Lusitania* was sunk off Old Kinsale Head, Ireland, with the loss of 1,198 lives, 114 of them American. A medal was struck to commemorate the deed in Germany, schoolchildren were released to celebrate the sudden death of 63 infants and children. Dr. Bernhard Dernburg, former Colonial Secretary, now in the United States as a "paid agent" (Lansing's description), dismissed the matter with the phrase "Anybody can commit suicide if he wants to." He referred to the fact that the German Embassy had warned Americans not to sail on belligerent liners. The German-language press in America scarcely bothered to conceal its rejoicing. Ambassador Gerard, expecting to be recalled, gathered that the Germans intended the sinking as a warning to the United States against further shipment of contraband. A plea to Congress for an embargo, backed by all the political forces the Germans could muster, had recently failed.

The large and vocal pro-Ally element, including most of the great newspapers, hoped the *Lusitania* incident would move Wilson from his pedestal. To Theodore Roosevelt it was "now inconceivable [that] we should refrain from action; we owe it not only to humanity, but to our own self-respect." Two nights later, however, the President, addressing four thousand recently naturalized citizens in Philadelphia, ignored the tragedy, ignored the war except in a backhanded way. This was his "too proud to fight" speech. Roosevelt was momentarily struck dumb. Lodge contemptuously allowed it to spread through Washington clubs and drawing-rooms that he considered the President too "womanish" to bear a manly part, and the characterization reached the White House. The speech overjoyed Münsterberg and George Sylvester Viereck, the leading German propagandist in this country; it persuaded the Berlin Government that it need give little weight to a protest on the *Lusitania* when it came.

Wilson's first *Lusitania* note, going forward three days after the Philadelphia speech, spoke again of "strict accountability," condemning the wanton destruction of civilians on the high seas in rounded Wilsonian phrases. Over the second *Lusitania* note, dated May 31, Bryan resigned as Secretary of State. The Cunard liner had carried a few cases of shells. This justified to Bryan her torpedoing without warning. The Great Commoner, who had been restrained from excursions into diplomacy except for his "cooling-off" treaties, now became the favorite orator of the German-American Alliance, the American Women of German Descent, and the German-American Peace Society. To Bryan, peace was an absolute good, in a class with Prohibition and the Genesis version of Creation.

The President was finding that, as usual, impeccable objectivity was gaining him and his cause no friends abroad. German rage against the United States, always easy to incite, ran like a fever through that country. Gerard found himself treated as a quasi-enemy. For several months the Kaiser violated protocol by declining to receive the American Ambassador. When, on Gerard's insistence, he was admitted into the imperial presence, William, hardly able to conceal his anger, announced that "America had better look out after this war. . . . I shall stand for no nonsense from America after the war." Arthur Zimmermann, the Foreign Affairs Under-Secretary, warned the Ambassador that there were 500,000 German reservists in America, who "will rise in arms against your Government if your Government should dare take any action against Germany." Gerard's reply, recounted in his book, *My Four Years in Germany,* was brief: "I told him that we had five hundred thousand and one lamp posts in America, and that was where the German reservists would find themselves if they tried any uprising." At about this time Gerard learned that Tirpitz was the author of an article in the *Frankfurter Zeitung* which promised that after the British had been knocked out by the submarine and had surrendered their fleet, the combined Anglo-German fleet would sail to America and there extract an indemnity paying the entire cost of the war!

We come to an amazing chapter in the Wilson-House
peace offensive. While in Berlin in March, 1915, the President's personal envoy was struck by an inspiration. He wrote
Page on March 27 that he was coming to London for a talk
with Grey on "a phase of the situation which promises results," adding cryptically: "I did not think of it until today
and have mentioned it to both the Chancellor [Bethmann-
Hollweg] and Zimmermann, who have received it cordially,
and who join me in the belief that it may be the first thread
to bridge the chasm." House's happy "thread" was freedom
of the seas, a concept which was Germany's meat and Britain's poison.

House tarried in Paris. By the time he reached London his
discovery had already been hallmarked by the Germans. In
their delight, the Foreign Office had wirelessed Count von
Bernstorff and Dernburg to initiate propaganda in America
on behalf of freedom of the seas. The British Foreign Office,
aware of this, treated the Colonel's promising proposals with
distinct reserve. Dropping it there, House carried his notion
back to the White House. The British would have rejected
the proposals in any case, as House, had he possessed even
rudimentary knowledge of sea power and its historical development, might have guessed.

Freedom of the seas as understood by House and subsequently by Wilson (to the confusion of our naval authorities
and the alarm of the British) meant abandonment of the
blockade, which, as it transpired, was the decisive weapon in
that war—a weapon that had served the British well also
against Napoleon, and the North against the South. In employing that weapon the British inconvenienced American
commercial and shipping interests, just as in the period
1861-65 the American blockade annoyed and angered the
British. The precedents established then were called into use
again. In the Civil War the North, devising the doctrine of
continuous voyage, blockaded the North American continent, capturing ships bound for Cuba and Mexico and se-
questering the cargoes on the presumption that they were
destined to be transshipped for Confederate ports. The

American rule was that ultimate destination was what counted, and if goods were bound from Liverpool to Savannah by way of Havana the United States called that a continuous voyage. The doctrine established by the United States in the 1860's proved a boon to England in 1915. Applying it, the British blockaded the European continent, regulating the flow of neutral commerce presumably bound for Germany through neutral ports on the Continent.

Theodore Roosevelt in 1906 and 1907 and House in 1915 would have deprived England of this weapon, deprived the United States also, for once in the World War, we enforced the blockade with relentless severity. In the Civil War the blockade contributed to the development of the ironclad. In the First World War it stimulated use of the submarine as a retaliatory force.

6

Late in March, 1916, a U-boat sank the *Sussex,* a Channel passenger steamer, forty lives being lost. A needless act, it corresponded hypothetically to the blowing-up of a passenger train carrying civilians. Wilson's note of protest (one of the series) was this time ultimative, reading: "Unless the Imperial Government should now immediately declare and effect abandonment of this present method of submarine warfare against passenger and freight carrying vessels, the Government of the United States can have no choice but to sever diplomatic relations with the German Empire altogether." Gerard, delivering the note, believed it meant war. The Tirpitz party seemed to have the upper hand over the moderates led by the Chancellor. But as Gerard sat in his office "in a rather dazed and despairing state," an invitation arrived to visit the Kaiser at the Great General Headquarters, then at Charleville in occupied France.

After a long conversation, in which William assured the Ambassador that "as Emperor and Head of the Church" he wished to make war in a "knightly manner," Gerard returned to Berlin. Within a few days the Wilhelmstrasse delivered a note pledging the German Government to observe the rules of war—to sink no more ships without warning. This was early in May. Except for a few "mistakes," the Germans adhered to the promise for some time.

In October, however, Gerard, reaching the United States on leave, was convinced that resumption of illegal warfare was only a matter of weeks, despite a turn in the tide of war toward the Central Powers. By December 6 Bucharest had fallen. Haig's offensive on the Somme had failed at a cost of 500,000 casualties. Asquith confessed in the House of Commons that no effective means had been found to check U-boat ravages. From August to December the monthly toll of tonnage lost rose from 230,000 to 355,000. On the Western Front the trench warfare was stalemated for another muddy winter; at sea the British faced dreary months. In Germany Tirpitz was promising victory within three months, given unrestricted U-boat warfare. General von Ludendorff, nominally second in command to Marshal von Hindenburg, had the ear of the All Highest, and Ludendorff favored resumption in the interest of a swift victory.

But first there would be a diplomatic diversion. On December 12, 1916, Chancellor von Bethmann-Hollweg, "in a deep moral and religious sense of duty toward this nation and . . . humanity," suggested a peace conference of the "hostile Powers." A week later Wilson, effecting a plan matured before the German offer, called upon the belligerents to state their terms as a means toward peace. The President asserted as a fact that the "objects which the statesmen of the belligerents on both sides have in mind . . . are virtually the same, as stated in general terms to their own people and to the world." "That one sentence," said House truly, "will enrage them."

In Paris, Georges Clemenceau remarked bitingly in his paper, the *Homme Enchaîné,* that the "moral side of the war has escaped President Wilson." J. L. Garvin, in the London *Observer,* thought a "memorable mistake has been made at the White House . . . [in the] strange and almost inexplicable wrong which Mr. Wilson does to the traditions of his own country, the truth of recent history and the conscience of

mankind." Otherwise the British press, which had never forgiven the President for not recognizing England's moral motive in going to war over Belgium, gave vent to explosive
rancor. "Everybody is mad as hell," Lord Northcliffe told
Page, who reported that the King, "expressing his surprise
and dismay that Mr. Wilson should think that Englishmen
were fighting for the same things in this war as the Germans,
broke down."

Balfour had succeeded Grey as Foreign Secretary in the
shake-up that brought Lloyd George to power. The Allies,
under Balfour's leadership, formulated their war aims generally as "restitution, reparation, and guaranties of future
security." Specifically, they listed demands roughly approxi-
mating those which were to survive Versailles. The Germans,
declining to state terms, stood on their offer of December 12,
which the Allies regarded as a "trap baited with fair words"
(Lloyd George's comment) and which Maximilian Harden,
in the liberal *Berlin Zukunft,* deplored as having "no semblance of sincerity in the enemies' eyes," having been
"preceded and accompanied by an array of blunders and
stupidities."

The American press (other than the German-language organs) condemned the Germans for abruptly—in the words of
the *New York World*—"closing the door, leaving no basis for
further discussion." To the *New York Times* the German
answer had the "look of insincerity," and the *New York
Tribune* believed the Berlin Government had "coolly, skill-
fully, completely . . . turned that document [Wilson's note]
to its own ends."

Peace by negotiation seemed far distant. The Kaiser, noting the Allied terms, stormed: "Our enemies have dropped
their mask. . . . After refusing . . . our honest peace offer, they
have now, in their reply to the United States, gone beyond
that and admitted their lust for conquest, the baseness of
which is further enhanced by their calumnious assertions."
But the President would not be discouraged. On January 22,
1917, addressing the Senate, he submitted peace terms of his
own. He called for a "peace without victory," for a "peace

between equals." The speech contained much that later appeared in the Fourteen Points: self-determination of nations, freedom of the seas, reduction of armaments, what was construed as the charter for an independent Poland, and the satisfaction of Russia's desire for the Straits. He likewise advocated an international organization to police his reforms. Wilson, it appeared, while unwilling to intervene in Europe's war, was bent on intervening in Europe's peace.

A chorus of approval arose from the pro-German press. "Upon the principles enunciated by the President must be based the only saving peace," said the *New Yorker Staats-Zeitung;* and Viereck's *Fatherland* found that whereas "Lincoln emancipated merely the African Negro . . . Wilson's speech sets free men and minds in every part of the globe." Senator Robert M. La Follette hailed this as a "very important hour in the history of the world." Taft, actively propagating the League to Enforce Peace, thought the speech marked "an epoch in the history of our foreign policy," but Theodore Roosevelt, dwelling on the passages on the freedom of the seas, remarked that "until this Government has taken an effective stand to prevent the murder of its citizens by submarines on the high seas, it makes itself an object of derision by speaking for the freedom of the seas." Cannily, the *Boston Transcript* feared that the freedom-of-the-seas infusion was the "mixture of blood in the dish of barley-sugar which the President set before the world."

A favorite theme of editorialists in this country was that Wilson had announced a "Monroe Doctrine for the world." Abroad, the press prevailingly agreed, holding, however, that in seeking to extend the American doctrine to Europe the President had abandoned it on behalf of his own country. In Madrid the *Epoca* called the address the "funeral oration of the Monroe Doctrine." To the Petrograd *Novoye Vremya* it seemed that Wilson had "cast aside the security of the Monroe Doctrine for a dream." The *Zürich Nachrichten,* rather more bluntly, believed the President had "violated the spirit of the Monroe Doctrine in his pretended meddling with European concerns." The London *Mail* re-

garded a "Monroe Doctrine for the world as hopelessly vision-
ary," a sentiment also voiced in Paris by the *Journal des
Débats.* Such discussion, indeed all talk of peace, soon became academic.

On January 31, 1917, Germany announced a return to
unrestricted U-boat sinkings. The United States, having recovered from its slump of 1914 and early 1915, was at dizzy-
ing heights of prosperity. From J. P. Morgan & Company's
office at the Wall Street "Corner" to the farthest Nevada
village, the country was riding high, with wheat at around
$2.50 a bushel, cotton crowding 35 cents a pound, copper,
oil—all raw goods—at new highs. Jobs were plentiful, wages
abundant. The country was making munitions; Grey's Allied
"reserve arsenal" had become active. We had already made
loans of $2,300,000,000 to the Allies for war supplies.

On February 1 the boom was placed in peril by resumption of ruthless submarine warfare. In London Page, fearful
that Allied purchasing power had already been exhausted,
noted that the "submarine has added the last item to the
danger of a financial world crash." In Berlin Foreign Secretary Zimmermann repeated assurances to Gerard at a supper
party: "Everything will be all right. America will do nothing,
for President Wilson is for peace and nothing else. Everything will go on as before. I have arranged for you to go to
the Great General Headquarters and see the Kaiser next
week . . . and everything will be all right."

In Washington the White House saw an odd spectacle—
the President and House grimly playing pool. House, hurrying to Wilson's side upon receipt of the news, found him
"sad and depressed," but "insistent that he would not allow
it to lead to war if it could possibly be avoided." "It would
be criminal," said Wilson, "for this Government to involve
itself in war to such an extent as to make it impossible to
save Europe afterward." On the day before when the German
announcement was placed before the President, Tumulty observed a swift change of expression: "first blank amazement,
then incredulity, then gravity and sternness, a sudden grey-

ness." Apparently the President had discredited Gerard's confident warning, which had been renewed by cable after he returned to Berlin.

Outside the White House newsboys cried papers with black headlines screaming of "piracy" and a "return to murder." In New York the *World* called the German note a "declaration of war against the United States," the *Post* saw in it a warning that Germany was about to "run amuck on the high seas." Garvin wrote in London that the "hour when the United States enters the war will seal Germany's doom." On that day the United States, a nation of 113,000,000, had a merchant fleet of 8,500,000 tons (to England's 13,000,000), gold reserves larger than Great Britain, France, and Russia combined, as much pig iron as the rest of the world, a copper output twice that of all other countries.

The President, pale, manifestly tired, met his Cabinet on February 2. At once he asked what should be done—"Shall I break off diplomatic relations with Germany?" Without pausing for a reply, he made what his Secretary of Agriculture, Houston, regarded as a "somewhat startling statement," which as Houston recorded it in his memories of the period ran like this: "He would say frankly that, if he felt that in order to keep the white race, or part of it, strong to meet the yellow race—Japan, for instance, in alliance with Russia, dominating China—it was wise to do nothing, he would do nothing, and would submit to anything and any imputation of weakness or cowardice."

Houston was taken aback by this Kaiserlike utterance, "a novel and unexpected angle." However, the Secretary of War, Newton D. Baker, and the Secretary of the Navy, Josephus Daniels, seemed "much impressed with the President's long look ahead." The President was still neutral, still clinging to the shreds of the high impartiality from which he had hoped to judge, moderate, and reorganize the wicked world. In the general Cabinet debate over the suitable reaction to the German challenge the President was asked which side he preferred to see win. Promptly he replied that he "didn't wish to see either side win, for both had been equally indifferent to the rights of neutrals, although Germany had been brutal in taking life and England only in taking prop-erty."

On February 3 the President broke relations with Ger-many in a brief address to Congress. Informed of the action by the Associated Press, Bernstorff said he was "not surprised. My Government will not be surprised either. The people in Berlin knew what was bound to happen. There was nothing else left for the United States to do." Four days later the Senate, by a vote of 78 to 5, approved the severance. In the country at large, already overwhelmingly pro-Ally, the de-parture of Bernstorff was taken as merely a token of the war that was bound to come.

A mingled assortment of pro-Germans and pacifists began uttering demands for a referendum on war, a move termed by the *New York World* the "expiring gasp of German propa-ganda in America." However, many of the German-American societies and German-language newspapers hurriedly bespoke their allegiance to the United States. On February 8 the German-American National Alliance, in convention at Phila-delphia, endorsed the rupture of relations, and its president, Dr. Charles J. Hexamer, urged the local units to "organize German-American regiments . . . for defense of the flag." "Unqualified approval and commendation" was voted the President in his stand by the Hoboken City Commission, and in Omaha the German *Tribune* declared that "our allegiance belongs to America first, last and all the time."

7

With the renewal of indiscriminate U-boat warfare the First Battle of the Atlantic was fairly on. The loss of tonnage, British and neutral, mounted in February to 540,000. De-spairingly, the *Spectator* conceded that Britain now had "command of the sea in name only," while the London *Nation,* resorting to understatement, likewise admitted that "unless we can sink submarines faster than they are being built and build British merchantmen faster than they are

being sunk, we are approaching the margin of peril." Losses
continued to climb. Plainly, England was marked for starvation and defeat; and more (it became increasingly patent to
Americans) was at stake than England's position in Europe—
her possible military surrender in northern France.

The sea ascendancy of Britain was being put to the hazard
of the surreptitious submarine. The American people, often
indifferent to the claims of the sea, were being made aware
(in ways more subtle than obvious) that they too faced the
loss of the Atlantic; that the Atlantic System, more felt and
taken for granted than rationalized, was under crucial attack.
The realization was borne home in February as it became
apparent that the Berlin declaration had wider implications
than it was at first supposed. A challenge to American national dignity, it presaged danger and increased destruction
on the Atlantic, but in addition it was blockading American
ports. In extending their counterblockade, the Germans at
the same time were locking up American harbors, and crip-
pled as England was, the blockade of America proved another
horrible blow. Nothing could have demonstrated more con-
clusively the essential community of interest in the Atlantic
world. The Germans had, of course, planned it that way;
they hoped the notice of February 1 would hold neutral
shipping in American ports. What they had not fully reckoned on was that the denial of the Atlantic to America would
inevitably impel that Sea Power into war.

As February wore along the indirect blockade threatened
to bring the whole American economy into collapse as well
as smother England. As early as February 2 the New York
press noted that American and neutral transatlantic liners
were canceling their sailings. P. A. S. Franklin, president of
the American Lines, announced that his flagship, the *St.
Louis,* was being held up until he could get guarantees of
protection from the Government. Ten days later he began
to dismiss his crews and unload cargo from all American
Line ships, passenger and freight-carrying. The Government
had told him, said Franklin, that he might arm his vessels,

but "you can't buy 6-inch guns in any store," and he had no
gunners in sight. Defense was a Government monopoly.

Soon the harbors of New York, Boston, Philadelphia, Baltimore, and the minor Atlantic ports were cluttered with
freighters under United States, Scandinavian, and other neutral flags. Neither shipowners nor seamen were willing to risk
the Atlantic passage for money alone. The ships of the Allied
belligerents came and went, their men having a patriotic incentive, but belligerent bottoms were by no means sufficient
to deliver Allied war needs. As tonnage languished in the
ports, the warehouses and piers filled up; then the railroads
could not unload cars at the seaboard terminals. With freight
yards crowded, a car shortage rapidly developed and the railroads became clogged as far west as Pittsburgh and Buffalo.
On February 16 the railroads placed an embargo on shipments to Atlantic ports. Whereupon the price of food
mounted, creating housewives' riots. Women streamed out
of lower East Side tenements in New York City, overturning
pushcarts, sprinkling kerosene on the stocks of outdoor deal-
ers, marching on City Hall with demands for food. It was
thought that some of the agitation was inspired by German
agents. If so, their intrigues worked in fertile soil. Coal also
became scarce, the price pyramiding.

The "paralysis of overseas commerce" threatened grave
social consequences. For the first time since Napoleon, Americans were shut off from the sea, and as far west as the wheat
belt, in little inland towns where the Atlantic was only a
name, people realized anew their dependence on salt water.
As fear spread, Spring-Rice reported to London the "stop-
page of trade, congestion in the ports, the widespread dis-
comfort and even misery on the coast . . . even bread riots
and coal famine." Had the jam at the ports not been broken,
the towering structure of war prosperity certainly would have
toppled in a matter of weeks. Furthermore, England would
have been smashed. The blockade control port of Kirkwall
in the Orkneys, heretofore crowded, saw few neutral flags
in February and March, 1917.

In the Cabinet discussion grew heated. With Wilson doubt-

ing, on February 24 whether the country would support
strong measures, William Gibbs McAdoo, Secretary of the
Treasury and the President's son-in-law, Franklin K. Lane,
Secretary of the Interior, and Secretary Houston pressed
for immediate, warlike action. The Senate isolationists,
led by La Follette, O'Gorman, and William J. Stone of
Missouri, were making menacing noises out of proportion
to their votes or the public following they commanded. "Congress or no Congress," pleaded McAdoo, this was "no time
for hesitation." Lane urged the President to inform the public about the treatment of American consuls' wives in
Germany, the State Department having received reports of
indignities. In Berlin the Foreign Office had attempted to
extort from Gerard his signature to a remarkable treaty
exempting the numerous German nationals in this country
from operation of certain American laws—in effect, conferring extraterritorial privileges—on penalty of having American citizens detained in Germany. Turning on McAdoo and
Lane, the President accused them of an appeal to the "code
duello." In justification for his attitude the Chief Executive
quoted Governor McCall of Massachusetts, who, calling that
day, had advised him that the people wished the Government to "go slow."

The relations between the President and his constitutional
body of advisers grew strained as the more resolute Cabinet
members sought to bring the reluctant intellectual to a decision. Houston put the argument on grounds of national
interest. The United States could "not afford to let Germany
intimidate us, or cut England off and crush France—we would
be the next. Germany would be mistress of the world, and
her arrogance and ruthlessness would know no bounds."

Two days after this session the President asked Congress
for permission to arm merchant ships. Backing and filling
in his address to Congress, Wilson denied "proposing or contemplating war, or any steps that may lead to war." The
spectacle of a Chief Magistrate treading softly in the presence
of an arrogant senatorial minority was by no means new. Nor
would Wilson be the last President to palaver with a vocifer-

ous bloc in the Senate. A bill was introduced with the evident approval of the country (Gallup's fever chart of public opinion was not then a national institution) providing $100,-000,000 for the equipment of merchant vessels with guns and crews.

On March 1 the Administration made public the Zimmermann note, which became at once a casus belli. Zimmermann, who had been promoted to be Foreign Minister, had been in search of friends in the Americas. To that end he had instructed the German Minister in Mexico to offer the Mexican Government Germany's assistance in reclaiming Texas and the Southwest from the United States as the price of a military alliance. The Germans hoped, of course, that an embattled Mexico would divert this country's effort if war came. An absurd endeavor on Herr Zimmermann's part —testifying anew to the German Government's ignorance of the United States, its spirit and power—he compounded the offense, from a propaganda point of view, by making full confession after his journalistic backers in this country had strenuously branded it an "English forgery." This note had passed in code through the American State Department's own communication system, being detected and decoded by the British secret service.

After being formally assured of its authenticity by Wilson the Senate majority chose to make of the Zimmermann note an overt act. With the press blazing wrathfully, the House passed the armed merchantman bill 403 to 13. La Follette and ten other Senators filibustered it to death in the Congress expiring on March 3, with 75 of the 96 Senators fuming in the cloakrooms and signing a protest against the demonstration of the minority. In his second inaugural address Wilson brought his gift for measured invective to bear, denouncing La Follette, Stone, O'Gorman, and their associates as "a little group of willful men, representing no opinion but their own" who had "rendered the great Government of the United States helpless and contemptible."

On March 9 the President, having been supplied with a citation of authority derived from an act of 1797, ordered

the ships armed. At the same time he called a special session
of Congress to meet on April 16, 1917, later advanced to
April 2. Only one step remained—the declaration of a state
of war. On a rainy spring night, with the Capitol dome
bathed in mist and a guard of cavalry from Fort Myer surrounding his carriage, the President rolled down Pennsyl-
vania Avenue to invoke war against the Power that had
sought to hem America in from the sea. All reservations had
vanished now (although only yesterday Lane had noted in
his diary that the President "goes unwillingly") as he vowed
"we will not choose the path of submission." Edward D.
White, the Chief Justice, himself a Confederate veteran, led
the cheers, tears streaming down his cheeks.

It was to be "force, force without stint, force to the utter-
most." To what end would this force be applied? In 1776 the
colonies fought for political independence, in 1812 the
United States fought for its rights on the high seas; in 1861 the
North fought to preserve the Union, the South for separation; the Spanish-American War was prosecuted for the deliverance of Cuba and the expulsion of Spain from the hemisphere. All these were limited objectives. Now Wilson was
summoning the nation to war for "mankind . . . the world
must be made safe for democracy." Early in his Administration the President, in an otherwise unimportant speech, described the American flag as the "flag of humanity." The
phrase had been taken as a bit of harmless rhetoric. No
longer a figure of speech, the concept was now clothed with
the majesty of a war aim. A dispute that began over America's safe access to and command of an ocean was suddenly
enlarged into a cosmic conflict between good and evil.

8

With his usual eloquence, Walter Lippmann recently
argued that the United States went to war in 1917 to preserve
the Atlantic System, as he put it, "to defend America by
aiding the Allies to defend the Atlantic Ocean against an

untrustworthy and powerful conqueror." [1] In 1917 Lippmann was one of the editors of the *New Republic;* he had access to the President, a circumstance attested rather querulously in a letter from Taft to Lord Bryce, in which the former President enumerated three or four advisers, including Lippmann, and referred to them as "men of . . . triumphant, graceful and charming phrasing." At the moment Taft was complaining over what he thought a Wilsonian tendency to wage war by "joint debate." But when in the article cited Lippmann attempted to "prove" that the Administration went to war for the Atlantic System, he only established that the editors of the *New Republic* understood almost better than any of their contemporaries the reasons that impelled the United States to that fateful act.

He quoted from editorials published in February, 1917, the month of decision, which in hammered, realistic sentences disclosed our good and sufficient motives. The article of February 17, for example, under the title "The Defense of the Atlantic World," declared that

if the Allied fleet were in danger of destruction, if Germany had a chance of securing command of the seas, our navy ought to be joined to the British in order to prevent it. The safety of the Atlantic highway is something for which America should fight. Why? Because on the two shores of the Atlantic Ocean there has grown up a profound web of interest which joins together the western world . . . if that community were destroyed we should know what we had lost. We should understand then the meaning of the unfortified Canadian frontier, of the common protection given Latin-America by the British and American fleets.

Proceeding to our specific grievance against Germany, the writer continued:

It is the crime of Germany that she is trying to make hideous the highways by which the Atlantic Powers live. That is what has raised us against her in this war. . . . When she carried the war to the Atlantic by violating Belgium, by invading France, by striking against Britain, and by attempting to disrupt us, neutrality of spirit or action was out of the question. And now

[1] *Life*, April 7, 1941.

that she is seeking to cut the vital highways of our world we can no longer stand by. . . . A victory on the high seas would be a triumph of that class which aims to make Germany the leader of the East against the West, the leader ultimately of a German-Russian-Japanese coalition against the Atlantic world.

The prophetic insight displayed in the foregoing also depicted with startling clarity the American situation in relationship to a Nazi victory in the Second World War:

. . . with Germany established . . . [as] mistress of the seas, our trade would encounter closed doors on every hand. . . . The sooner we should cancel the Monroe Doctrine the safer for us. . . . The passing of the power of England would be calamitous to the American national interest . . . [America would] be morally and politically isolated. . . . As a consequence of its isolation, it will become alarmed as never before. In its fear, it will arm until its territory is spotted with camps and its shores bristle with guns and battleships.

Lippmann and his associate, the chief editor of the *New Republic,* Herbert Croly, deserve all honor for extricating from the tangled skein of myth, propaganda, and moral and hysterical rationalization the true cord of vital interest that led us to the night of April 2, 1917. Who else of that year discerned what has become so apparent now that the second, grosser phase of the great war brings out the strategical outline of the first? Wilson? There is no doubt that Lippmann presented the Atlantic thesis to him; there is equally no doubt that Wilson's utterances are bare of evidence that he comprehended, or if he understood, believed. Theodore Roosevelt, as infatuated with his subjective "righteousness" as Wilson with his "humanity," was engrossed with a symptom—the "murder" of American citizens on the high seas—rather than a system. Page had an approximation of the truth, although he narrowed it to Anglo-American ascendancy. Henry Adams, a paralyzed invalid but still able to pluck harmoniously at the strings of history, penetrated again to first causes, writing a friend in England his gratification because "I find the great object of my life thus accomplished in the building up of the great community of the Atlantic

Powers, which I hope will at last make a precedent that can never be forgotten."

A disciple of Mahan's strategical doctrines, Lippmann was likewise in accord with Adams's systemic contribution. The British, acute in matters of sea power, gathered our less obvious reasons without difficulty. Spring-Rice, who for years had fondly addressed Adams as "uncle," was certain in April, 1917, that "it is, of course, impossible now to separate the interests of England and the United States, so far as regards the Atlantic." When Grey of Fallodon came to write his memoirs, he expressed what he thought was a truism: "But for the German submarine war on merchant vessels, the United States would not have come in on the side of the Allies." Winston Churchill in his history of that war, *The World Crisis,* gave full weight to the "virtual arrest of United States shipping through fear of German attack"—the self-internment of neutral vessels that threatened the well-being, as it shamed the dignity, of the United States in the early spring of 1917. Suspicious of general ideas, however, the British authorities underestimated the preventive part of the American motives—the determination that another nation, one the United States had often regarded as hostile, should not gain command of the other shore of the Atlantic.

Contemporaneously another American publication, the *Seattle German Press,* antedated the findings of the Nye Committee on the causes of war, stating in April, 1917, that the "entire nation is opposed to war. Wilson has been sandbagged by the Jingo press, which is kept by the financial interests of the country. . . . British gold, Wall Street, the ammunition makers and the indifference of the people are solely responsible for this national catastrophe."

Although the First World War President failed to recognize the Atlantic System in word, he did so in deed. In February, 1916, at a time when it first appeared that Germany's unrestrained U-boat warfare might impair, if not destroy, Britain's mastery of the Atlantic, Wilson had unexpectedly called for "the most adequate navy . . . incomparably the greatest navy in the world." Speaking at Kansas City and St.

Louis on successive nights, the President, who had been resisting the outcries of the preparedness advocates led by
Theodore Roosevelt and Major General Leonard Wood, demanded, with rare vehemence, that the United States (which
never, in the health of the British fleet, had considered a
navy of more than second rank) prepare to seize the trident
for itself.

The specific fears actuating Wilson's uncharacteristic aspiration were obscure. Ambassador Jusserand later would
warn House that, Russia and Japan having formed an alliance into which Germany might gravitate after the war,
the United States had better help France now if it wished
for help then. The aggressive behavior of Japan in the Far
East had already caused misgivings. Wilson himself in July,
1916, questioned whether England could be depended upon
for "even-handed" treatment in postwar trade rivalries. But
in February the underlying reason cannot have failed to lie
in a novel and general apprehensiveness concerning the
American future in a world from which the prop of the British Navy had been withdrawn. Only twice in American history has the country bestirred itself for the "greatest navy in
the world," or its substantial equivalent, a "two-ocean navy."
On both occasions British command of the seas was in peril.
Wilson's navy speeches gave his high sanction to preparedness. The Naval Bill of 1916, adopted on August 29, authorized ten battleships, six battle cruisers, and one hundred and
forty other vessels of all types, including fifty destroyers of
the class traded to Britain in 1940.

In the Senate debate on the war resolution La Follette
(one of the six who voted no) placed his opposition on the
ground that England, being the original blockader, was the
worse offender. The Wisconsin Senator likewise urged that
in the absence of a referendum the President had no mandate
to bear the country into war. The inference from his first
argument was that if the United States was to enter the
hostilities at all, it should be on the side of Germany. Few
Americans had ever considered that as a possibility. As a

nation-wide referendum was foreign to American institutions, there being neither precedent nor machinery for such a counting of noses, the second consideration seemed mere obstructive demagogy. As for the first, the country failed to agree that exercise of the right of blockade (even if burden-some to shippers and at times improperly administered) was as opprobrious as the sinking of passenger liners without warning. Lodge, whose "heart was more moved by the thought of a drowned baby than an unsold bale of cotton," reflected the sentiments of Americans more accurately than La Follette, whose memorable speech indeed expressed the case for the Wilhelmstrasse syllable by syllable.

This review of the entry of the United States into the First World War has minimized the protracted controversy with England over shipments within the blockade. It has also passed by the equally long record of illegal U-boat depredations, which, moving Wilson to protest, slowly stirred the American people to wrath. On April 2, 1917, the blockade issue became academic. The U-boat record, while dramatic, seems little more than incidental to the basic war cause, which, as it has appeared here, was the possible loss of control—of command—of the Atlantic. In this version, the United States went to war in 1917 not because of the rape of Belgium, not to repay the debt to Lafayette, not in revulsion against German militarism, not for "humanity" or for small European nations, not even for freedom of the seas. England too had prevented the "free" use of the seas by America. The United States took up arms in the last analysis because it seemed likely that without American intervention the scepter of the Atlantic would pass from the hands of English-speaking peoples into those of a stranger. Of England the Americans had no genuine fears; the stranger might provoke them into a far more terrible war—with perhaps the Continent and a subdued Britain behind him—to settle the ascendancy of the Atlantic Ocean, and, beyond that, this Western Hemisphere.

To Americans heedful of future security, the reiterated demand of Admiral von Tirpitz for the Channel ports as springboards for the conquest of England and America was more than a newspaper headline. The bleak pattern of conquest outlined in the Brest-Litovsk Treaty, by which Russia made a humiliating peace with Germany, and in various private renderings of war aims to Gerard and others, was by no means a figment to such Americans as House, McAdoo, Lane, Houston, Henry Adams, Page, Lippmann, and the United States Navy high command. In a moment of sharp perceptiveness Theodore Roosevelt had seen in 1911 that the United States was already enmeshed in the European balance of power. He wrote:

If Great Britain failed . . . the United States would have to step in, at least temporarily, in order to re-establish the balance of power in Europe, never mind against which country, or group of countries, our efforts may have to be directed. . . . In fact, we are ourselves becoming, owing to our strength and geographical situation, more and more the balance of power of the whole globe.

In the backward glance, it seems amply demonstrated that America fought in 1917 to ensure that the balance should not fall against her. Where the Atlantic was involved the United States was precisely as isolated as Belgium. For generations England, in the interest of her peace and well-being, had promoted a balancing of powers on the Continent. With the shrinking of the oceans, the demonstrated power of the submarine, and the incipiency of air warfare, the balance of world forces became of vital concern to Americans. For their own ends they chose as partner the Power holding command of the eastern North Atlantic, and their traditional friend.

VIII. Partnership on the Seven Seas: The Long Truce

THE NEWS THAT the Germans had signed the terms of the Armistice in Marshal Foch's railway car in the forest of Compiègne reached Woodrow Wilson early on the morning of November 11, 1918. Reaching for a White House memorandum pad, the President penciled this commentary on the triumph of Allied arms:

The Armistice was signed this morning. Everything for which America fought has been accomplished. It will now be our fortunate duty to assist by example, by sober, friendly counsel, and by material aid in the establishment of just democracy throughout the world.

Wilson exhibited no jubilation. In the hour of victory his mood was one of responsibility, his thought didactic. Yet a creative satisfaction might well have mingled with his severer emotions, for essentially the Armistice was his own. The fresh force of America had clinched the decision, but the Germans, deserted by their allies and facing military disaster, had sued for peace on the basis of the Fourteen Points which Wilson, in his Moses-like capacity of lawgiver, had handed down unilaterally in a speech before Congress in the preceding January. Lloyd George and Clemenceau, consulted belatedly after the fact, had agreed—with reservations—and in France soldiers on both sides of the line ceased firing with the American President's name on their lips.

Whatever was to happen to the peace, the truce was Wilson's. Unhappily, no one in that cozy White House study in the blackness of a November morning could foresee that the peace too would be merely a truce, although lasting for two decades. The President had made the Armistice unmistak-

ably his through a great show of firmness. At times an implacable man, the schoolmaster-statesman had sought to bend the
flexible will of Lloyd George and back down the "Tiger" of
France by an immediate resort to the pressure of force. A
word of dissent brought from him a threat to desert the concert that had accomplished victory. The Anglo-American sea-
power accord weighed nothing in the scale against submission to the President's formulary in toto. Wilson, in truth,
had shown a disposition to spurn the Atlantic tie before the
victory had been reduced to legal form at Compiègne, a fateful attitude to which we shall soon return.

The American war aims, said the presidential statement,
had been accomplished. Now for the peace. What had been
the American war aims—for what had America really fought?
Few passages in American history have provoked such prolonged and bitter controversy. No misunderstanding has had
such lasting effects. Did the Americans go to war for reasons
vital to their country, to save their own skins? Or did they
fight to "make the world safe for democracy"? Were American interests engaged, or only those of humanity?

Such questions troubled American relations with Europe,
complicated the American approach to reconstruction,
soured the country on the Allies, disillusioned the Allies with
America. And because in 1918 war and peace aims were inex-
cusably scrambled, many Americans in 1941 have a blurred
view of the second phase of the World War. "We fought
once," they say, "to establish 'just democracy throughout the
world' and 'to crush autocracy everywhere,' and look what
happened! We destroyed Kaiserism and got Nazism. What
will we get if we crush the Nazis?" This perplexity is under-
standable. America is paying now in the befuddlement of the
national will for the lack of clear definition in 1918, a confusion for which Wilson, quite apart from the undoubted
nobility of his vision, must bear the principal blame.

It seems clear from the evidence in the preceding chapter
that primarily the United States fought not for the betterment of mankind but—to reduce the matter to its simplest
terms—for command of the Atlantic. It fought in defense of

its own security, its well-being, its prestige, and its familiar Atlantic world. A powerful, far-reaching enemy had brought the war to American shores, closing the Atlantic to our commerce, virtually blockading our Atlantic ports, and threatening to shatter American economy. That enemy seemed likewise about to conquer the eastern bastion of the Atlantic world—the British Isles.

This enemy happened to be a dynastic, militarized state, an "autocracy," as Americans lightly put it in 1918 before they came to know how profoundly evil an autocracy could be. The American war aim was the defeat of that enemy. We may now scarcely doubt that our aim would have been the same had the enemy been a republic or a constitutional monarchy. To that end America mobilized her man power, wealth, and productive capacity, sending, 2,000,000 soldiers to fight in France.

While Americans fought, their President, not satisfied with the bare, objective, selfish reasons for the tremendous effort, evolved peace aims also. Amid the battle he announced the formularies for a new, democratic order which he hoped the expected victory would enable him to impose on the old, autocratic order. The idea that the United States was embarked upon an ideological crusade was, of course, an afterthought. The Germans were as autocratic in 1914 when they violated Belgium, as militaristic in 1915 when they sank the *Lusitania,* as in April, 1917, and, until the President replied with war to the renewed submarine campaign he had professed himself unable to distinguish between the belligerents as to their virtue. America went to war in 1917, to be brief about it, because then and not until then the Atlantic was threatened. The command of the Atlantic was America's safety line, just as with the British the fate of the Low Countries brought their vital interests into question. Unless the Americans were extraordinarily smug, therefore, they could scarcely maintain that their entrance into the war transformed the Allied struggle for survival into a moral crusade. It was the magic of Wilsonian verbiage that performed that deed.

On the morning of November 11, 1918, the Atlantic System had been defended successfully. The time had arrived for the President to translate his words (which, incidentally, had been a propaganda weapon of value against the morale of a Germany being slowly reduced by the blockade and military pressure) into a bright new political edifice. In less than four weeks the President was on the liner *George Washington* bound for Paris as chief of the American commission to the peace conference. With him went the blueprints for a new order, a high sense of his historic mission, and contempt for the Old World "politicians" he was soon to encounter. The liner also carried two of his colleagues, Secretary of State Robert Lansing and the veteran diplomatist Henry White, as well as the commission's staff of experts—economists, geographers, historians, and lawyers. Colonel House and General Tasker H. Bliss, the other commissioners, were already in Paris. One day as the party neared France the President addressed the staff. Dr. Isaiah Bowman, the distinguished geographer, noted the gist of the presidential remarks: "that we would be the only disinterested people at the peace conference, and that the men whom we were about to deal with did not represent their own people."

That conclusion displayed a relaxed grip on reality. It was Wilson's own credentials, not those of the Europeans, which were open to doubt. Only a week before the Armistice the American people had administered what Lansing was to term a "popular rebuke to Mr. Wilson for the partisanship shown in his letter of October." Wilson had called for a Democratic Congress; both houses went Republican. In December Lloyd George won his "Hang the Kaiser" election by a staggering majority. In a test of Clemenceau's leadership two weeks after Wilson's arrival in France, the "Tiger" carried the Chamber of Deputies four to one, the issue turning on the full satisfaction of France's claims at the forthcoming conference. As long as the British and French Premiers stood for a punitive peace and huge reparations they represented their own people quite accurately. The Italian Premier Orlando likewise understood his people better than did Wilson, as was disclosed by the President's appeal to them over Orlando's head in the Fiume matter. Overnight the Italians, who had so recently strewn flowers at Wilson's feet, rose up to execrate him for obstructing their dubious ambitions in the Adriatic. If any of the Big Four at Versailles misread the postwar mood of the plain people, it was Wilson and not his fellow peacemakers.

A stereotype has been widely imprinted on the American mind to the effect that Wilson fell among the thieves of old-school diplomacy on the road to his new order. According to this image, the innocent prophet was robbed of his elevated aspirations for humanity while his assailants were smothering his principles. Wilson himself did not create this impression, which is more flattering to his purity of motive than his sagacity, and he repeatedly rejected such a construction on the speechmaking trip that brought his collapse. Nor do the facts about the League of Nations, the heart of the new order, bear it out. Lord Robert Cecil, General Jan Christian Smuts, the Prime Minister of South Africa, and Lord Phillimore, a noted international lawyer, carried drafts for a society of nations to Versailles; the Covenant reflected their thought also. There never was doubt of British support. In truth, the anti-League cabal in the Senate and anti-English writers generally failed to give Wilson due credit for launching the League of Nations, preferring, when it suited their purpose, to depict him as the victim of an English plot to foist a superstate on America.

The truth of the legends of Wilson's humiliation and frustration at Versailles has been sufficiently assessed by careful authorities and is not, moreover, a part of our narrative. But whatever his fate was at the peace conference, there can be little doubt that Wilson approached Europe with a minatory and forbidding mien. Winston Churchill, who was not sympathetic with the President, was to recall later that it seemed he came to Paris "to chasten the Allies and chastise the Germans."

Wilson's behavior in Paris and London was unbending. London's millions poured into the streets to honor him on the day after Christmas. The demonstration failed, however, to warm the President into comradeship. A banquet followed at Buckingham Palace. Wilson spoke with "measured emphasis and cold tones," producing on the Prime Minister, as he related in his *Memoirs of the Peace Conference,* a "chill of disappointment." The President omitted what would have been a normally generous reference to the sacrifices and heroism of the British share in the recent joint enterprise; there was, Lloyd George noted, "no glow of friendship or of gladness at meeting men who had been partners . . . and had so narrowly escaped a common danger." Between that occasion and a subsequent speech in the Guildhall, Lloyd George had Lord Reading subtly suggest to the President that the British would appreciate a kindly reference to their war effort. Wilson withheld even that minimum acknowledgment of hospitality. His frigidity would have had little meaning had it been merely a lapse of graciousness. Its significance was far wider, affecting the relationship between the English-speaking Powers in a time pregnant with the future.

It may be that the President resented Lloyd George's refusal to accept Point Two (freedom of the seas) of the Fourteen Points before the Armistice, a conflict with which we are soon to deal in detail. It may be that both the President and the Prime Minister were mindful of an episode of the past spring, a difference that had not improved their cordiality. After the crushing German offensive in March, 1918, Lloyd George had asked Ambassador Page (according to a cloud of witnesses quoted by that industrious diarist Clarence W. Barron) if he might not get former President Taft and A. Lawrence Lowell, president of Harvard University, to come to England for some speeches. The British had just suffered nearly 300,000 casualties, and Lloyd George no doubt truly felt that words of reassurance from these two influential Americans would bolster the home morale and create fresh hope of victory. When the Prime Minister's request reached the two American leaders, they went to the White House for what they expected to be perfunctory approval.

The President, who earlier had asked the British Embassy to send home some of the English lecturers abroad in this country, objected. He called to Taft's attention that there were several million Irish-Americans and German-Americans, loyal to this country but anti-English, adding: "I think we have already been too close to England, and I hope to see the relationship less close after the war." Taft and Lowell had no choice but to decline the English invitation.

In Europe now, preparing to set the world to rights, Wilson obviously still saw small value in the English-speaking bond. Indifferent to strategy and even geography, disdainful of nationalism, mistrusting England as he mistrusted Republicans, and acutely aware of self-interest in everyone but himself, the President seemingly knew little and cared less about the Atlantic System. In his *History of the American People* he had ignored this country's hemispheric status and relationship, making no attempt to interpret the strategical significance of the Monroe Doctrine or the body of thought from which it came. His preoccupations were verbal, not factual, with doctrines and not deeds, and at the moment his scope transcended the merely national or continental. Nothing short of a global reconstitution of international relationships would do.

2

The pre-Armistice dispute between Lloyd George and Wilson over the freedom of the seas had fractured the Anglo-American sea-power concert, which by intensifying the blockade and convoying the army and supplies to France was winning the First Battle of the Atlantic and helping to decide the issue in Flanders. Intent on a literal acceptance of the Fourteen Points, the President, through Colonel House, was in effect proposing that the British scrap their navy at the hour of its greatest triumph. More than ever before Britain, battered and exhausted on land, rejoiced in her mastery of the seas. Wilson, although aware of this, acted with characteristic single-mindedness in pursuit of his purpose, not hesitating to employ severe language and threats against the great Sea Power with which America was linked more closely than at any moment since 1775.

At the time of their utterance the Fourteen Points represented a blueprint for the kind of world Wilson thought it desirable to work toward at the end of the war. They were a statement of Wilsonian peace aims and, to the considerable extent that the President may be said to speak for the country, of American peace aims. Such they remained until October, the endorsement of the Allied statesmen being neither sought for nor volunteered. It was only after Prince Max of Baden, Germany's Chancellor in the hour of disaster, appealed for peace on the promise of the Fourteen Points that the Allied Prime Ministers were asked to underwrite them.

Lloyd George and Clemenceau took the situation with fair grace, but elsewhere, both in America and in Europe, the predicament of the Prime Ministers aroused sympathy. It was felt that Wilson had shown a highhanded attitude. Some critics even suggested that he had been collaborating with the foe to present his Allies with an ultimatum. Taft, a loyal supporter of the American war effort, expressed this point of view in a letter to a friend, one strongly condemning the President for failing to consult the Allies before replying to Prince Max. He added: "He would never do that—that is just the kind of man he is. He recognizes no obligations of partnership or of decent courtesy. He thinks he is running the whole show himself. I do not know whether Lloyd George and Clemenceau now have the courage to tell him what is what, but if they do he will turn tail." It seemed to Taft that the Chancellor's "peace offensive was most ingeniously baited" to gratify the President's "vanity."

Wilson's exclusive negotiations with Prince Max can best be justified on the hypothesis that he believed the United States had a moral ascendancy over the Allies; that it had gone to war to rescue them from the results of their own misdeeds, and proposed now to set them straight with or without their consent. According to this hypothesis, the United States had fought for no material stake. This might be called the crusade theory. To that construction Wilson and his co-believers were to adhere more and more closely. The pretensions arising from this viewpoint account for the President's scorn for the Allied "politicians" and his refusal to extend the comradely hand. Although the crusade theory offended the Allies, they dissembled their annoyance. The authority of America was too overshadowing to be called into question. Harold Nicolson, who was with the British Foreign Office advisory staff at Paris, records in his book *Peacemaking* his impression that "the President possessed unlimited physical power to enforce his views. We were all, at that date, dependent upon America, not only for the sinews of war, but for the sinews of peace. Our food supplies, our finances, were entirely subservient to the dictates of Washington. The force of compulsion possessed by Woodrow Wilson . . . was overwhelming."

The weight of Wilson's authority had encountered Britain's determination to retain her sea power in the last week of October, 1918, when the Fourteen Points were officially laid before the Allied Premiers. Point Two at once became the stumbling-block. It read: "Absolute freedom of navigation upon the seas, outside territorial waters, alike in peace and in war, except as the seas may be closed in whole or in part by international action for the enforcement of international covenants." The seas were universally free in time of peace. In time of war international usage sanctioned the blockade, a maritime counterpart of the land siege. The blockade was a belligerent right, its rules changing with circumstances, as we have seen. As a weapon the blockade's usefulness devolved on command of the seas. It was one of the strongest weapons in Great Britain's armory, the weapon which had humbled Louis XIV, frustrated Napoleon, and was now reducing the Central Powers. To strip away the right of blockade "would virtually prohibit offensive use of British sea power altogether," as Harold and Margaret Sprout concluded in their book *Toward a New Order of Sea Power,* "and would largely nullify the advantages of England's incomparable strategic position *vis-à-vis* the Continent of Europe."

That result was, of course, what Wilson and House, who was in Europe as Wilson's "personal representative" on the Supreme War Council, intended. The discussion over Allied acceptance of the Fourteen Points came to a head in Paris on October 28. At luncheon with Lord Reading and Sir William Wiseman that day House warned the British Government that unless it yielded on the freedom of the seas the British "would bring upon themselves the dislike of the world." The United States and the other countries, House was confident, would not tolerate England's "complete domination of the seas" any more than they had suffered Germany to dominate the land, and "the sooner the English recognize this fact, the better it [will] be for them." The account of House's remarks to Reading and Wiseman are taken from the House diaries; his version is used for this whole episode.

House, Clemenceau, Baron Sonnino (the Italian Foreign Minister), Lloyd George, and Balfour met the next day at the Quai d'Orsay. Lloyd George was firm. He could not accept Point Two "under any conditions." To do so meant that the "power of blockade goes; [and] Germany has been broken almost as much by the blockade as by military methods. . . . This power has prevented Germany from getting rubber, cotton and food through Holland and the Scandinavian countries." The American suggested that England's blockade had alienated the United States in the early years of the war. A similar blockade might throw the United States into the arms of Britain's enemy the next time.

The British Prime Minister still balked, whereupon House casually observed that the President would have no option in case of Allied refusal to embrace the Fourteen Points but to call off his negotiations with Germany and seek his own arrangements. Did that, inquired Clemenceau, imply a separate peace? House agreed that it did. "My statement," House noted, "had a very exciting effect on those present." Well it might. The hostilities were still under way. America's withdrawal in force, or the intimation of such a move, would have had unpredictable consequences. The Germans might even have been rallied for a stand on their own soil. Nevertheless, Lloyd George gave no ground, replying to House that "if the United States made a separate peace we would be sorry, but we could not give up the blockade . . . as far as the British public is concerned we will fight on." Clemenceau signified his agreement, complaining that he could not understand the "meaning of the doctrine . . . war would not be war if there was freedom of the seas."

Before the Supreme Council met on October 30 Wilson had armed his negotiator with an ultimatum by cable. It read: "It is my solemn duty to authorize you to say that I can't take part in the negotiation of a peace which does not include freedom of the seas, because we are pledged to fight not only Prussian militarism, but militarism everywhere." The President's threat conveyed in his closing sentence—"I hope I shall not be obliged to make this declaration public" —did not avail, however, with Lloyd George.

English navalism and Prussian militarism were to Wilson and House on the same footing, as the President's agent made clear to Lord Reading when he protested at a subsequent interview that the British were taking the "same attitude that Germany took in the spring of 1914 regarding her army." Although House pleaded that in his opinion the right of blockade was not to be extinguished, but only modified to ensure the "immunity of private property at sea in time of war," the Britons had no doubt that Wilson's aim was enfeeblement of the British at sea as well as prostration of Germany on the land. It was in that sense, said Lloyd George, that the Germans understood Point Two, and Wilson was proposing to accord the enemy a truce on that understanding.

The negotiations hung fire. At House's suggestion Lloyd George prepared a memorandum in which he reserved "complete freedom" on Point Two at the peace conference. He also amended Wilson's conditions to strengthen the provision for reparations. Clemenceau made the Lloyd George draft his own. Thereupon Wilson sent further threatening cablegrams to House, proposing to lay Britain's position be-

fore a Congress which he was sure would be unsympathetic
with the thought that "American life and property shall be
sacrificed for British naval control." To Wiseman, House
ventured the opinion that "all hope of Anglo-Saxon unity
would be at an end" and "there would be greater feeling
against Great Britain at the end of the war than there had
been since our Civil War" unless the Prime Minister receded.

Although House threatened now to eclipse the British
Navy if the British held out, Lloyd George still refused to
endorse the principle. In answer to talk of American naval
building he observed only that "Great Britain would spend
her last guinea to keep a navy superior to that of the United
States or any other Power." In the end House had to be content with a simple declaration by the Prime Minister. "We
are quite willing," Lloyd George said, "to discuss the freedom of the seas and its application."

In spite of this defeat, on November 5 House reported to
the President "a great diplomatic victory," all the more remarkable in his opinion because accomplished "in the face
of a hostile and influential junta in the United States and
the thoroughly unsympathetic personnel constituting the Entente Governments." Despite Wilson's determination, the
minimizing of sea power for which he contended dropped
from sight on the road to the new order. Freedom of the seas
was not discussed at the conference. Someone misleadingly
told the President that under the League of Nations there
would be no neutrals in future and hence no necessity for
safeguarding neutral rights at sea.

In the heat of this conflict, the English Prime Minister
might have been pardoned for wondering if the decline of
German sea power meant the rise of a new and hostile force
overseas. It was apparent that something had gone wrong
with the prophecies of Jefferson, Chamberlain, Carnegie,
Richard Olney, and Admiral Mahan. "Fighting once more
in the same cause" had not tended to knit English-speaking
affections, if Wilson and House were any measure.

We may only guess at the intellectual forces that spurred
Wilson's fight for Point Two. In his cabled remonstrances

against the British position he called it "one of the essentially American terms" from which he could not "recede." The doctrine was not unfamiliar in the United States, for it was a shibboleth of foreign policy dating from the days of American weakness, but one which had been clothed with meaning only during the general wars produced by Napoleon and by the Germans under William II. In the 1860's and in 1898 the United States had not hesitated to close the seas to others, employing and extending the right of blockade. America fought in 1917 not for the freedom of the seas but to uphold command of the seas and, once in, she cheerfully enforced the blockade against the remaining neutrals. The matter was demonstrably one of expediency, not principle.

The President may have believed a radical change in the rules of war necessary to keep the peace, yet he proposed no alteration in the rules of land warfare. He may have honestly believed that the British Navy menaced the security of the world. Yet the British had not been aggressors in the war just ending, nor had they provoked Napoleon, and the century between had gone by under the name Pax Britannica without a general war. The arguments of Wilson and House during this controversy, as disclosed only in House's diary, tend to the conclusion that both wished England's sea dominion brought to an end. There is no indication that either weighed the reduction of British sea power in relation to the interests of America, with respect to either the strategical problems of this country or the protection of the security of the Atlantic world against the rise of future aggressors in Europe. Yet in 1823 a strong British fleet had been regarded as a buffer between the New World and Europe. In 1898 the British fleet stood between the Continental Powers and the United States. The Mahan school, dominating naval thought, had for twenty years predicated its defense calculations on the existence of a British fleet screening Europe, and America demonstrated in 1917 her strategical association with and reliance on the British navy. These lessons seem not to have been considered by the President.

Freedom of the seas was a traditional doctrine, but the sea-power collaboration of the United States and Great Britain likewise had the sanction of usage and history. Plainly, Wilson hoped in a general way to dispense with all power apart from his projected league. The attack on British sea power unfortunately affected the status and security of his own country as well. The United States, as Mahan had pointed out, was also an island, dependent on command of its seas for its security. No society of nations—short of the millennium—could relieve America of a certain concern with the question of who was to command the eastern Atlantic.

3

The sea-power dispute at Paris merely ruffled Anglo-American relations. Soon they were to be genuinely vexed. Before sailing for the peace conference in the first week of December, in his annual message to Congress Wilson had given his blessing to naval expansion. Point was immediately added to this endorsement by a bill embodying the recommendations of the General Board for naval increases which if carried out would give the United States unquestioned supremacy on the seas—in strength afloat—within six or seven years. The bill called for twelve superdreadnoughts and six-teen battle cruisers. Under the current building naval act of 1916, ten dreadnoughts and six battle cruisers were within reach. The programs of 1916 and 1918 therefore envisaged a total of forty-four post-Jutland capital ships, embodying the lessons of that battle and far superior to any vessels then in commission.

Although England had emerged from the war in the "highest position" navally that "she has yet attained," as Churchill pointed out, the projected American fleet could have driven her from the seas. Not since Henry VIII had the British Navy so dwarfed Continental rivalry, yet at the Armistice the Admiralty listed only forty-two first-line capital ships and these were of pre-Jutland types. Germany's fleet was interned in Scapa Flow, soon it would be scuttled and out of the way,

and the Admiralty had settled back for a time of recupera-
tion, of study, adaptation, and leisurely replacement.

The 1918 American naval bill shook the complacency of
the Admiralty rudely. If authorized and built, these ships
would transport the trident across the Atlantic, and Britain
would be put to it to keep in sight of the Americans. House's
purring pre-Armistice threats, it seemed to the Ministry, had
not been idle. Moreover the Secretary of the Navy, Josephus
Daniels, confirmed the intentions of the Administration in
Washington. Before the House Naval Committee Daniels
urged "incomparably the greatest navy in the world," assuring the committee that the President favored the 1918
program. In the London *Times* Daniels was quoted as defy-
ing England to head off American ascendancy at sea, promising that "the United States will lay two keels to every one
that Britain does, or five to one if necessary."

British government and naval circles were amazed and
shocked. They now understood the cold realities behind
House's admonition in Paris that this country had the
"money, men, and natural resources" to outbuild the Royal
Navy. Amid the startled reaction in London a comment
made by Wilson was scarcely found reassuring. On December 21 the President stated for the *Times* of London that
he considered it "essential to the future peace of the world
that there should be the frankest possible coöperation, and
the most generous understanding between the two English-
speaking democracies. . . . We fully understand the special
international questions which arise from the fact of your
peculiar position as an island empire." The President "understood," but, it was noted, he had failed to acknowledge
England's "peculiar position."

The British, relating Wilson's advocacy of the greatest
navy to House's blunt assertions, saw evidence of a power
maneuver, a bit of strategy calculated to strengthen his trading position at Paris. This impression was confirmed by
Daniels, who disclosed in the *New York Times* of December
31 a hint from the President that "nothing would so aid him
in the Peace Conference as Congress's authorization of a big

navy." In February, 1919, a report was to be widely circu-
lated in Europe and only inconclusively denied that the
President had cabled the House Naval Committee that failure to pass the 1918 bill would be "fatal" to his program at
Paris. The committee speedily adopted a favorable report
in order to enable the President, in the language of the *New
York Sun*, to "lay his cards on the table in respect to com-
petitive armaments." To the Europeans, accustomed to the
devices of power politics, Wilson's feinting—if it indeed was
that—appeared both reasonable and realistic. It was, however,
felt in informed quarters that the navy pressure was super-
erogatory, his moral and material influence being already sufficient to carry the day if intelligently applied. Here and
there it was suggested that in resorting to "Yankee bluff" the
President was stepping down from the pedestal, but the season of disillusionment, when a British journalist would remark that the prophet "spoke like Our Lord but behaved
like Lloyd George," was not yet at hand.

Meanwhile the formal opening of the peace conference at
Versailles on January 18 had reduced the sounds of Anglo-
American sea-power rivalry to off-stage shouts and murmurs.
It is true that with the arrival of Daniels in March Admiralty
officials took a rather vehement hand in behind-the-scenes
parleys. The Secretary of the Navy subsequently described
these exchanges as the "naval battle of Paris." But in the
work of the conference, especially that crucial job of formulating a society of nations for the better world ahead, the
Anglo-Saxon delegations collaborated with a unity of spirit
distinctly unwelcome to Clemenceau. Wilson and House for
the Americans, Lord Robert Cecil and General Smuts for the
British, presented a united front in the commission charged
with framing the League charter. The draft Covenant was
the product of the American and British legal staffs; a French
draft was tabled on February 3 at the first session of the commission, under the chairmanship of Wilson. It was Cecil, a
son of the late Lord Salisbury, who bore the brunt of supporting the Anglo-American case on the floor, on one occa-

sion seeking to cudgel French agreement by the threat of English and American withdrawal into an Anglo-American alliance as the postwar substitute for a league. He did this without dissent or rebuke from the American conferees.

Although the political delegates had shelved the naval issue, the naval staffs had not. Daniels's arrival awoke the slumbering antagonism of the sea dogs. Dropping punctilio, Admiral Sir Rosslyn Wester-Wemyss, First Sea Lord, stormed in upon the Secretary at his hotel, putting the case for Britain's continuing mastery of the seas with quarterdeck emphasis. He inquired with scant ceremony why the United States, with such limited responsibilities, desired the largest navy afloat. His opposite number, Admiral W. S. Benson, chief of the American naval delegation, matched the Sea Lord's tones at a later, more orderly conference, where he demanded parity for the American fleet. An evidence of the mutual mistrust between the services was a memorandum prepared by Benson for the President which set forth ominously that "every great commercial rival of the British empire has eventually found itself at war with Great Britain—and has been defeated."

Walter Long, First Lord of the Admiralty, took up the controversy with Daniels, falling back before the Secretary's firm demand for "equality of naval strength" between the English-speaking Powers. Daniels rested his claim on the ground of world peace. The Wilsonians soon would be justifying a great navy as a counterweight to the British in ensuring that the League of Nations would not be reliant solely on British sea power. But gradually out of the Anglo-American naval dispute would emerge not a reduction of armament on the sea, nor a change in the rules of warfare, but a vigorous, healthy American desire to have a fleet as big as the next fellow's—however rationalized. And while, to the English naval authorities at Paris parity with America was an evil almost as inconceivable as American supremacy, a decade later such parity would be accepted, as we shall observe, as the norm.

During the discussion, Long intimated (or so Daniels understood) that American naval ambitions had chilled Lloyd George's zeal for the League of Nations. The Prime Minister was to deny this, adding nevertheless that the League would be a "mere piece of rhetoric if we continue to build dreadnoughts"; but in April he employed an aspect of the League as a weapon against American naval expansion. Wilson had returned home to sign bills at the close of Congress early in March. While there he felt the mettle of the opposition to the League. It seemed to him and his advisers that the omission in the Covenant of any reference to the Monroe Doctrine was the strongest club in the hands of the irreconcilables. Wilson returned to Paris determined to write into the League charter a recognition of that doctrine.

Lloyd George, the approval of the League by his Government having been too complete for a reversal even if he had such in mind, chose to take a stand against incorporation of the Monroe Doctrine. It was assumed that he did so for trading purposes, hoping to extract in exchange from Wilson a modification of the alarming American naval program. His avowed reason was that such an inclusion might exempt the United States from full responsibility under the Covenant, granting to that country a privileged position and opening the way to agitation for the recognition of other regional declarations. Lloyd George's colleagues, Balfour and Cecil, gave House to understand that they lacked sympathy with this viewpoint.

In his exhaustive and scholarly exposition of Wilson's course, *Versailles Twenty Years After,* Dr. Paul Birdsall of Williams College characterizes the Prime Minister's objection as an attempt to "levy blackmail." To Birdsall, expounding the theory so stanchly advanced by Ray Stannard Baker, the Wilson biographer, of the good prophet beset by wicked and wily men, Lloyd George was the "slippery Premier." To others it has appeared that the adroit Welshman was making a legitimate use of the Monroe Doctrine pawn against Wilson's big-navy knight in a chess game involving national interest. Lloyd George wished to retain the trident and avoid a naval race. Wilson believed that the Monroe

Doctrine concession (it was nothing more to him) would assure the ratification of the Covenant by the Senate. To the Briton, a naval race might upset the peace of the world; the American believed that defeat of the League in America would be a universal calamity.

The chess game went to a draw. House and Cecil arranged the capitulations. Wilson agreed to recommend that Congress shelve the 1918 program. This represented no actual sacrifice, since Congress had shown an increasing reluctance to press on with naval expansion. Further, the President was willing to have his Government talk over future naval plans with the British. In return Lloyd George waived all objections to the Monroe Doctrine clause. The truce was embodied in an exchange of memoranda between Cecil and House on April 9, 1919. It was only twenty-nine years since Cecil's father had promised Victoria that England could "always catch them [the Americans] up" in naval competition.

The Paris truce was not made public at the time. When news of it reached America a month later, the Anglophobic press, led by Hearst, railed at the President for "selling out" to Lloyd George. In announcing withdrawal of the 1918 program Daniels optimistically declared that existence of the League of Nations made it unnecessary to "impose on the taxpayers of America" for more capital ships. This was late in May. The Treaty of Versailles would not be signed until June 28, but already signs were multiplying of dissatisfaction with the projected League Covenant, so Daniels coupled a warning with his assurance to the taxpayers. Unless we accepted the League we must continue building until we had "incomparably the biggest navy in the world." There was, he said, "no middle ground."

Thereafter Wilson used the threat of a huge navy and costly militarism as a club over the isolationists. Again, as with the Allies at Paris, the size of our navy became an instrument of high Wilsonian policy. Repeatedly Wilson and Daniels uttered the terms of the choice: the League of Nations or "great standing armies" and an "irresistible navy."

The form of political pressure exerted by the Administration encouraged big-navy elements—such as shipbuilders and patriotic societies, as well as naval officers themselves—to provide reasons why America should outstrip the British at sea. The necessity also arose of identifying potential perils and enemies, and again England became the traditional foe at a time when doughboys and Tommies were still guarding the bridgeheads of the Rhine.

By January, 1919, America was deep in the psychological embroilment that accompanies and aggravates a naval race. The aggressive tone used toward England in the United States evoked like expressions on the other side of the water. House noted with alarm that the "relations of the two countries are beginning to assume the same character as [those] of England and Germany before the war." England again became the football of American politics. The attack converged from two sides. While the Senate "battalion of death" excoriated the British for deluding Wilson into a plot to give the British Empire six votes in the League Assembly (the Dominions each had a voice) to our one, the big-navy phalanx deployed from the right to swear that we must rule the waves or allow "Great Britain to be the bully of the world." In the Senate all the familiar changes were rung on the theme of "perfidious Albion." The British had "threatened our interests oftener and more seriously than all the other nations on earth." The United States had had "more wars and complications with England than with all the other nations . . . combined." While the "pride of England might be hurt by her slide into second place amongst the naval powers," she was advised that competition with America was hopeless. So went the debate.

As for the British, they were bewildered by the sudden American demand for superiority at sea. For twenty years, since Sir Edward Grey explained to a German diplomat that the English never reckoned on the American fleet as a hostile force, they had taken Anglo-American naval accord more or less for granted. It was assumed at the Admiralty that the two fleets would never be turned on each other. Moreover,

Britons acquainted with the strategical aspects of the case could not understand how the United States would dispose the vast fleet contemplated by the General Board. It had no bases outside the continental United States except at Guantánamo and Hawaii. Its strategical responsibilities were not extensive. Of the great sea gates—those narrow passages where the trade routes of the world come together—America held but one, Panama. England had the North Sea and the English Channel, commanding the sea movements of Northern Europe, Gibraltar, Suez, and Singapore, as well as the southernmost capes, Good Hope and the Horn. Strictly speaking, the United States owned no life line; England's life lines ran for thousands of miles around the globe.

The only hypothesis upon which the British could understand American naval expansion was that of intended imperialism. Unless, they reasoned, the United States proposed embarking on a world-wide course of grabbing territories and the bases which alone make naval operations feasible in far waters, there was no point to its having the largest navy afloat.

As the discussion progressed in both countries, the wartime entente of the peoples began to disintegrate, the old antipathies to revive. Many Americans, taking their cue from the Anglophobic press and the cries of the Senate irreconcilables, came to suspect that they had been lured into war by the British for British ends. Contributing to such suspicion was the obscurantism which had jumbled American war motives with the Wilsonian peace objectives. The British, forgetting—if they ever actually knew—that America had gone to war for reasons strictly American, affected to regard the United States as a partner with equal liability to the cause; a tardy and reluctant partner who came late to the fray, tarrying on the way to grow enormously rich at the other partner's expense.

In each English-speaking country the immediate postwar reaction to the other was ugly. There should be no desire to crowd fresh blame on the memory of the peacemaking President, but it must be clear that Wilson's conduct produced a major share of this ill will. He it was who most authoritatively propagated the crusade theory of the American war effort, misleading both Europe and America. It was his employment of the naval program for purposes of diplomacy and domestic political persuasion that aroused the fear and distrust of England and helped fan the coals of the persistent Anglophobia in the United States. That situation was instinct with irony. In pursuing the ends of international co-operation the President called out at home the forces that traditionally seek to block such co-operation, and between England and America he produced estrangement. In striving for a world order he impaired accord between the world's greatest Powers. One cannot escape the feeling that in these matters the President acted irresponsibly; that in reaching for the greater he threw away the less and in the end had nothing.

4

The broad outlines of that vast, praiseworthy, and doomed experiment in world power relationships, the League of Nations, are not pertinent to this study. Engrossed in the development of the Atlantic System, our attention is caught, however, by speculation on the fate of the League had Wilson organized it from the bottom up rather than from the top down. How would the League of Nations have fared in this country had it been built on the experience and power structure of the Atlantic System? Suppose the President, consulting American tradition, had treated the Monroe Doctrine as a cornerstone instead of accepting it as a mere amendment to the League Covenant? These questions, bearing directly on the power problems that will arise out of the war begun in 1939, have more than historic interest.

On June 28, 1919, when the commissioners of the victorious Powers and Germany signed the Treaty of Versailles, the states of Pan-America and the British Commonwealth stood intact, uninvaded, politically stable, their peoples fed and secure. At the head of these groupings England and America were, moreover, unchallengeable if they chose to act together upon the seas. Alone of the white Powers except for France, amid the fall of dynasties, revolutions, starvation, poverty, and national frustration they possessed political vigor and economic reserves.

Within the boundaries of the Atlantic System and the empire lay 40 per cent. of the land area of the world, a third and more of its population, and considerably more than half its industrial productivity and available resources. Here, within one potential power bloc, was the gold of South Africa, Canada, and the United States; the oil of the Americas and the Middle East; the wheat and meat of Argentina, Australia, Canada, and the United States; coal, copper, cotton, rubber, tin, sugar, coffee, tea—all the materials needed or coveted by man in lavish abundance. Outside the Soviet Union there were no important surplus-producing areas not controllable from Washington, London, and New York.

A war-shattered Europe, unable even in peace to feed itself and supply its workshops with raw materials, was more than ever dependent upon the outside world. The relationships of continental Europe with that world depended, in the final analysis, upon sea power, a vast instrument in the hands of the English-speaking Powers. No such aggregate of military weight and economic power had ever before been joined with the opportunity to create a peaceful, thriving order for the earth. Years after Versailles, Stanley Baldwin, addressing a meeting in Albert Hall, spoke of what might have been after 1919, having always, he said, "believed that the greatest security against war in any part of the world whatever would be the close collaboration of the British empire with the United States. The combined power of their navies, their potential man power, the immediate economic power of a uniform blockade and their refusal to trade or lend money would be a sanction no power on earth, however strong, dare face."

But that was in 1935. A rearming, infatuated, tribal Germany was placing herself outside Western civilization. The United States and Great Britain, earnestly desirous of "peace in our time," had missed the bus, and it was beginning to be apparent that they might have to fight for peace once more.

In 1919 the resources summarized by Baldwin were at Wilson's disposal. The British would have been his willing associates. No one else could have opposed him successfully had he chosen to reorganize his world on the solid basis of Anglo-American power, using the liberal principles he espoused but deferring to American tradition and reality by limiting responsibilities and sanctions regionally. Suppose he had organized a free society of nations, vanquished and victor alike, world-wide in legislative scope but "compartment-alized" along power lines already tested, a federal system with regional subdivisions; the continent of Europe charged with its metropolitan affairs; the Americas charged with their own; the English-speaking Powers united behind its general purposes and decisions?

Wilson had no lack of advice to that effect. Among the American voices offering formulas for White House consideration was that of Lansing, who as early as May, 1916, wrote of his concern over a possible collision between a world state and the Monroe Doctrine. It might, he thought, be wiser to establish "geographical zones . . . leaving to the groups of nations thus formed the enforcement of . . . disputes. I would not like to see European nations . . . cross the ocean [to] stop quarrels between two American republics. Such authority would be a serious menace to the Monroe Doctrine and a greater menace to the Pan-American doctrine."

Of all the counsel available to the framers of the League of Nations none was more temperate, informed, and penetrating than that of Dwight W. Morrow. A partner in J. P. Morgan & Company, Morrow had served during the war on the Inter-Allied Maritime Commission. Later as Ambassador to Mexico he was to embody the "Good Neighbor policy" before it reached the dignity of a phrase. A pragmatist, a gradualist in political reform, Morrow never lost sight of the attainable. In the overwrought weeks of the peace conference he published a book, *A Society of Free States,* which he hoped might be of guidance to those drafting the charter of the

League. His essay, first serialized in the *New York Post,* reviewed the long record of man's effort to substitute consent for force in the affairs of states.

Morrow knew that the Covenant as projected went beyond the "general desires" of the American people. He was aware of the strength of American attachment to the American system—the Atlantic System—and the profound dread of Americans of being entangled continuously with the complexus of Europe. He therefore proposed that the League of Nations, expressing its aims in world terms, proceed by intermediate stages. "The men and women of this country," he wrote, "would feel easier in having the United States accept the proposed covenant if it were known that military enforcement should be dealt with, in the first instance, in world compartments."

The Morrow arguments were addressed to the Senate as well as the peace commissioners. To Morrow the League, although it might contain glaring defects, was an essential "step towards coöperative organization." In an address at Columbia University in June, 1919, before the treaty was concluded, he suggested for a characteristic reason that "an interpretative declaration of what America understands the document to mean" should be attached to it by the Senate. "I think it vital," he explained, "that the people of the United States should *understand* their international obligations." [1]

That was not to be. A fateful feud between the White House and the Senate turned America back on herself. The Senate minority appealed to the cowardice, the selfishness, and the parochialism of the American people. Their place in history is not a proud one. But what shall be said of Wilson? They handed him back his treaty, revised and interpreted but still a treaty acceptable to Europe—and he refused it. "I shall consent to nothing," he said. "The Senate must take its own medicine." The body and the heart of the man were broken, but not his high, exigent spirit.

Because the men of 1919—Wilson, Lloyd George, the Sen-

[1] Italics ours.

ate irreconcilables, and all those Americans and Britons who had a hand in shaping the postwar world—failed to make intelligent use of the potentialities at hand, the men of 1940, Churchill and Roosevelt, had to mobilize the same forces for war once more. The tragedy of 1919 was to be fully revealed twenty years later.

5

Of the problems left unsolved at Paris two pressed for settlement in 1921 when Warren G. Harding succeeded Wilson in the Presidency, ushering in the brief reign of "normalcy." These were the Anglo-American sea rivalry, aggravated by the pseudo-navalism of Wilson and Daniels, and the threatening status of Japan in East Asia. Japan was now the third Sea Power and so a party to any consideration of both problems. To England the naval question had first claim, whereas in the United States a re-examination of the Far Eastern situation seemed equally desirable. The hopes of the English-speaking Powers were met by the Washington Conference on the Limitation of Armaments and Far Eastern Questions, which was convened on November 12, 1921, under the clear, objective, and decisive chairmanship of the Secretary of State, Charles Evans Hughes.

The impulses toward the conference came equally from both sides of the Atlantic. In both England and America the postwar depression had exerted a chastening influence; both were fed up with war and thinking of economy. These currents were easily channeled into feeling against the cost of dreadnoughts. In America the eloquent, unstable, and determinedly provincial William E. Borah, leader of the Senate "battalion of death" against the Versailles Treaty, first officially articulated the wish for abandonment of the naval race by introducing in December, 1920, a resolution calling for a conference. Next, when Harding was inaugurated on March 4, 1921, he expressed willingness to take part in such a gathering. But Borah was merely abreast of a trend and Harding actually behind it.

A strong movement, given point by the advocacy of Theodore Roosevelt, General Pershing, and General Bliss, was already at flood early in 1921. Roosevelt, referring to the British Navy as "probably the most potent instrumentality for peace in the world," declared in the *New York Times* that American needs required only a "second navy," and urged an understanding with Britain. Before the House Naval Committee Pershing called for a halt to naval competition before America was plunged "headlong down through destructive war to darkness and barbarism." The press generally agreed with the *New York World* that excessive navalism was a "crime." Such powerful agencies of mass persuasion as the American Federation of Labor, the Federal Council of Churches, and the League of Women Voters joined the agitation against naval expansion. General Bliss, also testifying before the House committee, specified a remedy, urging that a conference of the Sea Powers be held at Washington at the outset of which the United States Government should submit a "reasonable proposition tending to remove mutual fear." As we shall discover, Bliss's remedy was applied in detail.

The American campaign encouraged similar aspirations in England. Powerful individuals and groups called on the Ministry to seek an understanding with the United States. Added to the sentimental considerations, there was a practical motive weighing with the British Government. Although the 1918 program had been shelved, the British had no assurance that the United States, uninhibited by membership in the League of Nations or by any other international commitment, might not embark again on an aggressive policy aimed at mastery of the seas. The Ministry, hopeful of a shift in the American naval bent as a result of the change in administration, called the British Ambassador home in January, 1921, for a report on the prospects of a naval agreement. (In the fall of 1919 Sir Edward Grey, soon to be Viscount Grey, had been sent to Washington to sound the President, but he found Wilson too stricken and no one else empowered to converse with him.)

In February, 1921, Colonel Arthur Hamilton Lee, now Lord Lee of Fareham, was made First Lord of the Admiralty and charged with the task of coming to terms with America. Lee, whose numerous ties with the United States included marriage to an American, wished the initiative to arise in America. British sensibilities were still raw from the pummeling given England in the senatorial debates on the League of Nations. Lord Lee's first step was to announce on March 16, at a dinner of the British Institute of Naval Architects, that he gladly responded to the "hint thrown out" in Harding's inaugural address: "If an invitation comes from Washington," he added, "I am prepared personally to take part in a business than which there can be nothing more pressing in the affairs of the world." No invitation came. The Administration had not yet fixed a naval policy.

Undiscouraged, Lee tried a more circuitous approach through a private citizen, Adolph S. Ochs, publisher of the *New York Times* and a consistent advocate of good Anglo-American relations. Ochs, as was natural because of his position and frequent visits, had many friends in London. Amongst them were Lloyd George and Lee. While breakfasting with the Prime Minister at Number 10 Downing Street on April 22, 1921, the publisher was handed a note from Lee asking for an interview. When they met, Lee observed that it was a "crime against civilization and humanity for the United States and Great Britain to become [naval] rivals," and suggested that the publisher transmit his sentiments to the United States Government.

Lord Lee then startled Ochs by offering fleet parity, saying that the Ministry now agreed that command of the seas should be shared with America. This was news to the journalist Ochs, and hence stimulating. Lee went on to discuss a possible partnership on the seas, under which the United States Navy might be concentrated in the Pacific while the British took responsibility for the Atlantic. Ochs, delighted at the opportunity for an equitable settlement of a troublesome issue between the two countries, saw that his conversation with Lee reached Edwin Denby, Secretary of the Navy, whence the matter went to Harding and Hughes.

Certain writers on Anglo-American relations, ignoring the state of mind in America at the time, have cited the Lee-Ochs parley as evidence that here again the British Government was leading this country by the nose. The construction is naïve. For while Lee was proposing to Ochs a wide concession in order to gain naval peace, powerful pressure was being applied from many quarters in America toward the same end. Meanwhile Secretary Hughes was feeling his way to his own solution. A simple naval agreement with Britain was not enough, as he saw it. Japan had to be consulted about the future disposition of sea power. That led into the problem of Anglo-Japanese-American relations and the whole Far Eastern complex. Hughes determined to couple the problems, offering the British a naval conference in exchange for discussions on the Far East.

Japan was by no means eager for such a discussion. While the Allies and the United States were absorbed by the war in Europe, Japan had resumed her imperialistic march into China, appropriating Shantung from the Germans at the outbreak of the war and thereafter levying on China the notorious Twenty-one Demands, the effect of which was to destroy Chinese sovereignty. The United States Government, pursuing the general interventionist policy inaugurated by John Hay, had not condoned either the occupation of Shantung or the Twenty-one Demands. Adding to American distrust, the Japanese had manifested a pertinacious intention to absorb the Siberian maritime provinces during the civil strife that followed the Bolshevik Revolution. Wilson, induced to join the Allied expedition to Vladivostok, sought ways in which to checkmate the Japanese design and to preserve Russian sovereignty there. Hence the American and Japanese forces in Siberia worked most of the time at cross purposes. Moreover, as the price for their naval assistance in the Mediterranean the Nipponese had obtained from England and France their consent to picking up the former German islands flanking the American sea road from Hawaii to the Philippines.

At the Paris Peace Conference the Allies honored their agreements, including one approving the acquisition of Shantung. The issue of Shantung was one of the most troublesome before the conference. China's claim for return of the German sphere seemed to the Americans and the British morally and legally clear. Yet Japan stood on her wartime engagements, including an understanding pried out of Peking; she was likewise strongly in possession. Wilson retreated at the last moment, justifying his surrender on the ground that otherwise the Japanese might refuse to enter the League of Nations. Ironically, Wilson's moral lapse over Shantung aroused indignant protest from the anti-League forces in the United States, his enemies using Shantung as a stick with which to beat his otherwise high purposes.

In 1921 the Far Eastern policies of the United States, following a broadly consistent course from Hay to Hughes, had again carried America into sharp collision with Japan. The fresh evidence of her aggressive designs on the mainland, her grabbing of strategic islands to the disadvantage of America, her growing navy, and a current flaring up of the perennial Japanese exclusion issue—these had mobilized American public opinion against Japan. As usual the American people, shrinking from political responsibilities in Europe, contemplated action in Asia with approval.

In 1921, indeed, a large section of the American public believed that Japan was the next enemy and though war with England still seemed inconceivable, the Anglo-Japanese Alliance suddenly appeared as an inimical instrument which made even war with England less remote. That alliance, which was up for renewal in 1921, became widely unpopular in the United States. It was clear to Americans that whereas England's mortal enemy Germany had been defeated with American help, the most dangerous potential enemy of the United States, Japan, had been strengthened by the war, and one of the elements in her strength was her alliance with the other great Sea Power. As Hughes put it, the prospect of a renewal of that treaty "aroused no little uneasiness" in America.

Only Canada of the self-governing nations in the British Commonwealth shared the American aversion to the alliance. An influential section of English opinion saw it still as a safeguard to the immense British interests in the Far East and the Pacific. An allied Japan, it was argued, could be deflected from acquisitive glances in the direction of the Yangtse Valley, Hong Kong, and the Indian Empire, as well as being brought to overlook the Caucasian exclusiveness of the South Pacific Dominions. In the winter of 1921 the pro-Japanese party in England arranged a glittering reception for Hirohito, the Japanese Prince Regent (in 1941 the Emperor) on his first visit abroad. At an Imperial Conference opening in London in June Lloyd George and the Prime Ministers of Australia and New Zealand openly hoped for a renewal of the compact. Arthur Meighen, the Canadian Prime Minister, ranged himself more resolutely on the other side. Canada belonged to the American as well as the British political system; Canada's western provinces faced the same problem of Japanese immigration as the American Pacific States; and public opinion in the Dominion marched with that below the border relative to Japan.

The alliance was not allowed, however, to jeopardize American accord at London. In opening the conference Lloyd George affirmed it as the "cardinal policy" of the British Empire that America should not be alienated, and the Prime Minister gradually retreated before Meighen. Failing, because of Canadian and American opposition, in an attempt to broaden the alliance into a triplex agreement, Lloyd George finally surrendered and threw the alliance into the hopper of a prospective general conference. Harding called the conference on July 10, 1921, hurrying at the last in response to urgent cables from George Harvey, his Ambassador at London, who was fearful that Lloyd George, under parliamentary pressure, might act first and thus gain whatever prestige was involved in initiating the enterprise. Abandoned by her ally, Japan had no option but to accept the call to Washington.

6

Hughes took command of the Washington Conference within an hour of its opening. Incisive, crisply impatient with dissent, the Secretary of State executed a diplomatic coup by definitively outlining a 5-5-3 ratio for the capital ships of the Naval Powers—England, the United States, and Japan. With him on the American delegation were Lodge and Root. Balfour and Lord Lee led the British delegation, Balfour, filled with gracious dubiety, being frustrated in his attempts to act as "honest broker" between America and Japan by Hughes's brittle forthrightness.

Out of the conference came Anglo-American capital-ship parity (a rough equality in other classes would result from subsequent naval conferences); the Four-Power Treaty underwriting the status quo in the Pacific itself; and the Nine-Power Pact calculated to ensure China's territorial integrity. The Four-Power Treaty replaced the Anglo-Japanese Alliance—unsatisfactorily to both England and Japan. It was the best Hughes would grant. France was the fourth Power; invited in by Hughes presumably to widen the base and as an acknowledgment of France's position as a World Power. Aristide Briand represented the French at the outset in Washington. His delegation, which went to Washington convinced that the British and the Americans were verging on a rupture, remained to be sulkily persuaded that the whole affair bespoke an "Anglo-Saxon Alliance." In pique over that assumption, the French made common cause with the Japanese in the naval part of the parleys.

The assorted treaties went to Congress and the British Ministry in February, 1922. In his speech from the throne in that month George V rejoiced that "our relations with the United States enter a new and even closer phase of friendship." President Harding professed to view a breach in Anglo-American amity as "unthinkable." Ambassador Harvey thought that the greatest achievement of the conference was the revelation of "the complete mutuality of interest . . . upon the face of the earth" of the two Powers.

Harvey was not alone in believing that American insistence and English acquiescence in naval parity betokened the beginning of a power partnership extending over the seven seas; the press of both countries overwhelmingly applauded the new comity. The London *Times* pronounced it a "great day for all time in the history of the world." To the *Manchester Guardian* the result had "drawn close the English-speaking peoples." In New York the *Herald* called the conference "much the greatest of all time." The *Dallas News* viewed the outcome as a "demonstration of Anglo-Saxon unity," and the *Minneapolis Journal* expressed gratification at the "scrapping of the outworn prejudices between the two great English-speaking nations."

The Senate isolationists, led by the xenophobic Borah and Hiram Johnson of California, who as usual echoed Hearst's extreme views, opposed the treaties as a matter of routine. Their efforts were centered on the Four-Power Treaty. But the new Administration had firm control of the upper house, and the treaties were all ratified. There were, moreover, signs that the American people had had enough of the senatorial hermits. Although a wave of antiforeignism was sweeping America along with an aggressive antiradical movement, the old indictments of Britain's iniquity failed to reach their mark. Into the *Congressional Record* went a signed Hearst editorial, imputing to England in language now hackneyed an "arrogant disposition to employ the United States as a useful tool for the furtherance of her own selfish purposes. England has . . . always succeeded in destroying every great power that rivalled her . . . first Spain, then Holland, then France, then Germany."

But the old poison had lost its venomous effect. Objective observers saw evidence at Washington that the center of power in the English-speaking world had already begun to shift across the Atlantic. To the English it seemed that the United States had asked and been granted much. For the first time in centuries Britannia ruled the waves not alone but in partnership. Moreover, the British Empire had been required to exchange Japan, a reliable ally prepared to fight in support of the imperialistic structure in the Far East, for the unpredictable friendship of the United States in that quarter of the world. At Washington, Britain seemed not leading but led.

Into the Senate debate went a view sharply contrasted with that of Hearst. Borah, outraged, read on the floor a speech made by Paul D. Cravath, an eminent New York lawyer, before the New York chapter of the Council on Foreign Relations. It seemed to Cravath that an Anglo-American entente had succeeded the Anglo-Japanese Alliance. "Every member of the American delegation," said the indiscreet Cravath, had assured him that out of the "understanding" and "sympathy" exhibited at Washington had come a common assumption "that in all future emergencies they can both count on having the very closest coöperation." Cravath knew "definitely" that Balfour shared this opinion. Further, the technical advisers of both countries were positive that the British and American fleets would have no trouble in defeating Japan "in Japanese waters." The speaker was certain that "our naval position as against Japan had been improved rather than weakened."

As a result of a Senate outcry, Cravath telegraphed Lodge an unconvincing denial of the report as read. Hughes felt called upon to disclaim any secret understanding with the English. Root held his peace. Cravath, of course, had spoken advisedly. Anglo-American relations, never static, had been clarified and strengthened. The Atlantic System, disregarded under Wilson, who never accepted its tenets and implications, had been reinstated, and the outline of a Pacific System had been marked out for later filling in. Hearst in America and the editor of the *Saturday Review* in London each saw his country sacrificed to the ambition of the other, but Archibald Hurd, coeditor of *Brassey's Naval Annual,* concluded a bit regretfully in the London *Fortnightly Review* that "the trident of Neptune passes into the joint guardianship of the English-speaking peoples."

Characteristically, service opinion in all three countries deplored their naval "losses." Admiral Sir Rosslyn Wester Wemyss saw in Britain's peaceable ceding of parity "an act of renunciation unparalleled in history." Japanese naval officers complained that they had suffered a more grievous defeat at the conference table than ever they had experienced in battle. In America Admiral H. S. Knapp condemned the bargain by which the United States agreed not to develop bases west of Hawaii in return for Japan's acceptance of the 5-5-3 ratio.

The public in England and America preferred, however, to share Harding's sanguine faith that the Washington treaties had brought in a "new and better epoch in human affairs." It is impossible not to smile at the grave optimism of 1922, yet the Washington Conference was a success within the limitations specified by Hughes. Between the English-speaking Powers its naval agreement has remained in force. The British, if somewhat against their wish, were relieved of an alliance that might easily have proved embarrassing. Japan withdrew in force from Shantung (as indeed she had promised at Paris), and although her mainland ambitions were only temporarily set aside, the crisis atmosphere of 1921 in both Japan and America was relieved. For some time after the conference Americans stopped talking of the "inevitability" of war with Japan.

The participation of the United States followed the clear lines of its major policies, notwithstanding the querulous nonsense of the isolationists. America had reaffirmed her strategic, sea-power solidarity with the British in conformity with the Atlantic System. As for Asia, the United States had adhered with fidelity to the co-operative policy initiated by Hay. Whether wisely or not from the point of self-interest, we had again balked Japanese desires with respect to China, wringing from her another acknowledgment of the Open Door. Again America had conducted a purely moral intervention in China; exhibiting the faith in verbal pledges characterizing postwar diplomacy, she had enfeebled her power to enforce respect for her policies by giving up the right to strengthen the bases at Guam and Manila.

The United States had also demonstrated again its unwillingness to bear a part in European politics. The dualism which urges the country toward a decisive voice in Asia while it shrinks from the councils of Europe was never more dramatically exemplified than in Washington. At Paris Wilson, Lloyd George, and Clemenceau agreed on a tripartite defensive alliance designed to safeguard France from Germany until the League of Nations should become sufficiently entrenched. The Senate rejected that treaty along with the larger purposes of Versailles. At Washington the French doggedly sought guarantees from England and America in return for the discarded treaty. Hughes as stiffly sidetracked the attempts of the French to open the question of land armaments, aware that any discussion of armies led straight to the guarantees which neither English-speaking Power was at the moment prepared to concede.

The British too had withdrawn from Continental matters after Versailles. "At the very time that the United States Government repudiated the Versailles settlement legally," writes Dr. Birdsall, "the English people did so morally." The drift in Europe in the spring of 1922 could not, however, be entirely ignored by the British, although America would still escape political involvement then, and generally during the long truce.

7

Lloyd George, therefore, his hands freed by the naval peace, equilibrium in the Far East, and an armistice in Ireland, turned in the spring to the Continent. Two years of peace had been almost as ruinous as war. Germany was in the incipient stages of the inflation which was to liquidate the debts of the country and beggar the middle class. The psychological weight of reparation payments and war debts (little actually had been paid on German account after the deliveries to France and Belgium of livestock, railroad equipment, metals, and other payments in kind) hung over the economy of Europe, palsying all efforts at reconstruction. At this point the rigorous Poincaré succeeded Briand, the great European, on a platform calling for the stricter exaction of reparation payments.

In Lloyd George's opinion, the time had come for a general appeasement and the reintroduction of Germany and Russia into the family of nations. He therefore approached Poincaré on the project for a new "peace" conference to include Russia and Germany and, if possible, the United States. A Social-Democratic Government at Berlin, struggling against the contempt and opposition of the Junker class, the army, and the bureaucrats, was seeking a three-year moratorium on reparation payments. Lloyd George favored this respite; Poincaré set his face against it. The French statesman would agree to Lloyd George's conference only at a price—a defensive alliance with England. Lloyd George accepted the terms, prompting Edwin L. James, the Paris correspondent of the *New York Times,* to cable his paper that the United States had lost its influence in Europe and no longer held the balance of power. As plans reached maturity for the "peace" conference, to be held at Genoa, the Germans and the Russians met at Rapallo, to the surprise of Europe, signed their own pact of recognition and trade, and re-enforced Poincaré's worst fears.

The Genoa Conference of 1922, the first in a series of parleys aimed at redressing the maladjustments flowing from the recent war and the peace settlements, ended in failure. The United States, refusing to attend, resisted efforts by the Powers to intertwine reparations with the governmental debts owed to America. Thereupon American-European relations entered the phase epitomized in Europe by the quip of a Parisian journalist: "The Shylock strain seems to predominate in the cross-breeding of Uncle Sam."

Into this atmosphere was injected the Balfour memorandum on war debts, which placed the approval of statesmanship on the journalist's gibe. Balfour was created an earl in 1922. He stood at the pinnacle of favor, both royal and public; his utterance therefore carried the sanction of Britain.

What Balfour did was to announce to the Continent that England was prepared to ask only enough in payment of reparations and loans to the Allies to balance her payments to America. The effect all over Europe was to identify war debts with reparations. Between the lines, Lord Balfour was saying that England was a good fellow, willing to go easy on the defeated foe and her debtors, but that flinty-hearted Uncle Sam was barring such generosity. He further compounded what was in American eyes an offense by a misstatement, a lapse as often stressed by his own countrymen as by Americans. His gift for subtle ratiocination bore the great skeptic outside the boundaries of the factual when he indicated that England had borrowed in the United States for the other Allies, implying that the United States Government had required Britain's endorsement on loans for the Continental Powers. The truth was, of course, that all the Allies had equal access to the United States Treasury, buying freely of munitions, food, and other supplies and merely sending the bills on to Washington.

No British statesman of his time played as large a part as Balfour in Anglo-American relations; none had communicated such distinguished evidences of goodwill, none had practiced so inept a statecraft. It was Balfour who fumbled indecisively with Pauncefote's dispatch on the eve of the Spanish-American War, Balfour who joined with the Kaiser in the second Venezuelan incident. In 1917, heading the British War Mission, he appeared before a joint session of Congress while all official Washington, led by the President, sang "God Save the King" in a moving gesture of comradeship. Warmly received when he returned in 1921 for the Washington Conference, Balfour became to Americans the best-known figure in British public life. His attempt, therefore, to make the United States the scapegoat for Europe's reparation and debt tribulations was regarded in this country as the wound of a friend, hence harder to bear.

The controversy over the Balfour memorandum illustrated the misunderstandings that grew out of the confused statement of war purposes. On the hypothesis that America had fought solely to crush autocracy and vindicate democracy, the war had been American from 1914 onward, and the Allies had considerable basis for their reproaches that the Americans came late, contributed little but the promise of greater things in the future, withdrew after the fighting, and now demanded their pound of flesh. The American people, squirming under the implications of this hypothesis, felt instinctively that it was a wrong one. But wherever they turned they met the powerful phrases of the man entitled to state America's aims, and Europe was never slow to quote Wilson for its own ends.

Balfour's reflections, offending America, also injured Great Britain's interest there. Calvin Coolidge, who succeeded Harding in 1923 on the President's death, dropped into the discussion his famous rustic rejoinder: "They hired the money, didn't they?" A cold and inadequate dismissal of a profoundly troublesome international problem, the remark punctured Balfour's finespun structure of evasion to the satisfaction of millions of Americans. The funding commission under Stanley Baldwin, Chancellor of the Exchequer, was able to obtain only a minimum relaxation of terms in Washington, France and Italy doing much better. The British paid on the barrel head until the Hoover moratorium of 1931, continuing token payments through 1933. Their debt as funded in 1923 was $4,250,000,000. Altogether they remitted something more than $2,000,000,000. In June, 1934, when the British defaulted, they still owed $4,750,000,-000, the increase being due to compound interest and the fact that payments had reduced the principal insufficiently.

So went the years of the false peace. Poincaré, seeking to wring blood from the German turnip, invaded the Ruhr, a venture characterized by Lloyd George as "dismal and tragic." Briand, back in power, brought about surface reconciliations at Locarno in October, 1925. The new Italian dictator, Benito Mussolini, only just getting a total grip on his country, traveled to the conference spectacularly by train, racing car, and speedboat. Reparations and debts were eased,

western frontiers were redefined, Germany was invited to
enter the League of Nations. "It is ended," said Briand,
"that long war between us. . . . Away with the rifles, the
machine guns, and the cannon!"

Lloyd George gave way to Bonar Law, to Baldwin, to
Ramsay MacDonald and then to Baldwin again. Hoover
succeeded Coolidge, Franklin D. Roosevelt followed Hoover.
The Tory Baldwin had no settled American policy, Mac-
Donald, returning to power in 1929, was pro-American.
Hoover pursued the traditional path of collaboration with
the British. In 1927 a naval conference at Geneva came to
grief when the admirals to whom Coolidge and Baldwin
entrusted the negotiations collided in a celebrated dispute
over the displacement of cruisers. England wished 6,000-ton
cruisers with 6-inch guns (converted merchant liners in
wartime carry 6-inch guns) and the United States plumped
for 10,000-ton cruisers with a wide cruising range suited
to the Pacific. It appeared for a time that Baldwin's Government, bowing to the Admiralty, was seeking to renege
on parity, and Lord Robert Cecil resigned from the Ministry
in protest. A delegate at Geneva, Cecil had been overruled by
the admirals. An American lobbyist in the secret pay of shipbuilders took credit with his employers for wrecking the
conference, and Coolidge, finding fault with the British conduct at Geneva, announced the building of fifteen 10,000-ton
cruisers already authorized.

The Western world, sampling the incipient joys of a boom
in 1927, was little concerned over the cost of a few cruisers.
The skies over Europe were relatively cloudless, Adolf Hitler
was an obscure beer-hall cultist, a leader of street fighters, the
author of a dull and rambling book who had been in jail.
Germany was making an amazing economic recovery, thanks
to loans from the United States and England. Her steel
production rose to prewar volume, her merchant marine,
soon to boast the *Bremen* and the *Europa,* had grown from
400,000 tons to 3,700,000. France, stabilizing her currency,
was also gaining prosperity. In 1928 America's foreign trade
passed the $9,000,000,000 mark, approximating that of Brit-

ain. As the price of a huge export trade, the United States was exporting billions of dollars a year in capital and loans.

The Coolidge years (Westbrook Pegler's "era of wonderful nonsense") marked the heyday of the foreign lending policy, a species of economic imperialism which it was hoped might transfer financial sovereignty from London to New York. By 1929, when the bubble burst, American private investments abroad amounted to nearly $20,000,000,000—$2,500,-000,000 of it irreclaimably sunk in Germany. Sums loaned by the American investor to Europe found their way back to the United States Treasury in reparation payments and intergovernmental debt service. Optimists, unfamiliar with the elements which had made England the world's banker, erroneously supposed that Wall Street was to eclipse Lombard Street permanently. The United States lacked, however, a tariff policy enabling it to accept goods in payment for dollars; it lacked Britain's vast shipping, insurance, and dockage paraphernalia with which to service trade in all parts of the world; nor had it a tradition of colonial enterprise, with thousands of trained and willing young men available for management in the far corners of the earth.

Wall Street's expansive hopes caused a corresponding apprehension, however, in Lombard Street. Envy of America's economic might had been present amongst the British trading classes since the "Yankee invasion" led by the elder J. P. Morgan in the opening years of the century. It was England's lot to be ruled during the postwar years by men of business such as Baldwin and the sons of Joseph Chamberlain, Neville and Austen, whose attitude toward the United States was conditioned by their fears of Wall Street's self-confident competition.

It took MacDonald's return to power in 1929 at the head of a Labor Ministry to restore the transatlantic perspective of the British Government and heal the breach of Geneva. MacDonald finally settled the issue of parity. Preparing for a goodwill mission to this country, the Prime Minister suspended work on several men-of-war and assured the League of Nations Assembly that England and America were on the

road to complete naval understanding. As his contribution
to accord, President Hoover announced that the keels of
three authorized cruisers would not be laid pending a re-
examination of parity. While in America MacDonald sat on
a log with Hoover at the President's camp on the Rapidan
and delivered an invitation to a new naval parley in London.
Addressing the Senate, he declared he could foresee no situation under which "our arms, whether on land, on the sea or
in the air, can ever again come into hostile conflict." As for
parity: "Take it, without reserve, heaped up and flowing
over!"

At the London Naval Conference of 1930, full equality in
all categories was worked out for the English-speaking navies.
France, under pressure of Mussolini's imperialistic thrust
in the Mediterranean, fell out with the major Sea Powers,
and declined to accept the status allotted to her. The Japanese delegation came insisting on a 10-10-7 ratio, won concessions in cruiser strength, and returned home to face angry
public demonstrations and repudiation by the militarists.
Assassination being a common instrument of public policy
in Japan, the extreme militarists contrived the murder of
Hamaguchi, the Prime Minister, for upholding the London
agreement. The death of Hamaguchi, the "Lion" of Japanese
politics, signalized the rise of the brutal forces in Japanese
life toward an ascendancy which they were to maintain over
the liberal, parliamentary elements for the next decade.

Meanwhile, the New York Stock Exchange had undergone
in October and November, 1929, a succession of panic days
marking the end of the postwar boom. The ensuing breakdown of the world's interlocked economy supplied, as is now
apparent, objective conditions of disintegration out of which
came the breakdown in large areas of traditional civilization
itself in the 1930's.

8

In 1931 the postwar world passed into a prewar status.
Thereafter fear of the next great war supplanted regret over
the last one. Two events marked the transition. President

Hoover declared a one-year moratorium on war-debt pay-ments, a belated and futile effort to save the deflationary government of Chancellor Heinrich Brüning and so the German Republic. The Hoover intervention represented the final chapter in the long story of Europe's attempt to escape pecuniary payment for the war. It failed to save Brüning, Germany, or the postwar financial fabric. In a rough way, it settled the problem of intergovernmental debts owed to America, since our debtors thereafter repudiated their obli-gations. The other milestone of 1931 was the Japanese seiz-ure of Mukden, the prelude to the conquest of Manchuria.

Brüning's speedy fall put an end to reconstruction. Japa-nese aggression destroyed the hope of collective security, which had grown up in the Western world since Locarno, and more particularly after ratification by the Powers in 1928 of the Briand-Kellogg Pact of Paris. After Brüning, Germany was governed by presidential decree, paving the way for the personal government of Hitler. The conquest of Manchuria disclosed the decay of the democratic world and the paralysis of its will to resist aggressors—even, as in the case of France and lesser European democracies, of a will to survive.

An isolationist in 1941, Hoover took an active part in both the crucial occurrences of 1931. Having perceived a grave threat to American security and well-being in the premoni-tory happenings of that year, he now rejects the conclusions he once foresaw. His intervention in Europe followed the pattern of American postwar economic relations with the old continent. Contrary to a widespread impression, the United States did not wholly retreat into its shell after Con-gress adopted a separate peace with Germany. Faithful to its dread of permanent entanglements in the Old World, the United States abstained from political commitments, yet participated in such economic arrangements as the Young and Dawes plans. Wall Street, uncommitted by Washington's parting injunction, extended help throughout Europe. The English-speaking countries rendered enormous assistance, by and large, to Germany, assistance scarcely acknowledged and brazenly denied after the gutter forces had seized the

republic. Hoover's moratorium, therefore, followed the
policy of economic intervention.

Hoover's Far Eastern interference likewise pursued the
traditional path allowing the United States to exert its influence politically in Asia while withholding it in Europe. His
Secretary of State, Henry L. Stimson, bore the brunt of the
crisis over Manchuria. Stimson believed in collective security;
to him the Pact of Paris was a solemn pledge of a better day.
A vigorous idealist, he reacted boldly against events that induced pessimism elsewhere, the stresses of 1931 which sent
fear through the Western world. A blundering attempt by
the German and Austrian governments to create a customs
union (Zollverein) provoked militant French resistance but
foreshadowed what seemed to others an eventual association.
The credit structure of Central Europe was shaken when the
Creditanstalt, a huge Rothschild bank in Vienna, fell.
England had borrowed at short term in France and had
loaned at long term in Germany. When the French called
their English loans, England went off the gold standard. In
the gathering economic crisis Hitler's Nazis emerged as a
formidable parliamentary party, electing 107 Deputies to
the Reichstag and polling more than 6,000,000 popular votes.

Japan struck while Europe was thus distracted, and Stimson
alone of the democratic statesmen saw the world menace in
a clash between Asiatics in far-off Mukden. His warning that
the "new structure of international society" would be "in-
calculably damaged" unless Japan was brought to book
went largely unheeded and unanswered. The outburst of
Japanese aggressiveness at Mukden on September 18, 1931,
brought an immediate appeal from the Chinese Nationalist
Government. Stimson acted as promptly. Thereafter for
seven months the Secretary of State sought by every power
of persuasion to support China's territorial integrity, halt
the fighting in Manchuria (and later at Shanghai), and vindicate the principle of collective security. He negotiated directly with the feeble civil government at Tokyo, with
Ramsay MacDonald and Sir John Simon, the British Foreign
Secretary, and, at Geneva on behalf of the Nine-Power

Treaty and the Pact of Paris. Pledging parallel action with the League of Nations, Stimson called for unified diplomatic pressure, an appeal to "world opinion," and the imposition of economic sanctions if all else failed. The Japanese were more vulnerable to sanctions in 1931 than they would be in 1941. In the decade between the English-speaking Powers enabled Japan to buy huge reserves of oil, scrap iron, and dozens of other military essentials. Stimson likewise urged a policy of nonrecognition of Japan's ascendancy in Manchuria.

Stimson was compelled to make the best of acceptance by the League of Nations of his nonrecognition policy, together with a fact-finding commission under League direction. Geneva would go no further. One factor detracting from his position was the naval weakness of the United States. Another was his inability to get on common ground with the Soviet Union, a party of genuine interest. Hoover had neglected the navy and declined, alone of the heads of Great Powers, to enter into diplomatic relations with Moscow.

It was, however, the refusal of Great Britain to collaborate with Stimson that most effectively stymied his endeavors. England, passing through political change, entered in September, 1931, on the long, humiliating, and in the end mortally dangerous road of appeasement which was to carry Neville Chamberlain to Munich. In August, a National Government had succeeded MacDonald's Labor Ministry, with the Prime Minister still at the helm. Two months later MacDonald accepted a coalition Ministry, principally Tory, and was thereupon deposed as head of the Labor party. At the beginning of his physical decline (soon his memory and coherence would be noticeably affected in the House of Commons), MacDonald was the prisoner of his Tory colleagues. The temper of such colleagues as Neville Chamberlain—so anti-American that he reputedly declined to receive Americans visiting London—was averse to making common cause with Washington. Generally speaking, it was the middle-class, business type Tory, thinking first in terms of profit and trade advantage, that let the British Empire down in the prewar years. In fairness to the Ministry it should, however, be noted that the British climate in the 1930's was pacifist to the point of morbidity, the City, labor, and the intellectuals opposing commitments likely to lead, however remotely, toward war.

Simon, a great lawyer but a poor diplomat, was by nature a trimmer. Lloyd George remarked once that Sir John had "sat on the fence so long that the iron had entered his soul." Both the Prime Minister and the Foreign Secretary took refuge from Stimson's disquieting importunities behind the walls of the League of Nations. At Geneva it was not clear from day to day during the discussion of Manchuria whether Simon spoke for England or Japan, and Yosuke Matsuoka, there to plead Japan's cause, remarked that the Englishman had summed up in fifteen minutes what he had been trying for weeks to express.

In January, 1932—three weeks before the Japanese bombed Shanghai, fired the Chapei Neighborhood, and met the heroic Nineteenth Route army in battle—Stimson asked the British to join in a stern note to Tokyo, threatening non-recognition of "any situation, treaty or agreement brought about in violation of treaties." The British Foreign Office omitted the courtesy of a direct reply, issuing instead a casual communiqué to the effect that "His Majesty's Government have not considered it necessary to address any formal note to the Japanese Government on the lines of the American Government's note." Superciliously, the London *Times* shed light but no luster on the incident, saying: "The American Government may have been moved by fear that the Japanese authorities would set up virtually an independent administration in Manchuria, which would favor Japanese interests to the detriment of the commerce of other nations. It is clear that the Foreign Office does not share these apprehensions."

Whether the Foreign Office actually believed that Stimson's interest was confined to the Open Door or whether this was mere evasion never has been really clarified. Some time afterward it was semiofficially acknowledged that the communiqué had been a "slip," a subordinate having sent it off on the eve of a week end without waiting for the approval of a superior. On November 30, 1938, a letter to the *Times* which bore the marks of having been written by a Foreign Office functionary explained that the civil servant responsible for the action had not "realized until it [the communiqué] appeared in the press that it read like a rebuff to America."

Unrebuffed by the communiqué, the Secretary of State continued to press Simon. Obtaining no tangible support at long range, Stimson went himself to Geneva, where the Foreign Secretary and the Prime Minister were attending the ill-fated general Disarmament Conference. Face-to-face negotiations brought no better result. Although expressing "earnest anxiety for complete co-operation," MacDonald and Simon would not come to grips with the issue as Stimson saw it. As Japan consolidated her theft of Manchuria, establishing the puppet State Manchukuo, Stimson continued to utter warnings that this unrebuked aggression would stimulate like aggressions, endangering peace elsewhere.

Stimson's policy carried into the Roosevelt Administration. The President-elect, who was to take office in March, 1933, authorized Stimson in advance to announce that there would be no change. Nor, except for a less urgent tone with Tokyo, was there change. By 1941 Roosevelt and Cordell Hull, his Secretary of State, had borne the United States into a virtual alliance with China (nonbelligerent it is true), although contradictorily it furnished the sinews of war to Japan until midsummer of that year. And in 1941 Stimson, having correctly diagnosed the first symptoms of the totalitarian malady, was laboring as Secretary of War to help suppress the full-grown evil.

Eight years to the month after the Japanese took Mukden Hitler ordered the invasion of Poland. The stream of aggression rising in Manchuria had come to full flood. During those eight years tension mounted steadily as the regimes to be joined in the Rome-Berlin-Tokyo Axis progressively brought war nearer the heart of Europe. The Japanese

fought the Chinese, first in Manchuria, then in China
proper; they fought, not too successfully, the Soviet Union
on the Manchurian-Siberian border and in Mongolia. In
1937 the Japanese launched their undeclared, all-out war
on China that was still plaguing them four years later. Mussolini's mechanized legions overwhelmed the Ethiopians,
armed only for nineteenth-century warfare, and the Fascist
dictators, meeting Stalin's forces in Spain, enlarged civil
strife into a precursor of general European war while the
democracies looked on as if entranced.

The United States Government was not indifferent to
Mussolini's naked conquest of Ethiopia, co-operating with
the League of Nations in embargoing shipments of war
materials to "both belligerents." As America could have had
little access to Ethiopia with such shipments, the embargo
was plainly aimed at Italy. In truth, Hull and Harold L.
Ickes, Secretary of the Interior and oil administrator, exceeded the zeal of the League of Nations, attempting to halt
oil exports to the belligerents. The failure of the League to
apply oil sanctions and Stanley Baldwin's reversal of the
MacDonald Ministry's Ethiopian policy when he himself
became Prime Minister in 1935 momentarily dampened the
zest of the Roosevelt Administration for collective security.

The course of that Administration toward the world had
aspects of ambiguity during this period. Although in his
annual message of January, 1936, the President denounced
the aggressor nations, he accepted with little evidence of
distaste the elaborate and naïvely contrived network of neutrality laws which the isolationists in Congress patched up
session by session. The poverty of isolationist thought was
never more clearly displayed than in this legislation. These
laws, beginning with Hiram Johnson's bill interdicting loans
to governments in default to the United States, assumed that
history runs in undeviating grooves. Because America went
to war in 1917 after lending hundreds of millions to the
Allies, Johnson seemed to believe that the existence of the
loans had been a controlling factor in the decision. Because
the United States sold munitions to the Allies and American

vessels were sunk by U-boats, the isolationists considered the sale and the sinkings among the primary causes of its participation in that war.

The authors of such legislation were dealing entirely with surface manifestations. Congress, with surprisingly little opposition from the White House, was invading a field where it had no historical or constitutional business—the primary conduct of foreign affairs. Representing a vote of "no confidence" in Roosevelt's foreign policies, the enactments, as any thoughtful student of American affairs could have informed the isolationist members of Congress, failed to insulate America from the world. They did weaken the influence of the United States, and by so doing assisted the aggressor nations. Thanks to these laws, Hitler and his accomplices proceeded in full confidence that the most powerful nation in his path had for the time being declared itself a noncombatant in the conflict between totalitarianism and democracy. The isolationists had, moreover, struck ignorantly and dangerously at the national interest by attempting to serve notice that America would not defend the Atlantic System beyond her three-mile limit. Fortunately, the unrealistic mood giving rise to the neutrality laws yielded to the onrush of circumstance.

There is, of course, much to be said for the Americans who dreaded another "foreign" war. Since Versailles it had become a commonplace of mass thinking that the United States was duped in 1917 by the combined machinations of Wall Street, munitions makers, and English propagandists, and that after the United States had fought to redeem the Old World from its evil, monarchical, autocratic ways, the Old World had turned on America, dubbing this country "Uncle Shylock" and in the end refusing to pay its war debts. Senator Gerald K. Nye's munitions investigation proved that the Morgan firm had acted as British purchasing agent in this country and that certain industrialists made large profits out of supplying materials for war. Wilson's postulate that America had fought for humanity, a half-truth at best, came to be a bad joke. During the long truce the United

States was drenched with what Walter Lippmann has called "cynical histories" calculated to prove everything but the simple truth that America went to war for her own cogent reasons and that, in Wilson's words, "everything for which America fought [was] accomplished."

The myth that the United States had blundered in 1917 was in full currency in 1935. In that year the American people, if they were sure of any one thing, were positive that they would never be gulled into another "European" war. Yet within five years the United States, as a nonbelligerent ally of Great Britain and China, was at war in both the Atlantic and the Pacific in all but name and actual "shooting." The American people had not been gulled into this war. Wall Street was out of the picture. The "merchants of death" had retired, dismantling their plants, to the point where in 1939 the country had scarcely enough smokeless-powder capacity to supply the army for maneuvers. The United States had loaned no money abroad. Its ships were forbidden the war zone. The English, mindful of the American legend, endeavored to keep their propaganda inconspicuous. They only succeeded in botching it.

Something had happened outside the calculations of the isolationists of 1935. That something was the fall of France.

IX. "Atlantic Charter": Toward a Liberal World Order

ONCE THE NORTH SEA, English Channel, and Atlantic ports of the Low Countries and France had fallen in June, 1940, the Atlantic world lay constructively open to the Nazis. Only one bastion remained, hemming them in to the seaward. And who, in the stunned days of Dunkirk, dared hope that the thin line of British resistance, the Royal Navy, the Royal Air Force, and the stubborn gallantry of the British people, could stay the Teutonic tide for long? It was in those days, the grimness of which sobered and alarmed America, that the second phase of the modern struggle between England and Germany —between the classical, liberal, Christian civilization of the West and the primitive, reactionary forces of the Teutoburg Forest—burst the bounds of Europe, becoming a world war by definition and America's war in fact.

Thenceforward a wave of the future totally unlike the dark flood adumbrated by Anne Morrow Lindbergh began to bear the United States ineluctably into the conflict. It was then that "the defense of the security of the Atlantic world" became, in Walter Lippmann's phrase, "an inexorable necessity." In that historic moment America's vital interests were engaged. Until the barrier states of the West went down, only American sentiments were involved. Overwhelmingly, the American people detested and feared the new barbarism of the Germans; sympathizing with its victims, they wished to extend assistance to its enemies. To that end in October, 1939, only a few weeks after the wanton invasion of Poland, Congress repealed the mandatory provisions of the arms embargo, opening American industrial productivity to the Atlantic belligerents, England and France.

That act in itself did not identify the war as American. Although Americans understood the moral issues, recoiling from the swelling Nazi terror, it was only when the Germans stood on the opposite shores of the Atlantic that their defeat became directly essential to the American nation. The war had been revealed for what it was, "fundamentally," as Colonel Frank Knox put it, "an attempt by Germany to seize control of the seas from Great Britain." To that "vital" situation, the Secretary of the Navy added, the United States could not remain indifferent, any more than in 1917 it had held aloof when command of the Atlantic seemed likely to pass to a hostile, aggressive Power. England was again, as in 1823, as in 1898 and from 1917 onward, the eastern stronghold of the Atlantic world, and her fate was a matter of concern to America only relatively less important than our own.

Being no longer detached, if interested, bystanders, the United States promptly displayed by its acts recognition of the American stake in the war. Congress passed and the President signed the first peacetime draft act in American history. Billions were poured out unquestioningly for an army and an air force. Again, as in 1916, when it appeared that Britain might be subdued, America undertook the creation of a two-ocean navy. Those were defense measures calculated to fortify the United States at sea and on shore. But Administration and Congress went beyond such negative defense.

The United States Government proceeded almost automatically to Britain's help, thus signifying a conviction that the English were bearing the brunt for America and the American neighbors of the Atlantic world. Only on the hypothesis that England was the first line of security for the United States would the Government have been justified in alienating guns, ammunition, tanks, shipping, and aircraft or exchanging fifty over-age but serviceable destroyers to England for seven offshore bases from Newfoundland to Trinidad. (By their part in this trade, the English finally concluded the drama of their retirement in force from the American seas, confiding their North American and Caribbean possessions and interests to American guardianship. The British withdrawal was an unprecedented manifestation of trust by one nation in another. Nor was it merely a crisis measure. It crowned, as we appreciate from our observation of British policy, a long process of retirement.)

Another unprecedented action was to follow, this time on the American side. Early in 1941 the President and Congress, acknowledging even more directly that England was fighting the American fight, enacted the Lend-Lease Act, which for the first time in history placed the treasure of one country at the free disposal of another. Unless vital American interests were being served by the British the United States Government lacked the moral right to share with them the American sinews of war.

The fact was that the United States Government, Administration and Congress alike, was defending its country and the Atlantic world at the point of best defense—the other side of the Atlantic. American wartime policy became thereafter one of unified effort with Great Britain.

Congress passed the Lend-Lease Act only after a searching inquiry and a debate frivolously protracted by the isolationist minority. The relationship of Britain and America to the defense of the Atlantic world was made abundantly clear by witnesses testifying before congressional committees and in the debates in both houses. Among other responsible witnesses were the three Cabinet members most concerned with the war situation: Cordell Hull, Secretary of State, Henry L. Stimson, Secretary of War, and Knox. The testimony of these men left Congress and the public in no doubt as to where our interest lay. Said Secretary Hull: "Control of the high seas by law-abiding nations is the key to the security of the Western Hemisphere. . . . Were Britain defeated . . . Germany could easily cross the Atlantic—especially the South Atlantic—unless we were ready and able to do what Britain is doing now."

To Stimson, the statesman who had sought so steadfastly and heartbreakingly to nip totalitarian aggression in the bud, it was apparent that "the British fleet today stands alone as an obstacle to German control of the Atlantic." It remained, however, for Knox to spread before the House Foreign Affairs Committee in detail the historical and strategical reasons for the inescapable link of America with Britain. Because the Secretary's statement may be regarded as the official declaration of the United States Government on its relationship with England and the Atlantic world, we draw extensively from its text. The importance to America and the Western hemisphere of sea power could not, said Knox, be exaggerated, continuing: "It has been because of the existence of sea power, exercised by two nations, Great Britain and ourselves, that both the Atlantic and the Pacific have served as barriers against the acquisitive designs of aggressive powers." Not, it will be noted, the existence of the oceans as broad bodies of water but the identity of the Powers commanding them had guaranteed the security of America in the past. After specifying the three great sea exits from Europe, the North Sea, the English Channel, and Gibraltar, the Secretary proceeded by explaining:

Our entire western world has been safe from attack from Europe because the Brtish fleet has always stood sentinel at those three exits . . . and the British policy, for many years, has accepted and assisted us in the maintenance of the Monroe Doctrine. That has sufficed to make the Atlantic barrier secure.[1]

Turning to the Pacific, Knox recapitulated the rise of Japanese sea power, the strengthening of Japan during the First World War, and the transfer of our fleet to that ocean as a "check" on Japanese "aggressions." The United States, said the Secretary, was able to maintain its battle fleet in the Pacific only "because the existence and deployment of the British Navy gave us security in the Atlantic." The effect, Knox concluded, was that "both we and the British actually

---

[1] It should be recalled that from the discovery of America until the enunciation of the Monroe Doctrine, European Powers invaded the New World repeatedly and at will. Thereafter only the French in support of Maximilian actually occupied a part of the hemisphere; with the rise of American naval power and the growth of the Anglo-American accord, only Germany looked threateningly toward these shores.

have had a two-ocean navy, operated for a single peaceful purpose."

The Anglo-American sea-power partnership described by the Secretary of the Navy was not ended by the war. It has, in truth, been intensified. While the British Navy has been fighting, convoying, and patrolling in the Atlantic, the Mediterranean, and the Indian Ocean, the United States Navy has also been performing a military function by containing the Japanese Navy. Impassive, dogged, ready for battle, the American fleet by its presence in force has dissuaded the Japanese from opening a naval front in the Pacific or venturing a direct assault on Hong Kong, Singapore, Manila, the Netherlands East Indies, and Burma. Thanks to the partnership which, as we have seen, dates from 1922, the British have been required to keep only a skeleton naval force east of Suez. The United States Navy has been guarding what a London journal called the "ramparts of the democracies in the Pacific" as well as lending a hand in the Atlantic.

Owing to the failure of both governments to disclose their naval policies in detail, it has not been as widely understood as it should be that the most urgent field for American "exertions" in the common cause—as predicted by Admiral Mahan a generation ago—is the Far East. Yet it was not lost on students of the development that Winston Churchill in his world-wide broadcast of August 24, 1941, depicted the United States as the principal in the attempt to bring Japan to heel. The United States, said the Prime Minister, was patiently seeking a peaceable solution of the Asiatic problem, but if its efforts failed "we shall, of course range ourselves unhesitatingly at the side of the United States." Apparent from Churchill's words, as well as from the logic of the situation and other evidences, is the fact that in the Anglo-American division of labor the United States bears the primary responsibility for coping with the Axis in the Pacific.

Throughout the spring and summer of 1941, the United States pushed steadily across both oceans. The Alaska, Guam, and Manila bases were hastily strengthened, the fleet was placed in final readiness, the Philippine army was mustered into United States Army Service, and a unified army command established for the Far East. Increased help went forward to China, a joint plan of defense being concerted with the British and Netherlands commanders, and negotiations were opened, it was supposed, with the Soviet Government looking to a land and air front in Siberia. In the Atlantic the United States Navy moved eastward, taking over the protection of Greenland and occupying the Iceland base in conjunction with the British. As the arc of patrol of the navy was extended, it exerted increasing influence on the Second Battle of the Atlantic. Meanwhile the offshore bases were being hurried to completion, and in South America progress was made toward a unified hemisphere defense.

By the fall of 1941 the United States Navy occupied a position of menace in both oceans. The decision as to whether America should change her status from full-scale but nonbelligerent participation to all-out war now rested with the Axis, both in Europe and in the Far East. During the first nine months of 1941 the tempo of American participation rose. The flow of goods and food for Britain mounted week by week. It was the addition of American fighter craft to British production that justified the costly air offensive against Germany and the occupied countries in the summer. United States merchantmen were delivering supplies to the British Middle East command by way of the Pacific and the Red Sea. In August the President announced that the United States was undertaking the responsibility of ferrying planes to the Middle East by way of the South Atlantic and Africa—a significant step in the light of open American concern over the disposition of the French base at Dakar. This undertaking meant the establishment of an air base—under the civilian auspices of the Pan-American air lines—on the Atlantic coast of Africa.

2

With his country already deep in the war by midsummer of 1941, President Franklin D. Roosevelt made the peace

America's also by his epochal meeting at sea with Winston Churchill in mid-August. The Atlantic conference between those "two men of the sea," in the evocative phrase of the *New York Times,* was in a sense a fulfillment and an enlargement of the Atlantic System. By its suggestive setting "in a spacious, landlocked bay," as Churchill described it, the conference dramatized for the English-speaking peoples their solidarity on the sea. Meeting to consider broad oceanic strategy and the problem of supply, the seagoing statesmen charted also a Pax Anglo-Americana, which was, in point of terms, a broadening of the liberal practice of the Atlantic world—nonaggression, political and economic freedom—into a formula for wider application when the war is ended. "An Atlantic charter," as the Laborite London *Daily Herald* construed it, for world application; a phrase adopted by Churchill in the broadcast mentioned before as a title for the Eight Principles which he and the President had declared.

To statesmen familiar since youth with the sea-power theses of Admiral Mahan, as are Franklin Roosevelt and Churchill, the place of meeting was singularly appropriate. The fact that both the heads of government are students of sea power cleared the road to what Churchill termed their "comradeship," and in all likelihood prompted the Prime Minister's remark at the end of the Sunday service on the British battleship *Prince of Wales,* a remark attributed to him by *Time* magazine: "I'm not a religious man, but I thank God that such a man as you is the head of your Government at a time like this."

The conference was likewise symbolical, emphasizing as Anne O'Hare McCormick saw it in the *New York Times,* "the supreme importance of the Atlantic battlefield," and reminding the Nazi master of continental Europe that the command of the sea by the English-speaking Powers was still unbroken. A reminder also to the people of both countries that the Atlantic, in the words of the London *Daily Telegraph,* was no longer "an abyss dividing us" but "a means and a bond of union." In his report to the British Empire by radio on August 24 Churchill also mentioned the unifying aspect of the conference, saying that the meeting symbolized

in form and manner which everyone can understand in every land and in every clime, the deep, underlying unities which stir, and at decisive moments rule, the English-speaking peoples throughout the world.

Yet the significance of the conference lay not alone in the appropriateness of the meeting-place and the decisions reached there. Of equal import to us in appraising the event is the bare fact that a President of the United States and a British Prime Minister had entered into a joint undertaking in world affairs. Insofar as a President and a Prime Minister may commit their peoples, Roosevelt and Churchill had formed an Anglo-American alliance to administer the peace, and inasmuch as their program must wait on victory, they forged also an alliance for victory.

If the Atlantic Declaration meant anything, it clearly bespoke an English-speaking power concert, "openly arrived at." Those persons on both sides of the water who found little but a "vague" resemblance to Wilson's Fourteen Points in the Eight Articles overlooked the power implications of the conference. Where Wilson avoided the nettle of power, Roosevelt and Churchill grasped it firmly. In Article Eight of the "Atlantic Charter" the conferees proposed that the English-speaking Powers themselves disarm the aggressors and, in effect, police the peace; the material clause reading: "they believe, pending the establishment of a wider and permanent system of general security, that the disarmament of such nations is essential." [1] The President and the Prime Minister, as the *New York Herald Tribune* viewed it, intended "taking military authority into the hands of the democratic and non-aggressive powers."

That reading of Article Eight gained confirmation from Churchill's broadcast, wherein he said:

The United States and Great Britain do not now assume that there will never be any more war. . . . On the contrary, we intend

[1] The text of the Atlantic Declaration will be found in the Appendix.

to take ample precautions to prevent its renewal in any period we can foresee by effectively disarming the guilty nations while remaining suitably protected ourselves.

In that attitude toward power lay the most salient difference between Wilson's foreshadowing of the shape of things to come and the Atlantic Declaration. The First World War President treated disarmament as an abstraction, leaving its definition to a parliament of states. His disarmament point, Number Four, merely suggested "adequate guarantees given and taken that national armaments will be reduced to the lowest point consistent with domestic safety." Roosevelt and Churchill, being men of limited objectives, preferred to keep postwar fulcra of military power in the custody of the liberal nations, placing a "system of general security" later on their time schedule. In 1941 that seemed only good sense. It was the precise reverse of Wilson's policy. Wilson had not waited, as we have seen, even until the Armistice to begin dismantling the Anglo-American sea-power accord growing out of that war—in the interest of a general enfeebling of the Sea Powers. Although he could not at that time have had a clear perception of postwar relationships, alignments, and power problems, Wilson preferred trusting to the effectiveness and good purposes of a society of nations that had not yet taken form.

The statesmen of the Atlantic conference, it was clear, sought to conserve the solidarity of the English-speaking peoples and to avoid a division of their powerful forces. They had, it is true, the advantage of experience. Both Churchill and Roosevelt had had occasion to observe at close range what Walter Lippmann has termed the postwar "disintegration of Anglo-American power," a failure to harness the potentialities of the Atlantic and British power groupings for world security which Lippmann charges with the major responsibility for the current war. To Lippmann it was "separatism, isolationism, disarmament, a blind pacifism and a mean cynicism which, in the twenty years from the Armistice to the outbreak of the war, reduced the English-speaking nations from a position of invincible security to that of the desperate defensive."[1]

Although the President and the Prime Minister avoided the word and color of alliance, few thoughtful Americans or Britons doubted the essential nature of the sea-born agreements. There was little dissent from the conclusion of Dr. Edmund A. Walsh, S.J., an authority on international affairs at Georgetown University, that the Atlantic Declaration "changes our previous defensive relations into an out-and-out defensive alliance with Great Britain." In general the American press found in the conference what the *New York Times,* characteristically friendly to Great Britain, hailed as "the immense and inevitable fact of Anglo-American partnership." That part of the press supporting the country's foreign policy approved the new association, seeing it with Lippman in the *Herald Tribune* as a minimum and reassuring condition of national survival. "There is no turning away," wrote Lippmann, "from the fact that the independence and security of the English-speaking peoples require their close and unbroken collaboration."

Also typical of this point of view, the *St. Louis Star-Times* rejoiced that Britain and America had become "indissolubly united in self-defense against Hitler's evil New Order." In Atlanta the *Constitution* suspected that the linking of English-speaking fortunes at sea would take rank in historical importance with the signing of Magna Carta and the adoption of the Constitution of the United States. The *Syracuse Post-Standard* expressed gratification that the United States was committed to postwar reconstruction "hand in hand with Britain," and the *Galveston Daily News* was no less pleased that Roosevelt and Churchill were now "speaking for the Anglo-Saxon world."

No less alert to interpret the significance of the conference, the newspapers opposing our foreign policy took, on the whole, a captious line. The *Chicago Tribune,* which daily promises peace to "Chicagoland" in a world being racked to bits, meanwhile attempting to thwart the national defense

[1] *Life,* April 7, 1941.

program, was certain that "the country repudiates it" (Roosevelt's pledge of collaboration). The *Denver Post* wondered darkly what the Senate would have to say about the President's "entering into an 'alliance' . . . without consulting it," and the *New York Daily News,* which specializes in rallying religious and racial antagonism against the foreign policy of the Government, sought to score on the declaration on the ground that it omitted reference to that one of Roosevelt's "four freedoms" dealing with religion. In an address delivered earlier in 1941, the President listed political, civil, economic, and religious freedom as desirable goals toward which to work in a postwar order. This omission, the *News* supposed, must have occurred out of "deference to our new ally —Joe Stalin." A few days after the announcement of the conference, the President sent a copy of the Atlantic Declaration to Congress. In his covering letter he added a corollary to the Eight Articles, a stipulation pointing out that the Declaration self-evidently includes "the world need for freedom of religion and freedom of information. No society of the world organized under the announced principles could survive without these freedoms, which are a part of the whole freedom for which we strive." Wilson's Fourteen Points likewise were silent on religion.

It should be remembered that the anti-Communist animus displayed by congressional isolationists, the America First Committee, and that part of the press believing that defense begins at the three-mile limit was not directed at the Kremlin, or even the Communist sectaries in our midst. As long as the Nazis and the Bolsheviks were linked, the Communists enjoyed a like immunity with the Nazis from the attack of these groups. It was only when Hitler betrayed Stalin's confidence and invaded Russia in June of 1941 that the isolationists discovered that Russia's place in the war could be turned to use. Their motive was of course readily apparent. The support of England and America for the Soviet Union's military endeavors was a club with which to beat the Roosevelt Government, another ideological weapon at the disposal of the appeasement and defeatist forces in America.

A Washington dispatch to the *Chicago Tribune* brought the Atlantic Declaration under the fire of the Senate isolationists five days after its announcement. Upon his return from the meeting at sea Roosevelt conferred with Democratic congressional leaders. At this gathering, said the dispatch to the *Tribune,* the President disclosed "the grand strategy of the new Anglo-American-Russian alliance for the defeat and disarmament of Germany and Italy." Further, the President was represented as having told the leaders "that an invasion of the Continent would be necessary to accomplish this, and that an American expeditionary force would be required." In the Senate Alben W. Barkley of Kentucky, Administration leader, arose to deny the truthfulness of the report, charging that its author had "deliberately falsified" the President's disclosures.

Whereupon Senator Hiram Johnson, venerable bell-wether of the isolationist flock, took occasion to defend the Senate's prerogative in foreign affairs. A living link with the senatorial "battalion of death" that shamed the United States before the civilized world in 1919 by trampling under international co-operation, Johnson accused the President of violating the Constitution by entering into "an offensive and defensive alliance" with Churchill in disregard of the Senate. To the Californian the Atlantic Declaration was, moreover, a warlike document, Article Six seeming to him especially bristling. That article expresses the hope of the conferees that "after the final destruction of the Nazi tyranny" there may be "established a peace which will afford to all nations the means of dwelling in safety within their own boundaries and which will afford assurance that all men may live out their lives in freedom from fear and want." Johnson preferred to phrase the article in his own verbiage as follows: "That means—and no other construction or interpretation can be put upon the language—that after the destruction of the Nazi tyranny the two nations entering into this particular document and this particular commitment will have a new order based on righteousness and justice and decency and good government. And headed, I assume, though they do not say so, by Mr. Joseph Stalin."

A long Senate career had versed Johnson in the potentialities of debate. His introduction of Stalin into a discussion of Article Six exhibited that aptitude at its most cunning. The Senator concluded, not surprisingly, that Article Six could only be effectuated "by war." Among those who heard and read Johnson's words were some who were reminded of a passage in the late Clarence W. Barron's published diaries quoting from a talk purportedly given by Johnson to his intimate supporters during the 1920 Republican National Convention at Chicago. Johnson, fresh from his triumph in the Senate over such "righteousness and justice and decency and good government" as was represented by the League of Nations, was a candidate for the Republican presidential nomination. In the talk Johnson, according to Barron's informant, bade his workers remember that among his political assets was "the Irish and German vote."

Robert A. Taft of Ohio, Republican, and Bennett Champ Clark of Missouri, Democrat, joined Johnson in attacking the Atlantic Declaration. Clark wished the world to know that the President had "no authority" to commit the United States Government to anything without the consent of Congress. He condemned the President for boarding a belligerent warship, speculating with pious dread on the consequences had the *Prince of Wales* been sunk by a Nazi bomb at that moment. He supposed such an event "would have been an act of war against the United States." As for Senator Taft, he detected a "new commitment" in Article Four, pledging a joint "endeavor" and with "due respect for their exisiting obligations . . . to further the enjoyment by all States, great or small, victor or vanquished, of access on equal terms to the trade and to the raw materials of the world which are needed for their economic prosperity." Senator Barkley thought this only a general statement of a desirable policy, committing the United States to no departure from accepted practices. "I am sorry to say," said Taft, "that I cannot understand from the Senator's statement whether this is, or is not, an agreement." In reply to which Barkley disclaimed responsibility "for the Senator's lack of understanding."

It was on such a plane that the debate ended. A minor skirmish, a pedestrian exchange of parliamentary points totally irrelevant to the overshadowing issue of 1941—war or submission. The heavy malevolence of Senator Wheeler was missing from this discussion, the leader of the American appeasement forces being absent from the chamber. Although willing enough, neither Taft nor Clark could place the debate on the foreboding level of Wheeler, with his monotonous and chilling delivery, his inspired talent for distortion. Neither of the younger Senators would be quite capable of the raffish wit that gave rise to the quip about "plowing under every third American boy." Clark is a product of Missouri frontier politics, a school in which, as with the keelboat men of early Mississippi River days, no holds are barred—a primitive and personal politician, but not fundamentally a man to appease a foreign enemy. Like Wheeler and other isolationists, Clark is in part victim of his hatred for Roosevelt, an aversion which has been known to reach the proportions of a pathology.

Taft, a man of rigorous personal integrity, of courage and ability of a high order within the limitations of a rigid imagination, seems somehow not to belong with the irreconcilables of 1941, either by breeding or by character. Unlike Clark, who faithfully reflects the parochial record of his father, the late Speaker, in dealing with foreign affairs, Taft repudiates the course of his own father, the late President. Although deeply mistrustful of Wilson, the elder Taft was able to suppress his partisanship before, during, and after the First World War. The son is unable to concede as much to Roosevelt. The attitude of too many of the Senate isolationists seems not dissimilar to that of the French captain quoted in the book by Hans Habe about the French debacle, *A Thousand Shall Fall*. The captain "loved France more than he loved Hitler, but loved Hitler more than he loved Léon Blum."

The case of all the congressional isolationists, with their egotistical reliance on their own infallibility in opposition to the plain lessons of recent history, reflects on the utility of the parliamentary institution in time of emergency. As with the European parliaments of the Hitler period, Congress has proved unequal to the crisis. A history of the failure of Congress to grasp the national interest has yet to be written. It will make melancholy reading for those of us who have faith in the representative principle in American democracy.

Wheeler stands apart from the ruck of the Senatorial isolationists by reason of his superior force and his cynicism. Were the issues not as grave as national survival, one might admire the recklessness with which he has deployed his wilfulness against his Government's foreign policy. His suggestion that the armed forces might question the authority of the Commander-in-Chief, his willingness to see the country enfeebled in morale as well as the materials of defense, his guarded ventures into anti-Semitism in the Spring of 1941, the much-questioned use of his frank—all these indicate a profound opposition within Wheeler to the forces, spiritual and political, arrayed on the side of the free peoples. Hitler has openly counted upon disgruntled members of the elite in countries marked for destruction. Whether conscious of it or not, Wheeler's behavior has at times approximated the Nazi description of such forerunners of Fascism. The Montanan's point of view on his country's fate in a menacing world goes beyond the sciolism of a Lindbergh or the parochialism of a Nye. Should the United States forget its destiny and allow the triumph of Nazism, Wheeler's place in the history of his time will be unquestionably conspicuous.

Apart from the stormy isolationists in Congress and the Anglophobic utterances of the "keep-out-of-war" groups, the "Atlantic charter" met with a generally favorable public response in America. The Eight Articles conformed to American idealism and experience. There was warrant for believing, with Richard B. Scandrett, Jr., in his book *Divided They Fall,* that "the spirit of the American people" had not, since

the Gettysburg Address, been "more adequately expressed
than in that joint pronouncement of the British and American people for which their Prime Minister and our President
were but mediums of expression." The stark proposal that
the English-speaking Powers shall reorganize the world and
police the peace elicited surprisingly little dissent from a
public instructed more widely than ever before in the realities of world power relationships.

3

A rather grim disappointment that the Atlantic conference had not produced a definite pledge of belligerent action
from the President served to obscure its larger meanings in
England. Although the London *Daily Mail* characterized
the meeting as the "event of the century," suggesting that
"the fate of mankind for good or evil" now depended upon
Anglo-American decision, the British press made little attempt to bring the sea conference into historical perspective. In that beleaguered country there was a feeling, no
doubt, that such interpretations might await the end of the
battle. Nor was there much dwelling in the United States on
the place of the conference in the living stream of Anglo-
American relations. Few editors or public men thought to
take note with the *New York Times* that the "joint declaration was without precedent in Anglo-American history."

Yet so it was. Never before had the responsible head of the
United States Government committed this country to a long-
range course with the British Government (or any other government) in affairs outside their immediate, mutual interest.
In 1823, as we recall, John Quincy Adams interposed his
thorny will against the Canning proposal for an Anglo-American pledge of Latin America's security, arguing that to do
so would make the young republic merely a "cock-boat [a
tender] in the wake of the British man-of-war." That situation, giving rise to the Monroe Doctrine, developed in the
aftermath of the Napoleonic Wars. In all the years until the
next general war in the West there was no full-dress occasion

for an alliance. Although America joined with England and her Allies in the First World War, President Wilson held himself studiously aloof from even the name of alliance, calling the American relationship to the Allies an "association." Contrary to a widely prevalent opinion, as we have seen, Wilson shunned close quarters with the British after the war was well under way, and at its close placed no value on the accord between the English-speaking Powers.

A suspicion that those Powers were joined in formal undertakings persisted throughout the last half-century, as we have noted. In 1897 the Kaiser thought that England, America, and France were in league against Pan-German aggressiveness. Thereafter the sleep of German statesmen was periodically troubled—in 1898 during the Spanish-American War, at the time of the Samoan incident in 1899, and on several subsequent occasions—by dreams of a hostile Anglo-American combination. At both the Paris and the Washington conferences the French charged the Anglo-Saxons with concerting against them. That was so likewise at the London Naval Conference of 1930. In the United States, notably in the 1900 Presidential campaign and after the Washington Conference, opposition politicians sought to make political capital out of similar intimations. In none of these instances was there evidence of a genuine alliance. That remained for 1941.

The collaborations inspiring these reports and rumors served, nevertheless, to break ground for the Atlantic Declaration. Since the 1890's, as has been traced in preceding chapters, the drawing-together of America and Britain has followed a steadily progressive and rational course. That they should cohere in 1941 in the presence of the most affrighting world crisis in history seems according to the terms of what Bismarck meant by the "logic of history." It was in 1894 that Mahan prophesied the alliance of the English-speaking Powers when once they had identified their common interest in the sea. His prophecy gained vindication on the pitching decks of *H.M.S. Prince of Wales* and *U.S.S. Augusta* in August, 1941.

There were many progenitors of the Atlantic Declaration on both sides of the Atlantic. In the beginning Jefferson and Canning, Madison and Monroe, and in a wholly negative way John Quincy Adams prefigured such a démarche. A span of two generations and there were Salisbury and Cleveland, Richard Olney and Joseph Chamberlain, the rough-timbered antagonists over Venezuela. Then John Hay and Henry White, the tentative Balfour and Lord Bryce; and Carnegie and Cecil Rhodes, dreaming of English-speaking federation a half-century before Clarence K. Streit. On to Theodore Roosevelt, placing props under the Anglo-American accord while professing to be doing something else, and his devoted Spring-Rice. Finally Walter Hines Page and Lord Robert Cecil, with the accented and architectural prose of Henry Adams condensing the whole pattern of strategy, civilization, language, and a like respect for the sea into a phrase—the Atlantic System.

Of all the progenitors, Mahan's grasp on the realities underlying the Atlantic power concert was the surest. To him sentiment was the decorative design, self-interest the cement that held the structure together. To the austere Admiral the republic and the empire were "natural allies" because their interests touched without necessarily colliding, because England and the Dominions complemented this country strategically at so many points, and lastly because together—but not singly—they might rule the seas and thus hope to assure survival in a world of enlarging power magnitudes. More than that, Mahan knew that if the two giants with the one language were not friends, they might become enemies. From 1890, when Mahan's star rose into Salisbury's sky, until his death in 1914 the historian propagated that doctrine ceaselessly, confident that the day would come when the peoples of both countries were to accept its verity.

A half-century ago, it will be remembered, Mahan counseled Americans to abandon the isolationist habit of mind, describing it as one befitting only the "infancy" of the United States. He miscalculated the blind strength of isolationism, setting too early a date for the relaxation of its down pull on

American politics. The dead weight of isolationism was to retard the coming of age of the United States, subject it to danger from abroad, and injure the national spirit for more years than Mahan could contemplate. He did not foresee the sordid withdrawal from responsibility after the war of 1914-18 which helped to bring the United States in the 1940's face to face with war on all oceans and all continents, a war of probable exhaustion and not one for conquest or glory but one to be fought out of sheer necessity.

The doctrines of Mahan, it may be assumed, entered the calculations in the "Atlantic bay" of which Churchill spoke. Both the statesmen were bred to his rationalizations. No authority on the problems before them conformed more closely to their intellectual background, their predilections, and their concentration on sea power—surface, subsurface, and in the air. The principal weapon at their disposal was sea power. Without command of the seas, according to the Mahan thesis, they could not hope to win the war. With it, their chances were better than even. The conferees—Roosevelt, with his lively realization of history and his deep insight into the American story, and the historian Churchill—must have levied on the Anglo-American past and the evolution of the Atlantic System in attempting to map the future. Mahan would have been a mainstay there. In another aspect, the point of national interest, neither the Prime Minister nor the President needed a reminder from the Admiral.

It is one of the minor ironies of these times that the English-speaking countries should be brought into their closest connection since 1775 by statesmen who have never been prone to hands-across-the-sea sentimentalizing. One of the fallacies of the Anglophobe is that since he hates England, anyone who seeks a closer tie with that country loves England with a passion as unreasoning as his own. Such is not the case. Both Churchill and Roosevelt are confirmed nationalists. The Prime Minister, a round, bent, compact John Bull with a pink, shaven face and no side whiskers, was not on the Atlantic at personal risk and inconvenience to discuss the mutual heritage of Shakespeare. Nor was he there to sur-

render an imperial interest. The British Empire, it has been
said, is a living religion to Churchill. In its service he will do
battle with Turk or Christian, or make a league with the
Devil. Forty years ago Churchill, fresh from the Boer War,
delivered his maiden speech in the House of Commons. In it
he avowed a sort of Churchillian imperial creed. If the far-
flung dominions and colonies of the Crown were justly governed, prosperous, and healthy, then, said Churchill, "the
cause of the poor and the weak all over the world will have
been sustained; everywhere small peoples will have more
room to breathe; and everywhere great empires will be encouraged by our example to step forward into the sunshine
of a more gentle and more generous age."

A Tory in his latter years, belonging to the same party
with Chamberlain, unlike Chamberlain, Churchill placed
the British Empire above the considerations of any class, and
appeasement did not run in his veins. The son of an American mother, Churchill has not been inclined to an excess of
tenderness toward her country. Freely employing his King
James-version phraseology in the House of Commons and in
his writings, Churchill has not spared criticism of American
policy, especially the train of Wilsonian assumptions. His
zeal for British naval ascendancy, moreover, inpaired good
relations with America in 1927 when in the Ministry he
backed the intransigeance of the British admirals at Geneva.

As a candid nationalist, Churchill met his counterpart on
the Atlantic. If Churchill resembles a shorter, clean-shaven
but immensely shrewd John Bull, Roosevelt, tall, affable, hu-
morous, and likewise shrewd, would—given a goatee—bear a
fair likeness to the traditional image of Brother Jonathan. If
Churchill took a narrowly British attitude over the Geneva
naval dispute, Roosevelt derricked the London Economic
Conference of 1933, on which the hearts of the British were
set. It was also Roosevelt who took America off gold, Hoover
having declined to do so, to the detriment of the world trading position of the sterling bloc. No more than Churchill has
Roosevelt been given to meaningless fraternizing with the
transatlantic neighbor. On the other hand, neither brought

prejudice or suspicion to the conference table. The platform on which they met was not sentiment, but fused national interest.

4

The good fortune which brought Churchill and Roosevelt to the chief places in the English-speaking countries at this time of world crisis cannot be exaggerated. Men with bold and far-ranging minds, they not only comprehend the tremendous forces engaged in the present struggle but they also face up to the implications. The presence of these sea-power authorities at Westminster and Washington in 1941 testified anew to the sound public sense of the English-speaking peoples. Lesser leaders, men unfamiliar with the grand outlines of spatial strategy, might ignore or seek to evade the thrust of Germany's global aspirations. Roosevelt and Churchill understand that the "crucial question of the century," in the words of Dr. H. W. Weigert, a German émigré professor now at Hiram college in Ohio, is "whether domination of the oceans or the continents will prevail."

To Weigert, writing in *Harper's* for November, 1941, of Dr. Karl Haushofer's school of geopolitics, the Nazi invasion of Russia plus German-Japanese collaboration discloses

the tremendous goal of Hitler's armies: to develop a gigantic world pincers movement with the aim of outflanking the oceans, and, by the control of the continental spaces and their ports, to strangle sea power.

According to the Haushofer synthesis, painstakingly elaborated during the last twenty years at the Institute for Geopolitics, Munich, the Land Powers under Germany, and with Japan as a satellite, must necessarily vanquish the great Sea Powers to gain world leadership. Only then will the Anglo-American imperium give way to a Germanic New Order. To Haushofer, a geographer and a major general in the First World War, the task of overpowering the English-speaking nations on their chosen element is too formidable. His methodical talents have therefore been employed on a formula

which might enable a master of Central and Eastern Europe
to gain world hegemony without actually meeting and destroying the overwhelming force of the English-speaking Powers at sea.

That is the inner meaning of geopolitics. Only when
Haushofer's dialectic is seen in relationship to the broad lessons of Mahan does it take on reality to the Anglo-Saxon
mind.

Underneath the Alexandrine metapolitics of the German
power theorist, his inflated space concepts, and their gran-
diose application, may be seen the familiar outlines of the
struggle between a Continental System and the Atlantic System. The aim of Haushofer is to circumvent Mahan, not to
overthrow him by frontal attack. Hence he proposes a detour
into land conquest, a vast project bringing Europe, Asia, and
Africa under German domination; an attempt to offset sea
power by weight of land mass, man power, and raw-material
stocks needing little or no ocean transport.

In the light of Hausofer's rationalizations, the invasion of
Russia in June, 1941, takes on larger meanings. Hitler
struck not so much to remove the threat of the Red Army
in his rear, or to obtain wheat and oil, as in order to gain
ascendancy over the huge land bridge between West and
East. The Führer sought, fulfilling Clausewitz's classic definition of the purpose of war, to impose his will on Russia.
His objective was command of the "Heartland" of the
"World-Island" charted by Haushofer—the continents of
Europe, Asia, and Africa—the heart of that island being the
region from the Volga to the Yangtze north of the Hima-
layas. The "Heartland," by Haushofer's definition, is essential to the grand strategy of the Land Powers because of its
supposed immunity from the far-reaching tentacles of sea
power.

If we accept this interpretation of Hitler's march into Russia, the war in the East far transcends ideological conflict.
Under such circumstances the political creed professed at
the Kremlin became immaterial to the Atlantic world. In
going to the defense of the Soviet Union the Sea Powers were

not only helping to enfeeble Nazi strength; they were also protecting a flank. Both Roosevelt and Churchill, it must be assumed, gathered the full intimations of Hitler's march to the East. That insight no doubt accounted for the promptitude with which they dared domestic complications by pledging assistance to the Soviet Union.

The Haushofer concepts of the "World-Island" and "Heartland," it should be noted, did not originate in Germany. Haushofer borrowed them from an inimical source, from Sir Halford Mackinder, a Scottish theoretician. In 1919 Sir Halford warned the Allied statesmen at Paris against German domination of Russia and Eastern Europe. "Who rules East Europe commands the Heartland," he wrote in a book, *Democratic Ideals and Reality;* "who rules the Heartland commands the World-Island; who rules the World-Island commands the world." It was Haushofer's self-chosen task to adapt this warning out of the Atlantic world to a technique for the potential conquest of that world.

To what degree Hitler's course has been directed by Haushofer seems still speculative. Until the flight of Rudolf Hess, Hitler's discipleship was widely assumed. Legend ascribed to the Munich geographer the place of reigning strategist in the highest Nazi circles. The Nazi-Soviet pact of 1939 bore Haushofer's approval, his monthly organ *Zeitschrift für Geopolitik* blessing the rapprochement as a step toward absorption of the Slavic world into the Germanic orbit. Haushofer is understood to have opposed the substitution of conquest for accord as a long-range policy. If a difference existed, it seems to have been over method rather than objective. The invasion of Russia might be considered as a Nazi short cut rather than a repudiation of Haushofer's premises. It may be doubted, however, that the Eastern adventure represented a general policy of withdrawal in the West. The direct pressure on the Sea Powers was perhaps only momentarily relaxed. Hitler and his counselors would, quite naturally, prefer a quick decision in the Atlantic to the circuitous, long, and possibly exhausting flank movement across Asia and down into Africa.

The war, as of September, 1941, seemed still to hang on the issue in the Atlantic. Russia, for all the magnitude of the military operations there, was still a sideshow. In spite of Haushofer, sea power had still to be reckoned with by the master of the Continental System.

Roosevelt and Churchill, meeting at sea, manifestly found themselves in agreement on these matters: the strength of the liberal tradition, the value of Atlantic civilization, the virility of the English-speaking peoples, and the necessity to the well-being, peace, and order of the Western world of the utter extirpation of Nazi reaction. Though they agreed as to aims, there was a practical divergence between the English-speaking Powers on the means. Churchill, the leader of a people at war, brought the sound and fury of battle to the conference cabin. Roosevelt and his people were half in, half out of the war. America, as the London *News-Chronicle* put it, "is in the peace, although she is not yet in the war." That was, of course, a half-truth.

5

Throughout the summer of 1941 this country waited edgily on circumstance. To acute observers, the balance between quasi-peace and shooting war seemed so delicate that the slightest jar might tip us into war. As Churchill observed in the broadcast to which reference has been made, "one man," Hitler, had the answer to the question "When will the United States enter the war?" The President stood steadfastly by his determination that when hostilities came, they should come as the result of enemy action. He did not propose to fire the first shot.

On the night of September 11, the President broke the spell of indecision. In a broadcast commanding the largest audience yet granted a public utterance in America, Roosevelt informed the people that he had ordered the United States Navy to clear a large and undefined area of the Atlantic of enemy warcraft. The *U.S.S. Greer,* a destroyer, had been attacked by a German submarine at a point southeast of Greenland. To the President "this was piracy." The attack on the *Greer* brought to a head a series of German depredations on American shipping in the South and the North Atlantic, the Red Sea, and the Pacific. These were the acts of "rattlesnakes." The Nazis, it was apparent to the President, had evidenced a desire to seize command of the seas. Hence, the time had come for "Americans of all the Americas"

to stop being deluded by the romantic notion that the Americans can go on living happily and peacefully in a Nazi-dominated world. There has now come a time when you and I must see the cold inexorable necessity of saying to these inhuman, unrestrained seekers of world conquest . . . "You shall go no further!"

In defense of the Atlantic world, Roosevelt had ordered the navy to shoot at enemy vessels at sight. However palliated or attenuated, that was a warlike act. The response of the country was heartening. Not long thereafter the American Legion national convention, which in 1939 had adopted isolationist resolutions, declared for all steps necessary to defeat Nazism. As in the past, whenever the issue was plainly presented as defense of the Atlantic world, the nation rallied. The isolationists, driven by events, resorted to extreme and self-defeating methods. At Des Moines, Lindbergh disclosed his affinity with Nazi methodology by raising the anti-Semitic cry. The Jews, the British, and the Roosevelt Administration he charged with hustling the United States into war, forgetting that the Jewish minority had been divided, as have other racial groups in America, that the British are a negligible bloc among us, and that less than a year ago Roosevelt's policies had been decisively endorsed by the public. In Washington, Senators Nye and Bennett Clark likewise aped the propaganda methods of the Nazis by seeking to raise an anti-Semitic clamor against Hollywood. That was a measure of desperation, gaining the countenance of no responsible leader of American thought.

The President's bold words resolved many doubts. It was

time. The midsummer of 1941 had been a season of despair
for those Americans solicitous for their country's honor and
survival. Subversive forces had been encouraged, the agents
of disunion had gone unchecked until it seemed to one observer that the war was being lost in the confused and un-
comprehending hearts of the American people. Congress, a
not wholly responsible organ of national policy, was showing signs of disintegration. The unexpectedly dogged resistance of the Soviet Union, which lessened the sense of
urgency in this country, emboldened the Republicans in
Congress to play with the national safety, and the House of
Representatives, exhibiting an excess of partisanship and a
minimum of patriotism, came within one vote of disbanding
the army. The fact that such a vote failed to alarm the country more generally reflects no credit on the House. The lack
of alarm was due to the fact that the country took it for
granted that the minority members were merely angling for
votes in their districts.

A group of Republican leaders, including Hoover and Alfred M. Landon, a former Governor of Kansas who ran for
the Presidency on the Republican ticket in 1936, were also
encouraged in midsummer of 1941 to try out isolationism as
a party issue. They no doubt believed it possible to take such
a line because for the moment the emphasis in the war had
shifted from the Atlantic to Russia. And with the disregard
for objective logic characterizing the partisan mind, they
chose to take their stand against military aid to Russia at a
time when Russia's resistance made it possible for them to
venture into the open with an attack on the foreign policy
of their own Government.

It has been suggested that these Republican leaders, together with those in Congress who have been opposing the
defense program, hope for a reaction similar to that which
overcame Wilsonism in 1920. They should remember that
the Republican party has never thrived except as a nationalist party. In the prelude to the First World War it was the
Republican party, led by Theodore Roosevelt, Taft, Root,
Hughes, and other stalwarts, which most clearly saw the

national interest. The record of the party at the end of that war was unexceptional. It is only fair to point out that there is another type of leadership in the Republican party in 1941, exemplified by Wendell Willkie, whose insight into the problem of America's relationship to the world crisis has been deep and steady, and whose utterance of his views has been unfailingly forthright.

In the fall of 1941 the country was of three minds. First, there was the vast middle body of citizens, hating war and its impact on their personal lives, confused about America's precise responsibilities and her peril, but willing to defend her and their civilization whenever persuaded of the necessity. Inarticulate and undemonstrative, these were people who joined no peace or war societies and stayed home from the meetings of the opposed groups, who voted uniformly in the public-opinion polls against the abstraction war as they would have voted against the abstraction death or poverty, yet endorsed each separate step of the Administration toward defense, against Hitler, and in support of Britain. In general this middle group, which might be called the neutrals, trusted Roosevelt's leadership.

Next, on both sides, bidding for the favor of the neutrals were bodies of citizens known loosely as interventionists and isolationists. At the risk of oversimplification it may be said that those parties differed broadly along these lines: The interventionists preferred war to submission, the isolationists preferred anything, including submission, to war. Whereas the interventionist was unwilling to gamble his country's security, its independence, and its proud place in the world on the resistance of other peoples, the width of the oceans, or an internal collapse in Germany, the isolationist, closing his eyes to danger, was willing to gamble on any factor that supplied him with an argument. Another broad difference was that in general the interventionists believed in the liberal tradition, believed in their country and its mission, and were willing to sink party politics for the duration, while the isolationists were more influenced by personal or group than by national

interest. These considerations apply, of course, only to the
sincere isolationist who actually prefers the American way
of life to that of the Nazis—the antiwar man whose ground
is not merely hatred for Roosevelt or England, or both, or
a sympthy, conscious or unconscious, for the "wave of the
future."

The isolationist tent was wider than the interventionist,
and it sheltered along with sincere Americans opposed to
war and those optimists who relied on Hitler's benevo-
lence a heterogeneous collection of persons and groups at
heart inimical to the American tradition. Among these were
to be found unassimilated Germans and Italians of the immigration during the long truce, aliens repaying the privilege
of free speech by advocating the cause of the tyrants who suppressed it in their homelands. There were also the Communists, taking political instructions from Moscow, supporting
the American war effort only because the "workers' home-
land" lay in the path of the common enemy. There were the
small, subversive, pro-Fascist movements typified by the
Christian Front, which draws its doctrine from Father
Coughlin's propaganda organ *Social Justice*. The street fighters of that anti-Semitic band went into action in New York
City in the spring of 1941, according to the press, shouting
"We want Hitler!" and "We want Lindbergh!"—cries ringing ominously in the ears of those who recall the street brawl-
ing that accompanied the Nazi rise to power. It is one of the
most serious counts against Senator Wheeler and that ill-
starred young man, Lindbergh, that they have so recklessly
evoked the dark forces that lie under the surface of any society.

As for the sincere isolationists, they are as familiar a phenomenon of these days as the Nazism which has overrun their
counterparts in countries from Austria to heroic Greece.
They were the Englishmen who said: "Where is Czecho-
slovakia?" and the Frenchmen who saw no point in dying for
Danzig. They were the Dutch and Belgians who declined to
consult with England and France about a common defense.
They were the well-meaning, timid people all over Europe

who thought Hitler didn't mean them. In France they relied on the Maginot Line. In other European countries they counted on their own peaceable intentions. In America they rely on the Atlantic Ocean and their own wish to be let alone. The fact that they have misread the signs will not spare them in the United States should it resist too late, or too little. Nor does the fact that the sincere isolationists belong to an ancient tradition recommend them to those Americans who believe that the national interest demands all-out and immediate participation in this war.

The tradition to which the isolationists belong is negative and antinational. In the time of Washington their spiritual forebears were Tories, or worse, those pliant souls who managed to avoid being identified with either side. They condemned Jefferson for wasting good money on the Louisiana wilderness. They thought that in warning the Old World away from the New World Monroe was taking in too much territory. They opposed settling or claiming the Oregon Territory. As United States Senators they blocked the annexation of Texas so that it had to be accomplished (as later also in the case of Hawaii) by a majority vote of both houses. In the North during the Civil War they were, of course, Copperheads. In 1919 they opposed Wilson not on the legitimate grounds that lay open to them but on the general ground of Hiram Johnson and his band that they wanted no truck with foreigners, and that the President was carrying America beyond her depth.

America never would have been carried anywhere by the gentlemen of this tradition. It should be cold comfort to those statesmen who are playing politics with the destiny of the United States that the leaders of this tradition are so uniformly anonymous. Who except historians remembers individual Tories? The fame of the Founding Fathers, of Jefferson, Monroe, Lincoln, and Wilson, is secure; not so with those who sought to block their endeavors.

6

The attitude of the sincere isolationists has varied little from generation to generation. They fear risk, responsibility, hardship, and defeat—but principally defeat. Fortunately it is not necessary to theorize about the attitude of the gentlemen of that tradition in this crisis. A complete specimen is at hand in an address made by Henry Noble MacCracken, president of Vassar College, a week after the announcement of the Atlantic conference. Dr. MacCracken spoke in Carnegie Hall, New York City, before a mass meeting of the America First Committee, an antiwar organization which seems intent on persuading the people that England, not Germany, is the enemy of this country.

MacCracken spoke against war. In common with the spokesmen for the isolationist party generally he did not deal adversely with Nazi Germany. Owing to the necessity of minimizing the danger from that quarter, such speakers cannot stress the vicious dynamism of the conquerors of Europe. They are under no such inhibitions regarding England. So the president of Vassar warned his hearers against the evils of association with the British Empire. He intimated that that empire had not led a blameless existence. Ignoring the unmistakable implication in American national policy that England is fighting the war for the United States also, MacCracken hinted that the English were again striving to use America for their own purposes. He accomplished this innuendo by describing the Atlantic Declaration as the "Churchill treaty," although it is generally understood on both sides of the water that Roosevelt initiated the conference.

A commitment to the "final destruction of Nazi tyranny," said the speaker, means war. The "war party" and the "peace party" agree on that, but whereas the war party wants to get on with the job, the peace party "has no hope of crushing the Nazi rule at this time." What then was the peace hope of the peace party? "It looks for the democratic regeneration of Europe from within, after the fury of war shall have spent it-

self." The same hope no doubt would be extended to the
United States when, after a Nazi triumph, its appeasers and
defeatists shall have turned America into a satellite of the
Nazi New Order.

MacCracken, accepting defeat in advance, doubted that
the United States Army could vanquish the enemy. He questioned also the ability to sustain the home morale in a war
which he contemplates would be "fought in the East Indies,
in Egypt, in Morocco and Iran as well as in Europe." A fixed
idea ran through isolationist thought in 1941 that war in
America would be preferable to war elsewhere, and that
nothing would so sustain morale as feeling the blows of the
enemy in Boston, New York, or Pittsburgh. "We do not
know," said MacCracken, "of any authoritative military man
who has told us how Germany can land in America." That
curiously fatalistic notion likewise prevaded isolationist
thought in 1941. From Lindbergh to MacCracken to the unidentified spokesmen for Dr. Goebbels in our midst there
came the refrain of American invincibility to direct Nazi attack. That theory, when honestly held, grew out of unfa-
miliarity with the monstrously effective creeping tactics of
the enemy as well as the lessons and the strategy of sea power.

Had Dr. MacCracken ever thoughtfully considered the
military situation of this country should Hitler be master
of Europe and Africa and Japan in undisputed command of
Asia, with the oceans flanking the United States under the
control, outside our immediate waters, of those Powers? Had
he thought of the probable allegiance of South America under those conditions, of the prospect of a Quisling Canada
and a British Empire co-ordinated into the Nazi New Order
through the weapons of military defeat, potential starvation,
and the frustration that would come from the knowledge
that further resistance was useless? Would we undertake the
conquest of Canada when we had failed to stand with Canada
in defense of the Atlantic world? Is America prepared to
fight her way to the south, taking and occupying the lands
of her neighbors, with the man power and resources of Europe and Asia arrayed against her? How many years does

Dr. MacCracken think the United States could stand the
strain of standing in arms against the whole world outside
its own borders? And which party is to defend it then—the
war party, which wishes to fight now that America may have
resourceful allies, command of the seas, and access to all the
world outside Europe, or the peace party, which prefers to
wait until America has none of those factors in her favor?

Dr. MacCracken should be let in on a secret. A great many
Americans fear his associates of the peace party more than
they fear the Nazis in battle. A great many Americans believe, rightly or wrongly, that the appeasement forces which
have systematically sought to destroy this country's will to
resist, have tampered with the morale of the United States
Army, opposed in Congress every measure of defense, and
irresponsibly sought to divide the country on racial and religious lines do not intend now, or ever, to resist. Dr.
MacCracken should know that many Americans are confident
that Hitler would not need to land troops on American shores
to subdue our country should England fall. The appeasers
would invite him in. A good many of the appeasers know
that also. It is too bad that Dr. MacCracken does not.

The question goes beyond men's intentions. It comes down
to simple equations of power. Dr. MacCracken, speculating
for the moment on the consequences should the United
States win the war, supposed: "We should have garrisons in
Germany, Japan and Italy, commissars of raw materials all
over the world imposing an Anglo-American peace on the
world, with one indispensable condition as its basis, the integrity of the British empire." Without our pausing to wonder where in the Atlantic Declaration that outline of an
Anglo-American peace appears, the question arises and
should be propounded to Dr. MacCracken and his peace
party: Would he prefer German, Japanese, and Italian garrisons in the United States, with Axis commissars of raw
materials ordering our economy? Would he rather see the
"integrity" of the Nazi New Order or that of the British Empire maintained? Fair questions, those are by no means
rhetorical ones.

7

Whoever wins this war will reorganize the world. That is what Willkie means by his compact and summarizing observation that "after this war the capital of the world will be either Washington or Berlin—I want it to be Washington." The choice is limited, on any foreseeable basis. Either the peace will be made in Washington and London, or it will be made in Berlin. The New Order will be either Anglo-American or Nazi. After first reading his own construction into the "Atlantic Charter" the sincere isolationist Dr. MacCracken indicated his disapproval. Does he prefer a peace made in Germany? That is the alternative.

Since the Atlantic conference no one need be in doubt about the choice. It lies clear before Americans. They may vizualize the Nazi New Order from the writings of Hitler and his adjutants, from the Nazi record in governing their own people and conquered nations, and from the history of the German tribes. The Nazi regime is an escape into the primitive barbarism of the German tribes as noted by Julius Caesar and Tacitus. Opposed to this archaic movement, the spokesmen of the Atlantic world promise a continuation and a betterment of classical, liberal, Christian civilization. Behind the promise stand the political stability, the steady progress under law, the respect for individual rights, the civil liberties, the religious and racial tolerance, the rise in well-being, in the mature English-speaking democracies.

A Nazi order means the organization of human society on a hierarchy of races, against all the lessons of history and reason, with the Herrenvolk as masters, all others in varying degrees of slavery. The persecution of the Jews and the Poles and the assassination of hostages in France and other occupied countries have demonstrated to the world the savagery of the Nazis. Tacitus observed this same sadistic cruelty of the Germanic tribes toward their slaves and captives. "They often kill them," he wrote, "not from motives of systematic discipline but in the rage of passion." Caesar found what we now perceive as a spring of Nazi morality in the customs of the tribes toward foreigners. "Robbery," he wrote in the *Commentaries,* "has nothing infamous in it when committed outside the territories of the state to which they belong. They even pretend that it serves to exercise their youth and prevent the growth of sloth." In a Nazi world no human rights would stand against the arbitrary will of the Führer, the party, or the state. In the democratic state the state itself moderates as between the rights and privileges of citizens, even protecting the citizen from the state itself.

What does the "Atlantic Charter," with the Roosevelt corollary, offer in contrast to the reign of force, persecution, oppression, and atavistic culture which will be the lot of humanity if the Nazis and their allies prevail? The Eight Articles may be condensed as follows:

1. The dominant Sea Powers renounce any desire for territorial or other gain from the war.

2. They promise not to alter national boundaries (specifically, it must be supposed, not to dismember Germany) without the "freely expressed wishes of the people concerned."

3. Self-government, self-determination, and restoration of sovereignty and territories to the nations who are victims of the Nazis.

4. Equal access to trade and raw materials by all nations, including the vanquished. This is in reality a pledge of a worldwide Open Door.

5. Collaboration toward the freest exchange of goods to secure "for all improved labor standards, economic advancement, and social security." This is a declaration against autarchy.

6. Permanent peace.

7. Free access to the seas.

8. Abandonment of "the use of force" as an instrument of national policy, with a pledge on the part of the Sea Powers to disarm and keep disarmed the notorious lawbreakers and bullies in the society of nations.

And the Roosevelt corollary, emphasizing the desirability of freedom of religion, communication, and information.

Those are broad generalizations—"a simple, rough-and-ready wartime statement of the goal toward which the British Commonwealth and the United States mean to make their way," in Churchill's phrase—covering a scheme for world-wide reorganization. What credentials do the English-speaking Powers submit as evidence of good faith? Just this. While the Nazi cult has been perverting Germany and preparing to engulf the world under a tide of totalitarian imperialism, the English-speaking Powers have been relaxing their hold on Dominions, colonies, and protectorates. During the long truce the British Commonwealth was given legal form as an association of self-governing nations under the Crown. Ireland was allowed virtually to demit from the British Empire and reclaim complete freedom over her ports, to the present embarrassment of the British. The ties with Egypt were rendered easier to Egypt, and long strides were taken toward the goal of self-government for India within the British Commonwealth. In those years the United States beat a steady retreat from imperialism, both political and economic. Under Roosevelt's "Good Neighbor policy" America relinquished protectorates over Cuba and Panama and arranged to retire from the Philippines in 1946. Both England and the United States will carry better credentials to the peace table this time than they did in 1919.

A victory for the English-speaking Powers would strengthen the growing Pan-American solidarity. Since 1936 the relations among the three Americas—North, Central, and South—have been undergoing a steady maturing. A co-operative policy for the twenty-one American republics has taken satisfactory form. The Declaration of Lima in 1938 outlined a "common policy," which A. A. Berle, Jr., writing in the *Survey Graphic* of March, 1941, hailed as a transmutation of the Monroe Doctrine into a multilateral declaration. Since then the American republics have formulated and implemented a program for hemisphere defense under which one or more Powers would act for all. The growth of genuine peace and understanding in the Americas is a tribute to the patience and spirit of accommodation of Franklin Roosevelt and his universally respected Secretary of State, Cordell Hull.

On the other hand, no thoughtful observer can doubt that a Nazi New Order spells the end of the Atlantic System. The

Monroe Doctrine, which has been withering away under the co-operative policy, would be struck down by the Nazis. For forty years German publicists have been ringing the knell on the Monroe Doctrine. The ties binding the Americas into one world entity are not cultural; they are only incidentally economic. Until recent years the factor of cohesion was political similarity and a common reliance on Anglo-American sea power. Remove that command of the Atlantic, substitute for it Nazi command, and the pressure of trade would perhaps soon carry South America into the German orbit.

Americans may confidently predict America's status in a world organized under terms of the Atlantic Declaration. What might they expect in the event that the Nazis remodel the world system? They have had clues in the propagandistic writings of the Axis Powers to the projected role of the United States in a Nazified world. They know also from his own words and the testimony of Nazi deserters and others in what low esteem Hitler holds America. To Hitler the United States is the most decadent of the democracies, undisciplined, incapable of co-operative action, allowing indecent privileges to Jewish and Slavic immigrants and its native Negroes. The Führer, counting upon American disunity, "did not consider North America a decisive factor" at the outbreak of this war, according to Hermann Rauschning. Rauschning, a Junker intellectual and agrarian who embraced then rejected Nazism, reported in his book *The Redemption of Democracy* that Hitler "has repeatedly told his intimates that he was not afraid of the United States as a Power because it was his purpose to unloose upon the American Continent a revolution of unprecedented dimensions. . . . Sooner or later, America's hour would strike, to create a new future through breakdowns and turmoil on a gigantic scale."

The United States, we may gather from the speculations of Nazi theorists, would be allowed to retain its sovereignty, to exist in a restricted way, partly disarmed and having surrendered its Pacific and Atlantic bases and control of the Panama Canal—provided it installed a regime satisfactory to the Nazi high command and took its respectful place in the New Order. That would of course mean the introduction of racial laws; suppression of the freedom to comment on the Nazi regime except in complimentary terms; and acceptance of an economy, a currency, and a credit system linked to that of the Nazis. This would, quite naturally, bring about the end of the American nation as Americans have known it since 1789, bringing on a black night of terror, hatred, and suspicion such as the American people never have known. No one, whether worker, farmer, employer, professional man, student, or religious communicant, would be immune. The only gainers would be a few callously selfish businessmen and certain political adventurers capable of being Quislings.

Should the United States resist incorporation into a totalitarian world, the Nazis might elect merely to segregate it economically. A Nazi Europe, holding Africa as a tributary and in close association with a Japan dominating Asia, the East Indies, and Oceania, would have little or no need for the products of North America—none whatever if Canada had been incorporated and South America had been drawn into the Nazi order. American surpluses could be denied access to world markets except on ruinous terms, American industrial products be excluded altogether, and the whole American tariff system be destroyed overnight. Does that seem a lurid prognosis of the economic and political fate of America should Russia and the British fall? There is a growing and definitive literature on the subject of Nazi world aims and methods waiting to be consulted by doubters.

The isolationists offer Americans that dim and dreary world. In their hearts the appeasers (not all isolationists are appeasers, but all appeasers are isolationists) are indifferent to the question of who reorganizes the world so long as their corner is left untouched. From Lindbergh, fatefully attracted to an alien primitivism, to such representatives of the negative tradition in American life as MacCracken the message is of defeat, despair, and submission. As the *New York Post*, commenting on the MacCracken address we have discussed,

summed it up: "If the American nation today carries on with
no more pride and stamina than he pictured, then indeed
his voice of defeat spoke a timely warning." The *Post* rejected the MacCracken doctrine, characterizing it as "an un-
blushing proclamation of sterility and decline. . . . Dr. Mac-
Cracken wrapped himself in the bloodstained tatters of defeat as in the banner of his cause. It was, in fact, a shroud.
The people of this country, we say quietly, will take the
Stars and Stripes."

8

The *Post's* assumption has historical sanction. The American people have never preferred submission to victory. As a
nation they do not know the experience of defeat. On the
other hand, they have never—except perhaps in 1898—gone
eagerly to war. From the 1770's until the 1940's the road to
war has been rutted, winding, filled with obstructions.
Though Americans are always unwilling to take up the
sword, it is yet a terrible and decisive weapon in their hands.
They have never halted or turned back on the road. The
American will to prevail has been tested through the generations—in the seven years' war for independence, a war that
seemed a dozen times lost; in the terrible battles of the Civil
War, the most extensive and bloody war in history until the
First World War, a war of brothers won only when the South
found itself at last without food, clothing, and weapons. Nor
should it be forgotten also that 2,000,000 soldiers from this
peaceable land stood at arms in France when the last war
ended. They would not have been denied victory.

Moreover, the United States is more united today than in
the presence of any great war in its history. National unity,
the sense of nationhood, has followed a rising curve. Trace
out the story of faction and dissent in all the prewar phases
of the American past and see for yourself if this is not true.
All Americans are familiar with the division in the colonies
before—and during—the civil war we term the American
Revolution. Recall the resistance of New England, the luke-
warmness of New York before—and during—the remote chap-

ter of the Napoleonic Wars that Americans call the War of
1812. Lincoln's Cabinet was appeasement-minded; the draft
caused riots lasting for days and costing hundreds of lives in
New York; and the Union forces attained true unity and a
tempered will to win only in the third year of the War of Secession. In the thirty-one months of the First World War before our entrance Wilson's Cabinet was twice shaken by
resignations. But once in that war (as unsought and undesired
as this, its sequel), the united will of the American people
showed an unbroken front.

Happily, in the early autumn of 1941 victory was still
within the grasp of the Atlantic Powers. The forces mustered
against a Nazi New Order were on the rise. In man power, in
command of the seas, in production of the weapons of war,
the Atlantic Powers together with China and the Soviet
Union exceeded the Axis Powers. Once they were co-ordinated, once organized for victory, there could be no doubt of
the outcome. That meant war for America. To the isolationist that seems an unthinkable choice. It is dreadful, but not
unthinkable. Americans have fought in the past on foreign
soil. In the span of the nation Americans have fought in colonial Canada; in Cuba (twice); in Tripoli and Libya; in
Puerto Rico, the Philippines, and Samoa; in China, Siberia,
and Russia; in France, Belgium and Italy. They have fought
for independence, for the right to sail the seas unmolested,
for national unity, for territorial and strategical expansion,
for the national honor and prestige, and for the security of
the Atlantic world. Is it possible that Americans would refuse
to fight in 1941 when all these issues save expansion are involved and the alternative is slavery? The interventionist,
unwilling either to gamble or to treat with the powerful
forces contesting for domination over his country, regards
war, with all its personal terror, death, and destruction, as
the lesser evil.

In September, 1941, the forces of military concentration favored the Atlantic cause. In its favor likewise were the
imponderables, the moral factors upon which the great commanders of history have dwelt. Mahan, writing of the initial

disadvantage suffered by peaceable nations of loose, democratic organization when attacked by aggressors, held no
doubt that

in the end, the many will prevail. The immediate result [of such
bursts of warlike fury as the Nazis employ] is that the preponderant, concentrated force has its way for a period which may
thus be one of great and needless distress; and it not only has
its way, but it takes its way, because, whatever progress the world
has made, the stage has not been reached when men or States
willingly subordinate their own interests to even a reasonable
regard for that of others.

This was written in 1910. Since then the world has been
twice ravaged by the "preponderant, concentrated force" of
a German nation organized for the imposition of the will
of its rulers on other peoples. In his memoirs Bismarck declared the people known as Germans to be so heterogeneous
that they could be integrated only by dynasty or anger. Bismarck united them around the Hohenzollern dynasty, Hitler
by arousing their anger—their hatreds, their prejudices, and
the underlying brutality of man. Both were ancient and
regressive rallying-points. Both ran counter to their age. Both
Germanys were in reaction against the liberal, progressive
civilization of the West. A victory for Germany in 1918
would have carried the Atlantic world back along the road to
the Stuarts and Louis XIV. A victory for the Germany of today would plunge the Western world back into its pre-Chris-
tian infancy.

There can be no compromise between the Atlantic world
and German reaction. The true wave of the future bears
westward—if America does her share. A powerful Anglo-
American offensive, by the sea which the English-speaking
peoples providentially command, from the air and by land
once the English-speaking armies are forged, should bring
the "final destruction of the Nazi tyranny," preserve the Atlantic world, and return Western Europe to its traditional
allegiance to Western civilization. But victory may not restore to Europe its leadership of the Western world. Whatever the outcome of this war, France has been dealt a

staggering blow. Her decline from leadership in the West, apparent before the war, has been only dramatized by defeat. Unstable politically, France has, in any case, oscillated between the Atlantic and the Continental systems throughout recent history. Since 1789, it will be recalled, the French have been governed by two monarchies, two empires, and three republics. Neither France nor Germany can be counted on for leadership in a liberal postwar world.

The Europe emerging from this war, should it last another year or more, will be literally a shambles, starving, its cities shattered, its moral force demoralized, its will beaten and diffused. Only from the Atlantic world, from the Americas and the British Commonwealth, from that half of the white race which has learned to live in peace, can the regenerative factors spring. Rauschning's book, an apologia for his apostasy from Western culture, bore a subtitle, *The Coming Atlantic Empire.* Representative of a despairing mood that afflicts European intellectuals increasingly, his theme was the decline of the Old World, the rise of the New. To Rauschning it seems that "The centre of gravity is shifting westward. Around the Atlantic Ocean some new sort of empire of peace may grow up. The power nucleus of the new order is springing from a union of the Anglo-Saxon peoples. Europe will become a hinterland."

In such a New Order the English-speaking peoples must bear responsibility jointly. Jointly they can assure their survival, the health of the liberal tradition, revitalized by this ordeal, and peace. China may be helped to a unity and a strength equipping her for her rightful share in a new Asia. The Soviet Union, relieved of the fear of aggression and with the most convulsive phases of her experiment past, may be encouraged and tutored by the Powers committed to political liberty and progress by evolution. The German people, left territorially whole and granted economic equality, may find some other integrating core than dynasty or anger. The end of the last war did not bring Germany abreast of the modern liberal states. This war may accomplish that. All these assurances are implicit, some of them explicit, in the Atlantic Declaration. To make doubly sure, Churchill in his explanatory broadcast stipulated further that "instead of trying to ruin German trade by all kinds of additional trade barriers and hindrances as was the mood of 1917, we have definitely adopted the view that it is not in the interests of the world and of our two countries that any large nation should be unprosperous or shut off from means of making a decent living for itself and its people by its industry and enterprise."

The joining of British and American power in the postwar world need not, probably should not, be expressed in organic union. Many years ago, we remember, Mahan warned against the danger of formulating permanent arrangements between nations on the basis of temporary need or wartime sentiment. A general treaty of alliance, with subsidiary treaties covering matters of trade, tariffs, currency, immigration, and such points of possible conflict or co-operation, should provide a realistic framework for collaboration within the terms of the Atlantic Declaration. It should be borne in mind that while geography and other familiar factors dictate the general necessity of accord, Americans are not Englishmen, and vice versa. In detail, our customs and habits differ; an attempt to bring political union might easily be in itself divisive. The "ultra-American," the Anglophobe, and the sincere isolationist will not relish even so informal a linking as is proposed here. They must be convinced. Nor should it be supposed that the Anglo-American power concert will in future suppress or mitigate commercial rivalry between Americans and Englishmen. It has not done so in the past. The central fact to be kept in mind is that, in spite of such abrasive competition, the Powers have steadily grown nearer to each other politically since 1896—the year of their last quarrel.

The Anglo-American entente, symbolized by the Atlantic conference, as has been suggested in this book, is a product of organic growth. The result of natural cohesive forces, it has been conditioned little either way by the goodwill of the English-Speaking Union or the invidious provincialism of the America First Committee. Its time of maturing has been the last half-century, roughly since the United States signified an intention to return in force to the sea and to take a hand in affairs beyond its shores. Before the 1890's the Atlantic was an English inland sea; thereafter it became pre-eminently the sea of the English-speaking Powers. We have told the story of Anglo-American relations during these years with special reference to the Atlantic, to sea power, and to the persisting enemy of the peace and well-being of the Atlantic world— Germany. We have seen the English-speaking countries converge along lines of mutual interest in each time of crisis. We have seen a growing recognition of the essential solidarity of the great Sea Powers, but a recognition unexpressed in treaty or national declarations until the Atlantic meeting.

More is needed. The time has come to study the history, the structure, and the cohering factors in Anglo-American relations so that the reasons for alliance may be recognized frankly and defined in national policy in both the United States and Great Britain. The future of the Atlantic world depends upon that sort of recognition and definition.

For the immediate future America's course is plainly charted. An all-out military partnership with Great Britain and her Allies is a minimum condition of our survival as a great, liberal Power. Should ignorance, indifference, or factionalism in this country contribute to an Axis victory, the United States—the most advanced and powerful of nations —will almost certainly be reduced to a subordinate status, a position of tutelage in a world gripped by implacable reaction. Under "the law of the opposite shores," the United States cannot tolerate the establishment of a hostile Sea Power on the European side of the Atlantic. In the fall of 1941 it was apparent that our Government did not propose to tolerate it. The clock had struck with the fall of France. The exact hour in which our full force would be engaged in the struggle could not be foretold. That it would be so engaged could not be doubted.

Appendix

HEREWITH IS THE text of the Eight Articles as published by the President and the Prime Minister after their conference at sea:

The President of the United States of America and the Prime Minister, Mr. Churchill, representing His Majesty's Government in the United Kingdom, being met together, deem it right to make known certain common principles in the national policies of their respective countries on which they base their hopes for a better future of the world.

First: Their countries seek no aggrandizement, territorial or other;

Second: They desire to see no territorial changes that do not accord with the freely expressed wishes of the people concerned;

Third: They respect the right of all peoples to choose the form of government under which they will live; and they wish to see sovereign rights and self-government restored to those who have been forcibly deprived of them;

Fourth: They will endeavor, with due respect for their existing obligations, to further the enjoyment by all states, great or small, victor or vanquished, of access, on equal terms, to the trade and to the raw materials of the world which are needed for their economic prosperity;

Fifth: They desire to bring about the fullest collaboration between all nations in the economic field, with the object of securing for all improved labor standards, economic advancement and social security;

Sixth: After the final destruction of the Nazi tyranny, they hope to see established a peace which will afford to all nations the means of dwelling in safety within their own boundaries, and which will afford assurance that all the men in all the lands may live out their lives in freedom from fear and want;

Seventh: Such a peace should enable all men to traverse the high seas and oceans without hindrance;

Eighth: They believe that all of the nations of the world, for realistic as well as spiritual reasons, must come to the abandonment of the use of force. Since no future peace can be maintained if land, sea or air armaments continue to be employed by nations which threaten, or may threaten, aggression outside of their frontiers, they believe, pending the establishment of a wider and permanent system of general security, that the disarmament of such nations is essential. They will likewise aid and encourage all other practicable measures which will lighten for peace-loving peoples the crushing burden of armaments.

FRANKLIN D. ROOSEVELT
WINSTON S. CHURCHILL

Sources and Bibliography

THE AUTHOR'S DEBT to Admiral Mahan's published works needs little elaboration. That debt is acknowledged tacitly on each page of this book. Without the great power theorist's rationalization of Anglo-American sea-power solidarity, there would conceivably have been an Atlantic System —but the job of recognizing, depicting, and summarizing that system would be inconceivably more difficult. Of major assistance also were the excellent biographies of Mahan by Captain Puleston and Mr. Taylor and the searching, recently published studies of American sea power by George T. Davis and the Sprouts, Harold and Margaret. To Henry Adams the author manifestly owes the title as well as a running commentary on the creative period in American foreign policy. To A. Whitney Griswold he is indebted for an exhaustive account of America's part in Far Eastern affairs, and to Orestes Ferrara for the only comprehensive version of European diplomacy during the Spanish-American War.

Otherwise, government documents such as the State Department's *Foreign Relations* (issued down to 1922), Navy Department reports, and the *Congressional Record* furnished much of the bony structure. Also yielding rich structural material were the British parliamentary reports and *Die Grosse Politik der Europäischen Kabinette,* the German Foreign Office archives opened after Versailles. The contemporary press, daily and periodical, in England, Germany, and the United States was levied upon extensively for interpretation of deeds and popular moods. So was the large literature in diplomatic and naval histories, memoirs, letters, and biographies touching upon the affairs of the Powers during the last half-century and easily available to the student. A partial list of sources follows:

Adams, Brooks, *America's Economic Supremacy,* Macmillan, 1900
———— *The New Empire,* Macmillan, 1902
Adams, Henry, *The Education of Henry Adams,* Houghton Mifflin, 1918 (first pub. in 1907)
———— *History of the United States of America,* 9 vols., Scribner, 1889-91
———— *Letters of (1858-1918),* ed. by Worthington C. Ford, 2 vols., Houghton Mifflin, 1930-38
Alsop, Joseph, and Robert Kintner, *American White Paper,* Simon and Schuster, 1940
Arnold, William T. (Vigilans sed Aequus) , *German Ambitions As They Affect Britain and the United States of America,* London, 1903

Bailey, Thomas A., "Dewey and the Germans at Manila Bay," *American Historical Review,* October, 1939
———— *A Diplomatic History of the American People,* Crofts, 1940
Baker, Ray Stannard, *Woodrow Wilson and World Settlement,* Doubleday, Page, 1922
———— *Woodrow Wilson: Life and Letters,* Doubleday, Page (or Doran) , 1927-39)
Baldwin, Hanson W., *United We Stand,* McGraw-Hill, 1941
Balfour, Arthur James, Balfour, first earl of, *Retrospect: An Unfinished Autobiography, 1848-1886,* Houghton Mifflin, 1930
Barker, J. Ellis, *Modern Germany,* London, 1919
Beard, Charles A., *The Navy: Defense or Portent?,* Harper, 1932
Beer, George Louis, *The English-speaking Peoples,* Macmillan, 1917
Bemis, Samuel Flagg, ed., *The American Secretaries of State,* 10 vols., Knopf, 1927-29
———— *A Diplomatic History of the United States,* Holt, 1936
Berle, A. A. Jr., "Peace without Empire," *Survey Graphic,* March, 1941
Bienstock, Gregor, *The Struggle for the Pacific,* London, 1937
Birdsall, Paul, *Versailles Twenty Years After,* Reynal & Hitchcock, 1941
Bismarck, Prince Otto von, *Bismarck, the Man and the Statesman,* 2 vols., Harper, 1898
Bowers, Claude G., *Beveridge and the Progressive Era,* Houghton Mifflin, 1932

Brandenburg, Erich, *From Bismarck to the World War* . . . *1870-1914*, London, 1927

Bryce, Lord James, *America Commonwealth*, 2 vols., Macmillan, 1888

Bülow, Prince Bernhard von, *Memoirs*, 3 vols., Little, Brown, 1931-33

Bywater, Hector C., *The Great Pacific War*, London, 1925

—— *Sea-Power in the Pacific*, London, 1934

Carnegie, Andrew, *Autobiography*, Doubleday, Doran, 1933

Cecil, Lord Edgar Gascoyne-Cecil of Chelwood, *A Great Experiment*

Cecil, Lady Gwendolen, *Life of Robert, Marquis of Salisbury*, 4 vols., London, 1921-32

Churchill, Winston L. S., *The World Crisis*, 4 vols., London, 1927-31, Vol. 5, *The Aftermath*

Cleveland, Grover, *Presidential Problems*, Century, 1904

Coolidge, Archibald C., *The United States as a World Power*, Macmillan, 1927

Cortissoz, Royal, *The Life of Whitelaw Reid*, 2 vols., Scribner, 1921

Crecraft, Earl W., *Freedom of the Seas*, Appleton-Century, 1935

Davis, George T., *A Navy Second to None*, Harcourt, Brace, 1940

Denlinger, Sutherland, and Gary, Charles B., *War in the Pacific*, McBride, 1936

Dennett, Tyler, *John Hay*, Dodd, Mead, 1933

—— *Roosevelt and the Russo-Japanese War*, Doubleday, Page, 1925

Dennis, A. L. P., *Adventures in American Diplomacy, 1896-1906*, Dutton, 1928

Dewey, George, *Autobiography*, Scribner, 1913

Dugdale, Blanche E. C., *Arthur James Balfour*, 2 vols., London, 1936

Dunning, W. A., *The British Empire and the United States*, Scribner, 1914

Eliot, George Fielding, *The Ramparts We Watch*, Reynal & Hitchcock, 1938

Falk, Edwin A., *Togo and the Rise of Japanese Sea Power*, Longmans, Green, 1936

Fay, Sidney B., *The Origins of the World War*, 2 vols. in 1, Macmillan, 1935

Ferrara, Orestes, *The Last Spanish War*, Paisley Press, 1937

Fisher, H. A. L., *James Bryce*, 2 vols., Macmillan, 1927

Foster, John W., *Diplomatic Memoirs*, 2 vols., Houghton Mifflin, 1909

Gardiner, A. G., *The Anglo-American Future*, London, 1920

—— *The Life of Sir William Harcourt*, 2 vols., London, 1923

Garvin, J. L., *The Life of Joseph Chamberlain*, 3 vols., Macmillan, 1932-34

Gelber, L. M., *The Rise of Anglo-American Friendship*. Oxford University Press, 1938

Gerard, James W., *My Four Years in Germany*, Doran, 1917

Germany, *Outbreak of the World War; German Documents collected by Karl Kautsky*, Oxford University Press, 1924

Gillett, F. H., *George Frisbie Hoar*, Houghton Mifflin, 1934

Grey, Lord Edward Grey of Fallodon, *Twenty-five Years, 1892-1916*, Stokes, 1925

Griswold, A. Whitney, *The Far Eastern Policy of the United States*, Harcourt Brace, 1938

Gwynn, Stephen, L., ed., *Letters and Friendships of Sir Cecil Spring-Rice*, 2 vols., Houghton Mifflin, 1929

Hendrick, Burton J., *Life and Letters of Walter H. Page*, 3 vols., Doubleday, Page, 1923-25

—— *The Life of Andrew Carnegie*, 2 vols., Doubleday, Doran, 1932

Hoover, Calvin B., *Germany Enters the Third Reich*, Macmillan, 1933

Hornbeck, Stanley K., *Principles of American Policy in Relation to the Far East*, U. S. Government Printing Office, 1934

House, Edward M., *The Intimate Papers of Colonel House*, ed. by Charles Seymour, 4 vols., Houghton Mifflin, 1926-28

—— and Charles Seymour, eds., *What Really Happened at Paris*, Scribner, 1921

Houston, David F., *Eight Years with Wilson's Cabinet, 1913-1920*, 2 vols., Doubleday, Page, 1926

Howe, Quincy, *England Expects Every American to Do His Duty*, Simon and Schuster, 1937

Hurd, Sir Archibald Spicer, and Castle, Henry, *German Sea-Power: Its Rise, Progress, and Economic Basis*, Scribner, 1913

James, Henry, *Richard Olney and His Public Service,* Houghton
    Mifflin, 1923
Jessup, Philip C., *Elihu Root,* 2 vols., Dodd, Mead, 1938
Josephson, Matthew, *The President Makers . . . 1896-1919,* Har-
    court, Brace, 1940

Keesing, Felix M., *Modern Samoa: Its Government and Chang-
    ing Life,* London, 1934
Keim, Jeannette, *Forty Years of German-American Political Re-
    lations,* Dornan, Phila., 1919
Keynes, John Maynard, *The Economic Consequences of the
    Peace,* Harcourt, Brace, 1920
Kipling, Rudyard, *American Notes,* Lovell Company, 189-?
Krafft, Herman F., and Norris, Walter B., *Sea Power in American
    History,* Century, 1920

Langer, William L., *The Diplomacy of Imperialism, 1890-1902,*
    2 vols., Knopf, 1935
Lansing, Robert, *The Peace Negotiations: A Personal Narrative,*
    Houghton Mifflin, 1921
—————— *War Memoirs,* Bobbs-Merrill, 1935
Latané, John H., *America as a World Power, 1897-1907,* Harper,
    1907
Lindley, Ernest K., *Half Way with Roosevelt,* Viking Press, 1936
—————— *The Roosevelt Revolution,* Viking Press, 1933
Lloyd George, David, *Memoirs of the Peace Conference,* 2 vols.,
    Yale University Press, 1939 (English title, *The Truth about
    the Peace Treaties*)

McCoy, Frank R., "Our Common Defense," *Survey Graphic,*
    March, 1941
Mahan, Alfred Thayer, *Armaments and Arbitration* or, *The
    Place of Force in the International Relation of States,* Harper,
    1912
—————— "Hawaii and Our Future Sea-Power," *Forum,* Vol. 15,
    (1893)
—————— *The Interest of America in International Conditions,* Lit-
    tle, Brown, 1910
—————— *The Influence of Sea Power upon History, 1660-1783,* 15th
    ed., Little, Brown, 1898 (first published in 1890)
—————— *The Influence of Sea Power upon the French Revolution
    and Empire, 1793-1812,* 9th ed., 2 vols. Little, Brown, 1898

———— *Lessons of the War with Spain,* Little, Brown, 1899, pp. 1-11

———— *The Problem of Asia and Its Effect on International Policies,* Little, Brown, 1900

Marburg, Theodore, and Latané, John H., eds., *Development of the League of Nations Idea,* 2 vols., Macmillan, 1932

Marder, Arthur J., *The Anatomy of British Sea Power . . . 1880-1905,* Knopf, 1940

Millis, Walter, *The Martial Spirit,* Literary Guild, 1931

———— *Road to War: America, 1914-1917,* Houghton Mifflin, 1935

Moore, Frederick, *America's Naval Challenge,* Macmillan, 1929

Morrow, Dwight W., *The Society of Free States,* Harper, 1919

Mowat, R. B., *The American Entente,* London, 1939

———— *The Life of Lord Pauncefote,* London, 1928

Nevins, Allan, *Grover Cleveland,* Dodd, Mead, 1932

———— *Henry White: Thirty Years of American Diplomacy,* Harper, 1930

Nicolson, Harold C., *Dwight W. Morrow,* Harcourt, Brace, 1935

———— *Peacemaking, 1919,* London, 1933

———— *Portrait of a Diplomatist,* Houghton Mifflin, 1930

Olcott, C. S., *The Life of William McKinley,* 2 vols., Houghton Mifflin, 1916

Perkins, Dexter, *Hands Off: A History of the Monroe Doctrine,* Little, Brown, 1941

Pratt, Fletcher, *Sea Power and Today's War,* Harrison-Hilton, 1939

Pratt, Julius W., *Expansionists of 1898: The Acquisition of Hawaii and the Spanish Islands,* Johns Hopkins Press, 1936

Pringle, Henry F., *Theodore Roosevelt,* Harcourt, Brace, 1931

———— *The Life and Times of William Howard Taft,* 2 vols., Farrar & Rinehart, 1939

Puleston, William D., *Mahan: The Life and Work of Captain Alfred Thayer Mahan,* Yale University Press, 1939

Rauschning, Hermann, *The Redemption of Democracy: The Coming Atlantic Empire,* Alliance Book Company, 1941

Reuter, Bertha Ann, *Anglo-American Relations during the Spanish-American War,* Macmillan, 1924

Rippy, J. Fred, *The European Powers and the Spanish-American War*, in James Sprunt Studies in History and Political Science

Roosevelt, Nicholas, *America and England?* Cape and Smith, 1930

Roosevelt, Theodore, *America and the World War*, Scribner, 1915

—— *Selections from the Correspondence of Theodore Roosevelt and Henry Cabot Lodge, 1884-1918*, 2 vols., Scribner, 1925

—— *Theodore Roosevelt: An Autobiography*, Macmillan, 1913

—— *Theodore Roosevelt and His Time Shown in His Own Letters*, ed. by Joseph B. Bishop, 2 vols., Scribner, 1920

Scandrett, Richard B., Jr., *Divided They Fall*, Harper, 1941

Schieber, Clara Eve, *The Transformation of American Sentiment toward Germany, 1870-1914*, Cornhill Publishing Company, 1923

Siegfried, André, *America Comes of Age*, Harcourt, Brace, 1929

Smalley, George W., *Anglo-American Memories*, 2 vols., London, 1911-12

Sprout, Harold and Margaret, *The Rise of American Naval Power, 1776-1918*, Princeton University Press, 1939

—— *Toward a New Order of Sea Power*, Princeton University Press, 1940

Stevenson, Robert Louis, *A Footnote to History*, Scribner, 1892

Stimson, Henry L., *The Far Eastern Crisis*, Harper, 1936

Streit, Clarence K., *Union Now with Britain*, Harper, 1941

Sullivan, Mark, *Our Times*, Vols. 1-6, Scribner, 1927-36

Tansill, Charles C., *The Foreign Policy of Thomas F. Bayard*, Fordham University Press, 1940

Taylor, Charles Carlisle, *The Life of Admiral Mahan, Naval Philosopher*, Doran, 1920

Trevelyan, G. M., *Grey of Fallodon*, Longmans, Green, 1937

Tyler, Alice F., *The Foreign Policy of James G. Blaine*, University of Minnesota Press, 1927

Usher, Roland G., *Pan-Germanism*, Houghton Mifflin, 1913

Victoria, Queen, *Letters*, 2nd. ser. ed. by George Earle Buckle, 3 vols., Longmans, Green, 1926-28

Weinberg, Albert K., *Manifest Destiny*, Johns Hopkins Press, 1935

Wertheimer, Mildred S., *The Pan-German League, 1890-1914*, Columbia University, 1924

White, Andrew D., *Autobiography*, Macmillan, 1905

Wilhelm II of Germany, *Comparative History, 1878-1914*, Harper, 1922

————— *The Kaiser's Memoirs*, trans. by T. R. Ybarra, Harper, 1922

Williams, Mary W., *Anglo-American Isthmian Diplomacy, 1815-1915*, American Historical Association, 1916

Woodward, Ernest L., *Great Britain and the German Navy*, Oxford University Press, 1935

Young, Eugene J., *Powerful America*, Stokes, 1936

Index

This index includes: (1) all personal names (each time mentioned) except those to which there is only casual reference; (2) important place names and names of groups and events. Inclusive reference does not necessarily mean continuous reference.

Index